Poverty and prostitution

Frontispiece A sentimentalised version of a street-walker, adorning an Annual Report of one of the hundreds of Female Refuges operating throughout the country in the Victorian period. From the 34th *Annual Report of the Female Mission to the Fallen*, Charing Cross, London, 1892.

Poverty and prostitution

a study of Victorian prostitutes in York

FRANCES FINNEGAN

CAMBRIDGE UNIVERSITY PRESS

CAMBRIDGE
LONDON · NEW YORK · MELBOURNE

Published by the Syndics of the Cambridge University Press
The Pitt Building, Trumpington Street, Cambridge CB2 IRP
Bentley House, 200 Euston Road, London NW1 2DB
32 East 57th Street, New York, NY 10022, USA
296 Beaconsfield Parade, Middle Park, Melbourne 3206, Australia

First published 1979

Set, printed and bound in Great Britain by
Cox & Wyman Ltd, London, Fakenham and Reading

Library of Congress Cataloguing in Publication Data
Finnegan, Frances.
Poverty and prostitution.
Bibliography: p. 00.
1. Prostitution–England–York–History.
2. Prostitutes–England–York–Case studies.
3. York, Eng.–Social conditions. 4. Social
classes–England–York. I. Title. [DNLM:
1. Prostitution–History–England. 2. Poverty–
History–England. HQ117 F514p]
HQ186.Y67F56   301.41'54'0942843   78–68123
ISBN 0 521 22447 0 hard covers

Contents

Illustrations

Preface

In questioning the validity of much that has been written on Victorian prostitution in general this study draws on all the available evidence on individual prostitutes and brothel-keepers in a provincial city between 1837 and 1887. The enormous amount of detailed material in local archives relating to prostitutes has, until now, been neglected by historians who nevertheless have written and generalised on the subject, relying almost entirely on secondary sources. In contrast, this study has examined the lives and circumstances of the women themselves, both as individuals and as a class; and, since there is no reason to suppose that prostitutes in York were untypical of their kind, its findings have a wider than local significance and hopefully contribute to a clearer understanding of Victorian morality and society.

My attention was drawn to the widespread existence of prostitution in Victorian York during the preparation of my doctoral thesis on the development of the Irish Community in the city.[*] It was impossible to examine the lives of the Irish poor without becoming aware too of the existence of an equally deprived and unfortunate group – those 'fallen women' who, like the Famine immigrants, featured frequently in the newspaper Police Reports, were often applicants for poor relief and lived in the most squalid and insanitary parts of the city. Both groups, though distinct, were common victims of poverty.

I would like to thank the staff of the York Reference Library and Archives Department, in particular Mrs Rita Freedman the Archivist and her assistant Mrs Mary Thallon for their helpful interest in sorting the newly acquired records of the York Penitentiary Society.

[*] F. E. Beechey, 'The Irish in York 1840–1875', University of York, 1977.

I am also grateful to Dr D. M. Smith of the Borthwick Institute for supplying me with early references to the history of Grape Lane and to Major Tomlinson, Archivist at the York Barracks, and Sergeant Hawley of the York Police Force for their kind assistance. I am again indebted to Dr A. J. Wilmott of the Department of Computer Science, University of York, and would like to thank particularly Mr Steve Winnall for his generous help with the computer material.

My thanks are especially due to Mr Harry Hall, Senior Environmental Health Officer, for his unfailing kindness and for allowing me to draw upon his wide experience and knowledge of York's former slums; and also to the Department of Environmental Health for permission to reproduce many of the photographs in this book. Additional photographic material was generously supplied by the York City Archives and Mr David Wilde, and I am grateful to Mr David Whitely, University of York photographer, for his excellent reproduction of this material. I would also like to thank Mr S. S. L. Marshall, Managing Director of Vickers Instruments Ltd, York, for his hospitality and for allowing me to inspect the former premises of the Female Penitentiary, and those retired employees of the firm for their reminiscences of the Refuge and its inmates in the early years of this century. I am grateful, too, to my former husband Terry Beechey, A.R.I.B.A., for preparing the excellent map of mid-nineteenth-century York.

I would like to express my gratitude to Professor Harold Perkin for his encouragement and helpful suggestions, and Mr Peter Laslett for his expert advice in the later stages of the preparation of this book. I would like to acknowledge the assistance of the Twenty Seven Foundation of the Institute of Historical Research for a grant towards research expenses.

This list of acknowledgements would be incomplete without a special word of thanks to my daughters Sarah and Rachel for their assistance in coding much of the material for computer analysis and for their helpful understanding during the writing of this book. Finally, and most of all, I wish to thank Professor Eric Sigsworth for his scholarly advice, help and criticism, and his unfailing patience, encouragement and interest.

Frances Finnegan
Pocklington

Abbreviations

Annual Report	*Annual Report of the York Penitentiary Society*
Gazette	*Yorkshire Gazette*
Herald	*York Herald*
Poor Law	York Poor Law Guardians' Application and Report Books
Refuge Committee	York Penitentiary Society Ladies' Committee Books
Sessions	York Quarter Sessions Minute Books
Visitors' Books	York Penitentiary Society Ladies' Visitors' Books
Watch Committee	York Corporation Watch Committee Minute Books

1

Introduction

Much has been written about prostitution in the Victorian age, both in the period itself, when an abundance of literature on the subject was stimulated during the years surrounding the enforcement and eventual repeal of the Contagious Diseases Acts, and when hundreds of local societies were formed for the rescue and reform of 'fallen women'; and, more recently, when the problem has been examined historically. Most influential amongst the former seems to have been the work of Dr William Acton, whose books *The Functions and Disorders of the Reproductive Organs in Youth, in Adult Age, and in Advanced Life: Considered in their Physiological Relations* and *Prostitution, Considered in its Moral, Social, and Sanitary Aspects, In London and Other Large Cities: with Proposals for the Mitigation and Prevention*; both first published in 1857, have attracted a considerable amount of attention in recent studies, and have been instrumental in determining modern attitudes both to Victorian sexual behaviour in general and to prostitution in particular. Many of Acton's notions, particularly in the former work, are now generally regarded as having been rooted in ignorance or even fantasy, and his attitude to the sexuality of women, whom, as Steven Marcus observes, he rarely mentions in that book, have been quoted in recent work largely to illustrate the prejudices, fears and misconceptions of the man and his time. Thus his curiously contradictory statement, based on 'abundant evidence' that:

the majority of women (happily for them) are not very much troubled with sexual feeling of any kind ... As a general rule, a modest woman seldom desires any sexual gratification for herself. She submits to her husband, but only to please him; and, but for the desire of maternity, would far rather be relieved from his attentions. No nervous or feeble young man need, therefore, be deterred from marriage by the exaggerated notion of the duties required from him. The married woman has no wish to be treated on the footing of a mistress.[1]

has been much ridiculed, and dismissed together with one of his equally misguided and mischievous notions, on the grounds that Acton was 'the prisoner of the fictions of his age'.[2] Indeed, one suspects, in common with the town surveyor at Brighton who was infuriated at Acton's accusation that the whole of that resort's drains were insanitary because those in his own lodgings were bad, that Acton was 'basing a general charge on his domestic experiences'.[3]

Yet in spite of what has been variously described as the fiction, fear and ignorance contained in much of Acton's work, particularly with regard to women, it remains a fact that since 1964, when he was rescued from the obscurity into which he (perhaps deservedly) sank in the eighteen-seventies, William Acton has been regarded as the great authority and shatterer of illusions concerning Victorian prostitution. Steven Marcus, who first introduced Acton's work to modern readers generally, is much concerned with the fantasy, contradictions and confusions contained in his writing, and is aware of what he calls a 'dimmed consciousness' in *Prostitution*. Nevertheless, he describes the work as a very good book, which, he claims, not only explodes the popular myth of the prostitute's downward progress (which Acton maintained was the rare exception), but demonstrates, on the contrary, that most prostitutes sooner or later returned to a 'regular course of life', and that even when actively engaged in the activity, being endowed with 'iron bodies', they were freer from general disease than all other classes of females.[4] Similarly Peter Fryer in his introduction to the new edition of *Prostitution* published in 1968 states that Acton was the first to challenge the

conventional parable that prostitutes necessarily rotted in ditches, died miserable deaths in workhouses, or perished in hospitals. Such a fate was exceptional, he insisted. Most prostitutes were transients, who re-entered the ranks of 'respectable' society within a very few years: and an increasing number did so by getting married, sometimes 'above their class'. Giving evidence before the House of Lords' Select Committee on the Contagious Diseases Act in 1868, he was questioned on this point and took the opportunity of disabusing those of their Lordships who supposed that whores, when they 'lost [their] good looks' and retired, became brothel-keepers.[5]

In the same vein, in the introduction to the 1969 edition of *London's Underworld*, Peter Quennell states that Acton, like Mayhew, managed successfully to keep his survey 'matter of fact' and 'banish contemporary phobias'.[6] Finally, Keith Nield in his introduction to the 1973 edition of *Prostitution in the Victorian Age, Debates on the Issue from 19th Century Critical Journals*, shares the same unquestioning acceptance that Acton disposed of 'errors [which] were a litany of the conventional opinion about prostitutes'. He states that Acton 'showed' that

far from rapidly succumbing to disease and demoralisation . . . for many women, short periods of prostitution often culminated respectably in marriage or in business . . . The illusion was shattered that prostitutes sank more or less rapidly to the lowest grade of the profession where they soon died.[7]

It is a curious fact then that, while so much of Acton's work is regarded as questionable, his comments about prostitution are uncritically accepted; and opinions of other observers, some more experienced in the problem and apparently more balanced than he, dismissed as 'illusory', 'mythical', 'conventional belief' and 'vulgar errors'. It is true that, in recognising both that it was possible for a prostitute to redeem herself and begin a new way of life, and also that 'fallen women' such as unmarried mothers were not to be confused with professional street-walkers, Acton can be said to have displayed more sense and humanity than those of his contemporaries who regarded all 'unfortunates' in the same light, and all equally and permanently 'lost'. However, this was hardly a revolutionary doctrine – the hundreds of Rescue Societies, Homes for the Fallen, Female Missions and Guardian Societies operating up and down the country were a testimony to the fact that thousands of people already engaged in works of 'Rescue and Prevention' were aware of the distinctions between different classes of 'unfortunates', and were committed to the rescue and reform even of hardened prostitutes, well before 1857. Further, it is doubtful whether some of Acton's recommendations for the treatment of prostitutes were, as both Marcus and Fryer assert, 'in the direction of humanizing and rehabilitating them'. As one of the chief instigators of the Contagious Diseases Acts – whose infamous provisions he wished to see extended to the female population outside the garrison towns – his recommendations were, on the contrary, regarded by the Abolitionists as dehumanising, and of having the effect of both hardening and brutalising the prostitute and endangering the personal liberty and reputation of any female even suspected of being one. Also it may be doubted whether his scheme for the 'redemption' of unmarried mothers, who might otherwise be forced to resort to prostitution, was in fact particularly 'humanizing', or really designed for the welfare of the unmarried mother herself. In an attempt to promote the employment of such women as wet nurses, forced because they were poor to breast feed the offspring of women of superior classes (many of whom could perfectly well have fed their own infants), he betrays both his class interests and a lack of concern not only for the possible inclinations and emotions of the 'unfortunate' herself – whose function is reduced almost to that of an animal – but also for the fate of her own child, from whom she was frequently forced to be parted. In re-assuring his readers that:

> It is not street-walkers nor professional prostitutes we are speaking of. We are speaking of the young housemaid or pretty parlour-maid in the same street in which the sickly lady has given birth to a sickly child, to whom healthy milk is life, and anything else death. With shame and horror the girl bears a child to the butler, or the policeman or her master's son. Of course she is discharged . . . and of course, when her savings are spent, she will have to take, with shame and loathing, to a life of prostitution. Now, she is healthy and strong, and there is a little life six doors off, crying out for what she can give, and wasting away for want of it, and in the nursing of that baby is a chance, humanly speaking, of her salvation from the pit of harlotry.[8]

he assumes that the unmarried mother would automatically prefer to breast feed another woman's infant – often at the expense of her own baby – to a period of prostitution, even though such 'salvation' might last only as long as the continuance of her supply of milk. It seems likely that Acton's ignorance and phobias regarding the functions and disorders of the reproductive organs – expressed in a book which, as Marcus observes, is in reality almost totally concerned with male sexuality – extended to a similar lack of understanding regarding women's attitudes to their own bodies and babies. In the light of his statements made two years earlier, of course, Acton's assumptions regarding the attitude of women of the poor to prostitution (and especially those who, as unmarried mothers, were already 'fallen') are somewhat surprising. He had, after all, previously stated:

> I have every reason to believe, that by far the larger number of women who have resorted to prostitution for a livelihood, return sooner or later

to a more or less regular course of life ... Incumbrances rarely attend the prostitute who flies from the horrors of her position. We must recollect that she has a healthy frame, an excellent constitution, and is in the vigour of life. During her career, she has obtained a knowledge of the world most probably above the station she was born in. Her return to the hearth of her infancy is for obvious reasons a very rare occurrence. Is it surprising, then, that she should look to the chance of amalgamating with society at large, and make a dash at respectability by a marriage? Thus, to a most surprising, and year by year increasing extent, the better inclined class of prostitutes become the wedded wives of men in every grade of society, from the peerage to the stable.[9]

Others of their number, he claimed, by laying aside sums of money, became successful milliners, shop-keepers and lodging-house keepers. Thus in a few sentences Acton is alleged to have disposed of the errors in conventional opinion regarding the fate of prostitutes (though few in reality belonged to the 'better inclined' of their class) and, had his observations been based on fact, then prostitution might be regarded as a means of Victorian self-help and social improvement.

Prostitution, however, contains glaring contradictions. In describing the houses in which prostitutes lodge (and in which they all must speedily fall to the common level) Acton refers to the kitchens in which the women are to be found in the day – 'dishevelled, dirty, slipshod and dressing-gowned ... Stupid from beer, or fractious from gin, they swear and chatter brainless stuff all day ... as a heap of rubbish will ferment, so surely will a number of women thus collected deteriorate ... to the dead level of harlotry' – and affirms at another point, in contrast to the statement above, that whores have no thought of saving their earnings against an evil day. Further, he later states that, far from being healthy, at least one out of every four prostitutes in London is known to be diseased, 'spreading abroad a loathsome poison', with 'broken constitutions, sickly bodies, and feeble minds' being the result of their trade.

In a few words, then, prostitution consigns to a life of degradation thousands of our female population, ruining them utterly body and soul ... it is the cause of disease, premature decay, ultimately death.[10]

The basic contradictions in the book are apparent, and understandable if we bear in mind the fact that Acton was faced with the problem of alerting and alarming the nation regarding the spread of venereal disease, while at the same time stressing the inevitability of prostitution and the need for its recognition and regulation by the State. If it was indeed inevitable that certain men would always resort to prostitutes, it followed that such women were performing a service to society. It was therefore necessary to outline as unharrowing a picture as possible of the lives and subsequent fate of the many women who took part in the activity, in order that public conscience might not be aroused. Unfortunately Acton's preoccupation with the economic effects of the spread of venereal disease amongst the armed forces and with the safety of men in general, and his consequent advocacy of the Contagious Diseases Acts were obviously incompatible with his optimism regarding the prostitute's health. For according to him, she, rather than her clients, spread her 'loathsome' disease; and thus it was she who was compulsorily detained in the prison-like hospital accommodation provided by the new legislation.* It is obvious that had prostitutes been as happily situated and as free from disease as Acton at times chose to claim, and as others, using him as an authority, have since represented, there would have been no need for the enforcement of the Acts, and still less for their extension.

Other contemporary observers were not as optimistic as he regarding the ultimate fate of 'public women' – most of whom, of course, were common street-walkers. William Logan, for example, author of *The Great Social Evil; its Causes, Extent, Results and Remedies* published in 1871, produced much evidence based on local research which was directly contradictory to that put forward by Acton. He quoted information received from the Chief Superintendent of Glasgow in the eighteen-forties, for example, which stated that:

The average age at which women became prostitutes is from fifteen to twenty. – The average duration of women continuing prostitutes is, I think, about five years. The most common termination of the career of prostitutes is by death, and this is to be accounted for by the extremely dissolute life they lead. For the most part they live in a state of great personal filthiness – they have most wretched homes – they are scarcely ever in bed till far in the morning – they get no wholesome diet – and they are constantly drinking the worst description of spirituous liquors. In addition to these evils they are exposed to disease in its worst forms; and from their dissolute habits, when disease overtakes them, a cure is scarcely possible.[11]

---

* For a description of these wards and the frightening treatment received by prostitutes in them, see Acton, *Prostitution*, pp. 89–96.

Similar conclusions were reached by William Tait in his study *Magdalenism. An Inquiry into the Extent, Causes, and Consequences of Prostitution in Edinburgh*, first published in 1841. Add to the above the frequent prison sentences to which the prostitute was subject, and it will be seen that this description of the street-walker's life is far more in keeping with the evidence obtained for this study of York in the period than that generally represented as put forward by Acton.

William Logan, in common with Josephine Butler and other leaders of the campaign for the repeal of the Contagious Diseases Acts, was aware that the initial causes of women resorting to prostitution were overwhelmingly poverty, overcrowding, and poor pay, working conditions and employment opportunities for women. Though Acton too condemned these as being partially responsible for women taking to the streets, his was a different emphasis. He saw the source of supply as being 'derived from the vice of women' occasioned in the following order:

Natural desire. Natural sinfulness. The preferment of indolent ease to labour. Vicious inclinations strengthened and ingrained by early neglect, or evil training, bad associates, and an indecent mode of life. Necessity, imbued by The inability to obtain a living by honest means consequent on a fall from virtue. Extreme poverty. To this black list may be added love of drink, love of dress, love of amusement.[12]

As we have seen, Acton was aware too that seduction and desertion were often instrumental in forcing an unmarried mother on to the streets, and he felt that the fathers of illegitimate children should be made answerable for their actions. However, it is apparent throughout *Prostitution* that Acton is primarily concerned with protecting men, and that it is women whom he really fears and sees in the role of seducers. Thus

the seduction of a female, properly proved, should involve the male in a heavy pecuniary fine, according to his position – not at all by way of punishment, but to strengthen, by the very firm abutment of the breeches-pocket, both him and his good resolutions against the temptations and force of designing woman.

Such money, he continues, 'this bounty upon sinfulness – this incentive to a seducer', should not be paid to the mother, but put into a fund, half of which should be retained for the bastard child and the other half made over to the woman, only should she emigrate or marry. 'Such a law as this would be found materially to harden men's hearts against female seductions.'[13] Thus within a few sentences the guilt of the man is magically transferred to the woman.

In view of Acton's fundamental attitude to his own sex's part in prostitution – he seems to have regarded them as victims rather than seducers or even equal participants – together with his recommendations resulting in the enforcement and attempted extension of the infamous Contagious Diseases Acts, his reputation for displaying humanity towards both prostitutes and other 'fallen women' is, to say the least, undeserved.

Before briefly outlining the purpose and nature of these Acts, the obsessive desire for the enforcement of which obviously affected Acton's judgement, we should ask why the popular image of the prostitute as a demoralised creature treading the downward path ending in drunkenness, destitution and disease, was one which was so widely held, if it was untrue. Why was there such a 'popular myth' and 'vulgar error' regarding the plight of the common prostitute both in contemporary fiction and in the reports of other writers and rescue workers in the period; and why the necessity for the hundreds of Refuges and Rescue Societies (which, as we shall see, were hopelessly inadequate) if the prostitute could so easily be re-absorbed into society? The facts of the matter seem to be that Acton, far from 'exploding myths' or 'shattering illusions', was as ignorant about and prejudiced against prostitutes as he was about sex in general and female sexuality in particular. For some reason, however, his misconceptions regarding the former have latterly been accepted at their face value, without reference either to his own motives and contradictory statements or to the wealth of other conflicting contemporary opinion on the subject. More important, the mass of detailed evidence available, concerning the lives and circumstances of the prostitutes themselves, has been ignored; and it is in an attempt to examine one city's prostitutes, both as individuals and as a class, that the present study has been made. The results of this work suggest that if these women are in any way representative of Victorian prostitutes in general then Acton's views on the subject, far from being uncritically accepted, should rather be regarded as an interesting example of a middle-class Victorian male's ignorance, fear, prejudice and guilt.

The Contagious Diseases Acts of 1864, 1866 and 1869 were intended to diminish the alarming incidence of venereal disease amongst the armed forces, and as such initially applied only to certain naval and garrison towns,* though their supporters (amongst whom Acton was prominent) hoped that eventually their provisions would extend over the entire country. The main features of the Acts were the registration and supervision (by a special police force) of prostitutes; and, if found to be diseased, the compulsory detention of such women in special hospitals until they were cured. Women resisting examination were imprisoned with hard labour. The Acts were given the minimum amount of publicity, but, once fully appreciated, outraged opposition to their spirit and provision stemmed largely from two societies formed in 1869 – the Ladies' National Association for their repeal (led by Josephine Butler) and the National Association.[14] These enjoyed the strong support of Quakers, Wesleyan Methodists and Congregationalists, who emphasised the sexual discrimination explicit in punishing women but not men involved in illicit sex, which epitomised the 'Double Standard' of sexual morality; the class bias of the Acts, in so far as only lower-class prostitutes and street-walkers were likely to be detained; and the unprecedented powers of a police force able to arrest any woman on the mere suspicion of her being a prostitute and the obvious abuses implicit therein. Further, on moral grounds, they opposed the implied State recognition and sanction of a vice, and argued too that, far from rehabilitating her, the provisions of the Acts brutalised and degraded the prostitute still further. Finally, of course, and drawing on medical evidence contrary to that put forward by Acton, they demonstrated the obvious futility and injustice of attempting to control venereal disease by legislating only against street-walkers but not their clients, who remained free to spread infection, even to their wives. They were convinced too that prostitutes in danger of being detained for a period of up to six months (in conditions differing little from those in prisons) would be driven 'underground' and would no longer seek medication voluntarily as they had previously done. At the same time they feared (with justification) that the provisions of the Acts would become progressively more stringent and extend to an ever widening female population.

* York, though a garrison town, was not one of those dealt with by the Acts, though obviously, had their provisions been extended, it would have ultimately become so.

In spite of what Josephine Butler described as a hostile and 'silent press' the Abolitionists attracted growing support, including that of thoughtful working men who were well aware of the class bias in the legislation.[15] They mounted such a successful campaign that the Acts were suspended in 1883 and finally repealed in 1886. Though the campaign for repeal was given little publicity either in the national or local press (the National Convention held in York in 1874, for example, addressed by Josephine Butler and other prominent speakers and supported by leading York Quakers, was scarcely mentioned in the local press), the Abolitionists produced their own journal *The Shield* from 1870 to 1886.[16] At the same time, the literature in support of the Acts was published fairly freely, with articles concerning prostitution appearing in such journals as the *Westminster Review* and the *Lancet* throughout the period. However, with the exception of that written by Logan, who as a 'missionary' entered brothels and houses of ill-fame in order to talk to and hopefully rescue 'fallen women', Hemyng's account of prostitutes and their associates which appeared in Volume IV of Mayhew's *London Labour and London Poor*, and Tait's earlier account of prostitution in Edinburgh, the literature of the period was concerned less with the prostitutes themselves than with a general account of the problem. Similarly, modern studies, relying heavily on these nineteenth-century authorities, have tended inevitably to reflect this emphasis, the only individual prostitutes or courtesans receiving attention being those who, like 'Skittles' or Nelly Fowler, acquired particular fame or notoriety. Further, recent studies have generally been concerned with Victorian and particularly male sexuality, and with the nature of a society collectively upholding what have been described as the double standards of public as opposed to private morality, and the different degrees of sexual freedom and appetites allowed and attributed to men as distinct from women.[17] This of course applied only to the middle classes, however, since the prostitutes (who, as we have seen, were accorded more sexuality, even if less freedom, than their clients) were drawn almost exclusively from the ranks of the poor. There has thus been a concentration on the institutional aspects of prostitution rather than on the prostitutes and street-walkers themselves, who tend to have been neglected in the post-Freudian fascination with the Victorian male's apparent and impossibly high moral standards and consequent sexual repression and guilt. However, whether this assumed and self-imposed so-called respectability, which resulted in highly repressive behaviour that cloaked and it would seem even caused wide-ranging sexual irregularities, actually existed at a general level – and more particularly in the Victorian period than in any other – is open to doubt. All the evidence used for such interpretations is based on the opinions and observations of middle-class male doctors and writers many of whom, like Acton, were apparently fairly ignorant not only about sex and its consequences, but about the prostitutes themselves; and presumably being like Acton 'prisoners of their age' were anxious to discourage sexual activity not only before and outside, but even within marriage itself. Acton, for example, was chastening, both in his opening remarks to Chapter 7 of *Prostitution*: 'I cannot venture to hope that the sexual passion will in our time cease to operate or diminish very materially', and his recommendations regarding the infrequency with which intimacy between man and wife should occur. In spite of its limitations, however, it has apparently been assumed that this literature represented middle-class and indeed general Victorian opinion, whose moral tone (even if only in public) was as lofty as that of its authors. It has also been assumed that such highly specialised works as those quoted above, many of which were published in fairly obscure journals, were widely read and as such were responsible for forming as well as reflecting public opinion – affecting if not actually warping the sexual behaviour of the nation. Perhaps it is time that more attention be paid to the mass of other evidence on the subject, evidence based on facts rather than fiction, fantasy and impressions – evidence, that is, which examines the problem at the level at which it occurred. This can best be achieved in a detailed and comprehensive examination of local material.

With this in mind the present study examines all prostitutes and brothel-keepers found to be operating in the cathedral city of York during the first fifty years of Queen Victoria's reign. Four major sources of evidence have been used to enable these individuals first to be identified, and secondly, in many cases, to be brought vividly to life. This re-creation of prostitutes and their circumstances is achieved by combining the various references to individuals from the different records used, and results in hundreds of detailed pictures or case histories, extending in some cases over several years. Taken together, of course, this information provides too an insight into all recorded prostitution in the city over half a century, and thus throws new light on the problem of Victorian prostitution and sexuality in general.

The main evidence relating to local prostitution is drawn from the two weekly newspapers published in York throughout the period, the *York Gazette* and the *York Herald*, both of which provide detailed reports of the weekly magistrates' court proceedings and the Quarter Sessions. Prostitutes charged with soliciting or 'wandering abroad', as it was more commonly termed, fighting, indecency, picking their clients' pockets, or, as was often the case, with being drunk and disorderly, were regularly recorded in these police reports, with sometimes as many as fifteen or twenty street-walkers or brothel-keepers being listed in one week. Usually only the name of the offender, the charge, where the offence occurred and sometimes her address were mentioned; but if the case was particularly interesting or scandalous, or the prostitute an habitual offender, more information was provided. It is quite clear, however, that prostitutes and keepers of bawdy houses, even though they made an appearance at court, were not always reported as having done so – as is apparent from the history of Margaret Barrett, for example, the most frequent offender in the city and the prostitute most hounded by the police. Her case and her descent into drunkenness and destitution are discussed in detail in Chapter 5, but to illustrate the practice of under-reporting – which indicates that the recorded figure engaged in the activity is conservative – it is interesting to note that in one of her later appearances in court in the period (August 1887) she is described as having fifty previous convictions, and her next reported appearance before the magistrates is said to be her fifty-third.[18] Yet in all she was reported in the newspapers on only twenty-five of these occasions. Similarly, other prostitutes appear in the Court Sessions lists who were not reported in the local press.

The newspapers used various terms to describe women engaged in prostitution, such as common prostitutes, unfortunates, fallen women, women of ill repute, nymphs of the pave, the frail sisterhood, women of the town, abandoned females, etc., but readers were left in no doubt as to their occupation, particularly as many of the offences were described as occurring in brothels.

Prostitutes committing more serious offences such as assault or some types of theft were not dealt with by the magistrates but by the county court, and the records of the York Quarter Sessions yield information on additional individuals and further evidence relating to the activity.

The third major source of evidence used is the York Poor Law Guardians' Application and Report Books which cover almost the whole of the period. All individuals seeking financial or 'parish' relief from the Guardians of the Poor and applying to enter the workhouse are recorded in these volumes, which also provide details of the applicant's age, address, occupation, family, physical condition and reason for application. Euphemisms are not employed in this material and prostitutes are recorded as such. Since they are also invariably described as suffering from some form of venereal disease and are often admitted from a brothel, they are easily identified. In all, in the period there were 252 applications from individual prostitutes who sought relief at least once, and most of these were sent to the workhouse.

The final source of evidence used to identify prostitutes in the city during the period is the detailed material contained in the collection of documents relating to the York 'Refuge' or, as it was officially termed, the Female Penitentiary Society, opened in 1845 and continuing to shelter 'fallen women' until well into the present century. In the Minute Books, Reports of the Ladies' Committee and Annual Reports information was often recorded regarding the age, background and reason for the initial 'downfall' of many of the 542 prostitutes who, between 1845 and 1887, entered or applied to enter the Home in an attempt to reform. Many, of course, had previously appeared in the newspaper or Poor Law records, or, if they were dismissed from the Refuge because of pregnancy, disease, or misconduct and then resumed their 'life of sin', were subsequently to do so. This Refuge and its inmates, many of whom thus occur too in other sources, is the subject of Chapter 6.

These then are the four collections of evidence used to identify all prostitutes and brothel-keepers recorded in York throughout the period. Provided they were actually described as prostitutes – or any of the terms referred to above – or that they appeared in the records of the Refuge, they form part of this study; since every one of the hundreds of thousands of entries which occur in the above material between 1837 and 1887 has been examined, and all those relating to prostitution extracted and subjected to analysis by computer.

Other evidence used which provides further information about prostitutes or brothel-keepers with a known address is the material and photographs relating to York's Unhealthy Area and Slum Clearance schemes which took place largely in the nineteen-twenties and thirties. Many of the insanitary cottages and tenements then demolished had, as we shall see, been occupied by 'women of the town' in the previous century. In addition, provided a prostitute who had already been identified from one of the four sources referred to above remained in the same address for more than a few months, additional information about her and the household in which she lived can sometimes be obtained from the census enumerators' notebooks in the censual years 1841, 1851, 1861 and 1871. Such instances are comparatively rare, however, since residential stability was hardly a characteristic of the activity. As prostitutes and brothel-keepers never described themselves as such on the census (usually listing their occupations as dressmakers, servants, lodging-house keepers, etc.), it is unfortunately impossible to identify them from this source, which can only be used to supplement information on individuals already recorded as prostitutes elsewhere. In all, additional information on 153 individuals engaged in the activity was obtained from the census, 122 of whom were prostitutes.*

Thus, by linking together evidence from the various sources used, it is possible to obtain a very detailed picture of the circumstances, housing conditions, family background and career of the many prostitutes who appeared several times in some or all of the above; and at the same time the main characteristics of the total recorded prostitute community in the city begin to emerge. This is apparently the first time that such an examination of the subject, at the level of the prostitutes themselves, has been undertaken, or that material such as Poor Law records and reports of court proceedings have been systematically used for this purpose. Similarly, the records of the York Female Penitentiary Society (the Refuge) are used here for the first time. By a fortunate coincidence much new material relating to this institution was discovered in the cellar of a York solicitor's office,

---

* There were, in fact, two or three instances where girls not previously identified as prostitutes were thought to be such on the census and picked up accordingly. This occurred when, in the course of tracing an existing prostitute to her address on the census, she was found to be living in what was obviously a brothel or house of ill fame, in company with several other unmarried, unoccupied (or 'dressmaking') female lodgers, all of whom had already appeared as prostitutes or brothel-keepers in other sources. If in such a household (which was invariably in a notorious brothel area such as the Water Lanes) an additional young woman with similar characteristics was recorded, she was regarded as a prostitute even though never listed as such in this or any other source.

only a short time before the research stage of this work was completed.

This study of prostitutes in Victorian York then is not a repetition of the 'statistics' borrowed by one nineteenth-century authority on the subject from another, nor is it based on the impressions, opinions or bawdy anecdotes of middle-class gentlemen who were probably either ill-informed (even if well intentioned), prejudiced or warped. It does not attempt to explore the institutional or psychological implications of Victorian sexual behaviour, but is a pioneer study of the prostitutes themselves, the circumstances of their lives and the poverty in which, sooner or later, most of them were forced to exist. By examining, as it does, all girls and women actually recorded as prostitutes, who had thus necessarily fallen from the higher ranks of their profession (if indeed they had ever been anything other than common street-walkers), it is a study of destitution, drunkenness and disease. The women in this book were as far removed from the high-priced courtesans and 'pretty horsebreakers' in Hyde Park, or from the celebrated 'Skittles', one of the most famous prostitutes of the period, as they were from the fashionable society ladies who were the mistresses of the Prince of Wales. In fiction, their prototype was not Emile Zola's Nana, or Alexandre Dumas' magnificent La Dame aux Camélias, but rather Elizabeth Gaskell's prison-worn, drunken, prematurely old and degraded Esther. Poverty, therefore, the principal cause of these prostitutes' downfall and the condition in which most of them lived and were recorded, is the dominant theme of this book, which in no way substantiates Acton's claims, but rather gives proof to those 'popular myths' which he is lately alleged to have shattered.

In the half century between Queen Victoria's accession and 1887, the year following the repeal of the Contagious Diseases Acts, 1,400 individual prostitutes and brothel-keepers were recorded as operating in the city of York, together with a further 20 'infamous' persons, whose premises were known to the police to be the regular resort of prostitutes, pimps and thieves. Though large this figure undoubtedly underestimates the actual number of women involved and the real extent of the activity in the city, since it is clear that only 'low-class' prostitutes – such as street-walkers, those addicted to drink, girls who picked their clients' pockets or 'unfortunates' so destitute and diseased that they entered the workhouse or even attempted suicide – can be identified, together with the 542 girls who were admitted to or applied to enter the Refuge. Others, occupying a superior station in their trade and catering to the demands of the wealthier clientele – those 'kept women', courtesans or high-class prostitutes living in expensive lodgings or brothels and carefully watched over by the keepers of such establishments – may well have existed; however, they were neither 'nymphs of the pave' nor, if the brothel-keeper wished to preserve the good reputation of the house, petty thieves. Such girls as these were apparently rarely allowed to leave their establishments unless in the custody of an elderly servant of the house, or occasionally to accompany a trusted client to the theatre or some other entertainment.[19] Similarly drunken prostitutes could not be tolerated in 'respectable' houses, and though the sale and consumption of alcohol on the premises was, as will become clear, much encouraged, this was at the expense of and for the benefit of the client rather than his partner. Most damaging to the reputation of a high-class house, however, were diseased prostitutes, and any girls found to be such, or even pregnant, were summarily dismissed and either entered the employment of less particular brothel-keepers or went straight on the streets or into the workhouse.

Thus, though a few expensive and high-class brothels may have catered for the requirements of wealthier customers who either lived in or visited York, the girls in these establishments were neither drunk, disorderly, diseased or destitute, nor did they walk the streets or steal from their clients; and such was the discretion with which these houses were run that there is little evidence regarding either their number or the girls they employed. An occasional newspaper reference to such houses, however, and the fact that diseased or pregnant prostitutes were fairly frequently admitted to the workhouse from an otherwise unrecorded York brothel, indicate the existence of premises so carefully managed that they were apparently tolerated almost without comment. Twenty-four year old Elizabeth Baldin, for example, was admitted to and died in York workhouse in September 1845 having left 'Mrs. Maude's' establishment in Holy Trinity, King's Court, a square not otherwise associated with prostitution in the period.[20] Yet neither the girl nor the mistress of the house was otherwise referred to in any other records. Similarly, in December 1871, two prostitutes, Elizabeth Ridsdale aged twenty and Ann Holmes aged twenty-three, applied to the workhouse because they were sick and had venereal disease.[21] Both girls came from a 'Miss Walkington's' in Cross Alley, Water Lanes – the most notorious area for all kinds of vice in York throughout most of the half century. Yet again, no other references exist either to the girls (who, it would seem likely, had been engaged in the activity for some time) or to the keeper of the house.

It is impossible to estimate what proportion the 1,400 lower-class prostitutes and brothel-keepers who have been individually identified were of the total number of people engaged in the activity; but it is clear that throughout the period there were women in the city whose bodies were for sale, but, either because they were comparatively law abiding or because of evident police or other protection, they were not recorded as part of that 'unfortunate class with which the streets of York swarm at night'[22] and thus necessarily remain outside the scope of this study. One such, who almost escaped identification, was prostitute Maria Wrigglesworth, of whom only one brief but vivid glimpse is provided. Though fined five shillings for being drunk and disorderly in Spurriergate she was obviously no common street-walker, being described with unusual detail as 'a well-dressed female who sported a black silk dress and smart bonnet with white satin ribbons'.[23] Another was prostitute or brothel-keeper Harriet Mottley of North Street. She was charged in December 1862 with the theft of twenty pounds from farmer and innkeeper John West – a careless individual appearing in more detail in Chapter 3. The *Gazette* reported that Mr West maintained

> they were both *upstairs* together, but the prisoner said there was no upstairs, and the chief constable (who said he knew the house well) stated there was *no* upstairs, only two rooms in the house, one of which was entered by going downstairs.[24]

It is significant that not only was this prostitute dismissed on the evidence of the Chief Constable who 'knew the house well', but that she too, although evidently well established in her trade, remained otherwise totally unrecorded.

It was a fact well recognised by reliable investigators of the 'social evil' at the time that the active life of a top-class prostitute was relatively short, and that as such girls sickened, took to drink or became physically less attractive they inevitably took the downward path leading first to what were described as 'notorious' houses of ill fame, and finally to the streets or the workhouse. It is likely, therefore, that most of York's prostitutes, in the later criminal or impoverished stages of their lives at least, would have been recorded, and as such will form part of this book. Respectable brothel-keepers who enjoyed police protection or toleration, on the other hand, or those prostitutes fortunate enough to retire unscathed, without a criminal record and without ever having been even temporarily destitute (during an illness or confinement for example), were never, of course, placed on record under their true occupation and so can rarely be identified. In such a hazardous occupation, however, such women must have been relatively few.

In spite of the literature circulating at the time and that which has since been produced on the subject, it is still a generally held misconception that the Victorians, and in particular Victorian women, were kept in sheltered ignorance about various 'facts of life' including, of course, prostitution. However, it is quite clear that in York at least, this could hardly have been the case. As has already been observed, throughout the period there were two weekly newspapers (and for part of the time, four) each of which regularly reported the appearance at court of numerous prostitutes, brothel-keepers, and in some cases even their clients. In addition, the newspapers periodically printed various petitions, letters and descriptions concerning the disgraceful state of the city at night, referring to swarms of abandoned females prowling the streets, indecent and half-dressed women assembling and causing disturbances at various notorious houses and inns, and to certain localities packed from one end to the other with nothing but beerhouses, brothels and houses of ill fame. For much of the period too the press published the Annual Reports of the York Female Penitentiary Society.

Even without reference to the newspapers, however, it would have been virtually impossible to remain unaware of the existence of prostitution in a congested city like York – many of whose main thoroughfares were the regular haunt of the street-walkers who 'wandered abroad' from the early evening until far into the night, and, judging by the frequency of their appearances in court, caused much annoyance and embarrassment. Fig. 1 shows that Ouse Bridge, as well as being on the main route into the city from Leeds and the West Riding, was the only bridge over the river until that built at Lendal in 1863. Until that date anyone arriving in the city by train and wishing to reach the central part of York was also obliged to cross at that point, and throughout the period the old bridge, being more centrally situated, remained the busiest river crossing in the

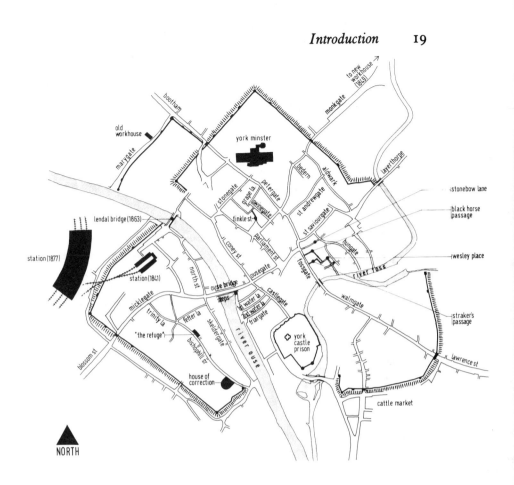

Fig. 1   York in the mid nineteenth century.

city. It, together with Low Ousegate and Spurriergate, was consequently the favourite haunt of prostitutes operating in the notorious Water Lanes and North Street areas, each of which was situated
close by, the former being described in 1858 as containing nothing
but 'dens of infamy',[25] and the latter (a small street but with an
almost equally bad reputation) having ten separate brothels closed
down by magistrates' order in one day in 1860.[26] Clients picked up on
the bridge, or around the corner in Nessgate or Castlegate, could be
whisked quickly into the sordid backstreets, but in the process there
was much soliciting and pestering of unwilling parties – as in
September 1855, for example, when prostitute Mary Smith was
sentenced to fourteen days for wandering abroad in Nessgate and

Fig. 2   Victorian Petergate – one of the superior streets in the city in which prostitutes were frequently charged with soliciting.

'seizing hold of persons and detaining them'.[27] Superior streets such as Petergate and Goodramgate were the scenes of similar annoyances, and since it was complained that gentlemen thus accosted were often accompanied by 'respectable females' it is improbable that even these could have remained blind to the attentions paid to their escorts by a certain type of unfortunate woman.

The term 'Victorian' when used to describe attitudes or behaviour, however, invariably refers only to the vocal middle classes, and tends to equate what is assumed to be their values and remoteness from certain conditions with those of the society as a whole. It has been shown that there could have been few women, even of the middle classes in York, who could have remained ignorant of the existence of prostitution in the city. The middle classes, however, were very much in the minority – the bulk of the population consisting of working-class men and women, many of whom, as Rowntree was later to demonstrate, lived in degrading poverty.[28] These people may not have had access to newspapers or even have been particularly literate, especially in the early part of the period. Nevertheless, they would have been only too well aware of an activity which was being carried out in the very streets in which they lived and the pubs they frequented and for which the women of their class were almost the sole source of supply.

In addition to the much publicised large concentrations of prostitution such as the Water Lanes and North Street, many 'houses of ill fame' – in effect the miserable cottages or tenements in which prostitutes lived – were scattered all over the poorer quarters of the city, particularly in the squalid and densely populated Walmgate and Hungate areas. It was here that the rows of back-to-backs and crowded courts and alleys, built and infilled in the early part of the century, were most congested; and here too that many of the lower-class prostitutes lived and carried out their trade. Amongst the poor living in such areas, therefore, there could have been few individuals without a neighbour, an acquaintance or even a relative who had not at some time accepted or at least contemplated prostitution as an alternative to destitution or the workhouse; and fewer still who could have been unaware of what was the last desperate resort of many of the women within their midst. Prison sentences, usually of seven to fourteen days, were an occupational hazard for the street-walker, and the frequent absences of these women (a few of whom had dependent children) could hardly have gone unnoticed. Nor too, could the permanent disappearance of younger girls, lured into what initially at least must have seemed an attractive alternative to domestic service or life in a dreary, overcrowded and insanitary slum.

Background details of many of the reclaimed prostitutes at the York Refuge reveal that, as well as seduction (often resulting in the birth of an illegitimate child) and 'falling in with bad companions', a frequent cause of girls becoming prostitutes was dreadful home conditions. Very often this meant that in addition to the poverty described above, the girl's parent or parents were recorded as drunkards, or that the re-marriage of a parent (a frequent occurrence in an age with such a high mortality rate amongst the poor) had resulted in cruelty to the stepdaughter, who left home for the streets. The history of seventeen year old Ann Boothdale, for example, admitted to the Refuge from York workhouse in December 1859 was described by the Ladies' Committee of the Penitentiary Society as follows:

Her mother is very disreputable, it is thought her drunkenness and evil habits made her husband leave her and go to Australia. The girl seems to have been driven by her mother into sin. She is anxious to be admitted and states it was 'contrary to her own wishes' that she has been leading the life she has done.[29]

The case of Louisa Harrison, also seventeen, was similar. She had applied to the Ladies' Committee in March 1861, but being too ill for admittance was sent to the workhouse. They reported that she had been brought to the Home from Doncaster by her father,

who seems a very respectable man, but her mother has been a sad drunkard for twenty years and with her daughter now keeps a bad house in Doncaster, to which the girl was taken by her mother. She was found by the clergyman's wife there, and by her has been rescued and has been two months in the Union.[30]

Another prostitute with a 'profligate mother' was Harriet Hardcastle, aged seventeen, who applied for admittance in May 1857. It was reported that her mother 'turned her out of doors and this was the immediate cause of her fall. She professes to be thoroughly disgusted with her past manner of life.'[31] Repentance for past sin was, of course, a necessary condition of entry – without it a prostitute could hardly hope to be admitted into an institution whose managers were as much concerned with rescuing her soul as her body. Miss Hardcastle's reform was temporary only, however, and in April 1860 the *Gazette* reported that she was keeping a house of ill fame in North Street.[32] Jane Scaife, an applicant to the Refuge in January 1858, had a stepfather who refused to have her in the house,[33] and a prostitute listed simply as 'Stubbs' in June 1859 was said to have left home because she and her stepmother did not agree. She knew a girl who kept a disorderly house and was thus 'led into sin'.[34] The vast majority of girls, however, had taken to the streets and were later to apply desperately for admittance to what was, as we shall see, a chilling and grim establishment, simply because they were absolutely destitute.

Few amongst the working classes, therefore, and especially the poor – of whom there were many in the city – could have been unfamiliar with the presence of prostitution in York; and many more must have had first-hand knowledge of its existence. Though little actual soliciting took place in their neighbourhoods (this offence, being naturally more rewarding in the main thoroughfares of the city) drunk and disorderly street-walkers with their companions were nightly to be seen in the back streets and slums, where fights between prostitutes, and even 'acts of indecency' in the ill-lit yards and passages, were not uncommon.

The existence of prostitution on so large a scale in such an historic and seemingly genteel cathedral city requires some explanation. Long before the nineteenth century certain areas of York had been associated with the activity, evidence relating to harlotry, fornication and licensed brothels in the central part of the walled city having been recorded since the Middle Ages. Grape Lane, for example, a narrow street only a stone's throw from the Minster itself was referred to in ancient writings and popularly known as 'Gropecunt' or 'Grapecunt' Layne',[35] because of its infamous reputation which survived even into the Victorian period; and adjacent Finkle Street, a place of similar character, was as late as the nineteenth century called 'Murky (or "Mucky") Peg Lane'.[36] Another traditional centre of prostitution was St Andrewgate – the church from which this street took its name having been converted after its partial demolition in the sixteenth century into a common brothel.[37] By the mid nineteenth century, however, according to indignant 'respectable' inhabitants of certain parishes and irate petitioners to the Lord Mayor, the problem of prostitution in York was becoming 'much greater than has scarcely ever been known to be the case at any former period',[38] and it was declared that there were 'few places in the country where an institution like the Female Penitentiary were more urgently required'.[39] The *Gazette* reported in 1860 that the streets of the city were swarming with 'these poor unfortunate girls', and stated that:

Almost every day some of these poor outcasts were brought before [the Lord Mayor] at the Guildhall charged with disorderly conduct during the previous night. From 11 o'clock at night until 1 or 2 o'clock in the morning these unhappy females prowled about the streets and being affected with liquor they conducted themselves in a riotous and disorderly manner and committed acts which were disgraceful to human nature.[40]

Between 1831 and 1881 the population of the municipal borough of York increased from 26,260 to 49,530, but throughout most of our period it could still be described as a pre-industrial city, with few premises employing more than a handful of workers. Apart from the railway carriage and wagon works, opened in 1842, most occupations were carried out in small workshop conditions in which craftsmen and unskilled labourers catered for the needs of the local gentry and the demands of the surrounding agricultural community. The largest single occupation in the city throughout the period was domestic service, which particularly dominated the female labour force. At the 1841 census, for example, out of a total occupied female population of 3,322, 2,216 or 68.5 per cent of employed women in the city were domestic servants and charwomen. The next biggest occupations were dressmaking, other needle trades and millinery work in which 381 women (11.9 per cent) were employed, followed by school-mistresses and governesses, numbering 82 (2.5 per cent). By 1871, when figures are available only for women over the age of twenty, there had been no change in this distribution of occupied females. Of the 5,175 occupied women in this age group, 2,271 (44 per cent) were domestic servants, charwomen and washerwomen; 812 (15.7 per cent) were dressmakers, seamstresses and milliners and 181 (3.5 per cent) were schoolmistresses and governesses. The only other female occupations to number more than 100 by 1871 were hotel and innkeepers (147) and agricultural labourers (112). For occupied females under twenty years of age the dominance of domestic service was even more pronounced, accounting, for example, for 76.5 per cent of their total by 1861. The prevalence of prostitution in the city, therefore, cannot be explained by the presence of factory conditions, which were so often condemned as causes of immorality amongst young working-class females; but rather by the lack of employment opportunities in York other than those associated with domestic service and the needle trades, both of which were notoriously badly paid and reputed to be fruitful sources of supply of women of the streets.

Evidence on prostitutes' birthplaces included in Chapter 3 shows that throughout the period over fifty per cent of York's whores came from elsewhere and, similarly, information regarding prostitutes' clients contained in Chapter 4 reveals that over forty per cent of those recorded were visitors to the city. Indeed, the number of such men referred to in the newspaper accounts of magistrates' court proceedings as being 'respectable gentlemen' in York on business, or farm labourers from neighbouring villages and towns, suggests that the city's position as a major marketing centre for the county was an important reason for its high number of brothels and street-walkers. More important, however, York, even in the mid nineteenth century, though declining in this respect, was still the most important social and cultural centre of the area, with the races, fairs, assizes, Assembly Rooms and theatre attracting both the gentry and humbler visitors, many of whom, apparently, spent their evenings in drinking and whoring. The races and fairs particularly not only attracted gentlemen and members of the lower orders, eager to sample the pleasures of the town, but also drew in prostitutes themselves, many of whom came specially for the occasions, from as far afield as Leeds, Bradford, Hull and even Nottingham, swelling the numbers of street-walkers already in the city.

On 2 May 1863, for example, the *Gazette* reported that three prostitutes, Mary Ann Smith, Susannah Pears and Sarah McMany, had been sentenced to three days in the House of Correction on a charge of 'wandering abroad with intention to pick pockets'. All of them, it was stated, had come to York especially for the races. Similarly on 30 November 1861 two abandoned females, Ann Taylor from Leeds and Mary Ann Brabiner from Nottingham, were picked up by the police for soliciting. They were both in York for the Martinmas Fair, and were discharged on promising to leave the city. Such occasions could even, apparently, be the cause of a girl's downfall. Sixteen year old Hannah Abbey, for example, who applied to enter the Refuge in July 1886 had come to York from the neighbouring village of Bolton Percy for the Gala in the previous year. She had 'been astray' ever since.

The railways and the development of York as a popular tourist centre also intensified the problem, again increasing both the number of prostitutes and the visitors for whom they catered. Thus in February 1887 Edward Martin of 9 St George's Terrace, Walmgate, was sentenced to nine months hard labour for keeping an immoral house, procuring and theft. It was reported that Elizabeth Bell and another young Leeds girl were induced by the man to catch the excursion train with him to York. He then took them to his brothel, and, when the girls eventually tried to leave, refused to let them have their clothes.[41] Another prostitute, Margaret Reece of Peter Lane, appeared in court charged with indecency in May 1870 and stated that: 'She was going to the railway station to meet the early trains, her object being to pick up any gentleman whom she could prevail upon to go home with her.'[42] The following week, having moved to Nunnery Lane, she was again charged with indecency, and three weeks later was sentenced to seven days imprisonment for the same offence. Within two months, now living at Toft Green, she was sentenced to a further ten days, and shortly after her release, having taken up residence in Trinity Lane, was fined five shillings for a similar offence. Exactly one year later, now having 'no fixed abode', she was again charged with indecency and within three months she was sent to the workhouse. By this time she lived in Hungate – in Wesley Place – a street which by the eighteen-seventies was competing with the Water Lanes as being the main centre of low-class prostitution in the city. She was described by the clerk to the Guardians as twenty-six years old, single, not able bodied and suffering from dementia. She was later removed to an asylum.[43]

The fact that York was a garrison town was also, of course, an acknowledged cause of the high number of prostitutes in the city, though, as we have seen, the provisions of the Contagious Diseases Acts were never extended to the city. Several of the girls at the Refuge were described as originally having gone astray after 'going to the barracks' and one suspects that there may well have been special (if unofficial) provision for their visits, though there is no evidence of this in any of the surviving military records.[44] In any event it is certain that as well as soldiers visiting the brothels in the town local prostitutes, and particularly very young girls, met them on their own ground. The Ladies' Committee of the Refuge reported in July 1863, for example, that Emma Clegg, aged only sixteen and admitted to the Home from the workhouse, though a 'hopeful case', had 'been in the habit of going into the barracks', as also had Elizabeth Ore, another sixteen year old, who had formerly been a domestic servant, and whose parents lived close to the Refuge, in Skeldergate. The Ladies had discovered that she had been 'induced by a girl who died recently to go to the barracks, and ultimately she left her situation and took to a sinful life'.[45] Only a month previously another sixteen year old prostitute, Mary Burgess, had applied for admission to the Home, but her 'state of health' – probably her pregnancy or the fact that she was diseased – had made her an unsuitable candidate and she was sent to the workhouse. She too, the Ladies had ascertained, had been a frequent visitor to the barracks.[46] Similarly in September 1862 Elizabeth Wales of Bootham Square, a prostitute aged only fifteen, had sought refuge in the Home. It was recorded that she had been 'sent early into service, but led by other girls went to the barracks, staying out late at night and at last she ran away from the place'. Another would-be inmate, Faith Wawn, withdrew her application in June 1860 and, according to the Ladies, 'Has again left her parents and is supposed to have gone with the soldiers when they left the barracks.'[47]

In addition, throughout the period there were many newspaper reports of prostitutes in company with soldiers, being charged with theft, indecency or drunk and disorderly behaviour. In July 1862, for example, street-walker Sarah Johnson, together with private Edward Taylor of the 10th Hussars, was charged with being disorderly and assaulting a policeman, for which offence she was sentenced to seven days and he was 'dealt with at the barracks'.[48] Another prostitute, Margaret Dodsworth of Friargate (one of the Water Lanes), was charged with disorderly behaviour in July 1867 and she, too, was in company with soldiers from the barracks.[49] In January of the following year 'unfortunate' Fanny Cass of St George's Terrace, Walmgate was charged with stealing a dress and chemise from the barracks,[50] and sixteen months later two street-walkers, Ann Saunders and Ann Hanson, both of North Street, were imprisoned for aiding and attempting to hide a deserter, private William Bloom of the 15th Hussars.[51] In September 1878 private John Burns of the 4th Dragoons was sentenced to three months imprisonment for hitting and stabbing prostitute Annie Dolbin 'when she was talking with another soldier',[52] and three years later another 'unfortunate', Elizabeth Convin of King Street (the first Water Lane), was charged with the theft of four pounds and fifteen shillings from private Robert Eastwood, of the Royal Marine Light Infantry. Eastwood stated that he had met her in the street on the Saturday night and then

accompanied her to a house in Hungate . . . He gave her half a crown for drink and entrusted the 'landlady' with a sovereign to change. Whilst the women were absent [his] suspicions were aroused and he secreted a purse containing four sovereigns and other money in his stockings which he rolled up and placed in his boot and then placed the latter under the bed. Having dealt out several items from the change referred to, he put the balance of five shillings in his trousers pocket and laid the trousers beneath the pillow. Next morning the pocket was empty and only threepence remained in the purse.[53]

Not only privates but occasionally officers too were reported as being in company with common prostitutes, though the infrequency with which this occurred suggests either that they had recourse to more discreetly run brothels in the city, or that they visited much superior establishments elsewhere. Further, of course, many of the officers, unlike the privates at the barracks, had their wives and families stationed with them. Two young officers of the 7th Hussars who did not, however, were W. W. Hope Johnstone and Lord Marcus Beresford, both of whom were single and aged twenty-two at the 1871 census. Beresford was later to become the intimate friend of the Prince of Wales, and his brother, Lord Charles Beresford (subsequently Conservative M.P. for York), was to involve the future king in one of the most damaging scandals of his career.* On 29 October 1870 the *Gazette* reported that the above two officers had been fined twenty shillings for disorderly behaviour in company with two prostitutes. Unfortunately and curiously, the prostitutes were not named.

During the mid nineteenth century much of the neighbourhood between the barracks and the city centre was built up to contain numerous working-class terraces, several of which housed some of the city's whores. Disturbances became so common in the area, and complaints regarding the conduct of prostitutes and soldiers so frequent, that in January 1885 the Chief Constable made the following recommendation:

Fulford being an important district on account of its proximity to the Barracks and the numerous prostitutes residing in the neighbourhood, I suggest that one inspector shall reside at Alma Terrace and take charge of the police station, with six night and two day men.[55]

This did not immediately have the desired effect, however, and the Ladies reported that young girls applying to the Refuge continued to have been catering to the needs of the barracks. They noted in 1887, for example, that Ann Elizabeth Medd, a seventeen year old pros-

---

* The Lady Daisy Brook/Lord and Lady Beresford affair (1889) in which the Prince of Wales played an active role and which was the cause of his rupture with the Beresfords.
   One wonders which (if any) of the York brothels was frequented by Edward's son and heir Albert Victor, Duke of Clarence and Avondale, who was stationed at York Barracks for four years (1887–91). During this period, which culminated in his brief engagement to Princess May of Teck (who, eighteen months after her fiancé's death in January 1892, married his brother – the future George V), Albert Victor was known by his parents and even by Queen Victoria to be leading such a 'dissipated' life that it was 'sapping his already feeble physical strength'.[54] According to other sources, he had by this time already contracted syphilis, was frequenting high- as well as low-class brothels; and in addition had been found and arrested by unwitting police when they raided a male brothel in Cleveland Street in London – an establishment staffed by telegraph boys and resorted to 'by the highest in the land'.

titute from Malton, admitted to the Ladies that she had just spent one month in a brothel in Ambrose Street, one of the terraces near the new police station.[56]

Even after our period the presence of soldiers in the city was recognised as hindering the work of those engaged in rescue and reform. In 1895 at the Annual Meeting of the York Association for the Care of Young Girls (a society formed in December 1881 which, in an attempt to 'attack the causes of Degradation in Women', had set up a Female Servants' Home and Employment Exchange at 16 Micklegate, a 'Preventive' Home for girls in 'moral danger' at 'The Lodge', 97 High Petergate, and a short-term 'Rescue' Home for prostitutes at Grove House, Monkgate) the President, the Hon. Mrs Maclagan, wife of the Archbishop of York, tactfully referred to the matter when calling for increased funds.

In making a special appeal to the wives of officers she said God forbid that she should dare to say that soldiers were worse than other men. She did not wish to think that for a moment, but they were much more attractive, and there was a glamour about a scarlet coat which turned the heart of a weak woman. She must honestly tell them that out of the cases that were brought to their rescue home, by far the larger proportion had been tempted and had fallen from the barracks.

The above illustrations suggest why the demand for prostitutes in York was always comparatively high, and indicate too that it may have been intensified seasonally. Further evidence in later Chapters indicates that, until the eighteen-sixties, the problem of prostitution in the city increased.

At the same time it is obvious that the prostitutes themselves were never in scarce supply, the main cause for this undoubtedly being the great extent of poverty in the area. As we have seen, domestic service was the major female occupation in York, with opportunities for other employment very limited. It was also the source from which prostitutes were most commonly recruited – since poor pay, hard and tedious work and often lonely hours exposed many of them to temptations they were unable to resist. There is limited evidence regarding the initial cause of individual women resorting to prostitution – that for York, as has been shown, being obtained largely from the records of the Refuge, in which a girl's alleged reason for her downfall was often carefully noted. The vast majority of applicants were in a state of extreme destitution, had already spent some time in the workhouse, and many had begun their working lives in service. Hannah Simpson, for example, a prostitute applying for admittance in November 1882, was nineteen years old and an orphan. She had been in domestic service, in the workhouse, and living a 'sinful life' for some months. Similarly Annie Short aged twenty-three was recorded in March 1884 as having been brought up in the workhouse. She had spent a very short time in service, went back to the Union, left of her own accord, had led a bad life ever since and had been imprisoned 'three or four times in the Castle'.

Another girl who came from a background of poverty and before becoming a prostitute had been in domestic service was nineteen year old Elizabeth Hansome. Her parents, described by the Ladies' Committee as very poor and with a large family, lived in a Hungate slum terrace – Carmelite Street – the address of several 'unfortunates' throughout the period. She had been employed in several country situations but had at times lapsed into a 'disreputable life' – the last time for more than six months. In January 1863 she was picked up in Hull for begging and imprisoned for twenty-one days, before being sent for by her mother and applying to the Home. Dinah Matthews, an applicant to the Refuge in April 1863, had a similar background. Again her parents who lived in York were 'very poor' and with a large family, but anxious for her to be taken off the streets. The Ladies reported:

The girl has been in service since she was nine years old, but frequently left her situations and when not required to sleep at them, resorted to a house of ill fame in Green Lane instead of going home to her parents as desired.

Chapter 4 which considers the clients of York prostitutes shows that the majority of those who were visitors to York came from the surrounding villages and towns; and this was overwhelmingly the case too with the prostitutes themselves. Elizabeth Ashton, for example, only nineteen years of age, was a girl whose history contained several of the elements already described as driving women on the streets. Her father and stepmother lived in the North Riding village of Hovingham from where she had been sent into service to the nearby small market town of Malton. There she was seduced and became pregnant, was forced to leave her situation and shortly afterwards gave birth to a stillborn child. Her stepmother had treated her unkindly and she had run away, ending up in a disreputable house in Walmgate. She soon became ill and went to the Union, there being told by the medical man that her recovery was doubtful. She became alarmed and began to read the Bible.[57]

Similarly, seventeen year old Ellen Wilson, who also applied to enter the Refuge from the workhouse, had originally left home after the re-marriage of her father, who lived in a small East Riding market town – Pocklington. She had spent two months in a brothel in Hull and had then made her way to York, where, being entirely destitute, she had slept out of doors and wandered about until a policeman took her to the workhouse where she lived for three months. Like so many of the desperate creatures who attempted to gain admittance to the Refuge, she was described as 'very ignorant, and without education of any kind'.[58] Eighteen year old Fanny Briscome, applying in December 1862, was another prostitute originating from a nearby village, Green Hammerton. She too had been in service, had taken to the streets and ended up destitute and in the workhouse. This was also the case with Margaret Dohele, a twenty-two year old servant from Ashton-under-Lyne, who, after prostituting herself in York for nine months, had been 'reduced to begging in the streets for a subsistence'.

Ironically, having been 'reclaimed', and, through the agencies of religious instruction, training in laundry work and plain sewing, 'reformed', the same girls, after two years in the Refuge, were once again 'placed' in service. Not surprisingly, it was noted that many of them returned to their old ways and 'vicious courses'. A few, however, as will be seen in Chapter 6, managed against incredible odds to regain their 'character' and make their way back into society, and, as the Penitentiary records show, a very small proportion of them even succeeded in marrying. Taking into account the probability that the inmates of the Refuge were prostitutes most favourably situated for reform, however, having such a strong desire for redemption that they entered the Institution in the first place, and voluntarily endured its spartan regime for two years; and bearing in mind that the rules of the Home admitted only those girls who were considered 'hopeful cases', were under twenty-five (and thus, it was hoped, not too set in their ways) and neither pregnant nor diseased, then it is unlikely that the rest of the prostitute population re-entered 'respectable' society and married, 'sometimes above their class' – let alone into the peerage – more frequently than they did. The claim that the majority of prostitutes, contrary to popular contemporary opinion, did so, ignores two fundamentally important conditions of their lives, demonstrated and discussed in Chapter 5. The first is the fact that many prostitutes were the victims of some form of particularly unpleasant disease for which there was no effective or permanent cure – hence the considered necessity for the Contagious Diseases Acts; and the second is the prostitute's invariable dependence on and frequent addiction to drink.

The fact that throughout the period women consistently outnumbered men in York is a further consideration in explaining the high number of them resorting to prostitution in a city with a surplus unmarried female population and, apart from domestic service, limited opportunities for employment. As will become clear, however, the overwhelming reason for their becoming whores was their background of poverty and deprivation, from which, sadly, even this desperate measure rarely provided permanent or even temporary escape.

For the vast majority of women in this book it can be stated with certainty that poverty was the result as well as the cause of their taking to prostitution, and it was also the condition in which they lived while engaged in the activity. However, it is clear that poverty itself was not necessarily sufficient to drive a woman on to the streets, for had this been the case then far more women would have been whores in a city in which, as Rowntree demonstrated, even at the turn of the century thirty per cent of the population were living below the poverty line. This would have been particularly the case, of course, with the large numbers of destitute Irish immigrants in York, from whom, however, a disproportionately low number of prostitutes was drawn.[59] Similarly, though there are a few instances of several women from one family walking the streets (illustrated in detail in Chapter 3) it was generally the case that only one member turned to prostitution while other females of the family, though presumably equally as destitute, failed to do so. Clearly then, though poverty was a characteristic common to all prostitutes, other contributory factors were relevant. According to contemporary observers these included ill treatment by parents or step-parents, seduction, the birth of an illegitimate child, desertion, widowhood and the need to support dependent children, lack of employment, bad parental example, being 'led astray by bad companions', intemperance, 'licentious inclination', love of dress and finery, indolence and lack of education. None of these, however, are necessarily causes of prostitution in themselves, and even when combined with poverty, need not result in a woman habitually selling her body for a livelihood. However desperate her circumstances, the fact that an individual took to and continued in prostitution must, in the final resort, be seen as a complex mixture of influences on that individual's personality. These, however, cannot be measured in the past.

2

Houses and haunts

Before discussing the aggregate characteristics of the total prostitute community in the city during the period, and examining in detail the lives and circumstances of individual brothel-keepers and women of ill fame, it will be useful to examine briefly the areas and types of houses in which they concentrated, so that places referred to in the text will be familiar to the reader, and York's prostitutes seen against the background in which they lived and worked. At the same time, of course, an examination of their housing conditions is relevant to an understanding of their material circumstances, and will hopefully cast new light on other aspects of the activity in the period.

The evidence assembled from all sources used in this study reveals conclusively that prostitutes in Victorian York overwhelmingly lived in those parts of the city most associated with poverty, and, further, that their clients too were drawn from the labouring rather than the middle classes. As has already been stated, between 1831 and 1881 York's population steadily increased from 26,260 to 49,530. At the same time the number of houses in the city rose from 4,955 to 10,733; and consequently there were re-distributions and concentrations of the population – particularly amongst the respectable working classes and artisans, who by the eighties had largely left the congested rookeries and slums of the central part of the city in favour of the new developments of small terraced houses in the Leeman Road, Nunnery Lane, Clementhorpe, Groves, Boroughbridge Road and Hull Road areas. During this period, however, there were still numerous complaints being made regarding the chronic shortage of cottage accommodation in the city, and Rowntree observed that even at the turn of the century the very poor were still for the most part inhabiting the insanitary yards, courts and tenements within the old walled city, or were crowded into the closely packed rows of dismal back-to-back slums of the Walmgate and Hungate district. Significantly, it was in these areas that most identified brothels were situated, and that the vast majority of recorded prostitutes drifted from one miserable hovel to another. Thus, as York's wealthier inhabitants continued their migration to the more healthy and desirable outskirts of the city, and the skilled and semi-skilled workers occupied the acres of houses recently built for the artisans, clear social distinctions became discernible, not only between different streets, but between whole neighbourhoods.

During this period of York's housing expansion fluctuations occurred in those areas most associated with prostitution, with certain areas becoming less or more notorious than had formerly been the case. The most significant development was the almost total elimination in the late eighteen-forties of the Bedern as a main centre of the activity; and the emergence in the eighteen-sixties and seventies of part of the Hungate district – and in particular Wesley Place – as the leading brothel area in the city, following the decline of districts such as the Bedern, Aldwark and St Andrewgate, and the partial demolition of the notorious Water Lanes. Walmgate, on the other hand, retained its deservedly infamous reputation throughout the whole of the period, and lesser centres of debauchery such as North Street, Grape Lane, Finkle Street and the Trinity Lane area continued in a more modest way to be the favoured haunts of both prostitutes and their clients. These centres of the activity in the period had various characteristics in common. Each of them was situated within the old walled city and all, to a greater or lesser extent, had become, by the early part of the century, the places which housed York's poorest and most degraded inhabitants. Further, with the exception of Wesley Place (built in the second quarter of the century), all had for many years been traditional centres of prostitution, and each of them contained or was situated close to a number of notorious beershops and public houses. As in other towns, then, poverty and the liquor trade were traditionally associated with prostitution in the ancient centre of one of England's leading cathedral cities.[1]

Until the early eighteen-eighties, when Clifford Street was built to relieve narrow and congested Castlegate and to link the Selby Road which skirted York Castle with Ousegate and Spurriergate, the Water Lanes area was undoubtedly the most notorious and criminal district in the city, and either housed or accommodated the largest number of whores throughout most of the period. With the Improvement Scheme, however, which not only plunged the new street through the upper portions of the Lanes but considerably widened the lower parts of both Middle Water Lane and Friargate, some of the most dilapidated and insanitary slums in York were demolished, and infamous beerhouses and brothels, the dingy and dangerous nests of vice which were the haunt of criminals, prostitutes and thieves, were razed to the ground.

This was late in the century, however, and for almost the whole of the period of this study the Water Lanes dominated the low-class night life of the city, and, as well as housing most whores, was the district in which most offences associated with prostitution, such as theft, drunkenness and assault, most commonly occurred. The three narrow Water Lanes which stretched from Castlegate down to the river's edge at King's Staithe were split between two parishes. First Water Lane or King Street was the nearest to Ouse Bridge, and was situated in the parish of St Michael Spurriergate. Second or Middle Water Lane and Third Water Lane or Friargate were in the parish of St Mary Castlegate, and these streets too were conveniently close to the bridge and Low Ousegate, which could then, as now, be reached from King's Staithe by steps. Hargrove described the Lanes in 1818 as dirty and so extremely narrow that only Friargate was wide enough to allow a cart down to the river at King's Staithe.[2] In the eighteen-fifties, however, the First Water Lane was improved and widened, so that after that date it was those parts of the district situated in St Mary's parish which were the most notorious, though King Street too retained much of its former evil reputation. Even before that street was improved, however, Middle Water Lane was undoubtedly the worst of the three, being the narrowest and the one containing a number of warren-like courts, yards and alleys, into whose dim and foul recesses respectable people and even the police were reluctant to venture. The evidence in the notebook of the census enumerator who attempted to do so in 1851 suggests that the poor man was the victim either of the hostility or the hospitality for which the district was noted, as by the time he had completed his unenviable task the entries were so confused and badly written as to be almost unintelligible. Similar unsuccessful attempts were made to penetrate the Lanes in the eighteen-seventies, when the Refuge Ladies decided to employ an 'earnest and Christian woman, who would visit and seek out the fallen in their homes'.[3] They were not successful in obtaining such assistance until 1873, and significantly their first and only attempt at this kind of missionary work was directed towards the Water Lanes:

Early in the year a Bible-woman was engaged to visit the Water Lanes, and although no great success attended her efforts, tracts were distributed and diligently read. At present the state of her health has compelled her to relinquish the work.[4]

Physically too the Water Lanes were notorious, and, according to contemporary descriptions, little was done to improve them before they were demolished. The properties, of various shapes, sizes and ages, were dilapidated, squalid and unfit – tiny cottages in the Lanes being crammed into insanitary yards containing stables and piggeries, and larger buildings being split into a bewildering number of hopelessly overcrowded dwellings, or used as low-class lodging-houses accommodating York's most destitute and criminal classes. Laycock described the Lanes in 1844 as having no water, except from the filthy river, no drainage and hardly any privies, observing too that: 'The scum of the country here come and sleep, and there is no discrimination of sexes.'[5] Within a few years the situation was worsened by the influx of the destitute and diseased Irish, hundreds of whom, men, women and children, crowded temporarily into the district before settling into equally insanitary but less notorious slums.[6]

In contrast to other areas which housed the very poor, the properties in the Water Lanes seem to have become more rather than less overcrowded as the century wore on, this being partly the result of an apparent reduction in the number of houses between 1841 and 1871, some of which, being in such a dilapidated state, literally fell down, and others proving so unsafe that they had to be demolished. Censual evidence on the number of separate households and houses in the Lanes is confused, and it is clear that the enumerators found it difficult to cope with this aspect of the returns,[7] especially for those larger houses haphazardly let off into a confusing assortment of separate but multi-occupied dwellings, entered by passages and flights of crumbling outside steps.

In 1841 the Water Lanes and their yards contained 147 houses and 713 inhabitants. Though the average number of persons per house was about five, however, some premises contained considerably more than this, especially in King Street, where one house sheltered

Fig. 3   Tindall's Yard, First Water Lane – one of the few photographs
of the district which was largely demolished in the early
eighteen-eighties. Congested yards such as this one, containing
tenements let off in single-room apartments, often grossly
overcrowded, were a nightmare to the census enumerators and a
constant source of disease and disorder. Throughout most of the
period the Water Lanes area was generally recognised as being
the lowest and most criminal quarter of the city, and that most
frequented by prostitutes and their associates. It was justifiably
described as containing little but brothels, public houses and
dens of iniquity.

15 and another 26 individuals. By 1851 the number of houses was
reduced to 134 and residents to 702. Again, however, individual
properties were badly overcrowded, with 15 and 18 occupants in
houses in King Street, and 39, 29, 26 and 17 persons crammed into
buildings in Middle Water Lane and Cross Alley. The situation in

1861 was very similar, with one establishment – 'The Green Tree', a notorious brothel, lodging-house and pub which furnished the workhouse with various destitute and diseased prostitutes and which featured in several court cases – listing 55 residents. By 1871 the number of houses was reduced to 123, and the average number of occupants per house had risen to 5.4. Again, however, particularly in Middle Water Lane and Friargate (which contained a house with 37 individuals), particular establishments were grossly overcrowded.

The residents of the area were characterised throughout the period by their extreme poverty – many of them being beggars, paupers, hawkers, labourers, field labourers, watermen and charwomen, and large numbers of them being regularly in receipt of parish relief. The majority, especially in 1851, were lodgers, and it was rare even for the householders to remain at the same address for more than a short period. It is clear, both from the newspaper reports of the magistrates' court proceedings and from the number of brothel-keepers' and prostitutes' addresses listed in the Poor Law records, however, that many of the so-called lodging-houses in this district were in fact, low-class brothels, the heads of households being brothel-keepers and/or prostitutes. Others, as the censuses and records regarding infringement of lodging-house regulations show, obviously combined their activities, having whole families lodging with them, but reserving some part of their premises for immoral purposes.

An indication of the area's notoriety is the fact that between 1847 and 1876 almost twenty-five per cent of offences associated with prostitution in the city were recorded as occurring in the Lanes, and these were largely theft from or assaults on clients, and the drunk and disorderly behaviour of street-walkers. Soliciting or wandering abroad, on the other hand, the most common charge brought against prostitutes in the period, rarely took place in the district – presumably because male visitors to the vicinity were already in the company of loose women. The reputation of the Lanes was such that few visitors would have gone to the area for other than immoral purposes. According to outraged petitioners, women of the streets were nightly to be found tipsy and with their clothes in disarray congregating with their drunken companions outside the many pubs and houses of ill fame in the area, or, worse still, on the corners of Castlegate itself – to the disgust and terror of its more respectable inhabitants. In addition to the high proportion of offences occurring in the area (and only those relating to prostitution have been taken into account here) analysis of brothel-keepers' and prostitutes' addresses extracted from the newspapers, the Poor Law volumes and the York Penitentiary Records show that, throughout the same period, one quarter of all those with known addresses were reported as living in the Water Lanes.

A man intimately associated with the district at the height of its notoriety was the Reverend Frederick Lawrence, the young rector of St Mary's Castlegate from 1871 to 1881. Shortly before the Improvement Scheme was carried out a letter of his, in which he complained of the disgusting condition of the buildings in the area (one of which had just collapsed); and the insanitary state of the Lanes, was published in the *Herald*.

There is a real want of light, air and ventilation. Some of the houses are supported by beams, others have huge cracks and holes in the walls. The lanes, courts and alleys, are close and narrow ... the drainage is defective, the paving consists mostly of large cobble stones, the surface either soaks in or stands in pools, the ashpits are foul beyond description; in some cases there are gratings immediately in front of the door or beneath the windows from which ascends sewerage gas.[8]

Also contained in the letter was a strange and, in the light of other evidence, unconvincing defence of the residents of this part of his parish, which was made up of the two most notorious of the Water Lanes and infamous yards such as Cross and Friars Alley. Of their inhabitants he wrote:

At the outset I desire to speak strongly in their favour. A return from the Police Office ... states that since January 31st there have been in this parish only five convictions, secondly there is not one resident woman of ill fame. That intemperance exists to a lamentable extent there can be no doubt, but this is, I believe, gradually diminishing ... that a large number of children seldom or never go to any day school is only too true ... a considerable number of the inhabitants are respectable people, working men and working women, widows with families, old men and women receiving parish relief, hard working Irish people, artizans who from the very great scarcity of cottages which prevails throughout the city, are obliged to take refuge in such places as they can get, watermen, coal-heavers, charwomen, match-makers, seampstresses and others.

It is apparent from the number of prostitutes who had addresses elsewhere in the city but who committed offences in the Lanes that there were indeed various street-walkers who, though non-residents, hired on a casual basis rooms which were set aside for immoral purposes in the area's many lodging-houses and even pubs. Since clients too were visitors to the area rather than residents, much of the district's notoriety can be said to have been imported and unfairly damaging to the reputation of those of Reverend Lawrence's parishioners who were poor, but respectable. The same, however, could be said of almost any low-class brothel district – and in this case the claim that the Water Lanes contained no resident women of ill fame is an extraordinary one, particularly in view of the vicar's peculiar knowledge of and missionary activities in the area. In 1877 (two years after the publication of his letter) detailed maps of the proposed Improvement Scheme Area, together with a key to the owners and occupiers of all the properties listed, were drawn up by the Local Government Board.[9] The owners of five of the properties in the two Lanes in Lawrence's parish and the occupiers of thirteen others were individuals identified from other sources as being at that time in some way associated with prostitution; and since lodgers were not included in the Table, the figure is undoubtedly a conservative one. Reverend Lawrence can hardly have been unaware of the occupations of such individuals, as their names and addresses were published frequently in the press. More to the point, however, Lawrence himself was included in the 1877 Table, and was listed as the occupier of two privies (shared by numerous other individuals) and of five different cottages and adjoining premises in Cross Alley, Middle Water Lane and Friars Alley. Two of these cottages, according to the document, were owned by Ann Render, a well-known brothel-keeper, and a further two by Elizabeth Air, another abandoned woman. Further, one of the cottages was said to be jointly occupied with Reverend Lawrence by James Moore, keeper of a house of ill fame, and another by Frank Dunlavy, also a brothel-keeper. Most of these characters are referred to later in this study.

Throughout his ten year incumbency of the parish Reverend Lawrence was actively engaged in missionary work amongst the poor and 'fallen', and this probably accounts for his strange 'tenancy' of certain of the most insanitary and even infamous properties in the Lanes. It does not, however, explain his denial of the area's deservedly notorious reputation, with which he was undoubtedly intimately acquainted. In October 1914 Frederick Lawrence, aged 74, died, having some time before given up the ministry in order to devote himself to various causes such as work amongst the criminal and destitute and sanitary reform. The *Herald*'s Obituary Notice is interesting both in its account of the Water Lanes in our period, and its tribute to Lawrence's unusual and demanding work.

The parish of St. Mary's during his incumbency, contained the three Water Lanes* which were then regarded as about the lowest parts of York. The Lanes were inhabited by many of the criminal classes, and the district had such an unsavoury reputation that few people cared or thought it safe to visit them. Mr. Lawrence was, however, one of the most assiduous visitors there, and he never hesitated to go into the most objectionable houses, and where there was considerable danger both from disease and violence, and carried on his work with single minded devotion. His missionary efforts were almost heroic, for he often took his life in his hands in penetrating on his errand of mercy purlieus which a single policeman dared not enter in those days. Much of his public work was extremely thankless, most of it against strong opposition and even hostility. So arduous and incessant were his labours in connection with the various movements which he inititated that his health gradually broke down under the strain.[10]

In later life Lawrence fell into 'financial stress' and a fund was set up to assist him, helped by friends and supporters in York and else-where. This scheme was initiated by his 'staunchest friend' and admirer, the York solicitor Mr F. J. Munby, who for many years was a leading figure in the management of the York Refuge for fallen women, and whose family home was actually purchased by the Society when they eventually vacated the Bishophill premises in 1919. It was, in fact, in his successors' firms records, that much of the material relating to the city's main Home for prostitutes was recently discovered. Both through personal missionary work and through his close association with Frederick Munby, then, Reverend Lawrence must have been as knowledgeable about local prostitution as anyone in the city. Though charitable, his defence of the Lanes' residents, many of whom he must have known to be actively engaged in the activity, and some of whom he probably knew well, is mystifying.

With the Improvement Scheme the most notorious area in the city was practically demolished. The Lanes' destitute and criminal classes, however, were simply made homeless and flocked to other unhealthy and overcrowded neighbourhoods such as the Hungate, Walmgate and Skeldergate districts, or to specific centres of vice such as North Street, Aldwark, Swinegate or Wesley Place. Appar-

---

* This is an error on the part of the *Herald*. King Street or First Water Lane was situated in the neighbouring parish of St Michael Spurriergate.

ently, too, in the late seventies various abandoned women began to settle in the area around the barracks. Before turning to these districts, however, an important point regarding the social status of the Lanes' nocturnal visitors should be emphasised. This district was undoubtedly the most frequented single centre of prostitution in the city. Yet, like other disreputable quarters, it housed some of York's most disgusting, insanitary and overcrowded slums. Further, as will become apparent in later Chapters, most of the whores in this neighbourhood were diseased, habitual drunkards and pick-pockets. Their associates were common criminals of every description and the district was, in effect, the centre of the city's underworld. As such, it could hardly have been the area to which local middle-class gentlemen – whether they were hardened whore-mongers or inexperienced adventurers – would flock for a night on the town. The reputation of the area was such that of those who had the means to pay for a less dangerous encounter, few but unwitting visitors to the city and those made completely reckless by drink would risk their wallets and health in the dingy alleys and foul lodgings of the Lanes. Apart from Mr Robinson's establishment (described in more detail in Chapter 4 – and this in any case was situated in the comparative safety of the corner of Castlegate) the area's houses of ill fame would seem to have borne as little resemblance to the conventional image of a well-appointed Victorian brothel, staffed by accomplished young females and frequented by the dissipated gentry, as did the two-roomed hovels in Hungate, which nevertheless, were also much visited whore-houses. It seems reasonable to suppose, therefore, that establishments such as these, which form the vast majority of those on record in the city, catered largely for the working classes and the poor; and that richer gentlemen 'out for a spree' resorted either to 'respectable' and therefore rarely identified houses in the city, or, in the age of the railway, had increasing recourse to those metropolitan establishments about which so much has been written and which obviously catered only for the privileged and the few.

Close to the Water Lanes but on the opposite side of the river, North Street and Skeldergate were other areas associated with prostitution, mainly because of their proximity to Ouse Bridge. Skeldergate was perhaps the most unsavoury and least frequented of all notorious districts in the city, with prostitutes living rather than working in the area and being housed mainly in the unhealthy yards off the main street. Any men returning with such women to their

Fig. 4   Entrance to Beedham's Court off Skeldergate – 'the habitat of
the pestilences of 1551 and 1604' and the yard, known as
'Hagworm's Nest', where cholera first appeared in 1831 and
1848. Several tenements in the yard were closed by Magistrate's
Order in 1903. Beedham's Court, adjacent to the gardens of the
Refuge, was the home of several low-class whores throughout
the period.

squalid lodgings, which can hardly be described as brothels, or even regular houses of ill fame, must have been almost as destitute as were the whores themselves; and completely regardless of their own safety, which was endangered by the likelihood of disease both from the women and their foul surroundings, rather than from any criminal activity in which the prostitutes or their accomplices might have indulged. Not surprisingly, very few offences connected with prostitution occurred in this neighbourhood, which is nevertheless worthy of mention as it illustrates the extreme degradation and destitution to which women engaged in the activity could be reduced. Throughout the period various women were described as living in Beedham's Court – a place with a reputation for poverty and disease dating back to the Middle Ages – 'the habitat' according to Laycock 'of the pestilences of 1551 and 1604', and the yard (commonly known as Hagworm's Nest) where cholera first appeared in the city both in 1831 and 1848 and in which an outbreak of typhus occurred in the same period. In single rooms in dilapidated tenements in this yard, whole families of the poor and the sick were crowded together with appalling sanitary consequences, and it was from the same buildings that various degraded street-walkers were reduced to apply for final admission to the workhouse.

In 1869 a Rescue Home for Fallen Women in need of temporary shelter was appropriately opened in Skeldergate; and higher up, in Bishophill, the long-term Refuge or Female Penitentiary already referred to had been in existence since 1845. Running down from Bishophill to Skeldergate was Fetter Lane, another narrow and disagreeable haunt of several well-known whores, and close to the junction of Fetter Lane and Bishophill, Trinity Lane housed a third Refuge for prostitutes in the period – The Home for the Friendless and Fallen, or 'St. Martin's' Home. In addition, several individual street-walkers lived in Trinity Lane, so that the Skeldergate area, though not as frequented by clients as other centres of vice, was nevertheless a district to which many low-class or discarded prostitutes turned at the end of the day.

North Street and its numerous yards along the river's edge were separated from Skeldergate by Micklegate, the western entry into the city leading to Ouse Bridge. North Street was famed for a number of its brothels throughout the period, and by the eighties neighbouring streets such as Tanner Row and Wellington Row were acquiring a similar reputation, though their houses of ill fame were

Fig. 5   Scriven's Court off Fetter Lane, one of the streets in the
Skeldergate district housing low-class prostitutes various of
whom, like Maria Nettleton and Elizabeth Shields, were
applicants for poor relief and were frequently admitted to the
workhouse.

far less numerous. Like many of the properties in the Skeldergate
area, houses here varied between ancient half-timbered cottages and
larger, more modern dwellings, behind which were courts such as
Hodgson's Yard in which prostitutes such as Maria Nettleton and
her family (appearing in detail in Chapter 3) struggled for an existence. Respectable parishioners of St John's Micklegate and All
Saints North Street made various complaints regarding the dis-

Fig. 6   Calvert's Yard, one of the many yards off North Street and
Tanner Row. As in the Skeldergate area, yards in this district
like Hodgson's and Letby's Yards contained various destitute
and diseased street-walkers. Several of these cottages were
occupied too, by more fortunate women of ill fame such as
Harriet Mottley, who enjoyed the acquaintance of the Chief
Constable.

orderly whores and public houses in the area, as, for example, in April 1860, when it was stated that ten brothels were operating in North Street alone.[11] These establishments were probably superior both to the notorious dens of the Water Lanes and to the miserable cottages to which street-walkers took their clients in the Hungate district, though particularly off the main street there were obviously smaller houses of ill fame, such as the two-roomed cottage in which prostitute Harriet Mottley entertained John West. Like Skeldergate, North Street never acquired the criminal reputation attached to the Water Lanes, or even to the Walmgate/Hungate area; and over the fifty year period less than seven per cent of prostitutes lived, and offences with which they were associated occurred, in this district.

Nearer the Minster were three other areas of prostitution – the Bedern, Aldwark together with St Andrewgate and three small adjoining streets, Finkle Street, Swinegate and Grape Lane. The last two areas particularly had, as we have seen, been associated with immorality and fornication since the Middle Ages.

The Bedern, which features only briefly but prominently in the early part of our period as a centre of prostitution had, by comparison, acquired its notoriety fairly recently. This small court, access to which until the early eighteen-fifties could be made only from Goodramgate, had formerly been the exclusive residence of the Vicars' Choral, who, though no longer living in the court still owned the once splendid dwellings which were now let out on leases. As early as 1818 Hargrove described the former mansions and their outbuildings which by then were sublet into a vast number of dwellings as 'the sad receptacle of poverty and wretchedness',[12] and in 1844 Laycock reported that:

Of 98 families living there, 67 have only one room for all purposes, 18 have two rooms, and 13 have three rooms or more. One entire building is let off in single rooms. The stair-case windows are so made that they cannot open, the rooms are low and confined, the light of day almost excluded, and the walls and ground damp and undrained. The building is occupied by 16 families, two abominably filthy privies being appropriated to all, and situate, with their accompanying 'ash-hole' or 'bog-hole', in a little back court. As might be expected, the smell in rooms of this kind is most disgusting and oppressive. Against the back wall of a cottage there is sometimes a dung-hill, the fluid from which soaks into the house. Indeed, this circumstance is repeatedly complained of by the poor people.[13]

In addition, adjoining the dilapidated dwellings in Bedern Back Yard there were piggeries and dung-heaps which contributed to the disgusting state of the confined neighbourhood. In spite of its appalling sanitary condition, however, and the chronic overcrowding of its wretchedly poor inhabitants, the Bedern, until its almost exclusive colonisation by the Irish in 1847, was a flourishing centre of prostitution – though once again the resident whores were low-class street-walkers who can hardly have been catering mainly for the local – or even visiting – gentry. As an indication of how concentrated the activity was in this early period, in November 1839 thirteen brothel-keepers in one day were charged with keeping bawdy houses in the Bedern.[14]

In spite of this action the activity obviously continued to flourish in the small court, however, as a petition to the owners of the property (the Ecclesiastical Commissioners) dated July 1844 testifies. The petitioners, various respectable inhabitants of neighbouring streets complained that:

The place called Bedern was the College of the Vicars' Choral, and more or less their residence; and by the ancient Statutes, they ought to reside there, and close the gates every evening at 8 o'clock to keep women out – that they have since leased the property out to various individuals and that in consequence of houses having been erected in the suburbs of the city ... nearly all the respectable part of the inhabitants, have left their residences and gone there.

That their late residences have all been let off in single rooms, many of them filled with whores, thieves, street-walkers, etc., thereby bringing great incumbrances upon the Liberty, besides great disgrace and scandal upon the Church of England by the Lessors continuing still to lease the said property after knowing the condition of the place, and that there is no remedy for the evil except by a complete renovation of the place ...

Your petitioners three years ago, in order to get the whores out of it, prosecuted one at great expense to the said Liberty, and with difficulty got evidence and a conviction for one month's imprisonment in the House of Correction – at the expiration of which time she went back in a Cab or Fly, preceded by a band of music and her associates flocked back double in number. The place is in that state that, if crime be committed, the inmates of it dare not give evidence for fear of their lives or property being injured by it.[15]

The prostitute referred to as returning to the Bedern in triumph was Mrs Sarah Heaton, who in July 1840 was charged for the second time with keeping a disorderly house there. Until 1839 she had occupied a house in Aldwark, but being one of the sixteen females removed from that street, she had set up residence around the corner in Bedern. According to the *Herald*:

She was followed by several prostitutes, the latter were removed, but she remained and the others returned ... and scenes of revelry, debauchery and prostitution were carried on with impunity ... at all hours of the night ... The cause of the noise and the frequency of the women of the town was the convenient brothel upstairs kept by Mrs. Heaton.[16]

Though the tenements in the Bedern were largely let off into single rooms there is some evidence to suggest that certain brothels in the court were larger than this, and could accommodate several whores. In November 1840, for example, two 'girls on the town', Mary Ann Walton and Sarah Dawson (alias Poppleton), were charged with robbing a 'Jew Hawker' of jewellery. Apparently he had been invited to step inside one of the houses of ill fame in the court and exhibit his wares, whereupon he was 'flocked around by four or five females who rifled his jewellery box'.[17] Sarah Poppleton was one of the thirteen brothel-keepers who in the previous year had been charged with keeping disorderly houses in the Bedern, and during the next five years faced various charges including theft, drunkenness and indecency. Earlier in her career of prostitution a certain Thomas Chappelow of Bedern, much to the indignation of the magistrates, preferred charges against this girl's elderly mother, who had smashed in his windows for harbouring her daughter in his house of ill fame.[18] By 1841 both Mrs Poppleton and her daughter were living in the Bedern. Sarah, however, along with two other well-known whores and eleven other individuals (some of whom may well have been 'on the town') was listed as living in the household of fifty year old Richard Richardson who claimed to be a labourer and his wife Elizabeth aged forty. Sarah Poppleton was aged twenty, and, like her two prostitute companions, was said to be of independent means.

Though with the influx of the Irish the Bedern became even more insanitary and overcrowded, and continued to be one of the most lawless and disreputable places in the city, its association with prostitution was almost completely destroyed and, as is shown in the following Chapter, only one brothel was reported as being situated there after 1846. Before that date however, and in the first decade of the fifty years with which this study is concerned, almost one quarter of all offences associated with prostitution in the city took place in this tiny, and, by all accounts, disgusting court. The proportion of prostitutes resident there was even larger. In 1843 the Chief Constable submitted a Return on the State of Crime in York to the City Council. Listing the addresses of the 118 prostitutes resident in the city in the previous year, he reported that thirty-three or twenty-eight per cent inhabited the Bedern.[19]

Nearby were two ancient centres of prostitution, Aldwark and St Andrewgate. The former, which ran parallel to the small court, was a long narrow street stretching from Goodramgate almost to the Hungate area, and for the most part contained small cottages (several of which were occupied by prostitutes throughout the period) and a few densely populated yards. Various of the larger properties in the street were used as brothels; and by 1839 Aldwark had become so disreputable that in one day sixteen brothel-keepers in the street were charged with keeping disorderly houses.[20] Leading from Aldwark into Colliergate was St Andrewgate; even the remains of the ancient church therein had, as has been observed, once been reduced to a common brothel. This street, which contained several elegant mansions, was noted for its larger houses of ill fame rather than, as in Hungate, the tiny cottages in which prostitutes lived and carried out their trade. Various complaints, particularly in the forties and fifties, were made regarding the immoral character of these houses, and of the abandoned women who lived in them. In January 1843, for example, complaints were made that in four houses in the street 'girls were exposing themselves in a most indecent manner'[21] and causing disturbance and disgrace to the whole neighbourhood.

In general, the houses in both Aldwark and St Andrewgate seem to have been slightly superior to those in the other main brothel areas in the city, though these too were staffed by common prostitutes and street-walkers, who, when necessary, took up residence in places of even worse repute. As in the Bedern, most offences in Aldwark and St Andrewgate occurred in the early years of the period, after which these streets lost much of their former notoriety. In all, between 1837 and 1846, twenty per cent of the city's offences relating to prostitution occurred here. In addition, the Chief Constable's Return on Crime in York, referred to above, revealed that in 1842 fourteen prostitutes lived in Aldwark and ten in St Andrewgate. Thus, in the early eighteen-forties, almost half the city's whores lived in these three adjoining streets and, between them, the Bedern, Aldwark and St Andrewgate accounted for almost half the city's early associated crime.

The establishments in Finkle Street, Grape Lane and Swinegate,

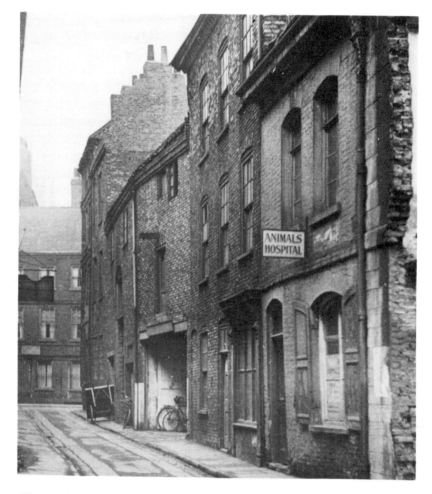

Fig. 7   An Edwardian view of Grape Lane, whose name and activities
had since the Middle Ages tended 'not a little to obscenity'.
According to Drake the place had been of old a licensed brothel,
and early examples of 'Grapelayne' prostitutes were Joan Abbot,
Katherine Lancastr' and Cecilia Egleston, all involved in cases of
'fornication' in 1437 (Dean and Chapter of York Court Book,
Folio 89). Amongst Victorian brothel-keepers with
establishments in the street were Thomas O'Garra, Mr Prior and
George Donaldson, the landlord of the 'Flying Dutchman'.
Resident prostitutes in the period included Elizabeth Smith,
Catherine Lacy, Mary Ann Bowman, Mary Ann Webster,
Elizabeth Ward, Charlotte Flint, Clara Garnett, Mary Ann
Henry, Sarah Booker Hirst, Elizabeth Horner, Ellen Fuesdale
and Florence Lickiss.

though comparatively few, were notorious and said by the magistrates to be run by 'the most disgusting and depraved women in the city'.[22] Adding to the infamous reputation of these three small lanes in the centre of the city was a number of public houses and beer-shops, such as Gill's Dram Shop and the Crystal Palace, which were not only the common resort of pimps, prostitutes and thieves, but apparently premises which were also used as brothels. The frequency with which licensees in the district were fined for allowing 'persons of a notorious character to assemble' and for harbouring prostitutes indicates a strong association between the activity and the liquor trade.[23]

Perhaps the most interesting area associated with prostitution in York, and the one which demonstrates the poverty both of the street-walkers themselves and the men who resorted to them, is the Walmgate/Hungate district. Unlike other notorious neighbourhoods, this was not cleared until the nineteen-thirties, and its reputation for both poverty and prostitution survived until well within living memory. The Walmgate terraces and courts particularly, which after the late eighteen-forties housed hundreds of destitute Irish immigrants, acquired a lasting reputation for poverty and drunkenness, and, following the decline of other brothel areas, the demolition of the Water Lanes and the consequent influx to the district of additional low-class whores, this general reputation for lawlessness became associated too with prostitution.

A detailed examination of prostitutes' addresses, location of brothels and where offences associated with the activity most occurred in the area, however, reveals that though the whole district had a deservedly notorious reputation, only parts of it were centres of prostitution. The Irish community, for example, though poor, contributed few women to an activity which actually declined or even virtually disappeared in areas colonised by the immigrants. Thus, as we have seen, in the late eighteen-forties what had once been a flourishing activity in the Bedern abruptly almost ceased and those parts of Walmgate such as Long Close Lane, Hope Street and Albert Street, which at each of the post-Famine censuses housed hundreds of the Irish poor, remained largely free from prostitution. Various of the sixty or so squalid little courts and yards branching off both sides of Walmgate and Fossgate were settled by the Irish too, but when this was the case, though drunken brawls and other disturbances were fairly common (and made much of in the local press), evidence

Fig. 8   Walmgate, about 1890. This street, the principal thoroughfare in
the whole of the Walmgate/Hungate district, contained the most
public houses and beershops in the city. In 1843 the Chief of
Police reported too that one sixth of the city's whores resided
here.

of prostitution in them was noticeably absent. The sixteen two-
roomed cottages in Britannia Yard, off Walmgate, for example,
contained 154 Irish immigrants at the 1851 census, and by 1871 they
exclusively occupied the yard.[24] Yet at no time was evidence of any of
its inhabitants' association with prostitution ever recorded.

At the same time, other parts of the district were notorious in this
respect, and Walmgate itself was one of the streets in the city in
which offences connected with prostitution, such as soliciting and
picking clients' pockets, most frequently occurred. In fact, for much
of the period, with the exception of a few houses of ill fame in Plow's
Rectory Buildings, behind St Dennis' church in Walmgate, the
brothels in the area were situated almost entirely in the larger houses
in Walmgate itself, and relatively few prostitutes lived or brothels

Fig. 9 Rear of Plow's Rectory Buildings, behind St Dennis' church, Walmgate. Various brothels such as 'Todd's' and 'Mrs. Varley's' were situated in this unwholesome terrace, and several diseased and destitute prostitutes entered the workhouse from this address.

were situated in the many courts off the main street or in the congested terraces between Walmgate and the city walls.

In 1843 the Chief Constable reported that of the 118 prostitutes resident in the city in the previous year, twenty-one lived along Walmgate and only six in the whole of the Hungate district.[25] It was reported shortly afterwards by the police that, since 'loose' women were tending to leave houses of 'general resort' and set up on their own account, there was a consequent increase in the numbers of houses of ill fame in the city, and it is clear from later evidence that

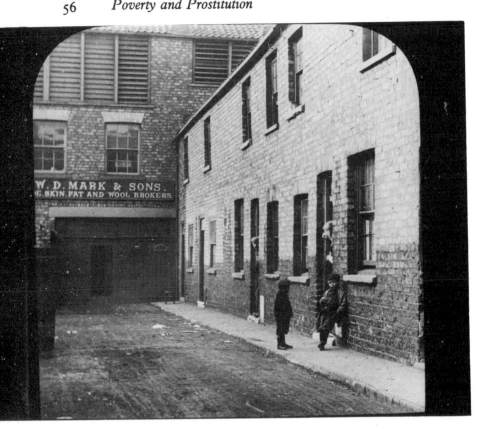

Fig. 10 A typical unpaved slum yard in York at the turn of the century,
access to which was through an arched passage. Note the houses
of the poor adjoin premises in which an offensive trade is carried
out. Other such yards in the Hungate and Walmgate areas
contained slaughterhouses, and several of these courts included
too the cottages to which prostitutes took their clients.

these were situated largely in the Walmgate/Hungate district at the
expense of all other notorious areas. Analysis of prostitutes'
addresses shows that by the mid forties thirty per cent of all prostitutes in the city for whom such information is available were living
in this neighbourhood, though the majority were concentrated in
Walmgate rather than Hungate. By the eighteen-seventies, however,
though the percentage of street-walkers living in the area was almost
the same, two thirds of these women now lived in the Hungate

district. Taking all offences for which a location was given over the
whole of the fifty-year period, 290 or twenty-seven per cent occurred
here. In this case, however, they continued to be concentrated almost
entirely around Walmgate.

The whole Walmgate/Hungate area, which contained densely
packed terraced houses, blocks of back-to-back cottages and notoriously insanitary tenements such as those in Bradley's Buildings and
Wide Yard, was described by Rowntree in 1901 as 'the poorest large
district in the city'.[26] Close to the houses of the poor, often backing
on to them or crowded into the same courts and yards, were dozens of
slaughterhouses and stables, and also in the district were various
offensive trades premises, piggeries and unhealthy grave yards. In
the vicinity too were the large cattle market – the beasts from which
were driven up Walmgate – the city's pig market, the gas works,
various light industries and one of the larger of the city's dungheaps,
draining its liquid contents into the river Foss, which wound its way
about much of the area and was given to frequent flooding. This
disgusting waterway was described by James Smith in his report on
the sanitary condition of York in 1850 as

a great open cesspool into the stagnating water of which the sewers of
near half the city sluggishly pass . . . It winds for more than a mile
about the city, and penetrates the low south-east side of it [the
Walmgate/Hungate area] among a crowded and poor population,
obstructing drainage, so as to make it impracticable in some parts, and
very imperfect in others, keeping the neighbouring land . . . continually wet and deteriorating the atmosphere around with mephitic
gases.[27]

By the end of the period little change had taken place, and though the
number of persons per house decreased after the eighteen-sixties (in
the previous decade numerous two-roomed cottages had contained
up to twenty-four inhabitants) sanitary conditions were still appalling and the area became even more built up. It was chiefly on the
inhabitants of the streets and courts of this neighbourhood that
Rowntree, a decade after the end of our period, based his study of
poverty.

This [Walmgate inside the Bar with Hungate] is the poorest large district
in the city. It contains . . . 6,803 persons . . . of this population no less
than 4,737 or 69.3% of the whole are living in poverty ['primary or
secondary'] . . . The district is situated in the old part of the city, and lies
entirely within the walls. It comprises some typical slum areas. A broad

thoroughfare [Walmgate] runs through one portion of it. Some of the houses and shops in this and in a few of the other streets are of considerable size, and are inhabited by comparatively well to do people; but a number of narrow and often sunless courts and alleys branch from these larger streets, and it is here that the poverty is chiefly found.[28]

In spite of its poverty, however, and its insanitary state (particularly if one ventured off the main thoroughfares) and the fact that though inside the walls it was by no means as central as the Water Lanes, Bedern, North Street or Grape Lane, the area, as we have seen, was the second most important centre of prostitution in York until the eighteen-sixties, after which it became unrivalled in this respect.

A major reason for this district's notoriety was undoubtedly its large number of public houses and beershops, which attracted prostitutes' clients and consequently the street-walkers themselves. Rowntree noted in 1901 that in the neighbourhood (within the walls) there were thirty-nine public houses – of which twenty-seven were situated along Walmgate and Fossgate – or one for every 174 of the population. This did not take into account the numerous beershops in the district, or the fact that just outside Walmgate Bar there were several other public houses clustered around the cattle market. In order to examine the area housing 'the middle-class of labour', Rowntree then grouped together parts of the Groves, Nunnery Lane and the Leeman Road areas, also containing slum property, and thirty-seven per cent of whose population were living either in primary or secondary poverty. These districts grouped together contained only nine public houses, or one to every 1,105 inhabitants.[29] Significantly too, these areas were practically free from prostitution. Thus it would seem that the public houses and inns along Fossgate and Walmgate, many of which dated from York's days as a major coaching centre, had an important effect upon the area's link with prostitution.

Though often referred to together, the Walmgate district was in fact separated from the Hungate area by the curving round of the river Foss and a short length of canal called Wormald's Cut. This section of the river could be crossed only at Foss Bridge, which separated Walmgate from Fossgate – a shorter length of street which in the nineteenth century led right to the corner of St Saviourgate almost in the city centre. Higher up St Saviourgate, by St Saviour's church, was the entrance to Hungate, which sloped roughly parallel to Fossgate, but in a wider curve, back down to the polluted river's

Fig. 11 Hungate, the principal thoroughfare in the district which, by the eighteen-seventies, housed the most prostitutes and contained the largest number of houses of ill fame in the city. The photograph is taken from St Saviour's church and is looking down towards the River Foss. On the right is the entrance to Lime Street and farther down is the narrow opening into Garden Place.

Fig. 12 Carmelite Street, looking towards Hungate. This dreary street in
the centre of the city's eventual main brothel area contained
various houses of ill fame, and was also the address of the
parents of several young applicants to the Bishophill Refuge.

edge. Thus most of the Hungate area, and particularly that relating to prostitution, was bounded on the south side by the Foss, on the west by Fossgate, on the north and nearest the city centre by a small stretch of St Saviourgate and on the east by the main thoroughfare in the area (a street much inferior to Walmgate and Fossgate) Hungate itself. In this small and unpleasant neighbourhood were situated all the Wesley Place terraces, Garden Place, Carmelite Street, Rusby Place and the various yards and small streets branching from the other side of Hungate such as Bradley's Buildings, and Haver Lane – each of which housed prostitutes in the period.

In spite of the river the Hungate district was within easy reach of Walmgate, for, once Foss Bridge had been crossed, three narrow yards or passages linked Fossgate with Hungate's most disreputable and probably most unhealthy streets. The first of these was Straker's Passage, a very narrow lane about half way along Fossgate, leading directly into Wesley Place itself. Nearer the city centre was Black Horse Passage which also, but by a more tortuous route, led right into Wesley Place; and finally, near the end of Fossgate and parallel to St Saviourgate, was Stonebow Lane, a tiny alley running from the now demolished church of St Crux in Fossgate to St Saviour's church on the corner of Hungate. These three passages, all within a hundred yards, played a vital role in low-class prostitution in the area since they directly linked the street containing the largest concentration of public houses in the city, with the district housing the most whores. Further, Walmgate and Fossgate provided other opportunities for soliciting, since they formed the main thoroughfare into the city from Hull, and were also conveniently close to the barracks. It is no accident then that the Wesley Place terraces (described in more detail in the following Chapter) became the most favoured residence of the Hungate whores, for clients picked up in the Walmgate and Fossgate public houses could, in a matter of minutes and by means of two secluded and ill-lit passages, be conveyed right to the doors of houses of ill fame, or to the general Hungate area – the district housing the most whores in the city.

The significance of Stonebow Lane varied slightly from the other two passages in that it did not lead, as did they, directly into terraces containing brothels, though it directly linked Fossgate with Hungate, a street in which several prostitutes lived. Instead, for at least twenty-five years of the period, six of the eight cottages in the lane itself were notorious brothels, and these properties were owned by

Fig. 13 Black Horse Passage, showing the entrance to Senior's Yard and Wesley Place. This narrow alley connected the many public houses in Fossgate and Walmgate with the brothels in and around Wesley Place, and was the scene of frequent robberies and 'acts of indecency'.

the church and leased and sublet by the Inspector of Police. The houses, which were minute even by Hungate standards, ran along one side of the Hungate end of the narrow little lane, and were known as Stonebow Buildings. (As an indication of the poverty of the area it is significant that at the lower end of the lane, almost on the corner of Fossgate, a large soup kitchen was opened, and by 1881 the Hungate Mission, situated in Wesley Place, was serving free breakfasts to destitute children.)[30]

The lease of Stonebow Buildings had been owned by Inspector J. Turner since before 1836 when he first entered the police force, yet, although it was to emerge in an enquiry that the cottages had for some considerable time been sublet to prostitutes and used as brothels, it is interesting that until the matter was raised in Council in 1855, the properties were never recorded as houses of ill fame, and their occupants never on any occasion brought before the magistrates. The scandal was first made public in a Council meeting in February 1855 and was reported in the *Gazette*. Mr Charlton, a member of the Watch Committee, declared that there was a great evil and disgrace that should be looked into.

He alluded to the fact of the Inspector of Police letting some tenements he had in Stonebow Lane to be used as brothels ... He had taken care to satisfy himself that what he stated had a good foundation. He accordingly visited one of these places himself and met with a young woman who was the mistress of the house and who, the moment he entered, shut and locked the door. (laughter) The fact is, that it being known who is the landlord of the houses and what is his position in the city it is required that these places should be conducted in a peaceable manner. (laughter) However, he obtained what information he wanted and then he wished to make his exit but he was told that he could not go yet as there had to be a lookout to see that the coast was clear and when that was the case he was allowed to depart.

In support of Mr Charlton, Alderman Evers stated that:

During the time in which he had acted as magistrate the circumstances referred to came under his own observation and he spoke to Turner and remonstrated with him on more than one occasion.[31]

The Watch Committee Minute Books contain further details of the affair; and though Inspector Turner pleaded in extenuation that he had made many attempts to 'keep his tenants respectable, had frequently discharged disreputable tenants and had had some of his cottages standing empty in consequence' – and even offered to

Fig. 14 Stonebow Lane from Hungate. The cottages on the left,
Stonebow Buildings, were brothels throughout most of the
period – the leases of which were owned by J. Turner, a York
Police Inspector who was the subject of a scandal in the
eighteen-fifties.

discharge his tenants or sell the cottages for the remainder of the lease if the Committee so wished[32] – he resigned in the following week, promising to part with the properties and until that time to keep them occupied by respectable tenants only.[33] This he clearly did not do, though the undertaking secured him his pension.

More than three years later, in November 1858, the *Herald* published the following letter from 'A parishioner of St Saviours'.

Seeing that an effort is being made to dislodge from one part of the city persons keeping disorderly houses, allow me to remark that unless such efforts meet with co-operation throughout the city, it will merely tend to the *whitewashing* of one neighbourhood by the *blackwashing* of another ... I have found ... that in a great many instances the owners of such property let to that class of persons that generally pays a greater percentage than be paid by a mechanic earning a livelihood by honest labour.

On reading the 10th Annual Report of the City Mission, I find it stated that the moral and spiritual state of the Hungate and Layerthorpe districts is fearful and that there are 28 houses of ill fame therein. In the parish that I reside in there are 6 houses belonging to the church and one belonging to a gentleman who is a member of the jail committee. These seven houses are of the worst description to be found in our city and scarcely a week passes that the police report contains an account of some robbery committed therein ... so dangerous has the road become that few people venture to pass through it at a late hour of the night.[34]

There is no doubt that the houses referred to were Stonebow Buildings, as the writer went on to state that the property was situated within sixty yards of the west end of St Saviour's church, and, as Mr Turner's cottages certainly were, 'in the immediate neighbourhood of four chapels'.

Two years later the houses were still being used for immoral purposes. The Watch Committee Minute Books reveal that in October 1860 J. Turner, 'late in this Force, be required to attend ... to answer charges against him of letting his houses situate in Stonebow Lane to prostitutes'.[35] Even this apparently had little effect. As will be seen in the following Chapter, at the 1861 census one of the cottages was occupied by a man called Thomas Simpson, his wife and three unmarried female lodgers. Mrs Simpson was a brothel-keeper and her three lodgers were all well-known whores.

It is clear that the physical condition alone of the three areas – the Bedern, the Water Lanes and the Walmgate/Hungate district – which, in different decades of the period, were the city's principal

Fig. 15 Layerthorpe Buildings. These 'wretched hovels of the poor' were situated in one of the several Layerthorpe yards which in the nineteenth century housed prostitutes such as Ruth Braithwaite, Ann Fox, Fanny Hodgson, Elizabeth Hodgson, Lily Maud, Ann Naylor, Ann Sutton and Kate Ward.

centres of prostitution, ensured that they would be the resort of the working classes and the poor, rather than the middle classes and the wealthy. This is confirmed by evidence on the social background of York's prostitutes' clients, contained in Chapter 4; and by an editorial in the *Gazette* published in 1849 following the second outbreak of cholera in the city during the period.

The respectable classes in this city can have no conception of the condition of certain localities. Take Bedern for instance and what do you find – filth, misery, drunkenness, disease and crime. Let those who doubt the proof of this assertion examine (if they have the courage) for themselves and they will find that no language can describe the feelings excited by observing the swarms of human beings hording together, without the slightest regard to the decencies of life. Let them for a short time inhale the close and pestilential atmosphere of these abodes of filth, and contemplate if they can without horror man in his lowest state displaying a brutal unconsciousness of his degradation. We need not tell our readers that Bedern is not the only locality in which these scenes of wretchedness abound. Medical men could inform the sceptical of other localities presenting scenes equally disgusting and disgraceful; they can tell of the fetid swarms who crowd the low lodging houses of Long Close Lane, Walmgate, the Water Lanes, etc.[36]

It is true that the Bedern had recently been abandoned by the whores, however Laycock's description of the court in 1844 indicates that even when it was the principal brothel centre in the city it was scarcely more inviting. At the time of this editorial, however, Walmgate and the Water Lanes had become the major centres of prostitution in York, yet these were described as equally disgusting and wretched – and localities whose horrors and misery could not be imagined by the *Gazette*'s readers. As was so often to be the case in this paper's observations, there was a sharp distinction between 'the respectable' and 'the poor'. Since prostitutes (like the rest of the poor in York) lived, as Logan rightly stated, in conditions of 'great personal filthiness' and in 'wretched homes' it is unlikely that their services were demanded largely by those more fortunate than themselves; and difficult to imagine, even if such women turned from a life of prostitution, how they could ever, in view of their poverty, enter 'respectable' society.

3

The prostitutes and brothel-keepers

By using the whole of the available evidence in the newspapers, the lists of Quarter Sessions, the Poor Law Application Books and the records of the York Penitentiary Society it has been possible to identify 1,400 individual prostitutes and brothel-keepers operating in York between 1837 and 1887 – the total, in fact, of all recorded individuals engaged in the activity in the period. Since no information exists regarding the exact point in time at which they all began and ended their careers, however, it is impossible to estimate from these sources alone how many prostitutes and brothel-keepers were operating in any particular year, or even to calculate with any exactness the growth or decline of the activity in the period. Further, as has already been observed, due to a certain amount of under-reporting, the weekly newspaper accounts of prostitutes appearing at the magistrates' court were not always comprehensive, and the extent to which omissions occurred may have varied from time to time. The extent to which prostitutes applied for Poor Relief too is an unsatisfactory indicator of the development of the activity in the half century, especially since changes in the Laws of Settlement, allowing relative newcomers to claim relief from their parish of adoption, did not take place until the eighteen-sixties. Similarly, the Quarter Sessions records, though valuable in yielding the names of a few otherwise unrecorded city prostitutes and in providing additional information about various of those already identified elsewhere, are limited and incomplete; and the Penitentiary records, though perhaps the most fascinating and providing the most detailed information about individual street-walkers and their lives, reveal little about the overall development of prostitution in the city.

Fortunately, however, for much of the period it is possible to state with complete accuracy the total number of common prostitutes and street-walkers recorded by the police as being 'at large' in the city, and also to know York's officially recorded number of brothels or houses of ill fame. (It may be noted at this point that neither the police nor the newspapers make any distinction between these terms, both of which are variously used to describe houses to which prostitutes resorted with their clients.) Some of this information is contained in the Watch Committee Reports to the City Council, and the rest is available from those of the Chief Constables' Reports on the Annual State of Crime in York, which from time to time were summarised in the local press.

It is clear from this evidence that the numbers of prostitutes and houses of ill fame in the city, already the subject of much concern in the opening years of the period, continued to increase until about 1860, after which there was a considerable decline in the activity. The first and most complete figures available are for 1842 and are contained in the *Gazette*'s summary of the Chief Constable's Return on Crime, submitted to York Council in February 1843.[1] The report contains the ages, addresses and place of legal settlement of all common street-walkers living in the city (these characteristics are discussed below) with the total number of such women listed as 119, and 39 houses of ill fame. By the following year the number of prostitutes had risen to 124 (no other information was given)[2] and in 1845 the figure was once again 118. The number of houses of ill fame in the city, however, though not recorded, was reported to be

greatly increased in number. This is however, rather attributed to the prostitutes leaving houses of general resort and taking small apartments in their own occupation than to any actual amount of prostitution.[3]

The next surviving statistics on prostitution relate to 1858, by which time the number of prostitutes in the city had risen to 173. In addition to this, but still with reference to the activity, there were a further 316 'suspected persons'. The number of houses of ill fame was now 88, and added to this were 324 houses of 'bad character'.[4] Within the next few years, due apparently to the 'increased efficiency and vigilance of the police force', the number of prostitutes was greatly diminished – in 1865, for example, there were only 71 whores at large in the city, 44 houses of ill fame, and three beershops and two coffeehouses said by the police to be the resorts of thieves and prostitutes.[5] Throughout the sixties these figures remained fairly constant, though the number of brothels in the city rose to 60 in 1871, but the late seventies saw a further decline in the activity, with only 14 houses of ill fame being listed by the police in 1877 – though this would seem to be a rather optimistic figure. Throughout this decade 'prostitutes proceeded against' rather than 'prostitutes at large' were listed, showing a steady decline from 134 in 1868 to only 53 in 1877.[6] No further comparable information was given after this date; however it is doubtful that the number of prostitutes and houses of ill fame increased appreciably during the last decade of the period. An analysis of all references to prostitution contained in both the newspaper accounts of the magistrates' court proceedings and the Poor Law Application Books (neither the Penitentiary records nor the Sessions lists cover the whole period) shows a similar pattern to that outlined by the police. The number of offences involving prostitution and of street-walkers applying for Poor Relief rose until the eighteen-sixties (in which decade 44 per cent of all references to the activity in the period occurred) after which there was a sudden decrease with only 4.8 per cent of the total taking place between 1877 and 1887. Even allowing for inaccuracies in police estimates, therefore, and these were reputed to be generally conservative in this respect, it seems clear that numerically at least prostitution reached its peak in York approximately half way through our period – an interpretation supported by the numerous complaints and demands for action published at this time.

The considerable decline in prostitution in the city during the eighteen-sixties and seventies may have been partly due to the activities of the York Society for the Prevention of Youthful Depravity, founded in 1860, many of whose members and subscribers were associated too with the Bishophill Refuge. The Society, which circulated tracts and publications to parents and employers pointing out the dangers to which children and young people were exposed, and which drew on the support of York Scripture Readers and the City Missionaries to distribute leaflets and preach sermons, took more positive steps to prevent the young particularly from entering prostitution. Rooms for the accommodation and refreshment of servants at the Hirings (an occasion recognised as being a fruitful source of supply for procurers) were opened at the Merchant Adventurers' Hall in Fossgate* – see Fig. 25; and at the request of the Society the

---

* The practice of hiring rooms for this purpose was continued by the York Association for the Care of Young Girls until the close of the century. It was reported, however, that though the

Directors of the North-Eastern Railway Company agreed to discontinue their practice of closing the Carriage Workshops on certain days during York races. The Society also attempted to have stopped the Sunday afternoon performances of the Military Band at York barracks believing (with some justification as the Refuge records demonstrate) that these had a 'very demoralising influence on young persons'. In this, however, they were not successful. Their most important objective from the point of view of preventing prostitution, especially amongst young women, however, was to secure as far as possible

not only the co-operation of the City Authorities, but the vigilance of the Police force, in order that decency and external propriety may be preserved in the streets. The adopting of judicious means for obtaining reliable information respecting the agency employed in ensnaring young people, and the places frequented by immoral characters; and when other means have proved unavailing, the taking of proceedings in law, or otherwise, for the suppression of immoral houses and for the punishment of offenders.[7]

Given that the Society included many of York's leading and most influential figures, both within the Council and outside it, these objectives must have had some effect.

The first Police Return on prostitution, drawn up in 1843, listed the place of legal settlement of 106 of the 118 common street-walkers living in the city. 46.2 per cent belonged to York, 41.5 per cent came from the rest of Yorkshire, 9.4 per cent from elsewhere in England and 2.9 per cent from Ireland. This information was not returned in later reports, but evidence on prostitutes and brothel-keepers identified in the three subsequent censuses reveals the birthplace of 123 women – 9 per cent of the total in this study. Over the period 31.7 per cent were born in York, 43.9 per cent elsewhere in Yorkshire, 16.3 per cent elsewhere in England, 4 per cent in Ireland and 3.3 per cent in Scotland. Thus, from an admittedly small sample, it would appear that even at the beginning of the period the majority of York's street-walkers were immigrants to the city – most of these coming from the surrounding small towns and villages – and that as the century wore on, and York's population increased, this tendency became more marked.

---

mistresses were unanimous in their favour of such an arrangement, 'to many of the girls the attractions of the Market place still prove irresistible'. (*York Association for the Care of Young Girls, Fourteenth Annual Report*, 1895, p. 14.)

Precise evidence regarding the social origins of York's street-walkers and brothel-keepers is scarce, since of the 153 identified on the census only 17 lived with their parents, thus enabling their fathers' occupations to be known. No such information is obtainable from the newspapers, and the Poor Law records are useful in this respect only on the rare occasions when a married prostitute (having supplied details of her husband's occupation) applied for relief on behalf of herself and her daughters, who subsequently became prostitutes themselves. Even the Penitentiary records provide limited information on the subject, with the result that from a combination of all sources it has been possible to identify the parental occupation of only 44 girls. With the exception of one woman, whose mother was listed as a schoolmistress, and another, whose father had been a schoolmaster, all came from the lower working classes. Thirteen were the daughters of small tradesmen such as tailors, shoemakers, engravers, saddlers, etc., 7 were the daughters of unskilled labourers, 7 were the daughters of persons such as charwomen, paupers, tramps and prisoners, 12 had mothers who were prostitutes and 3 (the young Nettleton sisters) were the daughters of a prostitute and a labourer. Though this sample is very limited, it is supported by additional evidence indicating that the majority of prostitutes in the city not only had working-class backgrounds but came from the ranks of the poor. This was certainly the case with most of the 542 fallen women who sought refuge in the Penitentiary (who acounted for over a third of the total identified in this study) who, quite apart from being largely destitute when they entered the Home, were repeatedly described as having been brought up in poverty and with little or no education. Few could read and fewer still write when first admitted; and it was stated in the Annual Report of 1900 that in over fifty years of the Refuge's history, inmates' backgrounds had invariably been not only poor, but disturbed, neglected and unsound. When recorded, the addresses of girls' parents provide further evidence regarding their humble origins. All had been brought up in those neighbourhoods already described as being occupied almost exclusively by the working classes, and though none had parents living in the Water Lanes, the families of many of the girls resided in those districts such as Skeldergate, Aldwark and Hungate noted not only for their poverty but for their association with prostitution.

A further indication of prostitutes' backgrounds is their own previous occupation, or, in the case of those identified from the enumerators' notebooks, the occupation they were allegedly engaged in at the time of the census. Since none of them admitted to being women of the streets in this source, its main interest is in how they saw fit to describe themselves – a reflection, perhaps, of previous occupations, however briefly pursued. Of the 66 prostitutes with occupations listed on the censuses, 25 claimed to be dressmakers, 17 servants, 5 laundry maids, 3 charwomen, 3 housekeepers and 3 seamstresses. The rest were allegedly in other occupations related to the needle trades such as staymaking, cap and bonnet making, etc., all of which, like dressmaking, because of their notoriously low rates of pay, were reputed to be fruitful sources of supply for prostitution. It is possible, however, that some of these women were claiming such occupations because they accorded most plausibly with their present circumstances, and were the ones least likely to be disproved, rather than because they had, in fact, previously been employed as such. Of the 56 prostitutes whose previous occupations were listed in the Penitentiary records, on the other hand, 41 had been servants – the majority of girls with occupations listed having thus been employed (or claiming to have been employed) in the two main female occupations in the city. Of the remainder, 5 had been millworkers, 3 barmaids, one a laundress, one a nurse, one a public house singer, one a tramp, one a sewing machinist and one, twenty-eight year old Elizabeth Irons who had been married at fourteen and had led a 'profligate life ever since', had travelled with shows as a horse-rider.[8] Only one of these girls claimed to have been a dressmaker. These girls, of course, had no reason to conceal their present mode of life (the Refuge was intended specifically for prostitutes) or to lie about their former occupations. The high number of domestic servants in this sample demonstrates even more than information about parental occupation, the humble origins of York whores – the vast majority of whom, according to statements made by the Penitentiary Committee, had worked as general skivvies not in well-run 'respectable' establishments but in situations of the 'lowest description'.

Of the relatively few prostitutes and brothel-keepers known to have been married, information on husbands' occupations has been found for only twenty-four individuals, all of whom belonged to the working classes. Six prostitutes and one brothel-keeper were the wives of labourers (one of whom also kept a brothel) and two prostitutes were married (in succession) to Henry Ashbrook of the Bedern, who claimed to be a house painter but who was in fact the keeper of a notorious house of ill fame. Two women were married to shoemakers (one of whom was a brothel-keeper), two to hairdressers, two to joiners, two to maltsters and one to a lodging-house keeper. The remainder, such as a sandgetter, a porter, a striker and a gardener, were employed in a variety of semi-skilled and labouring occupations.

The marital status of individual prostitutes and brothel-keepers was rarely included in the newspapers or court records, so that most of the 625 offenders referred to in these sources but not appearing elsewhere cannot be classified in this respect. The marital condition of Poor Law applicants and census respondents on the other hand was invariably given, and this information, together with that from the Penitentiary, indicates that few of York's street-walkers were married women, the majority, as magistrates and Lord Mayors were frequently to deplore, being young girls in their teens and very early twenties. Of the 252 prostitutes who applied at least once for poor relief in the period, the marital status of 233 was recorded. Of these, 213 or 91.4 per cent were single; 16 (6.9 per cent) were married and 4 (1.7 per cent) were widows. In addition 41 brothel-keepers were identified, though most of these were on record as prostitutes' land-lords rather than as applicants for relief. Since in many instances the surname only was given, the sex of 22 of these individuals is unknown; 10, however, were males and 9 were females. Only one of the men and three of the women can be said with certainty to have been married.

Of the 122 prostitutes identified on the census, the marital status of 113 is known. Of these, 98 or 86.7 per cent were single; 13 (11.5 per cent) were married and 2 (1.8 per cent) were widows. Thirty brothel-keepers were identified from this source, 14 of whom were men (all married) and of the 16 females, 6 were single, 8 were married and 2 were widows. From the evidence in these two sources then (which represents a sample of rather more than one in four pros-titutes in the city) about 90 per cent were unmarried.

Turning to the other material containing comparable evidence, the Penitentiary records, it is possible that the girls and women appear-ing here may be regarded as unrepresentative of the total prostitute community in the city, particularly in respect of age and marital status. Applicants over the age of twenty-five were not supposed to be admitted (though in fact, ten women aged between twenty-five and thirty years entered the Home) and though there were no rules restricting the admission of married women, such an age limit and the fact that the Home was a 'long term' Refuge, could obviously be expected to reduce their number – had there been a high proportion of elderly married prostitutes at large in the city. In fact, however, since it is clear that most street-walkers were single, and that the vast majority were in any case under the age of twenty-five, it is unlikely that the age limit imposed by the Institution had any great effect on either the age or marital status of those applying. Further, it must be emphasised that over forty per cent of all street-walkers identified in this study are to be found in this source; and that the Refuge material relates not only to those applicants remaining at the Home (and those who endured its rigours for two years might well have been untypical) but to all those too who, for various reasons such as misbehaviour while on probation, disease or pregnancy, were refused entry or stayed in the Refuge for only a short period of time. Between 1845 when the Home was opened, and 1887, 502 girls were admitted for varying lengths of time, and a further 40 made unsuccessful applications. Of these only 5 or 0.9 per cent were recorded by the Ladies' Committee as being or having been married. Of the 888 York prostitutes for whom information is available, therefore, more than 95 per cent would appear to have been single women.

With regard to ages, neither the Sessions nor the newspaper reports of magistrates' court proceedings are particularly valuable in this respect, though in the latter a prostitute's age is occasionally given, and street-walkers are frequently described as young, or very young girls on the town. Even without reference to other material these weekly reports over the half century give an overwhelming impression of the youth of most of the girls involved, and this is substantiated by contemporary observations and evidence from other sources. Prostitutes' ages are invariably recorded in the often detailed newspaper reports of the Quarter Sessions, however; and this information is usually included too, of course, in the censuses, the Poor Law volumes, and to a lesser extent in the Penitentiary material. Even so, this tells us nothing of the age at which a girl first resorted to prostitution, and only in the event of a street-walker's recorded death is it possible to state with certainty that she had left the activity.

In all, the ages of 524 individual street-walkers (43 per cent of the whole) were contained at least once in the above material throughout the period; and in the event of any individual having previously appeared on record as a prostitute – in court, for example – or subsequently doing so, it is possible to arrive at the age at which she was first and last reported as being on the streets. As both the Penitentiary records and the Poor Law volumes reveal, however, a considerable gap could elapse between a girl, or even a child, resorting to prostitution (particularly if she lived in a regular brothel rather than walked the streets) and her being picked up by the police or requiring poor relief – thus being placed on record. It was often the case that fifteen and sixteen year old prostitutes applied to the Refuge having already 'lived an irregular life' for some time, and others were admitted to the workhouse who were diseased or pregnant. While it is impossible to know for how long these girls had previously been engaged in the activity, it is clear that, before being recorded, they could already have been whores for some time.

As we have seen, for the 524 prostitutes whose ages were recorded at least once in the period it is possible, by referring back to their first and forward to their final appearance, to arrive at the outer age limits of their recorded time in the activity. Such a calculation clearly shows the concentration of prostitutes in the fifteen to twenty-five year old age group, with 437 (83.3 per cent) first appearing on record at York between these ages; and 398 (75.9 per cent) ceasing to be recorded under the age of twenty-five.

Table 1

Ages at which women were first and last recorded
as prostitutes in York, 1837–87.

Age	First recorded		Last recorded	
	Number	Percentage	Number	Percentage
Under 20 years	315	60.0	257	49.0
21–25	122	23.3	141	26.9
26–30	60	11.5	74	14.0
31–35	17	3.2	31	5.9
36–40	8	1.5	15	2.9
Over 40 years	2	.4	8	1.5

Fig. 16 This and the following three photographs, reproduced from *The Reformatory and Refuge Journal* 1899 and included amongst the York Penitentiary records, are of children 'found in the streets of a provincial city' in the eighteen-eighties and rescued from 'moral danger'.

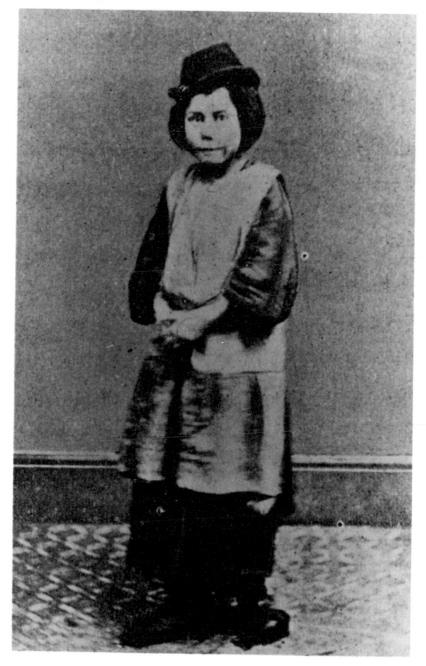

Fig. 17 This girl and her sister (Fig. 16) were found deserted by their parents. They were trained in an Industrial School such as the one in York, for which the Penitentiary inmates did the laundry.

Fig. 18 This child's mother was dead and her father, a labourer, locked
    her out of the room in which they lived so that she wandered
    about the streets each day. She had no bed or covering at night.

Fig. 19 This child was brought before the magistrates at the age of
eleven, dirty and in rags. Her father was dead and her mother in
prison.

A precise age distribution for all prostitutes at large in York in any one year is available only for 1842, and this is contained in the Chief Constable's Return to the Council, referred to above. In that year, it will be remembered, 118 common street-walkers were known to the police and the ages of all these women were recorded. Though there were fewer girls under twenty-one years in 1842 than was to be the case over the whole period, 75 per cent of prostitutes in the city were aged under twenty-six – a similar percentage to that expressed in Table 1. The precise age distribution for 1842 was as follows: 49 prostitutes (42 per cent) were aged twenty and under; 39 (33 per cent) were aged between twenty-one and twenty-five; 16 (13 per cent) were aged between twenty-six and thirty, and 12 (10 per cent) were between thirty and forty. Only two women (1.7 per cent) were over forty years of age. From both sets of figures then, it is clear that at least 75 per cent of prostitutes throughout the period were below the age of twenty-six, and that relatively few were still engaged in the activity after the age of thirty. A more detailed analysis of the under twenty year olds, however, shows important differences between the two sets of evidence, indicating either that in 1842 the police were unaware of the existence of very young prostitutes in the city, or that after that date younger girls were resorting to the activity. In 1842 only three prostitutes (2.5 per cent) were listed as being seventeen years old, and these were the youngest recorded in the city. Yet evidence relating to the whole period reveals that subsequently 5 fourteen year olds were prostituting themselves in York, 19 girls were aged only fifteen, 45 girls were aged sixteen and 52 were seventeen years old. Thus over the half century 121 (23.1 per cent) of York's street-walkers were aged under eighteen, compared with only 2.5 per cent in 1842. These figures for York prostitutes are similar to those produced by Tait based on an analysis of the ages of prostitutes admitted to the Edinburgh Lock Hospital between 1835 and 1842, and support his conclusion that: 'By far the greater number of prostitutes are between the ages of fifteen and twenty-five.'[9]

Apart from the five fourteen year old girls, three of whom were admitted to the Refuge there is no evidence for York of child prostitution of the sort encountered by rescue workers in other provincial towns in the period,* and exposed by William Stead in London.[10]

* The *Report on Female Prostitution* published in Edinburgh in 1857, for example, states that in Liverpool alone, there were at least 200 'regular' prostitutes under the age of twelve. A later Rescue worker reported to the York Penitentiary evidence of child prostitution in towns as unlikely as Shrewsbury and Hereford. 'Infant schools need very watchful care. As my first

However, it is obvious that by the eighties there were houses in the city containing very young prostitutes, and some of these, when applying to the Refuge, mentioned houses in Hungate and Walmgate which seemed to specialise in girls of their age. In February 1885, for example, eighteen year old Florence Mary Taylor described to the Committee Ladies how she had run away from home four years previously and gone to a 'bad house in Hungate'. She afterwards went to the Penitentiary in Hull for fifteen months, and then went into service. After only a month she returned to the Hungate brothel and was later admitted to yet another York Rescue Home – 'The Rest' in Aldwark,* from which she applied to the Refuge in Bishophill.[11] In the following year (June 1886) fourteen year old Mary Jane Sutherland applied to the Refuge. She had been in service for a short time in a public house in Hull and had associated with 'bad' companions. Her parents lived in Scarborough and she had come from there a month previously 'with a woman who took her to a house in Walmgate'. She had been rescued from the brothel by the police and she too had been to the Aldwark Home before applying to the Refuge.[12]

Regardless of the age at which they began or ended their careers in prostitution it is possible for those street-walkers referred to more than once in any of the sources to estimate their minimum recorded length of time in the activity. Such a calculation, however, is of limited value, as it is clear that many women recorded only once as prostitutes were experienced street-walkers who had for some reason eluded arrest, or who, though continuing in the occupation, were never referred to again. There were others who, though habitual street-walkers, stayed in York only briefly prior to or following an isolated arrest. Excluding those prostitutes who appear only in the

experience in the work was in being on the Committee of a Home for fallen children in another town, in Shrewsbury, I am always on the lookout for the children. Here we have had one as young as four years and many from eight years – one also of six from a very bad house which we closed. A majority of our girls are under eighteen and a large proportion under sixteen; thirteen, fourteen and fifteen are quite the usual age. Many of them are not only fallen but deeply depraved.'
Letter from Madeline E. Atkinson, Hon. Secretary of the Hereford Diocesan Society for the Rescue and Protection of Young Women and Children, to the Rev. A. S. Crawley, a Committee Member of the York Penitentiary Society and the Hon. Secretary for the York Diocesan Association for Preventive and Rescue Work, dated 1915; included in the York Penitentiary Society records.

* This was the original Rescue Home of the York Association for the Care of Young Girls. Within a few months it was transferred to larger premises at Grove House, Monkgate (see page 29).

records of the Penitentiary and for whom there is no other evidence, it is possible to assemble such evidence for 951 women. Of these, 665 or 69.9 per cent are recorded on only one occasion in the city, though many of these were described as 'well known to the police' or as 'old offenders'. 122 prostitutes (12.8 per cent) were recorded as remaining in the activity for up to two years; 76 (8 per cent) had records extending between two and five years and 59 (6.2 per cent) had records of between five and ten years. 23 women (2.4 per cent) were listed as being on the streets for between ten and fifteen years, and only 6 (0.6 per cent) remained in the activity for more than fifteen years. Thus, even bearing in mind the limitations of the evidence available, it would seem that contemporary observers such as Tait were correct in their assertion that the vast majority of prostitutes remained in the activity for less than five years.

It would be interesting to know the number of prostitutes both married and single who had children, and how many of these babies survived infancy and were brought up by their mothers. Also, whether such women resorted to prostitution before or after the birth of their first child, and whether illegitimacy was a cause as well as a consequence of the activity. This was said to be the case with some of the girls at the Refuge, the only source which provides any evidence at all on the causes of individual girls taking to the streets. Such information, however, is fragmentary, and almost all evidence available relating to prostitutes' families is that contained in the censuses and the Poor Law volumes, which do not, of course, necessarily indicate the number of times that an individual became pregnant, or the number of children that she eventually bore.

The newspapers, being concerned largely with the magistrates' courts and with offences in which prostitutes were involved, rarely reported whether or not a prostitute had children, or even whether she was married. Of the 374 street-walkers identified on the censuses or appearing in the Poor Law Application and Report books, however, fourteen were recorded as being the mothers of one child, five women had two children living with them, three women had three children and one had a family of five. In addition, entries in the Poor Law volumes for infants' funeral expenses reveal that four prostitutes were the mothers of children who had died. A further nineteen prostitutes applied for relief or admittance to the workhouse during their confinement for their only recorded infant. The Refuge records reveal that a further six prostitutes had had children – one of whom had had four, who had all died, three had had one child who had died, one had two children and another inmate had a baby of eleven months. In addition the Ladies reported that three of their applicants were pregnant. In all then, only fifty-five prostitutes were recorded as having borne at least one child or as being pregnant. Of this number, forty-one were single women, ten were married, two were widows and the marital status of two was not recorded.

Out of the total for whom this information is available (those prostitutes identified on the censuses, in the Poor Law volumes and the records of the Female Penitentiary) this figure, representing only six per cent, seems a very small proportion; especially in view of the nature of their occupation, the age of most of the women concerned and the inadequacy of contraceptive techniques available in the period. It was an opinion held by contemporaries that many street-walkers were barren or at least infertile. It seems more probable, however, that the low proportion recorded with children resulted rather from miscarriages, abortions, stillbirths and a higher infant mortality rate amongst prostitutes' children than those of other women, even of the very poor.[13] Several applicants to the Refuge, and even recently admitted inmates were turned away or dismissed because of what was obliquely referred to as their 'condition' or their 'state of health'. Though not included in the above figure, various of these were obviously discovered to be pregnant as well as diseased. Pregnancy, however, was a condition which the prostitute could afford even less than more virtuous women of her class. Obviously, when advanced it deprived her of her occupation; if she lived in a brothel she could be turned on to the streets or into the workhouse; and when the child was born its father would not maintain it or her. Tait was of the opinion that comparatively few prostitutes had children because, first, they were so subject to abortion that they rarely reached the full term of their pregnancies, and secondly because a high proportion of their infants died within a few weeks of birth as a result of syphilitic infection.[14] Chapter 5 which examines the physical condition of prostitutes in the city shows the reason for application of the 234 sick prostitutes requiring poor relief during the period. Nineteen of these, including five who were also suffering from venereal disease, were pregnant and confined in the workhouse. Because they had been unable to walk the streets they were all destitute, and most of them too were sick or not able bodied. Born to such women in such circumstances infants' chances of survival were limited, and coupled with terminated pregnancies, improper treatment and neglect arising from the women's mode of life – as well as destitution and disease – the small number of prostitutes with children is hardly surprising. Added to these was the allegedly common practice of baby farming amongst prostitutes, who would thus, of course, be recorded as childless in the censuses and probably the Poor Law records too. However, there was no evidence of this for York, and since the vast majority of street-walkers lived in lodgings or their own cottages rather than in regular brothels where children would probably not be tolerated, the necessity for such an arrangement would in any case be limited. Infanticide too was generally held to be common amongst prostitutes, but both Duchatelet and Tait, having witnessed the fact that prostitutes were 'exceedingly fond of their infants' thought such opinions 'greatly exaggerated'[15] and there is certainly no evidence of such women wilfully murdering their children in York. There were, however, occasional inquests held on and newspaper references to stillborn babies and dead infants found wrapped in paper, rags or clothing outside the hospital, workhouse, in churchyards or even in the river. Cause of death and how the child had come there were generally unknown, but it is probable that some of these little corpses were the weakly offspring of York's desperate women of the streets – and their indifferent clients.

Though so few prostitutes were recorded as having surviving children, an interesting aspect of the activity in the period is the fact that there were various street-walkers and brothel-keepers (and it is difficult to distinguish between the two, particularly in the case of those who left houses of 'general resort' and set up in business on their own account) who had relatives who were also 'on the town'. First there were notorious families such as the Varleys and the Bickerdikes, in which an ageing prostitute retired into the role of brothel-keeper, pick-pocket or procurer of clients, leaving the main business of the house to her daughters and other young women – who were sometimes even aided in their activities by a helpful brother. Other prostitutes again, though not apparently working with or for their mothers, were nevertheless the daughters of whores who had been notorious in their day; and others still had sisters who also walked the streets. Illustrations are used here only when such relationships are established beyond any doubt – when, for example, families appear together on the census, apply together for poor relief, or are described as such in the newspapers or Refuge records.

Nevertheless, in addition to the illustrations used, an examination of the computer print-out of all whores in the city reveals marked similarities in the surnames, ages and dates of appearances of numerous other women, and though family ties cannot be established suggests that there were a number of other prostitutes in the city who had relatives also in the trade.

The most interesting example of a family of prostitutes, and one illustrating the poverty and probable causes of its members taking to the streets, is that contained in the history of the Nettletons, whose misfortunes can be followed over a period of twenty-five years. They first appeared as applicants for Poor Relief in the December quarter of 1850 – Joseph, a twenty-two year old unemployed labourer and his wife Maria (sometimes called Mary Ann) aged eighteen and confined. Their address was listed as Douglas Buildings, North Street. Within a few weeks they made a further application to the Guardians, again on the grounds of Joseph's unemployment. Their baby Harriet was now one month old, Maria was nineteen and they had moved to Fetter Lane, off Skeldergate. Two months later they made a third application for relief, by which time they had again moved, and were now living in Hodgson's Buildings, North Street. Joseph was described as destitute and not able bodied.[16] The family must have moved again shortly after this as at the 1851 census they were recorded as living with Maria Nettleton's mother, a widow, once more in Fetter Lane. Also in the house was Maria Nettleton's brother, a twenty-two year old labourer. Within a few weeks (Harriet was now recorded as four months old) Maria was forced to apply to the Guardians again. She was still living in Fetter Lane, but it was recorded that she had been deserted by her husband.[17]

The next recorded appearance of Maria Nettleton was in Sessions, when she was imprisoned for seven days in June 1855 for being disorderly.[18] Two months later she was given a month for the same offence[19] and immediately following her release from prison, and described as a prostitute, she featured in one of the best reported and largest brothel robberies in the period.

Reference has already been made to the careless farmer and innkeeper Mr John West from Thorpe Arch, who mislaid twenty pounds while in Harriet Mottley's cottage in North Street, but who could not remember whether he had gone up or down stairs to reach the prostitute's bedroom. Seven years previously he had been involved in an even more disastrous experience in a York brothel, but had, as the papers pointed out with some amusement, failed to learn his lesson. On 21 September 1855 he attended the Howden Fair where he bought a prize horse, carefully placing the blue ribbon which the animal had been awarded in an inside pocket of his trousers, together with the remainder of his money. Arriving in the evening at Milford Junction, however, he found that he had missed his train to Thorpe Arch, and so instead journeyed up to York, reaching the city at about eleven o'clock. At this point, he still had the enormous sum of 330 to 340 pounds safely concealed inside his trousers. While passing over Ouse Bridge he met Maria Nettleton (then aged twenty-six) whom he accompanied into Middle Water Lane, where they were joined by John Hague (a twenty-six year old oysterman) and John McLoughlin, a twenty-two year old printer. According to Mr West, upon his stating that he required a bed, his companions obligingly took him to the house of a person named Prince in the Lane, and there the parties, together with prostitute Sarah Ann Hall, played 'teetotum' for half an hour for oysters, after which some gin was fetched. He then fell asleep in his chair, and when he awoke found that he had been robbed. The others gave a slightly different account of the night's events. After accompanying Nettleton to Mrs Prince's brothel, John West spent some time with the above assembled company, then gave two sovereigns to the prostitute, 'one of which she gave to Mrs. Prince'. After this he retired to bed with Nettleton, only to state on awakening that all his money had been stolen. In spite of the fact that the blue ribbon was found in Maria Nettleton's possession, she and her companions were dismissed through lack of evidence, though the Recorder's attention was drawn to the house, which 'appeared to be a den of thieves'.[20]

Nine months after this event (in June 1856) Maria Nettleton, who now lived in the Water Lanes, was once again reduced to applying for poor relief, and this time, since she was in labour and obviously destitute, was sent to the workhouse where her baby was born. Her occupation was now recorded as that of prostitute, she was said to be twenty-seven years old and described as single.[21] Within a couple of months (August 1856) she was charged with wandering abroad but was dismissed,[22] and in February, May and June the following year was imprisoned for one month, seven and ten days respectively for being a disorderly prostitute.[23] A few months after this, Joseph Nettleton reappeared on record and was fined five shillings and costs for drunkenness.[24]

The next reference to the family was once again in the Poor Law volumes and appeared in the December quarter of 1860. In spite of her husband's absence, Maria, once again described as married and also as a prostitute, now had five children: Harriet, aged ten, for whose birth the parish had given assistance; Thomas aged eight; Eliza, who had been born in the workhouse, aged five; Hannah, aged three and Emma, aged eighteen months. The family was once more living in Hodgson's Yard, North Street and Maria, now aged twenty-eight, was ill.

Within a few months further changes had occurred in the family's circumstances. At the 1861 census they were recorded as living in Letby's Yard, North Street and Joseph, now thirty-two and a sandgetter and labourer, was once more living with his wife. The four younger children were all recorded, with their ages correctly listed but ten year old Harriet was no longer present. She may have been sent into domestic service (one inmate of the Refuge had been a servant since she was nine years old) or she may well have died. The Nettletons were the sole occupiers of their cottage in the squalid yard.

Maria Nettleton's last recorded appearance was in January 1866 when she was once more charged with being disorderly and was sentenced to three days' imprisonment.[25] By this time she was about thirty-four years old and had been an active prostitute for more than ten years and imprisoned on at least six occasions. Nothing more is recorded of the family until 1875. In that year Mrs Nettleton's three younger daughters, all prostitutes and all with venereal disease, were sent to the workhouse. The sisters' applications were as follows:

March 1875, Emma Nettleton, prostitute, age 15. Single. Address Little Shambles ('Mr. Thompson's'). Destitute, not able bodied. Gonorrhoea. To house.[26]
June 1875. Hannah Nettleton, prostitute, age 18. Single. Address Feasegate. Not able bodied. Syphilis. To house.
June 1875. Elizabeth Nettleton, prostitute, age 19. Single. Address Finkle Street. Not able bodied. V.D. To house.[27]

The Nettleton family's history contains many of the characteristics so commonly encountered in this study of York's whores, yet in two respects Maria Nettleton was untypical of her kind. First, she brought up five children, all of whom survived infancy at least; and secondly, though on record for about ten years as a prostitute, she was never, apparently, arrested for being the worse for drink. In other respects, however, the family's record is depressingly familiar. Though not an unmarried mother, Maria was abandoned by her husband soon after the birth of her first child, and clearly poverty haunted this family, which began and ended its recorded existence in the shadow of the workhouse. The Nettletons moved with characteristic frequency from one sordid address to another, living always not only in miserable slums, but also in areas notorious for prostitution. In such circumstances and surroundings, it is hardly surprising that three of the daughters drifted early into the activity, with such wretched results.

The Bickerdike family was another in which the children were reared in an environment of prostitution and criminality, though their reputation was much more notorious than that of the Nettletons. Elizabeth Bickerdike was first recorded late in January 1870, when, described as a brothel-keeper of Finkle Street, she was acquitted of the charge of stealing a sovereign.[28] She was obviously a prostitute too, as one week later she was charged with indecency and probably sent to prison for a few days.[29] In her absence, her daughter Hannah, 'left in charge of the Finkle Street house while her mother was away', was sent to the House of Correction for seven days for disorderly behaviour, and she and her family were described by the *Gazette* as 'the most disorderly persons in the city'.[30] In both March and April 1870 Hannah, now listed as a prostitute, was fined again for being disorderly,[31] and shortly afterwards her mother, referred to as a prostitute and said to be 'one of the most abandoned and disgusting women in the city', was sentenced to one month's imprisonment for 'immoral and disgraceful behaviour'.[32] In May and August Hannah was again charged with indecency, and in October 1870 her mother received a three months prison sentence for the same offence.[33] In March, April and July 1871 Hannah Bickerdike was charged with indecency and disorderly conduct (for which she finally received two months imprisonment)[34] but in the meantime she was recorded on the census, from which further details of the family and household emerge. In this record Hannah claimed to be the head of the household (though in fact Mrs Bickerdike appears not to have moved into her new brothel in Palmer Lane, Hungate, until a few months later) and also to be a married woman, though her husband – if such a man existed – was not present. Her name was now Hannah Driffield, and, though she was imprisoned under her maiden name shortly

Fig. 20 Finkle Street or Mucky Peg Lane, from St Sampson's Square, c.
1880. This street contained several brothels including that run
by the notorious Bickerdike family – 'the most disorderly and
disgusting women in the city'.

afterwards, this was to be almost the last occasion on which it was used. According to the census Hannah was twenty-one years old, had been born at Wigginton, a village just outside York, and had a four month old son, named George Driffield. It is apparent that Mrs Bickerdike had raised at least two other children, as in the same household, and described as Hannah's brothers, were William Bickerdike, aged thirteen, and Richard Bickerdike, aged eight, both of whom had been born in Scarborough. Also present were Maria Driffield, Hannah's 'sister-in-law', a twenty-three year old unmarried servant, also born in Wigginton; and twenty-seven year old Ellen Harris, a single girl with no apparent occupation, who had been born in Essex. She was in fact a notorious prostitute, fined and imprisoned on several occasions in the early eighteen-seventies.

Although Mrs Bickerdike was not present in Finkle Street at the taking of the census (she may well have been serving one of her frequent prison sentences) and her daughter was said to be the head of the household, the older woman was still living there in the following July, when, described now as a common lodging-house keeper, she was convicted for allowing 'unmarried persons of opposite sexes to sleep in the same apartment'.[35] Within a few months, the family moved to Palmer Lane in Hungate, an area by then even more notorious for prostitution than was Finkle Street. From here in May 1872 Mrs Bickerdike was imprisoned for three months for keeping a house for immoral purposes;[36] and during her mother's absence Hannah, whose surname was once again Bickerdike, now twenty-two years old and claiming to be single, applied for poor relief for herself and her son George Thomas, aged two. Her occupation was recorded as that of prostitute.[37]

In May the following year Mrs Bickerdike of Palmer Lane was again charged with infringement of lodging-house regulations and with indecency,[38] and in January 1875, described as a keeper of a house of ill fame, she was involved in a brothel robbery.[39] In June 1877 in company with her nineteen year old son William Bickerdike, described as a labourer, and William Bean, a moulder of Thief Lane, she was charged with robbing and assaulting Thomas Cass Buck, a farmer from a North Riding village, who had visited her brothel.[40] Later in the year she made her fifteenth appearance at court and was described as a 'woman of immoral character' and 'almost beyond control'.[41] After this her fortunes declined rapidly. A few weeks later she was again brought before the magistrates, was described as a brothel-keeper, said to be forty-five years old and charged with being a common prostitute and with behaving indecently. It was stated at court that she had recently been charged too with being an idle and disorderly person; and on another occasion with being a rogue and a vagabond. She was sentenced to one year's hard labour.[42]

Neither she nor Hannah was recorded again, but William continued in a life of petty crime. In July 1882, now a hawker living in Hungate, he was charged with refusing to leave the 'Wheat Sheaf', a public house in that street, and also with stealing a bag of onions.[43]

Obviously, unlike Maria Nettleton, Mrs Bickerdike was a brothel-or common lodging-house keeper, rather than a prostitute, and both her daughter and at least one other well-known whore operated from her house. Nevertheless, she herself continued to be described as a prostitute until she was forty-five (one of the oldest in the period) and had no doubt by that time been in the business for several years. In common with Maria Nettleton, she was unusual in having brought up at least three children; but her family was untypical in that it did not constantly shift from one address to another, and in more than seven years lived only in Finkle Street and Palmer Lane. Characteristically, however, these locations were both well-known centres of prostitution. In one respect Elizabeth Bickerdike had more in common with most older whores in the city than did Mrs Nettleton. It is clear that by the mid seventies she began to be somewhat hounded by the police, and consequently served frequent and severe prison sentences.

Another family or families with a reputation similar to that of the Bickerdikes were the Varleys, though there may have been two distinct groups of that name involved in prostitution in the period. The first family was that of forty-nine year old Sarah Varley, a widow and a lodging-house keeper, who, at the time of the 1851 census, lived in Church Lane, Walmgate – the area behind St Dennis' church already referred to as being one of the few streets (apart from Walmgate itself) which contained brothels in the area. Mrs Varley had five children; Henry an agricultural labourer aged twenty-three, Ann a twenty year old flax spinner, Elizabeth aged eleven and a scholar, Jane also a scholar aged eight, and George aged four. Also present in the household were eight lodgers; four men, a married couple and two young women. None of these has been identified as having any association with prostitution. Two of Mrs Varley's three daughters, however, appear to have become street-walkers, and it is clear that by the late fifties the house was accommodating other prostitutes too. In 1859, for example, Maria Harrison, a prostitute, applied for poor relief from 'Varley's', Church Lane, Walmgate.[44] In the meantime Ann Varley, 'a woman of bad reputation', had been charged with theft in a Walmgate public house in September 1850,[45] by which time she would have been about twenty years of age. Seventeen years later the Guardians allowed thirty-three shillings funeral expenses for the burial of Jane Varley, a 'twenty-two' year old prostitute.[46]

The main Varley family lived in Hungate, and at the 1851 census lodged in that most squalid of slums, Bradley's Buildings, described and photographed by Rowntree in 1901.[47] These dilapidated tenements in a small closed court off the main street were acknowledged to be grossly unfit and overcrowded for many years, and, according to Rowntree at the turn of the century, contained numerous separate families and households, living in single-room dwellings built over common privies.[48] The Varley family consisted of Thomas aged forty-seven, a maltster from Wigginton, his wife Christiana aged forty from Scarborough, and their children John aged nineteen, Eleanor sixteen, Elizabeth eight and Richard four, all of whom had been born in York. Eleanor was said to be a servant. In the previous year, however, a girl named Ellen Varley was one of three girls, all 'less than sixteen years of age', charged with theft and described as prostitutes. She was imprisoned for fourteen days.[49]

In 1856 Ellen Varley was charged with soliciting,[50] and two years later, described both as a prostitute and 'an old offender', was charged with theft which had taken place in a Hungate brothel 'kept by her mother'.[51] By this time the family had moved less than a hundred yards down Hungate to Rusby Place, a sordid little street running unhealthily close to the river Foss, and linking the bottom of Hungate with the Wesley Place terraces. On the same day that Ellen Varley was charged with theft, two other prostitutes, Mary Smith and Mary Jackson, were charged with stealing a pocket handkerchief and six silver spoons from a man who had been 'persuaded' by Mrs Varley – 'the mother of the prisoner in the previous case' – to enter her notorious house in Rusby Place, where he met the two streetwalkers. Both girls faced various other charges in the period.[52]

Though the Varleys' activities were widespread from Rusby Place it should be emphasised that the whole neighbourhood was so poor, so insanitary and so offensive that it is doubtful that 'brothels' –

Fig. 21 Bradley's Buildings, Hungate, 1911 – the home in the
eighteen-fifties of the notorious Varley family. (a) shows the two
entrances to the court from Hungate, (b) the height and
dilapidated state of the tenements in the yard and (c) (similar to
the photograph used by Rowntree in *Poverty*) the entrances to
dwellings built above water closets. (In our period, of course,
these were dry privy middens.) They were grossly overcrowded
and unfit and described by the Medical Officer of Health in 1908
as the 'worst' dwellings in the district.

either in Bradley's Buildings or in the cramped cottages in the vicinity of the Foss – could have been much patronised by members of the middle classes. In April 1862, however, the Varleys apparently lured such a man into their humble home. Ellen Varley, alias Learman, aged twenty-five and her friend Sarah Stead aged twenty-seven were charged with obtaining a pint of brandy and four pounds ten shillings by false pretences from Thomas Wade, licensee of the 'Sportsman's Arms', Hungate, a public house almost opposite the dingy covered entrance to Bradley's Buildings. The girls (who provided their own decanter) told the landlord that the drink was for a 'gentleman' and Ellen Varley paid for it with a five pound note which she claimed belonged to a 'York gentleman who was afraid of being seen'. Mr Wade, who was unable to change the money, sent it to the 'Leeds Arms' at the end of Haver Lane. In the meantime Stead and Varley stated that the man would not go away as 'we have the gentleman locked in the house and we have the key with us'. The girls were given four pounds ten shillings change for the note, which was subsequently found to be a fake, but by the time they were apprehended they claimed that their client, having taken a portion of it, had already left. In spite of the fact that the defence claimed that they had been duped by an unscrupulous confidence trickster and in seeking to prove their innocence stated that neither girl could read nor write, Varley was sentenced to ten months imprisonment and Stead to five.[53]

Between 1858 and 1865 Ellen Varley was charged with a number of other offences, including theft, disorderly behaviour and common prostitution.[54] Her final recorded appearance was in January 1865 when she received her twentieth conviction – this time for annoying gentlemen. In the meantime her younger sister Elizabeth had been following in the family footsteps, and by October 1858 (by which time she was about fifteen or sixteen years old) she was applying to the York Refuge and expressing a strong desire to reform. She was apparently put on probation for two months, during which time she was frequently seen by the Ladies, who found her well behaved.[55] When she was formally admitted to the Home in December 1858, however, she was found to be 'in such a state of disease that she was obliged to be sent home'. In May the following year she was finally admitted to the Refuge, and though still ill her health gradually improved. She was in the Home for the 1861 census, and was described then as an inmate and a cook, aged nineteen and born in

York. A few months later she was found a situation as a washer-woman, but as this arrangement failed she was paid one shilling and sixpence a week for working in the Penitentiary laundry. Two months later she was placed in service at a house in Howden, in the East Riding.[56]

Like that of so many of the Refuge inmates, however, her reform was temporary only, and shortly after her sister's disappearance from the records, she re-entered a life of recorded prostitution. Between August 1865 and February 1868 she was charged with being a disorderly prostitute and an abandoned female, with wandering abroad and theft, and was variously described as living in Wesley Place, Garden Place and Palmer Lane – all of which were in Hungate and within a few yards of Rusby Place.[57] Her last recorded appearance was in April 1868 when, described as a twenty-five year old charwoman, she was charged with the theft of a silver watch and gold watch guard from a man who had accompanied her to a brothel in Palmer Lane – the door of which she opened with her own key. She was arrested at another house in the Lane, but was finally dismissed through lack of evidence.[58]

The French's were another mother and daughter team in which the man of the family (if there was one) was either a shadowy figure or absent altogether. Hannah French was first recorded in May 1839 having stolen various items including a waistcoat from her employer Robert Johnson, for whom she acted as housekeeper for a wage of five shillings a week. She claimed that she had committed the theft because of 'want', and that she had two eighteen year old daughters at home who were living in a 'very loose way'.[59] At Sessions, when she was committed to three months imprisonment, it was revealed that she was forty-eight years old and lived in Walmgate.[60] Immediately following her release, and described now as a married brothel-keeper of Walmgate, she was charged, together with her daughter Mary, with keeping a bawdy house for immoral purposes.[61] At the same time nine other Walmgate brothel-keepers were charged with the same offence. Mary French had already been sentenced to the House of Correction before her mother's imprisonment,[62] and a few weeks after the brothel-keeping charge was sentenced again for being a common prostitute, and for being drunk and disorderly in Walmgate.[63] At this point both women disappeared from the records, and Mary did not reappear until February 1843, when she was convicted for a similar offence, the charge being repeated seven months later – at which time it was combined with vagrancy and riotous and indecent behaviour.[64] At about this time Mary French obviously moved to the Bedern, and was convicted twice for being drunk and disorderly in the court in 1844.[65] Three years later the Poor Law Guardians allowed twenty-nine shillings for her funeral expenses. At the time of her death Mary French was described as twenty-eight years old, single, a prostitute and from the Bedern.[66] What became of Mrs French's other 'loose' daughter is a mystery since there are no references to other prostitutes of that name for sixteen years after the mother's first conviction. In February 1855 and April 1858, however, a certain Elizabeth French, 'a female of lost reputation', was convicted for loitering with felonious intent and for annoying gentlemen. There is no evidence connecting her with Mrs French, however, and had she been her daughter would have been about thirty-four years old – an unlikely age for a girl described as 'loose' at eighteen, to be first convicted.

Two sisters with a tragic history were Elizabeth and Sarah Eden. At the 1841 census they were living in Peter Lane, a narrow passage in which various individual street-walkers were known to reside and where, in 1870, George Richardson's beerhouse was found by the police to be harbouring thirteen prostitutes.[67] The sisters were the daughters of George Eden, a thirty-five year old tailor, and Eliza aged forty, both of whom had been born in the city. As well as Elizabeth aged ten and Sarah aged four, the family included George, a fifteen year old apprentice, and Nathan and Joseph both aged three. Also in the house was Frances Foundlove, a forty-five year old servant, though whether she was a lodger or employed by the family is unclear.

By September 1847 sixteen year old Elizabeth had already taken to the streets and wished to reform, but her application to enter the Refuge was withdrawn on account of her 'misconduct'. She reapplied in February 1848, still without success, and at approximately the same time (the March Quarter of 1848) she applied for relief from the Guardians of the Poor. At this time she was living at 20 Dundas Street (Hungate), was said to be seventeen years old, was destitute and was allowed two shillings and sixpence. A few weeks later, now recorded as sixteen years old and living in 'Watson's', Smith's Buildings, Hungate, she was found to be not able bodied and was sent to the Union hospital. Her occupation was recorded as prostitute. Also in that Quarter her brother George Eden, now a twenty-three year old tailor also of Smith's Buildings, was another applicant for relief. Whilst in the workhouse she again attempted to be admitted to the Refuge, but the Ladies felt that she should remain where she was for another month.[68] She obviously left the institution shortly afterwards, however, as in May 1848, described as a 'courtesan', she was charged with being drunk and disorderly.[69] Within a few months she returned to the workhouse, and from there in August 1848 she applied once more – again without success – to the Refuge. After this she was refused admittance even to the workhouse, and since the Refuge had no vacancies, she was eventually placed on probation in the lodgings of William Edwards, the temperance missionary.

By October, however, she was reported to be 'too ill in the hospital to make any application', and since there was still no room for her at the Refuge and she had 'no respectable home to go to' the Ladies required that she should stay where she was for a further few weeks. She was eventually fully admitted into the Penitentiary early in 1849;[70] her stay, however, was not a success. She remained 'idle while in the house', and in April of that year she escaped with two other inmates, Shepherd and Lockwood, all three girls returning 'to the worst neighbourhood'.[71] One year later, still aged only eighteen, in company with prostitute Ellen Gibson, Elizabeth Eden was sentenced to one month's hard labour for stealing a watch from Charles Theakston, a York maltster. He had apparently met the two girls and another 'female' in Walmgate and had accompanied them to the 'City Arms', where Eden picked his pocket, and shortly afterwards pawned his watch.[72]

By this time Elizabeth Eden's younger sister Sarah must also have begun to walk the streets. At the 1851 census she was a prisoner in the House of Correction, and was described as a sixteen year old orphan. Following this, in March 1852 her sister Elizabeth, now aged twenty, was ordered once again to the workhouse. She was described as a single prostitute, not able bodied and living in Wide Yard, Hungate (a place condemned for its poverty and wretchedness for almost a century).[73] Again her stay was temporary only, however, as within a few months she was charged with stealing five pounds in a Finkle Street house of ill fame. Shortly after this, in June 1853 her sister Sarah Eden, now described as a consumptive prostitute aged only nineteen, died in the workhouse. She had been living in Wood Yard, off Aldwark, and had been utterly destitute. Funeral expenses were allowed.[74] For the next five years Elizabeth Eden went unrecorded, until in August 1858 she was charged with robbery in a St Andrewgate brothel, kept by 'Lincoln Tom, a ticket of leave man'.[75] Her final appearance was in December 1859 when she was once again admitted to the workhouse. Her address was 45 St Andrewgate, she was aged twenty-four and was suffering from delirium tremens. Given her poor state of health (she was first sent to the workhouse hospital when she was only sixteen), the irregular life she subsequently led, her destitution and frequent stays in the workhouse and House of Correction, and bearing in mind the fact that she did not appear on record again – even for drunkenness – it is probable that, like her sister, she too died an early and horrible death.

The Eden sisters had a great deal in common with, and were in many ways typical of other women of their class. They resorted to prostitution at an early age and stayed in the activity only briefly. Unlike the 'general' prostitutes of Dr Acton's and their Lordships' complacent imaginations, however, they were not endowed with 'iron bodies', they were not elevated to a higher social class or riches as a result of having engaged 'harmlessly' in the occupation, and they did not retire, having made a 'dash' at a 'respectable' marriage. On the contrary, their careers were cut short as a result of destitution, drink and disease. Elizabeth made numerous and pathetic attempts to change her way of life – which were doomed to failure, no doubt because of her dependence on drink. It is particularly noticeable that like the Nettletons, the Edens lived all their lives not only in poor parts of the city, but in those, such as Peter Lane, Finkle Street, Hungate, Aldwark and St Andrewgate, which were also associated with prostitution.

Two other unfortunate sisters were the Hornsea girls, who, according to the 1851 census were the daughters of Matthew, a thirty-seven year old engraver and Martha, his twenty-nine year old wife. As well as Harriet, aged six, and Elizabeth, aged three, the family included a one month old baby, Emma. The family's poverty is apparent from its address – Beedham's Court, Skeldergate – already referred to in Chapter 2 as 'Hag Worm's Nest', the yard in which various outbreaks of pestilences, plagues and cholera had first occurred in the city.

Seventeen years after the census Harriet Hornsea, a sick prostitute claiming to be twenty years old, was given out-relief by the Guardians and was later admitted to the workhouse.[76] In 1876, by which

Fig. 22 Garden Place looking towards Hungate. Less than half the
   houses in this street were through dwellings and some contained
   only two rooms. Others backed on to stables, piggeries and
   workshops and most of those in the photograph faced or
   adjoined a large slaughterhouse. Garden Place, like Wesley Place
   which branches off to the left in the foreground, contained
   various notorious brothels such as 'Fox's', 'Mrs. Squires'' and
   'Mrs. Varley's'. Resident prostitutes included women such as
   Rose Ann McDermott, Elizabeth Hornsea, Ellen Varley, Mary
   Jane Barton, Clara Clark, Margaret Cooper, Rachel Lawson,
   Margaret Dodsworth, Mary O'Hara, Fanny Rickaby and
   Rebecca Stibbards.

time she must have been about thirty-two, she was again sent to the
workhouse. She was described as single, not able bodied and sick.
She had been found suffering from exhaustion on Ouse Bridge.[77]

Her sister Elizabeth had meanwhile been briefly admitted to the
Refuge in November 1863, but had left after only a few days,

Fig. 23 Four of the two-roomed back-to-back cottages in the Wesley
Place terraces and yards. These, 6–9 Bellerby's Yard, backed on
to identical dwellings in Lower Wesley Place, the street most
frequently associated with prostitution in York in the later part
of the period. Clients picked up in the Walmgate and Fossgate
public houses accompanied prostitutes back to these cottages via
the narrow and twisting alley ways which, like Black Horse
Passage, conveniently linked the two areas.

showing 'no desire to reform'. During the next few years she faced
various charges of indecency and in March 1875 applied to the
workhouse for relief. She was living at 'Fox's', in Garden Place,
Hungate, and was recorded as a prostitute, aged seventeen, sick and
suffering from venereal disease.

Garden Place was the home too, of Mrs Berriman, a widow, and
her son James, who seems to have assisted his mother in running her

house of ill fame. In July 1856 Mary Berriman, aged forty-seven, and her son James, aged eighteen, together with twenty-two year old prostitute Elizabeth Kinch were charged with the theft of three pounds ten shillings from John Abel, a retired farmer living in St Sampson's Square in York. He went to the Berrimans' house and, after they had had some drink, Mrs Berriman brought him the girl. They then had some more liquor and shortly afterwards the robbery took place. Kinch stated that she had stolen Mr Abel's trousers, that Mrs Berriman had locked her and them in the coal hole, and that James Berriman then took possession of the money, which was divided between them. Kinch was sentenced to one month and Mrs Berriman to three months imprisonment with hard labour.[78]

At the 1861 census Mrs Berriman and her son lived in Wesley Place, a block of three terraces and four yards, which, as described in the previous Chapter, though situated off Garden Place in Hungate, were directly linked with Walmgate and its many public houses and beershops. The properties in Wesley Place (or Lowther Street as the central block was originally called) consisted of tiny two- and four-roomed cottages which backed on to identical dwellings in the confined yards behind, access to which was through dingy, narrow passages. Most of the houses were only about eleven feet square and even those possessing two bedrooms were cramped, insanitary and unfit.* Though condemned as unhealthy in 1908, they were not vacated and demolished until 1932–3, by which time, though less overcrowded than they had been in our period, they were in an appalling condition. Probably the most unpleasant feature of these terraces and yards was their nearness to the river Foss (Wray's Yard and Lower Wesley Place went right down to the water's edge) which, as has already been observed, was in the nineteenth century an 'open sewer' – unfortunately given to frequent flooding. In spite of these disadvantages Wesley Place eventually became the most frequented centre of prostitution in the period; though again it is hardly likely that such sordid surroundings were the general resort of prostitutes' clients who were rich enough to go elsewhere.

---

* E. H. Smith, *Report on the Sanitary Conditions of the Hungate District* (York, 1908). The housing conditions in the whole of the Hungate district were condemned by the Medical Officer of Health in this Report because of the extreme narrowness of the streets and congestion of the buildings, the dark, damp, ill-ventilated, insanitary and dilapidated condition of the buildings, and the inadequate facilities in the cottage accommodation both in the streets and the back yards. These, he stated, were responsible not only for the general ill health of the occupants, but also for their *alcoholism, indecency, immorality and crime.* (My italics.)

Fig. 24 Lower Wesley Place running down to the right bank of the
River Foss (February 1933). Throughout the nineteenth and
early twentieth centuries these and neighbouring streets and
yards were subject to the frequent flooding of this river,
described in our period as: 'a great open cesspool into the
stagnating waters of which the sewers of near half the city
sluggishly pass' and into which was also drained the liquid
content of one of the large city dungheaps near St Margaret's
Church, Walmgate. The lower cottages on the left backed on to
those illustrated in the previous photograph. In spite of the size
of the houses and their insanitary condition, brothels in Wesley
Place became the most frequented in the city. As was earlier the
case with the Water Lanes, most of the whores identified in this
study lived in Wesley Place at some stage in their careers.

In one of these small cottages Mrs Berriman ran a brothel and lodging-house, at the time of the census living next door to another notorious keeper of a disreputable house, Harriet Squires, whose establishment contained at least three young whores between 1860 and 1864. (Two of these, seventeen year old Elizabeth Fogg and eighteen year old Ann Briskham, were admitted to the workhouse from Mrs Squires' brothel, suffering from venereal disease.)[79]

Living with Mary Berriman were her son James, now aged twenty-two and described as an unmarried cabinet maker, and two lodgers, Thomas Whitelock, a forty-two year old tailor and Elizabeth Brown, a married woman with no occupation listed. She was, in fact, a well-known prostitute, frequently charged with robbery and indecency in the Wesley Place and Walmgate neighbourhood.[80] Mrs Berriman was last recorded in March 1866, once more charged with keeping a brothel in Wesley Place.[81]

These examples indicate the extent to which mothers and daughters, or children from the same family, participated in prostitution – usually with disastrous results, in circumstances that were invariably associated with poverty. In addition to the families described above, the Penitentiary Ladies referred to various girls whose mothers were 'infamous' or 'disreputable'; or whose sisters, having been previous inmates of the Home, were obviously prostitutes too.* None of these girls can be said to have engaged in the activity harmlessly – indeed most pursued and ended their careers in tragic circumstances. Yet they have been included here, not to demonstrate the extent to which conventional opinion regarding the prostitute's fate, far from being a 'vulgar error', was based on reality (though this they undoubtedly do), but because they happen to be all those street-walkers in the city for whom there is positive evidence that members of their families too, were engaged in the activity.

There were also various husband and wife teams in the city, in which the man sometimes 'roughed up' clients and took part in the running of the brothel while the woman acted as prostitute, procurer of clients, mistress of the house and thief. John and Julia Bellerby, for example, kept a house of ill fame in Walmgate in which in 1838 one poor client, 'a simple looking lad', was robbed by the wife, while her husband 'threatened to break his head with the fire poker if he did

* For example, the Thackray sisters, see page 186. Inmates Mary Ann and Elizabeth Fletcher were also sisters and Louisa Harrison had both a sister and a mother who were prostitutes, see page 22.

not quit the house'.[82] By 1841 they had moved to the Bedern where they lived in a house containing thirty-four individuals, one of whom, Sarah Grimstone, was a much recorded whore. John Bellerby was thirty-four and claimed to be a 'joiner'. His wife Julia was thirty, and they had a five year old child, who, like his parents, had been born in York. The Ashbrook's brothel was also in the Bedern, and was the only one recorded in the court, after its colonisation by the Irish in the late eighteen-forties. Henry Ashbrook was himself Irish, though his first wife Ann had been born in York. In 1851 they lived in Milner's Buildings in the court, though this was not one of the large overcrowded tenements such as Snarr's Buildings which contained 138 immigrants at this census, or Pulleyn's Buildings which sheltered 117 Irish individuals. The Ashbrooks were, in fact, the sole Irish occupants of their tenement which seems to have been quite distinct from the rest of the Irish community. The Ashbrooks had two children and, though Henry described himself as a house painter, he was known by the Inspector of Nuisances to keep 'a very bad house', in which several male visitors were robbed. He and his wife, who figured frequently before the magistrates, were described in 1855 as 'two notorious characters'.[83] By 1861 Ashbrook had taken a new wife, Mary or Maria, aged only twenty-three and born in Ireland. During the late fifties she was frequently charged with theft from men who had accompanied her to her brothel in Bedern, and in July 1856 was involved in the garotte robbery of a young man whom she and another prostitute had taken to a house of ill fame in St Andrewgate.[84]

Michael and Bridget McHale (or McKale) were also Irish brothel-keepers, who appear to have been lodging-house keepers too. They apparently operated in two houses of ill fame, one in Fetter Lane off Skeldergate, and one in Middle Water Lane, in which most of their recorded offences occurred. They first appeared in court in March 1855 as witnesses in support of prostitute Caroline Smith, who had been accused of stealing a travelling rug from a man named Henry Stánsfield, a wool merchant from Layerthorpe, York. According to this man the prostitute had snatched the rug from him while he was walking in Castlegate, and had run down Middle Water Lane into the McHales' house, 'of whom the prisoner took a room'. According to Miss Smith, however, 'he had been with her for half an hour, and as he owed her something she should keep the rug'. The McHales corroborated her evidence, stating that she and the man had arrived together, had spent some time in her room, and that as Stansfield had refused to pay her she decided to keep the rug. The case was dismissed.[85] Shortly after this another prostitute, Catherine White, was charged with robbery at the McHales' house in Water Lane,[86] and in October 1855 Bridget McHale, aged thirty, was charged with the theft of three pounds from a man from a neighbouring village, who had accompanied Mrs McHale to her brothel in Fetter Lane, where he spent the night. Some girls who were 'lodging' in the house gave evidence that prostitute Mary Ann Hardisty stole the money while the man was asleep, and that Mrs McHale took part of the proceeds, which were then handed to her sister, Margaret Robinson of Middle Water Lane. Though described as an 'infamous character', Mrs McHale was acquitted, but the Recorder's attention was drawn to her house in Fetter Lane, which the foreman of the jury declared 'ought to be attended to'.[87] The McHales obviously continued to conduct a brothel in Middle Water Lane too, as in June 1857 and March 1863 respectively two prostitutes, Sarah Barker and Elizabeth Turnham, were admitted to the workhouse from their establishment. Finally in October 1863 Bridget McHale aged forty-one and John McHale aged twenty-four (said to be unrelated) were charged with stealing a watch from William Colley, a tailor from York barracks. Mrs McHale was sentenced to four months imprisonment.[88]

The Bellerbys, the Ashbrooks and the McHales all began their recorded careers as brothel-keepers in the city at a fairly early age – in their late twenties or early thirties – and had apparently retired from the business within about ten years. The Simpsons, on the other hand, were running a brothel in their advanced years, and were, in fact, the oldest individuals recorded in the activity.

At the 1871 census Thomas Simpson, a seventy year old agricultural labourer and his wife Jane, aged fifty-two, both from Tadcaster in the West Riding, lived in one of those notorious cottages in Stonebow Lane described in the previous Chapter, and possibly still leased by the former Inspector of Police. Also present in the house were their lodgers, three young women with no recorded occupation – Margaret Lee, aged twenty-six, Jane Quinn, aged thirty-three, and Sarah Fearn. Within a couple of weeks of the census, prostitute Margaret Lee, of Stonebow Lane, was charged with indecency, and Jane Quinn and Sarah Fearn – 'two disreputable women' – with obstruction.[89] Miss Fearn who had previously lived in Wesley Place had already been convicted in November 1869 and in April and June 1870 for indecency.[90] By January 1874 she had moved farther down Fossgate to Straker's Passage leading into Wesley Place, and was charged with the same offence.[91] Two months later the charge was repeated,[92] and finally in February 1876, making her fortieth appearance at court since 1869, she was sentenced to eight months imprisonment for indecency and for wandering abroad.[93] Jane Quinn, whose address was listed simply as Hungate, received similar convictions between February 1866 and April 1871.[94]

By December 1874 Mrs Simpson had moved to Finkle Street and was charged there as a brothel-keeper.[95] Two years later, her occupation still being recorded as such, she was sentenced to one month's imprisonment with hard labour for creating a disturbance and using bad language. It was stated that this was her sixth conviction and that she was 'known as a highly immoral character', a local clergyman describing her as 'a source of continual nuisance in the neighbourhood'.[96] In August 1877, now said to be 'an elderly woman and a keeper of a house of ill fame', she was charged with robbery from a farm labourer, and also with keeping an unregistered 'lodging-house';[97] and in the following year she was fined for the same offence. It was stated at court that 'a man and a woman were found by the police in a bedroom'; however Mrs Simpson's defence claimed that since hers was a house of ill fame, it could not be registered as a common lodging-house.[98] In May 1879, by which time Mrs Simpson must have been about sixty, she was again charged with the same offence.[99]

Acton, it will be remembered, is alleged to have 'disabused' their lordships of the notion that prostitutes, when they retired and lost their good looks, became brothel-keepers. Instead he claimed that they 're-entered' respectable society, and an increasing number married 'sometimes above their class'.[100] York prostitutes, however, did not achieve the latter state with any great ease, or in any great numbers, but some – and they were fortunate – did rise to the rank of brothel-keeper, though the term is generally used here to describe a female accommodating at most two or three low-class whores in a common lodging-house or cottage of ill repute, rather than a 'madam' actually employing such women. Rose Ann or, as she sometimes called herself, Harriet McDermott, for example, first appeared as a Poor Law applicant in 1867, at which time she was described as a single pregnant prostitute of Finkle Street. She was admitted to the workhouse in June,[101] and three months later a further entry records that she was granted thirty-four shillings towards the funeral expenses of her six week old twins, Lucy and Harriet.[102] In October 1867 she was re-admitted to the workhouse because of illness,[103] and in February 1868, now living in Garden Place, was charged with wandering abroad and indecency.[104] By 1869, however, she was obviously keeping a brothel. Described as a common lodging-house keeper of Cross Alley, Water Lanes, she was fined ten shillings for failure to register lodgers, and for having three abandoned girls and a man in two rooms.[105] In May the following year she was fined a further two pounds for allowing persons of both sexes to sleep in the same rooms. At the time of the 1871 census she was still living in Cross Alley, though she now described herself as a dressmaker. She was twenty-eight years old, her birthplace was Ireland, she was unmarried and had a two year old daughter.

Mary Holmes was another woman who changed her status. Though described as a common prostitute in September 1837 and June 1839, she was one of the sixteen Aldwark brothel-keepers convicted in August 1839 and of the thirteen keepers of houses of ill fame charged shortly afterwards in the Bedern.[106] Similarly nineteen year old Elizabeth Harrison, a destitute prostitute suffering from venereal disease, applied to the workhouse in the December quarter of 1862. Less than two years later, however, she was obviously keeping her own establishment. In June 1864 twenty-three year old prostitute Elizabeth Hough (or Huff) applied to the Guardians from her house. Though able bodied, this girl was syphilitic and sick. Miss Hough too subsequently became a 'lodging-house' keeper. She was convicted for accosting gentlemen in Castlegate in January 1865, and in October 1868 was charged with 'permitting persons of opposite sexes to sleep in the same room of her lodging-house'.[107] Similarly Annie Kendrew, who faced various charges for prostitution between 1871 and 1873 was identified in 1874 as being the landlady of eighteen year old Emily Foster, another syphilitic prostitute applying to the Guardians for relief.[108]

Throughout the period there were various other women who were described first as prostitutes and then as keepers of houses of ill fame, particularly after the fifties when, as we have seen, the police reported that it was no longer the case that street-walkers were concentrating in houses of general resort. By far the greatest number, however, remained prostitutes throughout the whole of their recorded careers. At the same time there were brothel-keepers or keepers of houses of ill fame who were never recorded as being prostitutes. Forty-three of these were males, twenty-two were of unknown sex and sixty-three were females. In addition to this there were, over the period, nineteen public house and beershop keepers who were variously charged with harbouring prostitutes and with allowing abandoned women to congregate on their premises, and six identified 'bully boys' or thugs, who assisted prostitutes in robbery and assault.

Like the prostitutes, brothel-keepers obviously supplemented their income (whether this was in the form of high rents for prostitutes' rooms, a percentage of the prostitute's takings, or the whole of her earnings in return for board and lodging – plus of course, profits on drinks consumed in the establishment) by various forms of robbery and theft. These were not only committed by the street-walkers, who often shared the proceeds with the keeper of the house, but, as will become apparent in the following Chapter, by the brothel-keepers themselves who very often stole clients' purses and made off with notes or sovereigns before any sexual activity had even occurred. Two brothel-keepers well known for such activities were Ann Render, who, it will be remembered, was recorded as occupying a cottage in company with Reverend Frederick Lawrence in one of the Water Lanes, and Elizabeth Shields, of North Street.

Ann Render was first identified on the 1851 census living at 27 Middle Water Lane. She was thirty-nine years old, and married to Thomas Render, a hairdresser. They had two children Thomas, aged nine and Mary Ann, aged two. By October 1857 she was obviously keeping a brothel as in that month Mary Ann White, a nineteen year old prostitute, was charged with the theft of one pound from James Porteus, a labourer who had accompanied her with two other men to Mrs Render's house. 'Some of them knew it was a brothel, and after having had something to drink, James Porteus gave the landlady a sovereign to be changed.' Mrs Render gave the money to the prostitute who failed to return.[109] In the following year Ann Render was sentenced to six months with hard labour for keeping such a disorderly house, and it was stated at her trial that she kept two bad houses in the Lanes, and had for this reason been discharged from her position as sexton of the parish church.[110] (This was during the incumbency of Reverend Lawrence's predecessor.) At the 1861 census she was recorded as a widow and like her son, now a labourer, had aged only seven years in the previous decade. In addition to her daughter, now twelve, there were also two females present in the house. One, a single 'dressmaker', was visiting from Cornwall, and unrecorded in other sources. The other was twenty-two year old Catherine White – a girl repeatedly charged with offences associated with prostitution between 1855 and 1860, and who, at the age of only twenty-four, was given a pauper's funeral.[111] Later in the sixties Mrs Render faced further imprisonments, but was still running a brothel in 1871. According to the census she claimed to be fifty-four (but must have been about sixty). Though her family no longer lived with her she had three 'lodgers' – twenty-four year old Kate Ward, a dressmaker, twenty-six year old Sarah Douthwaite, a staymaker and twenty-six year old Emma Stockhill, a servant. All three were convicted prostitutes.[112]

In contrast to Ann Render, who seems to have had a long and relatively trouble free career as a brothel-keeper, Mrs Elizabeth Shields was dealt with harshly by the authorities. She first appears on record as an applicant for Poor Relief in the December quarter of 1850. She and her husband Thomas, described as a thirty-one year old unemployed labourer, lived in Fetter Lane with their children Sarah aged eight and Thomas aged five. They were granted funeral expenses – probably for another child. In the following quarter, now having moved to Dodgson's Yard, North Street, Mrs Shields was again granted funeral expenses – 'for a child' who was almost certainly Thomas, as he was no longer listed as a dependant of the applicant. Sarah, however, who was now alleged to be six, was still present, though Mrs Shield's husband was described as 'absent'.[113] At the 1851 census the family was still in Dodgson's Yard, North Street, and now consisted of Thomas and Elizabeth, both aged thirty-one and Sarah aged six. Also present in the household were Hannah Fothergill, an eighteen year old unmarried 'visitor' from Stillington, a small West Riding village; and twenty-one year old Mary Allanson from Acomb, near York. Both these girls claimed to be house-servants, but were in fact, street-walkers – Miss Fothergill applying shortly afterwards both to the Refuge and the workhouse as a prostitute; and Miss Allanson having already been described by the *Gazette* as a 'courtesan'.[114]

Also at the census, in a neighbouring yard (Peart's Court) in North Street, lived thirty year old Elizabeth Beaumont, with her husband

Joseph, a thirty-two year old labourer, and their two young children William and Ann. In October 1852 Elizabeth Shields together with her neighbour Elizabeth Bowman 'alias Beaumont' (now said to be twenty-nine) and two Bradford women with previous convictions, Ann Sharpe aged twenty-one and Harriet Wilcox aged twenty-three, were charged with stealing two sovereigns, two half crowns and four shillings in silver from Mrs Ezra Hoyle, a Bradford beerhouse keeper. Elizabeth Beaumont, Harriet Wilcox and Mrs Hoyle had been witnesses at the assizes in a manslaughter case, and afterwards visited Mrs Shields's house, where they treated each other to 'a drop of gin'. During the evening one of the women observed that 'she had never seen Shields since Joey [probably Beaumont] was transported when they chucked an old man into the river and got a five pound note'. After more gin, Mrs Hoyle became 'very sleepy and was at length persuaded by Shields and Beaumont to go to bed'. She hid a box containing her money under her pillow, but this was stolen by Shields and Wilcox, and when Mrs Hoyle tried to stop them Elizabeth Beaumont 'laid hold of [her] by the throat and kept her on the bed until Shields got away'. Each of the four prisoners was sentenced to seven years transportation, at which Ann Sharpe, who was described as very violent, shouted to the judge: 'Thank thee, thou old bugger. I hope thou'll sit there till I come back and I'll bring thee a long tailed monkey to play with.' And Harriet Wilcox threw one of her shoes 'with great force' at Mrs Hoyle – narrowly missing Mr Dyson, a solicitor.[115]

Both Elizabeth Shields and Elizabeth Beaumont took up their former occupations as brothel-keepers after their return to York. In April 1860 both were charged with keeping houses of ill fame in North Street.[116] Perhaps they thought it prudent to move elsewhere after this, as that is the last recorded appearance of either of them in the city.

Only one brothel-keeper is on record as having subsequently become a prostitute. This was Mrs Bessie Mountain of Gill's Yard, Aldwark, who, in February 1855, charged Elizabeth Rathmell, 'a girl of lost character', with having robbed her of a gown, shawl and other articles. Rathmell had been lodging at Mrs Mountain's cottage for several months, Mountain having undertaken to 'feed her and clothe her for the earnings of her prostitution, but she had very indifferently fulfilled her contract'. Eventually the girl was discharged – 'a decision which elicited applause from the bystanders'[117] – but Mrs

Mountain continued her activities. In 1864, for example, Jane Saw-don, a seventeen year old diseased prostitute, was admitted to the workhouse from her establishment, by then in North Street. Three years later Mrs Mountain, now described as a fifty year old widow of North Street, occupation prostitute, applied for poor relief because of congestion of the liver.[118]

It is clear that female brothel-keepers, whether or not they were still or had previously been prostitutes, often supplemented their income with the proceeds of theft. This was less true of the forty-three male brothel-keepers in York about whom consequently there is considerably less evidence. Further, unlike female brothel-keepers, men who ran such establishments were rarely charged with keeping disorderly houses and seem to have enjoyed a greater degree of tolerance and lack of attention from the authorities, than did the eighty-four women brothel-keepers recorded during the period. In fact it is generally only through the applications of diseased or impoverished prostitutes to the workhouse that such men have been identified; and others, who like Henry Robinson or Edward Martin obviously ran flourishing and well-known establishments, would have remained totally unrecorded had it not been for a client's suicide in the house of the former, and prostitutes' complaints to the police regarding the latter.[119] Obviously, unlike many of their female coun-terparts, male brothel-keepers were not placed on record for offences arising from their own prostitution, but as well as this, the men seem to have kept better run establishments, of a superior kind, in which the client ran less risk of robbery (though not of disease) or involve-ment in disorderly behaviour.

Though resorting less frequently to theft, however, several male brothel-keepers were licensees of public houses, beerhouses and dramshops or gained additional income from selling (rather than serving) liquor on their premises. Edward Martin, for example, was sentenced to nine months imprisonment in 1887 not only in relation to the charge of procuring mentioned in Chapter 1 but also for brothel-keeping and selling beer without a licence.[120] George Gill, whose dramshop was in Swinegate, James Gibson, landlord of the 'Green Tree' in Middle Water Lane and William C. Herbert of the 'Cricketers' Arms', Toft Green were amongst licensees charged with having prostitutes living on their premises and whose girls some-times had to be admitted to the workhouse; and George Donaldson, landlord of the 'Flying Dutchman' in Grape Lane, David Shaun of the 'Red Lion', Peaseholme Green and Charles Needham, landlord of the 'Leopard' in Coppergate, were amongst those charged with harbouring prostitutes and allowing their premises to be used for immoral purposes.[121]

This Chapter has sought to outline the principal aggregate characteristics of the prostitute and brothel-keeping community in York in the period. Other aspects of their lives such as their criminality, their dependence on drink, their vulnerability to disease and their attempts at reform are discussed in the following chapters in which the histories of individual women are used to illustrate the statistical evidence contained in this section.

4

The clients

Since men resorting to prostitutes were rarely documented, information about them is inevitably more scarce than that concerning the prostitutes themselves. In spite of this, however, it has been generally accepted in recent studies of the problem that prostitution in the Victorian age was essentially the exploitation of one class by another – the vast majority of street-walkers, as we have seen, being recruited largely from the poorer working classes, but supposedly selling their bodies almost exclusively to men from the wealthier sections of society.* These, it has been affirmed, having invested their own wives and daughters with such 'purity' that they were placed beyond their reach, were thus compelled to satisfy their grosser sexual appetites with women of the poor, whose sexuality alone, it would seem, conveniently equalled their own.[1] The tendency during the period for men from the middle classes to postpone the age at which they married, in order to forestall the increasing financial difficulties involved in acquiring and maintaining all the necessities which such a change of status and enlarged establishment demanded, was at the time and has since been seen as an additional reason for their increasing recourse to prostitutes.[2] The habit, once acquired, was apparently difficult to discard, and even after his delayed marriage many a Victorian gentleman continued to enjoy illicit sexual relations with 'women of the town'. Thus a complex interpretation of Victorian sexual behaviour has emerged, in which middle-class men and working-class women are accorded comparative sexual freedom and enjoyment, while females of the middle classes (who indulged their husbands' modest demands reluctantly,

* This view overlooks the fact that the Contagious Diseases Acts were primarily designed to limit the spread of venereal disease amongst the lower ranks of the armed forces.

and then only for the purpose of bearing their children) are denied both. Studies such as Marcus's *The Other Victorians*, in which the diaries of a middle-class roué's escapades with common prostitutes and working-class women feature prominently, tend to support this view of one class's use of another.

While it is clear that one of the main characteristics of prostitution during this period was indeed the exploitation by the rich of the poor, and that it was largely because of poverty that most women resorted to the streets, such an interpretation based on the differences in sexual appetites and behaviour (particularly women's) in the various levels of Victorian society is too simple. One feels that even Acton's assertion that 'the majority of women . . . are not troubled with sexual feeling of any kind', has, for the middle classes at least, almost been taken at its face value; and one is left with the conclusion that middle-class husbands as well as bachelors resorted to the sexually uninhibited women of the poor, while their own wives languished between the fainting fits and hysterics brought about by the sexual frustration they subconsciously suffered as a result of being placed on rather dull pedestals of purity. The fact that many prominent women from the highest ranks of society, however, as well as from those a few grades down, were engaging in sexual affairs out of motives unconnected with financial gain, and also that many middle-class marriages were obviously very happy and fruitful, has been curiously ignored. More important with regard to this study is the fact that prostitutes, as well as supplying the needs of and being exploited by the rich, were catering too for their own class, and this aspect of prostitution has been much less emphasised.

Obviously the services of high-priced prostitutes and courtesans operating in expensive brothels, even though their own origins may have been humble, were to be bought only by those wealthy enough to afford them, and as such were well out of reach of the working man's purse. Famous rendezvous such as 'Kate Hamilton's' and the Argyll Rooms, and the man about town's 'Guides' which were barely disguised sex directories were also catering largely for the middle classes. But because attention has been focussed almost exclusively on these superior metropolitan establishments, the existence of the hundreds of thousands of much more sordid 'houses of ill fame' staffed by less desirable women, as well as the vast number of even lower-class prostitutes who haunted the streets of every town in the country, has been lost sight of in recent studies. Yet these desperate and frequently diseased creatures of the night, who, as we have seen, were often willing to sell their bodies for a few pence and who operated in the most insanitary and overcrowded of slums, could hardly have been the exclusive prey of men who could easily afford and would have been wise to pay for something better. It is clear that these women were being resorted to largely by men of their own class, particularly in those towns like York, which contained military or naval establishments.

The evidence relating to prostitutes' clients in York, though limited, suggests too another aspect of exploitation, namely that not only were the women of the streets being used by the poor as well as the rich, but it would appear that in many instances the prostitutes themselves were the exploiters. They may well have felt that through no fault of their own but poverty, or possibly seduction and the birth of an illegitimate child, they had been driven on to the streets, condemned by society and forced to make a living in the most degraded and dangerous of occupations. Given that their poverty was indeed the result of the exploitation of one class by another, and that many of them too, could no doubt trace their initial downfall to some abuse by the opposite sex, their resentment towards 'toffs' in particular and any men prepared to degrade and exploit their bodies and minds still further, is understandable. One can appreciate in such circumstances that a man prepared to hire their bodies was considered (as were they) fair game. He was prepared to risk (as was the prostitute herself) contagion; and if married presumably prepared to risk passing on the infection to his wife. In the process, however, he must also be prepared to lose his watch, wallet or purse, and in resorting to the prostitute be prepared to face (as she did nightly) the risk of physical violence. Police reports reveal too that men consorting with prostitutes were frequently drunk. No wonder then that the street-walker had scant respect for either the property or person of her client, who would undoubtedly have shunned her society once his passion had been satisfied and the effects of alcohol worn off, and who probably concurred – in public at least – with her frequent prison sentences and the spirit of the Contagious Diseases Acts. Inevitably then, the reports of the York magistrates' court proceedings, with frequent mention of thefts in houses of ill fame, brothel robberies and cases of prostitutes picking their clients' pockets, reveal the mutual basic contempt with which each regarded the other. These numerous prosecutions suggest that the gay reveller or the drunken fumbler of the previous night despised the woman he had so recently abused, and also that the prostitute loathed and was determined to wring as much as possible from the class and sex that had made her what she was.*

Upon examination of the evidence relating to prostitutes' clients in York, however, it soon becomes clear that the women did not discriminate between their victims. Indeed, far from robbing only middle-class, or, as the newspapers often termed them, 'respectable' gentlemen who accompanied them to brothels, or restricting their pick-pocket activities to those hardened profligates who may well have been responsible for many an innocent girl's 'ruin', prostitutes frequently exploited both physically and financially raw working-class youths – gullible hobbledehoys and foolish young farm labourers fresh from the countryside often being their prey. Obviously, the main reason for this was that the more innocent and inexperienced the client, the greater the opportunity for the prostitute to exploit him. Though it was sometimes the case that members of the middle classes and comparatively rich men were reported as having been robbed, such instances were rarer, though when they occurred the amounts stolen were substantial. There are three probable reasons for this. First, as we have seen, common prostitutes of the type identified in this study, operating in districts such as those described in Chapter 2, would be more likely to attract poor clients than well-to-do gentlemen. Secondly, it is obvious that a regular roué would have been aware of the risks involved and if he did resort to such women would, advisedly, have had few valuables about him, if going out with the deliberate intention of accompanying a prostitute to a brothel. An unsuspecting country lad on the other hand, having come to York with his wages in his pocket, could be lured into the back streets and robbed without ever even stepping inside a house of ill fame. Also it may well have been the case that, unless the amount stolen was particularly large, middle-class clients were understandably reluctant to press charges in such circumstances. It is probable, therefore, that brothel robberies and cases of pick-pocketing occurred which were never reported in the newspapers, those that were being largely related to poorer clients, to whom the theft of five shillings or even half a crown was a significant amount, or

---

* The fact that gentlemen resorted to prostitutes whom they frequently loathed is seen by Cominos to reflect and confirm the disassociation between sex and love in the 'Double Standard'.

to gentlemen who were strangers in the city. A 'respectable' local client, on the other hand, could obviously better sustain the loss of a few shillings or even pounds, and some preferred doing so to facing the embarrassing publicity of an appearance in court. This is demonstrated by a number of newspaper reports throughout the period of anonymous gentlemen who, after a night's debauch and finding their watch or wallet missing, rushed to the police station and brought charges against a certain prostitute or brothel-keeper. On reflection, however, and when completely sober, they refused to prosecute and the prostitute, who had been forced to appear in court, identified and charged with the offence, was dismissed.

Prostitute Sarah Heppel, for example, was charged in September 1863 with the theft of three pounds from a man in a brothel in North Street. As the man did not appear in court she was discharged.[3] Two months earlier Ann Shepherd of the Water Lanes (who in all was dismissed three times in similar circumstances) was accused of the theft of one pound from one of her clients, who also refused to press charges.[4] In June 1861 Ellen Murray, described on various occasions as a 'loose character' and a woman of 'lost reputation', was dismissed for the same reason, having been charged with the theft of seven shillings and sixpence from a Dewsbury man who accompanied her to another Water Lane brothel.[5] One year later another anonymous reveller who regretted drawing attention to his misdeeds for the sake of the recovery of two shillings and sixpence was said by the *Gazette* to be 'too ashamed to appear' – Sarah Pepper, his companion of the previous evening, being described as a 'female of ruined reputation whose progress in the paths of vice has detracted from her personal appearance'.[6] A certain Mr Wright, however, though he refused to prosecute and was 'ashamed of the transaction in which he had been engaged', was unable to keep his name out of print once he had accused prostitute Isabella Bramley of theft in 1852. She was a girl 'whose character will not bear the strictest investigation' and who a year previously, when only eighteen, had left Walker's brothel in George Street and, being destitute, entered the workhouse.[7]

In spite of the publicity as well as the domestic unpleasantness such cases must have occasioned, however, and also a certain loss of face (prostitutes' victims very often being regarded both by the magistrates and the newspapers as weak and foolish rather than sinful), a surprising number were, in fact, prepared to press charges

– indicating the high value placed on property and the undoubted existence of the 'Double Standard'. It is, of course, only through the somewhat astonishing persistence of these individuals that information about prostitutes' clients is available; for had they not been so determined to prosecute and to appear in court to do so, little evidence regarding this important aspect of Victorian prostitution in York would have emerged.

As has already been observed, willingness to appear in court (possibly at the Quarter Sessions as well as before the local magistrates) for the attempted recovery of a substantial sum of money or a very valuable watch or tiepin is, perhaps, understandable, in spite of the consequences of such publicity. Such was the case, for example, with John West and prostitutes Harriet Mottley and of course Maria Nettleton. A large sum of money was stolen too in April 1854 from Hugh McGiverin, a cattle dealer; though in this case the theft apparently took place before he and his companions went into a brothel. He and his friend John Foster, a cattle drover, being very drunk after the Fortnight Fair, were making their way along Walmgate when they were accosted by two prostitutes, Hannah Long, of Church Lane, Walmgate, and Mary Ann Stewart of the Water Lanes. They accompanied them to one of the many public houses in the district – the 'Half Moon Inn' – where McGiverin was robbed of two hundred pounds.[8] Other men visiting York were robbed of smaller, but still considerable amounts of money. In 1838, for example, William Lambert, a farmer from Murton (an East Riding village), accused prostitutes Ann Whitfield and Elizabeth Robinson, both of Walmgate, of robbing him of seven sovereigns, five pounds and some silver, when he accompanied them to 'Severs'' house of ill fame in Walmgate. The case went to Sessions and the women were found not guilty, Mr Lambert being advised 'not to frequent such houses' in the future.[9] Another adventurous farmer from a neighbouring village who paid more for his jaunt than he had anticipated was Michael Fletcher from Wheldrake. He was induced to escort Alice Anderson 'prostitute and thief' to her miserable cottage in Foundry Yard, Walmgate, where he was robbed of three bank notes, three sovereigns and three half-sovereigns.[10] Similarly, a 'respectable gentleman' named John Bennett, after being enticed into another Walmgate brothel by Harriet Wilson and Sarah Jenkins in May 1847, found his pocket had been relieved of ten pounds and eight sovereigns – only a short while before, a Mr Palmer of

Newton-on-Ouse having had a similar experience at another establishment in the same street. He had been in company with prostitute Elizabeth Todd, who had been charged on several occasions with theft from her clients.[11]

The appearances of middle-class clients prepared to press charges in such cases as these is more understandable than those in which the amounts stolen were comparatively small; as in 1869, for example, when Emma Farrah, a street-walker from North Street, was sentenced to three months imprisonment after robbing a pound from a gentleman who visited her house. Though he gave evidence the client in this case managed to remain unidentified. He was described as a York solicitor.[12]

Working-class clients too occasionally brought charges which were afterwards dropped, as in November 1864, for example, when prostitutes Elizabeth Herriman (who was to appear in court on twenty-two different occasions) and Kate Barnes, both of the Water Lanes, were dismissed on the non-appearance of the plaintiff, a labourer who had previously accused them of stealing sixteen shillings from his trouser pocket while he was at a brothel in which they lived.[13] More frequently, however, poorer clients, caring less for their respectable or professional image, and often, it would seem, having been robbed before actually transacting their business, were prepared to press charges. Amongst the gullible locals and foolish farm labourers who fell victim to York's more unscrupulous streetwalkers was a fifteen year old boy, persuaded by Irish prostitute Bridget Hanley to accompany her to a brothel in Middle Water Lane. There he was immediately robbed of four pounds fifteen shillings – 'half his year's wages'.[14] Another was farm labourer Mark Hedley from Pocklington, who, having been unwise enough to end his excursion to York in 'The Slipper' – a notorious public house in the First Water Lane – committed the additional folly of being seen to change a sovereign. His company was immediately solicited by prostitute Priscilla Barnett, 'but he declined' the invitation, and was suddenly aware of the woman's hand in his pocket and his purse being withdrawn. He instantly seized her arm and accused her of robbing him – which she denied – but the purse was found by the police, having been hidden under the form on which she was sitting. Miss Barnett's address was 'a vessel on the Ouse' in which she lived with her 'accompliss', a waterman Robert Lee.[15] Another young man who paid dearly for pleasure which did not materialise was 'a poor simple lad ... Robert Aunatun from Whixley', a West Riding village. One Saturday evening in October 1838 he met brothel-keeper John Bellerby in Gibson's beerhouse, Walmgate, and was persuaded to accompany him to another pub in Jubbergate. Here they played 'wisk' and the young man was soon 'duped out of forty-five shillings'. After this he was taken to Bellerby's house of ill fame in Walmgate, where, it will be remembered, his host and his wife robbed him of the remainder of his money and then 'threatened to break his head with the fire poker if he did not quit the house'.[16] Another 'simple looking lad' was George Smith, a farm servant from Church Fenton, a village between York and Leeds. He accompanied prostitute Mary Mullein to a brothel in Cross Alley and, after treating her and two other street-walkers to four shillings worth of gin, retired twice with Mullein to the bedroom. On the second occasion 'he fancied he felt her hand groping in his pocket', after which he discovered he had been robbed of nine shillings and sixpence.[17]

Amongst other farm workers and labourers who were robbed and brought charges in the period were Charles Perrin of Claxton Grange who in 1876 lost a pound while in company with Elizabeth Thomas at Mrs Thompson's brothel in Patrick Pool; and Thomas Walker, a labourer from St Ann Street, York, who accused prostitute Annie Walker of stealing his purse containing a sovereign at a brothel in nearby Finkle Street. Although she claimed in court that she took the money 'as the man had not given her what she wanted', Miss Walker was sentenced to one month's imprisonment.[18] Irish labourer Michael Brannan of Long Close Lane was another victim of prostitutes who combined picking pockets with their other activities, he having been robbed of his purse and one pound seventeen shillings after meeting Amelia Freer at the 'Half Moon' public house in Walmgate, and accompanying her to her house in Haver Lane. Since Brannan was a member of the York Irish community which was the subject of a detailed separate study,[19] he is one of the few York prostitutes' clients for whom there is extensive documentary evidence over a twenty year period. He featured prominently in various Irish fights and disturbances and was something of an alcoholic, having made thirty-nine appearances at court for drunken and riotous behaviour by June 1877, at which time he was still only forty-seven. He was, in fact, probably the most delinquent Irishman in the city. When the robbery took place he was twenty-six years old and had either recently married or was just about to marry Catherine, aged twenty-two. They had two children, and throughout the period he remained either a labourer or an agricultural labourer.[20]

Evidence relating to various other prostitutes' clients, who, like the anonymous solicitor, were not identified but had their occupations listed, suggests that though wide-ranging the majority came from the working classes. In May 1862, for example, labourer William Collins charged a Grape Lane prostitute Catherine Lacy with the theft of boots and a coat;[21] and in February 1855 'unfortunate' Caroline Smith was charged with stealing a hat from a Walmgate joiner named Lund, who had spent the night in her brothel.[22] Elizabeth Doughty, who met a private from Thirsk at the 'Shoulder of Mutton' beerhouse and took him to a Cross Alley brothel, was charged with robbing him of sixteen shillings;[23] and in May 1863 Margaret Carlton, making her tenth appearance in court, was accused of stealing one shilling and threepence from an Albert Street gardener.[24] In December 1853 Ann Johnson was charged with stealing seventeen sovereigns from a Tadcaster horse dealer;[25] and the landlord of the 'Barrack Tavern' in the Fulford Road was that victim of the Varley family who, as described in the previous Chapter, unsuccessfully attempted to conceal about his person six silver spoons and a handkerchief.[26] In addition, as we have seen, soldiers from the barracks were frequently recorded as associating with immoral women of the town, and examples of police constables too, who were reprimanded or dismissed from the service for similar behaviour, are provided in Chapter 5. In fact, one in every six identified clients was a policeman (a proportion exceeded only by labourers) and bearing in mind Inspector Turner's association with the activity, and the fact that he stated in 1855 that he had 'spent the best part of his life' on night duty, the number of unidentified constables consorting with prostitutes was probably much greater. This high proportion of policemen found to be patronising brothels is hardly surprising as they possessed powers, opportunity and knowledge of the trade, generally denied to other men.

As we have seen, prostitutes often worked in pairs for the purpose of fleecing their clients, many of whom to little effect resorted to all kinds of devices to avoid being robbed. In March 1856, for example, an unnamed man accompanied Ann Harrison and Ann Cooper to a notorious house in Petergate kept by the latter. Here he was relieved of five pound notes, seven sovereigns, some silver and a purse.[27] Similarly in September 1863 Ann Dennis and Mary Ann Cole were together charged with the theft of some clothes they had stolen from a man who visited Cole's brothel in the Water Lanes.[28] Street-walkers were also occasionally in league with male accomplices (sometimes their husbands) popularly referred to at the time as 'bully boys'.[29] An unfortunate client Francis Porter, for example, a farmer from Stockton-on-Forest in the North Riding was robbed of his purse and seventeen pounds in gold in 1887. He had been solicited by prostitute Mary Ann Maxwell of Bradley's Buildings, Hungate, who invited him to follow her to a house in that street, where he was told to wait and buy her a drink. He gave her a shilling and 'immediately after, the woman put her hand in his pocket and pulled out his purse ... after which she attempted to leave the room'. Porter tried to stop her, but was prevented by the sudden appearance of a certain John Lacy, a labourer from Aldwark.[30] Robert Swales, described as a general dealer, suffered a similar experience in May 1862. According to the *Herald* 'whilst going home on Wednesday night he was decoyed into a brothel in Lowther Street [Wesley Place] kept by prostitute Selina Martin', who in October 1856 had already been charged with theft at her former brothel in North Street and was said to have been assisted by her husband Thomas. On this occasion she was aided by militia-man John Hardy, who assaulted Mr Swales and robbed him of six sovereigns. Mrs Martin was remanded in custody while Hardy was given bail.[31] Robert Lappish, a farm servant, was one of the many unfortunate would-be clients who was both robbed and attacked before even entering a brothel. He had come to York from Church Fenton in November 1839 and while walking over Ouse Bridge early in the evening was accosted by two women, one of whom was prostitute Hannah Harrison. He accompanied them (doubtless into the Water Lanes) and before going very far noticed his money was missing. On 'giving the alarm' he was struck by a man who suddenly appeared out of the darkness.[32] Another poor dupe was the man who acompanied Ann Shepherd down Friargate in December 1861. Before he knew what was happening he was seized by two men and robbed of two pounds fourteen shillings, but was too stunned and alarmed to know whether they or the girl committed the theft.[33] A similar occurrence took place in October 1855 when a man was solicited by Mary Dowd and 'took her up a Walmgate passage'. Here, with the aid of Dowd's husband, who had presumably been stalking the couple, the unsuspecting gentleman was robbed of thirty pounds.[34]

In a final illustration of the frequent disappointment and danger involved in visiting a York brothel in the period we encounter again the notorious Finkle Street family already referred to in previous Chapters. In June 1877 Mr Thomas Cass Buck, having met William Bean and William Bickerdike in Market Street, accompanied them to the Alexandra Hotel, where he paid for a round of drinks. In doing so he was observed by his companions to possess a purse containing at least four pounds and some silver. They soon 'enticed him to go with them to a house kept by Elizabeth Bickerdike' and after a quarter of an hour in that establishment they asked him to pay for some beer. Mrs Bickerdike fetched a pitcher and while their generous client was trying to find a sixpence:

She clutched his purse out of his hand and ran out of the house ...
She returned in a minute and threw the purse at his feet. It then contained only five shillings. He was proceeding to run after her when the two male prisoners caught hold of him and threw him on the floor and kept him in that position for about a quarter of an hour. He at last escaped and gave information at the police station.[35]

The illustrations above indicate that many recorded York prostitutes resorted to picking pockets, theft and even violence in order to gain as much profit as possible from their clients. They stole from their own class, the poor, as well as the rich; and like their own seducers, were quite unscrupulous regarding the youth, inexperience or gullibility of the green but nevertheless willing victims they lured into the back-street brothels or yards. These, it would seem, were lucky to retire from their adventure unscathed. The more of a bumpkin the client, the less likelihood of his receiving value for money, and the greater the chance of his being robbed or hit over the head. Moreover, like the more experienced profligate, he also risked infection. It is obvious too that there was a submerged class of petty criminals in York, an underworld of disreputable beer- and lodging-house keepers, fences, thieves and thugs who assisted the prostitute in her work.

In addition it is clear that prostitutes frequently encouraged prospective clients to consume as much liquor as possible, partly, no doubt, to excite their interest and induce them to shed any reluctance they may have felt at the prospect of so risky an encounter, but also to render them so drunk and befuddled that they could more easily be rooked and hoodwinked. In the process, of course, the prostitute, who was more often than not herself a hardened drinker, if not actually an alcoholic, would be treated to a welcome dram. This aspect of the prostitute's life, emphasised in contemporary literature and observation and confirmed by the continual appearances at court of drunk and disorderly street-walkers, such as Margaret Barrett, Martha Stephenson and Elizabeth Herriman, is discussed in the following Chapter.

At the same time, of course, as contemporary observers and writers on the general problem of prostitution were continually complaining, and as is demonstrated by evidence relating to this study, clients were often affected by drink even before they came into contact with the prostitute. We have seen that street-walkers frequently urged their clients to spend money on liquor and even made free with their victims' purses – both to make them unwary and also no doubt to ensure that the man really had with him enough money to pay for his pleasures.* It was maintained too, and evidence from York material would seem to substantiate this, that prostitutes often earned commission on drinks which their clients bought in certain beerhouses, pubs and other notorious establishments. For various reasons then, it was in the interest of the common prostitute or street-walker to encourage her companion to drink as much alcohol as possible – provided, of course, that he could then be conveyed reasonably quietly to their destination and that his drunkenness did not actually endanger the prostitute herself. Thus, as has been observed, the two areas most associated with prostitution in York – the Water Lanes and the Walmgate/Hungate districts – contained the heaviest concentrations of beershops and public houses in the city; and in smaller areas such as North Street, Grape Lane and Finkle Street there were throughout the period numerous references to notorious drinking houses where both prostitutes and their clients assembled for the purpose of meeting. In such establishments nothing, it would seem, could excite a prostitute's interest more than the customer who paid for his drink with a bulging purse or wallet, or who even required a sovereign to be changed.

Clients affected by drink were no match for the wily street-walkers who frequently rendered them embarrassingly helpless. Tait was of the opinion that

the lowest class of prostitutes are almost all thieves; and no man who speaks to them, and ventures to accompany them to their wretched

---

* Occasional cases were reported of prostitutes not having been paid for their services by clients, who alleged that they had no money. See pages 105 and 129.

hovels, is sure of escaping with money in his pockets. Saturday evening is considered by these miserable creatures as a blessing; for they generally make as much on that evening as they do on all the other days of the week. If a poor man ventures into the streets in a state of partial intoxication, one or more of these women have their eyes at once upon him, and dog him from place to place, till they get him induced to go along with them to a tavern or their lodgings. They soon learn whether or not he is in possession of money; and the search is generally made without any regard to justice or shame. It is no very unusual thing for individuals thus entrapped to be stripped of every article of clothes, and to be turned out to the street in a state of perfect nudity; or, if they be fortunate enough to escape with their clothes, their bodies have to suffer for their empty pockets. They are sometimes tossed over a window or down a stair, without a moment's warning or ceremony.[36]

An incident of this type occurred in September 1863 when Michael Booth, another farm servant from Church Fenton, accompanied David Snaith and prostitute Ann Dennis to the brothel of Mary Ann Cole in Cross Alley. Here he was asked to pull off his boots and other articles of clothing and being 'a good deal in liquor' he shortly afterwards fell asleep, only to find on awakening that his clothes had disappeared. It was stated at Sessions that these had been distributed to various dealers and pawnbrokers throughout the city – Miss Dennis and Mr Snaith disposing of the articles and Mary Ann Cole, the brothel-keeper, receiving half the proceeds. Ann Dennis, a Leeds prostitute, was said to be 'one of the worst characters that ever entered York'. She had been sent by some ladies to the York Refuge but 'her conduct there was so bad that she only remained part of a day as they would not suffer her to remain any longer'. She was sentenced to twelve months imprisonment, Snaith to two months and Mary Ann Cole was acquitted.[37]

A similar incident occurred in 1853. Richard Fawcett, a cattle jobber from Lofthouse near Wakefield, 'entered a house of ill fame in North Street under the impression that it was a public house'. While he was sleeping prostitute Ellen Wilson ran off with his trousers from which she stole fifty-two pounds. He chased her downstairs, but was struck by a man who helped the girl to escape. Miss Wilson was sentenced to six months imprisonment.[38] Other visitors to brothels had their trousers temporarily removed while the contents of their pockets were stolen.

As Tait observed, any gentlemen palpably the worse for drink were the obvious prey of street-walkers such as Jane Dixon (alias Jane Antiss) 'well known to the police' and who had already been convicted five times for soliciting in York by September 1876. In that month it was stated by Police Constable Varley that he and another policeman (while in plain clothes) were accosted by Dixon in Micklegate. Upon following her they noticed that she solicited other men, especially those who were intoxicated.[39] The link between drink and prostitution is well illustrated by a case which occurred in 1857. In October that year an unnamed gentleman went into a riverside public house on King's Staithe, and was served beer by prostitute Mary Kilgarry. Prostitute Mary Ann Lockett then served him more drink, after which he accompanied them both to an adjacent brothel in one of the Water Lanes, in which establishment there were also 'two or three other females'. He was then robbed of three pounds, and though the police afterwards found Mary Kilgarry and her associate Alfred Bethany (in whose trouser pocket the missing purse was discovered) in bed together in another house in the Water Lanes, all three were discharged through lack of evidence.[40]

It is apparent from some of the cases reported in the newspapers that some men, though in possession of quite substantial sums of money, were prepared to resort to that lowest, most degraded and presumably cheapest class of street-walker who performed her services out of doors. These were the prostitutes who were either so destitute or undesirable that they had no access whatsoever to even the most disreputable brothels or houses of accommodation, or who, because they wished to remain totally anonymous – in the cases that were recorded, presumably because they intended to rob the client in the first place – did not wish to risk identification by being associated with any particular establishment or address. In either event, the services of such a prostitute, who did not have to share her meagre earnings with a brothel-keeper, were obviously to be bought at a very low rate; though the attendant risks involved from discovery or infection could hardly make such an encounter an attractive proposition. One can only assume that in most cases the client (who in fact often found the cost of such a dangerous transaction was more than he had anticipated) was drunk. Surprisingly, street-walkers who committed thefts in such circumstances were frequently traced, identified and forced to appear at court, though in common with most other recorded offences relating to prostitution in the period, it is likely that these incidents represented only a small proportion of the total number actually taking place.

Ill-lit courts, yards and alleys with which the poorer parts of the city abounded were the usual scenes of these 'acts of indecency'. In January 1858, for example, prostitute Ellen Kilner was charged with the theft of thirteen pounds from a man she had met in the 'Spotted Cow' public house in the old cattle market, who then accompanied her into a passage off Heslington Road. She was discharged because of lack of evidence.[41] Similarly an 'unfortunate' Margaret Carlton of Heslington Road was discharged in 1868 after having been accused of stealing a watch from a man who went with her into a passage near Penley Grove Street.[42] The general undesirability and desperation of prostitutes reduced to attempting to sell their bodies in such circumstances (as well, of course, as that of those clients prepared to purchase them) is illustrated from the history of this prostitute, who at the time of the above incident must have been about forty-five and, to say the least, past her prime. Eight years previously, when she first appeared in the York newspapers, sentenced to seven days for 'annoying persons', she was already an old offender, having 'recently spent nine months in Leeds prison'. Two years later, in May 1862 she was sentenced to three days in the House of Correction for wandering abroad in Fossgate, and in the following year, with an address in Bishophill close to the Refuge, was fined two shillings and sixpence for the same offence. One month later, making her tenth appearance in court in York, she was charged with the theft of one shilling and threepence, and three years after that (by which time her address was Barker Hill) she was recorded as making her eighteenth appearance – again for annoyance. Her next recorded offence was the incident described above in the passage in Penley Grove Street, and five years later, by which time she was fifty years old and living in Wesley Place, she was sent to the workhouse. She was recorded as being of 'unsound mind'.[43] Dr Acton and many of his colleagues, of course, were of the opinion that any woman who was strongly sexually motivated was demented or 'suffering from a form of insanity which those accustomed to visit lunatic asylums must be fully conversant with'.[44] It may be, therefore, that having lived a 'sinful life' for so many years prostitutes like Margaret Carlton were automatically assumed to be mad. Prostitutes were rarely recorded as being so in the Poor Law records, however, even though they were frequently admitted to the workhouse. It is far more likely that Margaret Carlton had been walking the streets because of her poverty and desperation rather than 'sexual excitement terminating even in nymphomania', and that by 1873, given the miserable circumstances into which she had sunk, the poor woman's mind really was unhinged.

Similar incidents in back streets and alleyways were reported throughout the period. Prostitute Elizabeth Robinson, for example, was accused of stealing a silver watch from a man 'she had enticed to follow her into a passage' in December 1857; and in the same month Jane Mallow and Margaret Perkins were each sentenced to seven days imprisonment for the theft of nineteen shillings from a man who had accompanied Perkins into a passage in Fetter Lane.[45] Four years later, Sarah Cowling of North Street was charged with the robbery of eleven pounds from a client who 'went with her into a yard'; and also in 1861 prostitute Jane Kirton (whose history is contained in Chapter 6), in company with a man called Henry Cowl, was prosecuted for indecent exposure in King's Square.[46] Similarly in October 1876 Ann Whitley of Thief Lane was sentenced to six months imprisonment for robbing her client John Rudd of Mothergill, whom she met in Railway Street and 'induced to accompany her along Rougier Street and across Tanner's Moat to an archway underneath Lendal Bridge'. Here, it was stated, she robbed him of a gold watch and 'made off'. On the following day she succeeded in raising a loan of two shillings and sixpence on the watch, which was subsequently taken to Inspector Worcester, and she was brought into custody. According to Miss Whitley the man had given her the watch 'because he had no money'[47] and indeed similar incidents indicate that clients did occasionally refuse to pay for services received.

More often, however, it was the prostitute who attempted to cheat the client, either by robbing him or accepting payment for services which were not then performed. Some prostitutes picked even the pockets of men who had rejected their solicitations. Street-walker Elizabeth Earley, for example, was imprisoned for a month in 1860 for the theft of a purse and eight shillings from a man she 'bumped into in Walmgate';[48] and in the following year Ann Shepherd (who appeared in court on three other occasions) was charged with stealing fourteen pounds from 'an old man she accosted in the street'. Later that year Ann McShaun, of Church Lane, Walmgate was charged with a similar offence, having stolen a purse from a man who did not wish to accompany her, and whom she had accosted in Castlegate.[49]

Reference has already been made to the York Society for the Prevention of Youthful Depravity founded in 1860, and its provision

YORK MARTINMAS FAIR.

THE FARM SERVANTS'

CHEAP

TEA & COFFEE ROOMS,

Will again be Opened at the

MERCHANTS' HALL, FOSSGATE, YORK,

On MARTINMAS-DAY and the Saturday following.

Good Hot TEA or COFFEE, at 1½d. per Cup,

On the shortest notice: Other Refreshments may be had equally cheap.

The comfort and welfare of those attending the Martinmas Hirings, especially females, is the only object contemplated by the promoters of these Rooms, and it is hoped that young people especially will avail themselves of the advantages they offer.

As many who come to the York Hirings are under the necessity of carrying their Year's Wages, and other money about with them, and thus are exposed to being robbed of their all, provision has been made this year whereby money may be left in safe keeping. Any sum, large or small, may be placed in the care of a Gentleman who will act as Banker during the time of the Rooms being open, such money to be returned at any hour the Depositor may wish,—the **only** charge being a penny for a receipt stamp.

GOOD FIRES, and all accommodation for general Comfort
Will be provided.

Fig. 25 Poster produced by the York Society for the Prevention of Youthful Depravity in 1861, designed to protect farm servants from the dangers they faced at the open Hirings. Female servants were vulnerable to the snares of procuresses and male servants to the attentions of prostitutes who were also pick-pockets.

of accommodation and refreshment at the Merchant Adventurers' Hall in Fossgate for servants attending the Hirings. As the poster reproduced in Fig. 25 illustrates, the Society was concerned not only with the comfort and welfare of young females who, it was reported, were frequently lured into prostitution on such occasions, but also for the welfare of young male servants who, being in possession of more money than they were accustomed to, were obviously the prey of street-walkers and pick-pockets. The dangers and temptations were thought to be so great, in fact, that the Society actually set up a bank for the temporary safe keeping of servants' earnings from their previous employment 'As many who come to the York Hirings are under the necessity of carrying their Year's Wages . . .'.[50] The need for such precautions is well illustrated by a robbery which occurred only a year after the Society was formed. William Lee, a farm servant from Tadcaster in the West Riding, came to York in December 1861 'for the purpose of attending the Hirings. He had nearly the whole of his year's wages – two five pound notes and a sovereign – in a purse in his trowsers pocket.' He and another farm servant called Newton were going to the station when they met Sarah Cowling (alias Cooley) in North Street at about seven o'clock in the evening. According to the men she picked Lee's pocket of all his money and ran off; though the prostitute produced evidence – supported by the Matron of the House of Correction – which brought about her dismissal.[51]

Only in one instance was the attitude of a client's wife recorded. In September 1837 a Mrs Henderson, owner of two houses in Aldwark, charged a woman called Mrs Hornsey with damaging her property. One of the houses was let and used as a brothel, and the enraged Mrs Hornsey, having found her husband in bed 'with a girl of the house', had hurled stones at the windows, breaking glass in these and those of the adjoining property.[52]

In spite of the fact that the combination of evidence from various sources can result in fairly detailed information about individual prostitutes, and that photographs, slum-clearance schedules and maps produce an accurate picture of the areas and even houses in which they lived, detailed information regarding clients, together with the interior and organisation of the brothels they frequented, is rarely obtainable – particularly for those superior establishments which, as has been suggested, were so discreetly managed that their owners and staff rarely appeared before the courts. In January 1878, however, in a sensational suicide case, the *Herald* provided a detailed account, not only of the running of such a house, but, equally important, of three of its patrons.

On Thursday 28 December 1877 Frank Arthur Clerk, a twenty-five year old medical assistant to Dr Wright of Stamford Bridge in the East Riding, told his friend Mr E. L. Nottingham, a farmer from the neighbouring village of High Catton, that 'he had the idea of going on a spree for a few days' and that he would pawn his watch and chain for the purpose. The two men journeyed by train to York, took a cab at the station, and after visiting a pawnshop, went to 'a brothel at the corner of Water Lane and Castlegate, kept by Henry Robinson'. There they stayed for three nights, and on the Saturday visited several public houses in the city, in which, according to the evidence of Nottingham, Clerk had been 'very free' with his money, standing champagne two or three times to the company. He was quite 'fresh' when they returned, but afterwards went out with a Mr Robert Henry Rockliff, a provision dealer from Tadcaster, who was also staying at the brothel, 'and both of them had their whiskers shaved off'. On their return they drank more champagne before retiring to bed, at which time Clerk appeared to be very lively. On the Sunday, however, he complained of feeling unwell and did not get up until the evening – returning to bed almost immediately. Nottingham stated that he slept with Clerk that night, and that he appeared to be suffering from the effects of drink. In spite of that, at about two o'clock in the morning the two of them in company with prostitute Marian Gibson, 'who slept on the floor without a bed', drank a further bottle of champagne between them, the following day Clerk again remaining in bed, but taking breakfast and consuming more champagne at four o'clock in the afternoon, with Nottingham and two prostitutes. After Clerk had finished his drink he threw the glass on the floor and seemed 'jolly and inclined for a lark'. Mr Nottingham did not see him alive again.

Mr Rockliff, who then gave evidence, stated that later that evening he went upstairs and asked Clerk if he would have some soup, but seeing a bottle labelled 'strychnine' on the table close to the bed, asked him what he had been doing with it. Clerk replied that he had taken some and Rockliff immediately fetched a surgeon Mr Hood, who, however, arrived too late to save the young man. According to the testimony of the surgeon, Clerk 'was suffering from severe mental depression after his debauch, but not from delirium tremens'. His suicide was obviously premeditated, however, as he had stolen enough strychnine from his employer at Stamford Bridge to kill a hundred and fifty persons. Marian Gibson, 'with whom the deceased cohabited while at Robinson's', admitted that he had been depressed at times and cried. The verdict returned was 'suicide while in a state of temporary insanity'. The Coroner stated that:

It is greatly to be deplored that a place such as Robinson's should exist. It appeared to be a place which was much frequented by young men, who could be supplied with champagne and other liquor *ad libitum* and the practice was much to be deprecated ... steps ought to be taken by the authorities to do away with such places.

Mr Roe, the lessee of the house, maintained that when he had discovered that Robinson was using the premises for immoral purposes, he had given him notice to quit – which he would do shortly.[53] It is clear, however, that he did not, and that if Mr Roe had really been unaware of what was obviously quite a large and flourishing establishment in one of the city's main brothel districts, he must have been an extraordinarily unobservant man. In the following year, as we have seen, detailed maps were compiled and lists drawn up of all the owners, lessees and occupiers of the properties in the proposed Castlegate Improvement Scheme Area. At the top of Middle Water Lane and on the corner of Castlegate were two premises owned by Mary Taylor and leased to Richard Roe. He occupied one himself and sublet the other to Henry Robinson – who was thus his next door neighbour and a close neighbour too of Reverend Lawrence.

Though limited, the evidence on prostitutes' clients in York suggests that they came from varied social backgrounds and were prepared to resort to all classes of those lower grades of street-walkers reported in the newspapers and Poor Law records. In spite of the risks involved, they frequented what must, by any standards, have been low-class brothels and houses of ill fame, patronising too those women of the streets who had sunk so low in their occupation as to have no access even to these.

Forty-three per cent of all recorded prostitutes' clients in the period were visitors to York, some of these obviously being fairly wealthy. The comparative frequency at court of these individuals suggests that because they did not live in the city they were ignorant of the notorious reputation of the more sordid haunts they were induced to visit, and possibly too that they did not share the reluctance middle-class residents of York might have felt at seeing reports of their nocturnal activities in the local press. In just the same way it is possible that some of the city's casual and unskilled labourers were perhaps more willing to press charges against prostitutes for theft than were York's more 'respectable' citizens – for it is unlikely that, even if literate, their friends and families were regular subscribers to either the *Herald* or the *Gazette*. In spite of the publicity and its consequences, however, it is evident that, if the cheated client felt sufficiently grieved, he was prepared to press charges, regardless of his social standing or where he lived.

Although the social status of those clients for whom there is information was fairly widespread, however, it is clear that the majority were not members of the gentry or the 'respectable' middle classes about whom so much has been written and surmised in connection with prostitution, and particularly with regard to their exploitation of working-class women and their hypocritical use of their 'Double Standard' of sexual morality. On the contrary, seventy-three per cent of all men recorded as associating with prostitutes belonged to the working classes or the poor – though again it should be noted that this may to some extent be a reflection of an understandable middle-class reluctance to face publicity in such circumstances. Having made this reservation, however, it is surely hardly surprising, in view of the appalling sanitary conditions of those brothels and their surroundings described in Chapter 2, and the degraded and diseased state of the majority of low-class whores operating in them – to say nothing of the other risks involved in frequenting such unsavoury neighbourhoods – that York's recorded prostitutes were patronised more by their own class than any other. The poor, unhappily for them, lived amongst and were accustomed to the disgusting filth and squalor, the vermin, the overcrowding and the offensive sights and smells of the insanitary slums in the 'low' parts of the city – localities of whose horrors the more fortunate classes had 'no conception', but in which almost all the prostitutes identified in this study were forced both to reside and carry out their trade. Further, of course, the working man who sought the company of prostitutes could probably not afford to frequent superior establishments, wherever these might be – unlike wealthier men who could afford to pay for comfort and comparative decency and safety. Finally, the contention that prostitution was in fact, being supported by working-class rather than middle-class demand is reasonable – in view of the relative sizes of the populations involved.

At the same time, it is clear from the evidence put forward in this book that the existence of prostitution on so large a scale in York was fundamentally the outcome of class exploitation – the vast majority of identified street-walkers having taken to and remaining in the activity out of necessity. Recorded prostitutes' clients on the other hand, unlike the women themselves, came from all walks of life, ranging from the aristocracy to the humblest labourer, police constable or soldier. All classes, therefore, conspired to make use of the prostitute. Yet it was the widespread prevalence of poverty – condoned and even worsened by those in whose power it was to remedy the situation and who, while abusing her, were most vocal in their condemnation of the prostitute and instrumental in punishing her – that was largely responsible for women of the poor taking to the streets in the first place. Homes for the Fallen, Female Missions, Refuges, Shelters and Penitentiaries such as those operating in York throughout much of the period, religious tracts, city missionaries and societies such as that for the Suppression of Youthful Depravity were the sincere attempts of a few middle-class ladies and gentlemen to deal with an appalling situation. They were well intentioned, and as will be seen, even reclaimed and reformed a few individual prostitutes. By concentrating on the past sin and future spiritual redemption of their charges, however, rather than on the root causes of their way of life – the desperation, misery and moral degradation of life in filthy, overcrowded slums; and the tedium, vulnerability and exploitation facing the thousands of young girls working as domestic servants, needle women or in factories – such societies seem now to be as inappropriate as they were ineffectual. They merely scratched at the surface of a vast problem with which they and their managers, together with the rest of society in the period, failed to come to terms.

5

Drink, destitution and disease

The physical condition and extent of disease amongst prostitutes is of fundamental importance when considering their general circumstances, since it is clear that a woman obviously sick, suffering from venereal infection or habitually drunk would find some difficulty in obtaining clients and would, as her condition worsened, in all probability, be reduced to destitution. Keepers, even of the lowest class of brothels, were naturally unwilling to employ girls in an obvious state of syphilis, gonorrhoea, consumption or even pregnancy, and the best such an unfortunate could hope for after she had been turned out on to the streets, was to lure some raddled drunkard into one of the many ill-lit yards or passages of the poorer neighbourhoods, where hopefully her condition would go unobserved and she could resort to occasional petty theft. Otherwise there were few alternatives but the workhouse, since Refuges and Female Penitentiaries were reluctant to take on the responsibility of applicants addicted to drink, in a very poor state of health or pregnant, many of whom having been engaged in prostitution for some time were in any case considered unsuitable candidates for reform. Ill health then, which must surely be regarded as an obvious occupational hazard of prostitutes who not only lived in the most squalid and insanitary of neighbourhoods (as indeed, did other women of their class) but led irregular and dissipated lives and were nightly exposed to the various infections of their clients, is of vital significance in considering general poverty associated with the activity. Further, since, as we have seen, the vast majority of prostitutes were single women, even temporary poverty arising, for example, from sickness, pregnancy or a spell in prison, could be peculiarly acute for such women, who had no husband and often no family to turn to in times of need.

Margaret Barrett, prostitute, drunkard, thief, syphilitic, vagrant and eventually violent convict, must have been as familiar and shocking a figure to York magistrates and readers of the local press as she undoubtedly was to nocturnal frequenters of the city's seamier neighbourhoods. For more than a quarter of a century she staggered from one conviction to another, appearing on fifty-three different occasions at court, and serving prison sentences which by 1887 totalled more than nine years. Obviously an extreme though not unique example of the depths to which women in her situation could sink, her case is nevertheless an interesting illustration of the link between the common prostitute and destitution, drink and disease.

She first appeared on record in York in September 1863 (though it later emerged that she had been 'perfectly incorrigible' since 1851, at which time she must have been about fourteen years old). Describing her as a ruined character, the *Gazette* reported that she had been charged with the theft of seven shillings (presumably from a client) at a house in Wesley Place. It is probable that her companion decided on reflection not to press charges, as this was one of the few occasions when she was dismissed without either a fine or a prison sentence.[1] For the next four years her activities went unrecorded – though it is reasonable to conclude that she continued in what for her, at least, was a particularly unrewarding profession – as in her next appearance at court, in September 1867, she was described as a prostitute, though it emerged that she had been reduced to stealing a sack of rags and bones from Frank Dunlavy, a labourer from the Water Lanes.[2] Her sentence of one month with hard labour was subsequently increased to five weeks; and on the day of her release she immediately became so drunk and disorderly in Walmgate, where she now lived, that she was re-arrested and sentenced to pay five shillings and costs or face a further fourteen days imprisonment. Accounting for her drunkenness, the *Gazette* reported that she had just received a postal order from her husband in Leeds and added that Mrs Barrett had already spent nine months of that year in prison 'through drink'.[3] Seven months later, now living in Elmwood Street, she made her sixteenth appearance at court – this time for wandering abroad and indecency – and was fined five shillings.[4] A few weeks later, having moved back to Walmgate, she was sentenced to seven days with hard labour for the same offence, and in the following month was accused of stealing a watch, but was discharged.[5] It is obvious that many of her appearances at court went unrecorded in the local press – during the next six months, for example, she must have faced five other charges, as in February 1869 she was reported as making her twenty-fourth appearance before the Bench. At this time she was living in the Water Lanes and was sentenced to fourteen days on the unusual charge of being a prostitute.[6] Within eight weeks she was again imprisoned – this time for two months with hard labour, because of indecency;[7] and the charge and sentence were repeated in the following September.[8] Only a week after the expiration of her sentence she was remanded for what was now the thirtieth time – once more on a charge of being drunk and disorderly. On being informed that Mrs Barrett had a relative who would immediately take her with him to America, however, the magistrates decided to discharge their prisoner, with the proviso that if the story were untrue she would again go to jail for two months.[9] It seems likely that she did in fact leave the city, as it was not for another nineteen months (until May 1871) that Margaret Barrett's name again appeared in the Police Reports in the *Gazette*, during which time, however, she had faced two other charges. On this, her thirty-third appearance, she was sentenced to seven days for indecency,[10] and within a week of leaving prison was given a further month for the same offence.[11] She celebrated her release on that occasion by becoming so drunk and riotous that she was again immediately arrested, but was discharged after promising – perhaps at the magistrates' suggestion – that she would leave the city.

If the authorities hoped they had seen the last of this particular prostitute, however, they were mistaken. In the quarter ending December 1871, only a few months after her expected departure, Margaret Barrett, now living at Kilby's Yard in the Water Lanes, applied to the Guardians for Poor Relief – though whether she actually wished to enter the workhouse is uncertain. She was reported as being thirty-four years old, able bodied and suffering from syphilis. Her application, however, was 'not entertained'.[12]

Following this, incredible as it may seem of an already diseased, apparently alcoholic prostitute, who had been refused shelter or treatment even at the workhouse, encouraged to leave the city, hounded by the police and who had already served dozens of prison sentences, her miserable career grew progressively worse. In December 1871, now 'with no fixed abode', she was given the unusually heavy sentence of three months imprisonment for indecency,[13] and in the following April, having faced a couple of further charges in the few weeks since the expiry of her last reported sentence, she made her thirty-ninth appearance at court. She was charged with disorderly behaviour.[14] This was followed by another unrecorded appearance before the Bench, and a further sentence at the end of May (by which time she was again living in Elmwood Street) of three months for indecency.[15] By April 1873 she had moved back to Walmgate, and in the next two months faced four other charges, the last being indecency again, for which she served a further three months imprisonment. It was reported on this occasion that this was her forty-fifth appearance in court since February 1860, and that she had served thirty-six months and seventeen days in prison.[16]

During the next couple of years Margaret Barrett disappeared from the York records, possibly she left the city; but in January 1876 it was reported at the Quarter Sessions that she had stolen a bottle of brandy from a Mr Dewse, landlord of the 'Lonsbro Arms' in Petergate. Her friend, prostitute Martha Stephenson, was charged with receiving the same, knowing it to be stolen. Mrs Barrett was said to be thirty-eight years old and:

The character of the prisoner was traced from 1851 to 1875, as being perfectly incorrigible. The various imprisonments showed that sufficient warnings had been given and she appeared incapable of reformation . . . whilst it was a matter of pain to have to pass sentence on females, the sentences would be heavy.

Both Margaret Barrett and Martha Stephenson were sentenced to two years imprisonment with hard labour.[17]

After having completed slightly more than half her sentence at York Castle, Margaret Barrett, now a 'middle-aged woman', was once more brought to the court. She was charged with assaulting the Matron and doing wilful damage to property belonging to the Castle. On the 19 April 1877, on entering Margaret Barrett's cell, the Matron had been knocked down by a violent blow and kicked by the prisoner, who then began to break up the furniture, and smashed every pane of glass in the window with a stool. The Governor stated that she was so violent that he had been obliged to put her in irons and keep her in solitary confinement. During her imprisonment she had destroyed sixteen pairs of stockings, and had been more trouble than all the rest of the prisoners put together. The damage to property was estimated at one pound. Mrs Barrett admitted the charge but said in her defence that she had been badly treated. The Governor, however, 'showed this to be entirely untrue' and she was fined one pound and costs for the damage and sentenced to an additional six months imprisonment for assault.[18]

Although she was released from York Castle late in 1878, Margaret Barrett was not recorded again until 1883, though in fact, as will emerge, she served several additional sentences in the meantime. In May that year she was charged with being drunk and disorderly in St Sampson's Square, and with having committed a similar offence in the previous week.[19] She had no fixed abode, and was given the choice of paying a fine of ten shillings and costs, or going to prison for one month. In the following year (January 1884), now said to be living in Aldwark, she was sentenced to one month with hard labour for the same offence, and one month after her release was charged with the theft of seven glass dishes, nine saucers and four cups from Walter Watson of York. She now had forty-nine previous convictions (as opposed to appearances at court) and the Recorder stated that her career of crime had begun in 1860, since when she seemed to have done nothing for a livelihood. Readers were then acquainted with Mrs Barrett's history since she had left the Castle. She claimed that she had worked hard for the past seven years for respectable people in the city, and was, in fact, described by the *Gazette* as a charwoman. The Recorder, however, disagreed with this account, stating:

In 1876 you were tried here and got two years ... that would not expire until 1878 and then you were taken up seven times for drunkenness and disorderly conduct and had a month each time. I must pass sentence upon you of five years because you deserve it and it must be a warning to you. And you will have to have two years police supervision.[20]

She did not, in fact, serve the whole of this sentence. In August 1887, once again having no fixed abode, she was convicted for the fifty-first time – once more for being drunk and disorderly, and two months later, now living in Aldwark, she made her fifty-third appearance at court – again for the same offence. It transpired that Mrs Barrett was 'out on ticket of leave – having still seventeen months of her sentence to serve'. On this occasion, however, 'the Bench was lenient' – committing her for only one month to York Castle.

By this time, and at the end of our period, Margaret Barrett must have been almost fifty years old. She had apparently been a prostitute from the age of about fourteen, and by her mid twenties at least was obviously a hardened drinker and sufficiently destitute to resort to the theft of a few rags and bones. How long she had had syphilis before applying to the workhouse is uncertain, but it is clear that for at least two years after needing treatment for the disease (which was refused) she continued to walk the streets, and even her later bouts of drunkenness were probably financed by prostitution. Apart from the fact that she had a husband who lived in Leeds (she was described as a married woman as late as 1887) and that she made some attempt to become a charwoman, few other details of her background are clear, other than her obvious poverty and dependence on drink. Her destitution is apparent from where she lived. For more than twenty-five years she drifted from one notorious slum to another – her most permanent residence being a cell in York Castle – and on several occasions she was actually homeless. Her drunkenness is obvious from her repeated appearances at court – though whether alcoholism was the cause or consequence of her becoming a prostitute is unclear. The severity of her prison sentences must have been unendurable to someone in her condition, so that her violent, though uncharacteristic conduct in York Castle is understandable.

Margaret Barrett's friend, Martha Stephenson, was another destitute and alcoholic street-walker, who between 1864 and 1876 made at least thirty-nine appearances at court and who, as in April 1869, for example, was frequently imprisoned for fairly long periods, immediately following her release from jail.[21] By September 1864 (when she was only twenty-two years old) she was already sick and destitute, and, having no home, was sent to the workhouse.[22] During the next two years, living in Walmgate and Hungate, she faced various charges for indecency, prostitution and annoyance, and in March 1867 – by which time she claimed to be thirty, not able bodied and suffering from rheumatism – she again applied for poor relief. Six months later, now apparently only twenty-seven and living in the Water Lanes, she was again not able bodied and was sent to the workhouse.[23] In the following few months she made various other appearances at court, some for drunkenness, as in May 1868 when she was bleeding and said she had been beaten by a man.[24] During this period she moved back to Hungate, but when re-admitted to the workhouse in December 1868, again ill and now claiming to be only twenty-five, she was once more homeless.[25] In the next two years she was convicted on various occasions for indecency, and during this time lived in several of the main centres of prostitution in the city such as Hungate, North Street and Peter Lane; though by 1872, when she was once more admitted to the workhouse being sick and not able bodied, she was again homeless.[26] As had been the case with Margaret Barrett, her prison sentences became increasingly severe until, as mentioned above, she was sentenced to two years in York Castle for receiving a bottle of stolen brandy. Unlike Mrs Barrett, Martha Stephenson was unmarried and obviously in a very poor state of health over a fairly long period. No further reference to her exists in the York records, and it is possible that she did not survive her harsh prison sentence.

Sabina Bulmer was another pitiful woman of the streets whose drunken habits caused her to be repeatedly imprisoned, and whose only recorded address was the workhouse. In December 1876 she made her thirty-second appearance before the magistrates – on a charge of drunk and disorderly behaviour in Coppergate. She had no fixed abode, and, unable to pay the five shillings fine, was sent to prison for seven days.[27] On the day of her release she was charged with stealing a basket containing a spice loaf, a bottle of rum, a piece of beef and other articles, belonging to a Mr John Senior of Fossgate. She was remanded in custody. In the following year, now an 'elderly woman', she was convicted for the thirty-second time – once more for drunkenness; and four years later, though no longer described as a prostitute, was a full-time resident of the workhouse. Reporting on her drunk and disorderly behaviour in Fossgate, the *Gazette* stated that whenever 'this aged widow' was allowed to leave the workhouse she 'fell into bad company and got drunk and the police were quite beaten with her'. Though she now had forty-two previous convictions, she was discharged on promising never to leave the workhouse again under similar circumstances.[28]

Regardless of whether these women, and dozens of others like them in the city, were actually persecuted by the police or magistrates – and they were certainly unfortunate both in the frequency of their arrests and the severity of their sentences – their numerous imprisonments seem to have been inevitable. Their predicament was like that of Esther in *Mary Barton* who declared:

I could not lead a virtuous life if I would . . . I must have drink. Such as live like me could not bear life if they did not drink. It's the only thing to keep us from suicide. If we did not drink, we could not stand the memory of what we have been, and the thought of what we are, for a day. If I go without food, and without shelter, I must have my dram.

Oh! You don't know the awful nights I have had in prison for want of it.[29]

Such women were trapped, however, for even their fear of jail and its absence of alcohol could not prevent them from desperately turning to drink as soon as they were released. To finance this craving they were forced to break the law – by stealing or walking the streets – and having satisfied their thirst, usually to the point of excess, broke the law again and faced further imprisonment.

William Logan, temperance reformer and author of *The Great Social Evil*, must be regarded as an authority on the subject of prostitution since he personally investigated the problem in Dublin, Edinburgh, Aberdeen, Inverness, Greenock, Paisley, Kilmarnock, Liverpool, Newcastle upon Tyne, Hull, Leeds and York* as well as a number of smaller towns in England and Scotland, visiting hundreds of brothels and notorious houses, and interviewing literally thousands of women of ill fame. Unlike Gladstone, however, who, regardless of personal danger, seized every opportunity to remonstrate with and befriend fallen women whom he met in the streets,[30] Logan more prudently visited them only in their 'dens of iniquity' in the early afternoons, stating that:

As a matter of prudence I seldom if ever entered into conversation with fallen women on the street with the view of reclaiming them. More harm, perhaps, than good has resulted from conversation with this class on the public thoroughfare, especially after dusk.[31]

Though recognising that among the principal causes of women resorting to prostitution were the prevailing and limited conditions of female labour, which sometimes resulted in near starvation wages – followed by seduction, overcrowded and squalid housing conditions, bad parental example, disagreements between daughters and parents and step-parents and lack of education – Logan was convinced that the major reason for women taking to and remaining on the streets was drink. As a temperance leader he naturally stressed the connection between these 'twin evils', using as evidence material from the work of another temperance writer, Professor J. Miller, who in 1859 had published an article entitled 'Prostitution Considered in Relation to its Cause and Cure'. In support of this view he quoted extensively too from the work of Dr William Tait, House Surgeon to

---

* Unfortunately Logan gives no details about his missionary work in York.

the Edinburgh Lock Hospital, who had for many years treated prostitutes suffering from venereal disease, and whose book on the subject, already referred to in Chapter 1, was first published in 1841. Unlike Logan, however, Tait – though recognising its importance – seems to have regarded drink as a consequence as much as a cause of women taking to the streets, dividing their number between those who were either congenital alcoholics or had themselves

first formed the habit of intemperance, and subsequently resorted to a life of prostitution in order to procure the means of satiating their desires for stimulating liquors;

and those who drank as a result of prostitution, in order to: 'Drown remorse and shame, and expel from their mind all uneasy feelings regarding their awful situation'.[32] From whatever the cause, however, and whether street-walkers became drunkards because of the miseries of their profession, or took to the streets in order to satisfy their craving for drink, observers of the 'social evil' and temperance reformers alike were agreed in recognising that intemperance and prostitution were invariably associated, and that, though all inebriates were not prostitutes, most prostitutes (and in many cases their clients too*) were either habitual drunkards or periodically under the influence of drink.

According to both Logan and Tait, comparatively few women's initial seduction had been brought about without the help of a few glasses of intoxicating liquor, whose soporific powers, as the prostitute progressed in the paths of dissipation, became more and more vital to her existence. Recommended and consumed at first merely as a remedy for 'low spirits', to embolden the hesitant or inexperienced street-walker to solicit clients or as an effective barrier against the remorse which might accompany more sober reflection, drink, and in particular strong spirits, soon became a habit which the prostitute, even when resigned to her position, could scarcely live without. Thus:

By and by the unfortunate grows a hardened prostitute; and then, what made her so, keeps her so . . . Drink then becomes the necessary to

---

* 'Full many a man is led captive to the impure embrace of the harlot, who would have stood firm against the temptation, had it not been for the previous act of intemperance, which, while it stimulated his animal desire, obscured his reason, and depressed his moral power' (Miller, quoted in Logan, *op. cit.* p. 59). This must surely have been the case with those men resorting to ageing whores and diseased street-walkers such as Sarah Pepper, Margaret Barrett, Sabina Bulmer, etc.

maintain the prostitution, and prostitution must be continued to provide the drink. Terrible reciprocity![33]

Logan, Tait, Miller and even Acton believed that few women of the streets remained outside this vicious circle for long, and that from whatever the cause, the habit of intemperance was 'all but universal among prostitutes'. Even the limited amount of alcohol allowed to girls in 'respectable' brothels rarely prevented this course, since prostitutes engaged in the activity for any length of time invariably found such restraint irksome and drifted into inferior houses or on to the streets where they could 'revel and dissipate at pleasure'.

The frequency with which offences connected with prostitution in York occurred in public houses or beershops; the fact that such premises were obviously regarded as the hunting ground of both the harlot and the whore-monger; evidence relating to brothels and their patrons illustrating that, in all types of identified houses of ill fame in the city, alcohol was consumed freely by both the prostitute and her clients – and indeed, that 'treating' the assembled company was a common if not actually obligatory part of the transaction – and the various references to applicants' former intemperance contained in the records of the Penitentiary Society, indicate that contemporary observers were justified in stressing the connection between liquor and prostitution, and that most unfortunates, in York at least, must certainly have had regular recourse to alcohol. The extent to which they did so, however, obviously varied according to the circumstances of the individual, and it is impossible to estimate what proportion of York prostitutes were actually addicted to drink, or to say little more than that as a group they were probably more dependent on liquor than were other women of the poor. Statistical evidence from the Quarter Sessions or the newspaper reports of the magistrates' courts is hardly conclusive in this respect, since the fact that a prostitute was prosecuted for drunkenness – even several times – does not of course prove that she was an alcoholic, yet on the other hand the fact that many of the city's street-walkers were identified for this study through other causes – because they were destitute or were prosecuted for indecency or picking pockets, for example – is hardly an indication that they were not. Only in the case of women like Margaret Barrett, Margaret Riley or Sabina Bulmer who were repeatedly prosecuted for drunkenness, is it reasonable to assume that they were indeed addicted to drink.

In spite of these reservations, however, figures relating to York

Fig. 26 Social reformers, those concerned with the rescue of fallen
women and temperance workers were aware of the connections
between poverty, prostitution and drink. This photograph was
used to illustrate these themes in lectures entitled 'Drink and the
Social Question', given in late Victorian York.

prostitutes appearing at court on charges connected with drink in the
period are as follows: of the 602 individual prostitutes arrested
(including those who were also at some stage in their careers
described as brothel-keepers) 179 or 30 per cent faced at least one
charge involving drink. Of these, 44 (7.3 per cent of the total) were
reported in the newspapers (usually in retrospect) as having been
convicted for drunkenness on at least ten occasions, and can thus be
classed as habitual offenders. These figures, however, are not only

inadequate in revealing the general relationship between prostitution and drink, but also fail to show the serious nature of many individual street-walkers' alcoholism. It will be recalled that Elizabeth Eden, for example, had only one charge of drunkenness recorded against her, and from this evidence she would not, therefore, be included as an habitual drunkard. Yet at the age of only twenty-four she was admitted to the workhouse with delirium tremens.[34] Other prostitutes, on their only recorded appearance in York, were so affected by drink that they tried to kill themselves, or went berserk in the police cells, yet they too are not included as habitual offenders.

Further it is clear that prostitutes, like other individuals, could consume large and regular quantities of alcohol without committing an offence or being arrested, and that it was only those women who staggered about the streets in drunken disorder, or who caused a disturbance while under the influence of intoxicating liquor, who were charged under this heading. Many others no doubt, in the privacy of their squalid lodgings, quietly drank themselves into a stupor, in the common kitchen of a low-class brothel or lodging-house, 'dishevelled, dirty, slipshod and dressing-gowned [grew] stupid from beer, or fractious from gin'; or, in the bedrooms of slightly superior houses of ill fame, greedily consumed, at their clients' expense, countless glasses of champagne. While it is impossible, therefore, to be certain how many prostitutes were regular drinkers, it is clear that few, if any, were totally abstemious.

It is apparent too that the law was not enforced either impartially or over-scrupulously in this respect, and that while certain women who might otherwise have appeared at court on a charge of drunkenness (or any other offence) enjoyed police protection and were arrested only if a complaint was filed against them, others, like Margaret Barrett, seem to have been pursued with extraordinary zeal. On various occasions in the period police constables were reprimanded by the Watch Committee, and often dismissed from the force for keeping company with known prostitutes, and in many of these instances, acts of indecency were associated with drink. In August 1846, for example, Police Constable Boyes was fined one week's wages and cautioned for absenting himself from his beat and being found drunk in a brothel; and in the following month, having repeated the offence in a house of ill fame in Aldwark, was immediately dismissed.[35] Three months later Police Constable Clark, reported for being off his beat at four o'clock in the morning and

Fig. 27 York City Police Force in about 1880. One in every six identified clients in the period was a policeman.

found reposing in a brothel in the same street was dealt with similarly.[36] In October 1849 P.C. Whitwell was fined one shilling a week from his pay for ten weeks for having been found in the 'City Arms' public house in Walmgate while on duty, and having indecent intercourse with prostitute Isabella Ogram in a passage in Castlegate,[37] and two years later P.C. George Franks was dismissed for drinking, smoking and whoring in a brothel in Wenlock Street at three in the morning.[38] William Horbury and George Armitage were dismissed from the force in November 1856 for their misconduct in entering a public house in North Street with two prostitutes (according to the *Herald* the women were treating the men to drinks); and in the following year P.C. Thomas Rainsdale was fined one week's pay for neglecting his beat in order to visit a brothel – 'not in the discharge of his duty'.[39] The case of Constable Duffy, summoned before the Watch Committee in 1866, is a further illustration of the link between the policeman on the beat, prostitution and drink. In March that year Mrs Smith, wife of William Smith of the 'Shoulder of Mutton' beerhouse in Water Lane, complained that the constable entered the house and asked for a glass of ale, at the same time stating that he had no money. When Mrs Smith pointed out that he had just been paid, he replied, 'I have no money, but I will pay you another time. You had better, it will be better for you.' She supplied him with a drink, and he then demanded the loan of half a crown 'to go and get a sweetheart with'. Since it emerged that Duffy repeatedly frequented the house, 'which is one of ill fame', he was dismissed.[40]

Police Constable King, found in a disorderly house in Albion Street (off Skeldergate) in the early hours of the morning, P.C. Pinkney, in company with a prostitute at a house in Stonegate, and P.C. Dacre, found drunk in the company of prostitutes at 'Liddells'' in Marygate, were dismissed in 1870, 1871 and 1874 respectively;[41] and in 1871 P.C. Maude was charged with neglecting his duty in not taking prostitute Elizabeth Claxton into custody – even though a complaint had been made against her. She was accused of robbing Edward Dent at the 'Hand and Heart' in St Sampson's Square, a public house which she was in the habit of frequenting regularly and which, it emerged, was kept by the police officer's father-in-law.[42] Illustrations such as these suggest that policemen in the habit of drinking and consorting with prostitutes would, understandably, have been reluctant to take them into custody, and may well have chosen to ignore the public misdemeanours of those with whom they were on such intimate terms.

As we have seen in Chapter 2, those areas most commonly associated with prostitution in York, containing the largest concentrations of brothels and being the neighbourhoods in which offences connected with the activity most frequently occurred, were precisely those in which many of the city's public houses and beershops were situated, particularly those enjoying a dubious, or more often infamous reputation. The undoubted association between drink and prostitution, however, is even more apparent from the number of publicans or beerhouse keepers charged with harbouring prostitutes, or allowing persons of a notorious character to assemble on their premises. It is clear that not only were many such houses frequented by street-walkers and their prospective clients as convenient meeting places, but that occasionally the premises themselves were used for immoral purposes, with the landlord either allowing part of his establishment to be used as a brothel, or employing prostitutes who were also required to serve drinks. As we have seen, one of the most notorious of these was 'The Green Tree' in the Water Lanes, a public house kept by the Gibsons who also used their premises as a lodging-house and a brothel, which furnished the workhouse with various destitute and diseased whores. Another was the 'Cricketer's Arms' in Toft Green, the landlord of which, William Herbert, was charged with allowing the house to be used as a brothel after a local watchmaker gave evidence that he had been in the habit of taking a room there for immoral purposes.[43] Various licensees of public houses in the Water Lanes used prostitutes as barmaids, and Margaret Smith, a beerhouse keeper of North Street, had a similar arrangement. In January 1864 she was charged with assault by Emma Farrer and a Miss Button. They were both described as being in her employment as servants and prostitutes.[44] In other disreputable houses, though prostitution did not apparently take place on the premises, customers requiring more than a drink were introduced to the services of women who lodged nearby or used neighbouring 'houses of accommodation'; in return for which the landlord received a share of the prostitutes' takings. Other licensees had similar arrangements with neighbouring brothels and acted as suppliers both of clients and alcohol. Most often, however, 'infamous' public houses and beershops were merely those in which prostitutes and their companions were known to assemble and where opportunities for soliciting and general dissipation went unchecked by landlords, who were not too particular about the class of clientele they served, and who did nothing to discourage such activities, so long as they increased custom. Two such houses in Swinegate, for example were the 'Ploughboy's Rest' and the 'Crystal Palace', both of which were notorious in the eighteen-fifties. The former was, as we have seen, a dramshop and brothel combined, described by the magistrates in January 1853 as a 'disgrace to the city, and the haunt of thieves, prostitutes and strolling vagabonds'.[45] The 'Crystal Palace' too, was obviously a favourite rendezvous of local whores. Charged in February 1857 with allowing an unlawful assembly of twelve prostitutes on the premises, the landlord Henry Thornton replied that had the police arrived half an hour earlier, they would have found twenty-four.[46] Amongst other notorious houses in the centre of the city were the 'Punch Bowl' in Stonegate (where on one occasion in the eighties when the publican was charged with keeping a disorderly house, twenty-four 'immoral characters' were found on the premises)[47] and a beerhouse in Peter Lane. In 1870 George Richardson the landlord of this establishment was charged with harbouring prostitutes. Five were discovered in rooms on the west side of the house, and thirteen in rooms on the east.[48] David Dixon's beerhouse in Black Horse Passage (leading from Fossgate to Wesley Place) was another haunt of both prostitutes and thieves, as was the 'Red Lion' at Peaseholme Green and the Alexandra Hotel in the Market Place. Perhaps most notorious of all, however, was the beerhouse at the corner of First Water Lane and King's Staithe, kept by Mary Megginson. She was repeatedly charged with allowing prostitutes on the premises and on one occasion in January 1860 the police found fifteen abandoned girls and five convicted thieves in one room.[49] A few yards away was another infamous house. In October 1862 John Ramsey, a sailor from the Shetland Islands, met twenty-three year old prostitute Phoebe Child at the 'Ship Inn', King's Staithe where he treated her and some other girls to drinks. He then went to bed with Miss Child 'in a house in the yard' where he was robbed of seven pounds.[50] In Mrs Megginson's house it was more often the case that clients met 'ruined girls' and accompanied them to houses of ill fame in the Lanes – often in Cross Alley. Such illustrations, together with those used in Chapter 4 showing the frequency with which clients were robbed in various other public houses and beershops and even in brothels when they were engaged in buying drinks for the assembled company, demonstrate that prostitution in York was closely allied to the liquor trade, with a great deal of soliciting actually taking place in pubs, and large amounts of alcohol customarily being consumed in brothels and houses of ill fame at the clients' expense. Further, and more particular to the prostitute, however, the evidence concerning charges brought against street-walkers for drunkenness indicates that individual women relied heavily on drink, not only as a means of meeting and disarming clients or extorting additional funds out of them in the form of commission on alcohol purchased – but also to satisfy their own undoubted personal need.

Among prostitutes who were the most frequent offenders in York in connection with drink were Jane Garbutt, who in 1865 was charged for the twenty-second time with being drunk and disorderly,[51] Catherine Fowler of the Water Lanes, who in 1864 made her fifteenth appearance before the Bench;[52] and Sarah Dawson, alias Poppleton, common prostitute and brothel-keeper who was repeatedly drunk, disorderly and riotous.[53] Ann McDonald was another prostitute evidently addicted to drink. Formerly from Glasgow, by December 1864 she was living in Peter Lane and from there moved to Walmgate and Navigation Road. Between 1864 and 1877 she received twenty-two convictions – several for drunkenness – as, for example, in January 1877 when she was apprehended lurching down Walmgate with 'a sickle in her hand and flourished it above her head alarming persons who happened to come near her'.[54] Like Margaret Barrett, she was no sooner released from fairly long prison sentences than she was re-arrested in a wildly drunken state. Similarly, Margaret Riley of Skeldergate, Palmer Lane and Toft Green made thirty-five appearances at court between 1867 and 1883 and had at least thirty-one convictions, most of them for the drunken disturbances which she caused at various times in almost every part of the city.[55] Another inebriate was Martha Snowden, a married prostitute from Hungate who was convicted for the forty-seventh time in 1886;[56] and another habitual offender was Julia Gray who was sentenced to one year's imprisonment with hard labour in September 1877 for prostitution and indecency. She had no fixed abode, had had at least fourteen previous convictions and was obviously a hardened drinker, being described as of similar character to prostitute Margaret Riley.[57]

Other women, though with fewer convictions, were nevertheless obviously very heavy drinkers. Margaret Thompson, for example, 'a woman of immoral character' was arrested for drunkenness in November 1879 and tried to strangle herself in the police cell by tying a handkerchief tightly about her neck. As it was not safe to liberate her she was remanded in custody for a week, after which time:

She had improved very much in appearance . . . [and] expressed regret for what had happened and said she would endeavour to rejoin her friends in Ireland with whom she had not communicated on account of the disgrace into which she had fallen.[58]

Similarly Ann Dixon made a third attempt at self-strangulation in the police station in September 1843,[59] and Julia Walker was another prostitute who attempted suicide in the police cells. This occurred after her re-arrest only one day following her release from prison. It was reported in the *Gazette* 'that her great failing seemed to be in getting too much to drink', but she was discharged on promising to go to the workhouse. In one of her many bouts of drunkenness she had violently assaulted a policeman in Walmgate, and she too, was an associate of Margaret Riley.[60] Sarah Rhodes was another prostitute who frequently took to the bottle, sometimes with violent results. In 1848, after being arrested for drunk and indecent behaviour, she 'seized the policeman and struck him in the face with her fist'. In January 1867 she made her eighteenth appearance at court for drunk and disorderly behaviour, and in the following month she died.[61]

Such women were by no means unique and were recognised by rescue workers as being the most difficult class of prostitutes to reform – 'being generally regarded as unhelpable'. It was stated in the quarterly pamphlet *Notes on Work Amongst the Fallen*, circulated to Rescue Homes and Female Penitentiaries throughout the country from 1887 onwards, and included with the York Penitentiary records, that among commitments to prison for drunkenness in Great Britain in the eighteen-eighties, though less than one third of the number were women, imprisonments of 'habitual offenders' were fifty per cent more frequent among women than men; and that of female commitments, eighty to eighty-five per cent were for drunkenness combined with 'importuning and disorderly conduct'. By 'habituals' the pamphlet was referring to persons who had at least ten imprisonments recorded against them:

But the names of habituals can be given who have been convicted *one, two, three, four, five and six hundred times* ... and in *one* year there are a number of individuals convicted of drunkenness, *thirty* up to *fifty-two* times, and a larger number six up to thirty times.[62]

These figures, prepared by the Reformatory and Refuge Union for a Memorial to the House of Lords, were taken from the prison records of London, Glasgow, Liverpool, Birmingham, Manchester, Dublin, Durham, Edinburgh, Dundee, Belfast, Greenock, Carlisle, Cardiff, Swansea, Hull and other provincial towns. York, therefore, was not unduly unfortunate or unusual with regard to its regular offenders, as it would appear that most other large towns in the country contained women who were repeatedly convicted for offences combining drunkenness and prostitution; and who, on the same day or the day following their release from prison, were re-arrested and returned to jail. This imprisonment took place, according to the Report:

after a debauch, the effects of which have hardly passed off before they are at liberty to repeat with impunity the offence for which they have so frequently been convicted ... these habituals look upon the gaols as national Sanatoria, in which they can sojourn for a brief period without performing any but the most perfunctory work – their condition, in many cases, not admitting of labour.[63]

The Reformatory and Refuge Union, believing that a change in the police regulations in dealing with these 'wretched beings' was absolutely imperative, and that short-term imprisonments were worse than ineffectual, advocated 'long-term remedial and reformatory treatment'. Given the prevailing punitive attitude of middle-class reformers towards insobriety, however, and the general ignorance and prejudice regarding the causes, effects and consequences of drunkenness – to say nothing of alcoholism in the period – it is difficult to see how such 'habituals' could have been saved. The National Society was strongly opposed to 'short-term' Shelters for prostitutes (such as the Homes in Skeldergate and Trinity Lane referred to above) regardless of whether such women were addicted to drink, holding the view that only in institutions such as the Female Penitentiary in Bishophill, where a fallen woman had to remain for two years, could her rescue and reform be effectively and permanently achieved. As we shall see in the following Chapter, however, the Refuge at York did not admit prostitutes known to be addicted to drink, and had a limited success rate, even with those who were not. Habitual drunkards and alcoholics, then, could hardly have been rescued or cured in such establishments since they were discouraged from entering them in the first place; the Homes lacked the medically trained staff necessary for such treatment and, equally important, they operated on a system whereby the inmates entered voluntarily and were ultimately free to leave if they wished.

Further, since the main purpose of *Notes on Work Amongst the Fallen* was the circulation of an up to date, strictly confidential 'Cautionary List' which contained the names and descriptions of prostitutes already dismissed from Homes for being especially troublesome and whose applications matrons were strongly advised to reject; and since girls with 'confirmed drunken habits' were included in this category, it is difficult to believe that by 'long-term remedial and reformatory treatment' the Refuge Union was advocating anything other than long-term imprisonment.

For Margaret Barrett and other women like her, however, ageing, homeless, diseased and without hope, such a 'remedy' was useless. Even a term of two years in jail with hard labour, solitary confinement and being put in irons did not fit them for society or make them less degraded than they had already become. It failed even to teach them to curb their need for drink, and in consequence, prostitution became the necessity to provide it.

As we have seen, the passing of, and to a far greater extent the controversy surrounding the eventual repeal of the Contagious Diseases Acts focussed the nation's attention on various aspects of prostitution, which were discussed and investigated more widely than in any other period of the country's history. Consequently, in support of the Acts, evidence was produced demonstrating the financial losses incurred by the nation as a result of venereal disease amongst the armed forces (particularly the lower ranks) and the danger too, facing the civilian population – both of which evils were seen to emanate from the prostitute. For without the enforcement of the Acts, she was as free to spread her 'loathsome poison' as were her far more numerous clients. In stressing the need for the state regulation of prostitution, however, its advocates were placed in a difficult position, since on the one hand they emphasised the dangers facing men who resorted to prostitutes without the 'sanitary' protection of the law, while on the other they sought to play down the harmful effects of the activity on the prostitutes themselves. Thus, those very aspects of the prostitute's life which common sense demands should be regarded as prejudicial to her physical well-being were represented by the supporters of the Acts (and in particular the Select Committee of the House of Lords, quoting extensively from Acton) as being proof of and reasons for prostitutes' good health and vigorous constitutions. Consequently, low-class whores, who in all weathers and far into the night prowled the streets and were repeatedly imprisoned, together with their more fortunate sisters who passed most of their time drinking and debauching in smoky, overcrowded taprooms and brothels, were described as leading healthy, outdoor lives; and women who, as was generally recognised, had appalling diets – preferring to go without food in order to buy alcohol – were described as well-fed. Girls like the vast majority of those reported in the York Penitentiary records as applying to the Home in a pitiful state 'with hardly clothes to cover them' and their superiors who sallied out at night in flimsy finery, were said, by their Lordships, to be well-dressed. Strangest of all, however, prostitutes, the recipients as well as the donors of disease, the group whom the law demanded should be regularly examined and if necessary compulsorily treated for venereal infection and from whom their clients had to be protected by stringent and degrading sanitary measures, were alleged to 'enjoy better health than other women of the class from which they are chiefly supplied'. It was concluded that they were more robust and resistant to disease than their poorer but harder worked sisters, and that they 'passed through the furnace of a dissipated career less worse from wear than their male associates'.

The evidence produced in this study reveals conclusively that this was not the case, and that their Lordships (if they really believed such nonsense) were severely misled. Nevertheless, their fanciful utterances have subsequently been regarded as established fact.

Unfortunately the extent to which ill-health was responsible for or contributed to the poverty which characterised prostitution in York can be calculated only for those prostitutes who were recorded in the Poor Law Guardians' Application and Report Books, or who appeared in the records of the York Female Penitentiary Society, since it was only in these sources that the physical condition of prostitutes was systematically recorded. The physical state of every Poor Law applicant, whether or not he or she was admitted into the workhouse, was always noted – in greater detail, of course, if the application was made on grounds of ill health – yet in only two or three instances out of the hundreds of thousands of entries in the period were individuals other than prostitutes reported to be suffering from venereal disease. Obviously other people in the city were infected, the large number of York whores who continued in their profession after having contracted disease would have ensured this, but either because they received private medical or quack treatment, were attended to at the hospital, or because they failed to recognise or seek a remedy for their symptoms, they were not reduced to requesting poor relief for their complaint. It is possible too that, apart from prostitutes, various other of the applicants for parish relief were, in fact, suffering from venereal disease, but since they required assistance on the grounds of say, unemployment, desertion, or some other illness or disability, and because they were not known to be prostitutes, they were presumably not examined for the condition, which could therefore have remained undetected. This would seem to imply that prostitutes recorded by the Guardians as diseased must have been in a fairly advanced and obvious state of illness, a supposition borne out by the fact that almost without exception they were described too as destitute – no doubt because their condition had deprived them of their usual livelihood.

Throughout the period, 234 individual prostitutes (nineteen per cent of the total identified) were recorded in the above source as sick or ill, and since they were all entirely without means, the vast majority were admitted into the workhouse. In addition, twenty prostitutes sought relief for reasons other than ill-health, one of them listing her grounds for application as 'want of employment' and the remaining nineteen being simply destitute or having no reason recorded. Of the 234 who were ill, well over half were suffering from venereal disease (listed as gonorrhoea, syphilis, V.D. or diseased) and about one eighth were simply recorded as sick or ill. The precise figures are as follows:

Venereal disease	124
Sick/Ill	32
Pregnant/Confined	14
Not able bodied	14
Deceased	10
Lame	6
Unsound mind	5
T.B./consumption	5
Venereal disease and confined	5
Smallpox	4
Fever	3
Others (including disabled, paralysis, itch, etc.)	12

Of the 234 sick applicants for relief, the ages of 181 were recorded. 105 or 58 per cent were aged between fifteen and twenty years, and 53 (29 per cent) were aged between twenty and twenty-five. In all therefore 87 per cent of sick prostitutes applying for relief were in the fifteen to twenty-five year age range – a slightly higher proportion than those in the same age group for the prostitute community as a whole. It is probable that, in addition to the 129 women who had venereal disease, various others, including those pregnant or confined (several of whom were described also as sick) were suffering from complaints brought about as a result of their profession.

It has been suggested that many of the women and girls with venereal disease must have been infected for some time before applying to enter the workhouse, and since a large number of these were admitted direct from brothels and houses of ill fame in the city, it is clear that though diseased, they had continued in their occupation until their condition had absolutely prevented it. However, even low-class brothel-keepers had no use for incapacitated prostitutes and rid themselves of such women as soon as they were no longer able to work. Logan recalled, for example, that on one of his visits to the Bradford workhouse he met a girl who had been a whore for four years, and who told the matron shortly before she died:

The mistress of the brothel was everything to me when in health, but when unwell I was turned out of doors without mercy, and the doctor said that I might have died any moment.[64]

Until they reached this stage, however, many girls were obviously retained in inferior brothels who were, to the client at least, an undetected but virulent source of venereal infection. In all, forty of the above prostitutes with venereal disease were recorded as being admitted straight from named brothels; however, given the additional number of such women whose address was the Water Lanes (and in particular Cross Alley) or other notorious streets which contained a high proportion of infamous houses, it is likely that others of them too came straight from brothels. Some girls were obviously very ill when taken into the workhouse, and it is unlikely that either they or their employers could have been unaware of the nature and advanced state of their condition. Twenty-four year old Elizabeth Baldin, for example, who had come from 'Mrs Maude's' in King's Court, was one of those who actually died soon after being admitted; eleven others were recorded as being ill as well as having venereal disease and five more were so sick with disease that they were classed as 'not able bodied'. Yet all of these were received straight from named brothels and must, therefore, have been responsible for a considerable spread of disease. In addition, their subsequent appearances at court show that at least thirty-one whores with venereal disease continued to prostitute themselves after only a short stay at the workhouse; and given the limited effectiveness of treatment in the period, they too must have infected a considerable

number of clients. Harriet Atkinson, for example, was admitted to
the workhouse with venereal disease in 1861 and was still walking the
streets eight years later;[65] and similarly sixteen year old Ann Mul-
downey who had venereal disease in 1859 was still engaged in prostitution in 1863.[66] Another sixteen year old, Elizabeth Smith, who
was admitted to the workhouse in 1864, though diseased, continued
as a prostitute until 1873,[67] and Anne Walker, Elizabeth Watson,
Elizabeth Wilson and Jane Wood were among other diseased prostitutes who continued to walk the streets for varying lengths of
time.[68] Other women, though not necessarily admitted from a
brothel were obviously horribly afflicted with venereal infection by
the time they applied for relief. Twenty-one year old Catherine
Connolly, for example, was so badly diseased with syphilis in 1874
that she was 'scarcely able to walk';[69] and a second Elizabeth Smith,
who had been allowed half a pint of brandy in April 1868, died from
the disease in the following month.

As well as the sick prostitutes referred to above, there were undoubtedly many other street-walkers in the city who were the victims
of ill health resulting from their way of life, but who for some reason
did not apply to York workhouse for relief. One reason for this may
have been that until 1861 when the Law of Settlement was amended
all those prostitutes who had lived in the city for less than five years
and were ineligible for relief could be removed back to their parish of
origin – hardly an attractive proposition for a fallen woman whose
diseased or swollen body loudly proclaimed her shame – though a
convenient way for the city authorities to rid themselves of such
undesirable immigrants. In 1865 the period for acquiring settlement
was further reduced from three years to twelve months, so that after
that date, only those who had fairly recently taken up residence in the
city would be deterred from applying for relief. Since York was a
centre of prostitution which attracted from a fairly wide area both
hardened street-walkers and young girls who would shortly be drawn
into the activity, it is probable that in the earlier part of the period at
least there were various such women who, rather than apply to York
workhouse, either sought treatment elsewhere or whose complaints
went unattended.

Though not necessarily included in this Chapter, evidence on
almost all the women identified as prostitutes in this study points to
the fact that poverty, disease and drink, either separately or combined, were common elements in their lives. Some of the girls, like

the three young Nettleton sisters, were recorded as being both destitute and diseased – they may well too have been heavy drinkers. Others, like Martha Stephenson, Margaret Riley and Ann McDonald, though not recorded as diseased, were habitual drunkards and at times destitute; and others still, like Margaret Barrett and Elizabeth Eden, suffered all the combined miseries of their trade. The records of the York Penitentiary Society show that many of the girls who applied to enter the Refuge were also not only destitute, but in a poor state of health – some being so ill, diseased or pregnant that they were refused admittance, and others though they entered the Home were subsequently found to be so ill that they had to be dismissed. In addition there were those who, like Elizabeth Eden, were so weak after remaining in the Home for the required two years that they were not fit for ordinary situations and had to be found special 'light' employment. Of the 542 individual women recorded as applying to, or entering the Refuge in the period, 81 or 15 per cent were recorded as being ill, with 24 (4.4 per cent) being refused entry and 28 (5.2 per cent) subsequently dismissed because of their condition. The precise nature of a girl's complaint was rarely recorded by the Committee of Ladies, however, who generally preferred to use euphemisms such as 'poor' or 'delicate' state of health, and 'unfit to be received' or 'her condition requires that she should leave the Home immediately' about those who were found to be diseased or pregnant. Only towards the end of the period were girls described as 'being in the family way' or 'in a terrible state of disease'. Of the fifty-two girls who were either rejected or hastily dismissed from the Home because of ill health, only thirteen subsequently sought relief for their condition at the workhouse – a further indication that the Poor Law records by no means reveal the total number of sick prostitutes in the city. Of the remainder, two were sent to other workhouses, twelve went to hospital (including one to Scarborough) and two were admitted to lunatic asylums. Six were returned to parents or relatives and five were found especially light employment because of their infirmity.* For those sick prostitutes in the city who neither applied to the Guardians for relief nor entered other institutions, there were few alternatives. Opportunities for finding 'respectable' employment must have been almost negligible, and without some sort of medical treatment and reasonable diet it is

---

* One of these, Margaret Richardson, soon became paralysed and died in a state of 'hopeless bodily affliction'. See page 185.

difficult in any case to see how their physical condition would have allowed this. It is probable that some simply drifted away from the city and that others, destitute and in an age with an appallingly high rate of mortality amongst the poor, died, either from diseases directly associated with their occupation, or from any more general infection which their weakened and sickly constitutions were unable to withstand.

Many of them, even though diseased or pregnant, by resorting to various shifts such as begging, scrounging, stealing or finding an occasional day's work in occupations of the lowest description, were able too, perhaps, to scratch the barest of livings until either their health temporarily improved or they died. Since such women were invariably dependent on drink, many no doubt preferred this kind of existence to the punitive atmosphere of the workhouse. Others, especially among the younger girls (and as we have seen, 87 per cent of the recorded sick prostitutes in the city were under twenty-six years old), may have been fortunate enough to have family or friends willing to receive or support them in their misfortune. It may well be that the attitude of the poor towards prostitutes and fallen women – particularly those who had relatives who were such – was much more sympathetic than has generally been supposed. None, after all, could have been more aware than were they of the difficulties of remaining 'respectable' in the appalling and overcrowded conditions in which they lived – of the dangers and temptations facing desperate, deprived or dissatisfied women; or of the slender division between what was so often described as the general immorality of the poor and an individual woman's ruin. Possibly, modern interpretations of Victorian morality, as in so many other respects, have been too narrowly confined to the 'respectable' middle classes, who may well have regarded as already deceased, any of their women folk who took to the streets, but who in fact, would rarely have had reason to do so. This may have been the reaction too, of those of the 'deserving' and 'respectable' working classes whose daughters had lost their virtue, but again, as we have seen, prostitutes were comparatively rarely drawn even from this section of society. The evidence from this study and the records of the Penitentiary Society show that on the contrary most street-walkers and inmates of the Home:

have had in their parents bad examples which they only too naturally followed; and some have been actually initiated in sin by those who should have been their protectors from evil influences.[70]

Further, in 1900, by which time 560 girls had been admitted into the Refuge and hundreds more rejected or dismissed as ineligible, the Committee reported of the inmates:

There is not one who can be charged with having sinned in spite of opportunities for good, and in defiance of watchful care, and in utter disregard of sound teaching and loving counsel.[71]

There were in fact several instances in the Penitentiary records of parents who were willing to take home their fallen daughters, especially if they had been 'reformed and trained'; but these, of course, were expected to be self-supporting. Even so, such cases indicate that the Victorian horror of fallen women – even if not confined to the middle and respectable working classes – could not have been the general attitude of the very poor, particularly those living in urban communities of great deprivation, who are known to have been largely irreligious,[72] and described in York as 'sunken and depraved in their squalid lairs'.

Having made this reservation, however, it remains unlikely that many diseased, pregnant or even destitute street-walkers could have returned to their homes – however indifferent their families may have been to the conventions of respectable morality, and however strong and widely held were ties of sympathy and family affection amongst the poor. As the Penitentiary records show, it was generally the case that daughters had left home and taken to the streets precisely because of bad home conditions, such as drunken parents, neglected and deprived childhoods, cruelty or frequent quarrels and fights with parents or step-parents, or simply poverty. In addition, many of the girls were described as orphans and 'entirely without friends' and others, even though they had relatives still alive, came from such poor and overcrowded backgrounds that it is unlikely that in their present incapacitated state they would have been a welcome addition to an already large and impoverished family. Further, some of the older Penitentiary applicants had obviously become prostitutes because, like Maria Nettleton, they had been deserted by their husbands, had been widowed or had had illegitimate children. These, had they been able to return to their parental home, would surely have done so before resorting to the streets, not afterwards, when their health had been broken by the activity.

It would seem then that, as well as those prostitutes who applied for parish relief in the city and who were recorded by the Guardians as diseased and destitute, there were others in York equally unfortunate who did not go to the workhouse, but who scratched the barest of livings or fell back on friends, remaining untreated until they died. For all of them opportunities for a better way of life and improved health must have been relatively rare.

6

Rescue and reform

As it is impossible to follow through to their conclusion the lives of all the individual prostitutes identified in this book, it is impossible to estimate what proportion of their number re-entered respectable society and returned to a more 'regular course of life'. Acton, concluding that the vast majority of prostitutes did so, was undoubtedly influenced by the work of the French authority on the subject, A. J. B. Parent-Duchatelet, who was described in 1842 as the 'Newton of Harlotry'. It was Duchatelet who first made the assertion, subsequently echoed by Acton, that prostitutes were endowed with 'iron bodies' and that they were healthier and more resistant to disease than average mothers engaged in ordinary domestic work; and who, basing his statements on a tendentious interpretation of the Parisian Police Registers of prostitutes listed between 1845 and 1854, painted such an optimistic picture of their brief lives in the profession, and the ease with which the vast majority were able to leave it.

The opinions of Acton and Duchatelet were accepted and re-iterated by the Select Committee of the House of Lords on the Contagious Diseases Act, 1866, which affirmed that 'prostitution is mainly a transitional state through which thousands of British women are constantly passing',[1] and that:

The fact is, the average mortality of prostitutes while living as such is not greater, as is commonly affirmed, but is probably less than that of respectable women of their own rank of life. The most attractive kind of physical beauty is that which is at once the result and expression of a well-developed and thoroughly healthy organization; and it is precisely the possessor of such an organization who is most exposed to the temptations of the seducer, and who, therefore, is most likely to be led or driven, sooner or later, to adopt a life of prostitution. Horrible as the truth may be, it is we fear indisputable that the ranks of this section of civilized communities are, to a great extent, recruited from the finest women of their order, seduction being the means by which the healthiest and most vigorous are selected. They live an idle life, pass much of their time in the open air, are generally well clothed and well fed, and thus proceed in their career with a capacity of withstanding the attacks of disease and of bearing its results, which is denied to their more respectable but poorer and harder-worked sisters. 'Notwithstanding,' says Mr. Acton 'all her excesses (and legion is their name) the prostitute passes through the furnace of a dissipated career less worse from wear than her male associates.'[2]

The Committee reported that in France, as in England, a considerable proportion of erstwhile prostitutes became domestic servants in families of every social grade:

Thus ceasing to act as prostitutes by commencing or recommencing a 'respectable' career, women who a little time before would have been regarded as outcasts too debased to be spoken to, are admitted into the houses of the refined and affluent classes, are entrusted by mothers with the care of their children, become the attendants and probably not seldom the confidants, of their daughters just blooming into womanhood, and, in short, entering every department of domestic life, have confided to them, at one time or another, the most important or the most cherished interests of a considerable section of society.[3]

At the same time, they utterly rejected the views of other leading doctors and writers on the subject, which were represented by them as follows:

It has been confidently stated and frequently repeated that English prostitutes sink rapidly from one grade of their wretched life to a lower and lower one, until they reach the lowest depths of misery and infamy; that only in extremely rare and exceptional cases do they ever escape from their degraded position; and that from the time they enter their fatal career their lives are seldom prolonged beyond three or four years. Mr. Tait says, that 'in the course of three years very few can be recognised by their old acquaintances, if they are so fortunate as to survive that period'; he believes that not above one in eleven survives her twenty-fifth year, and that 'perhaps not less than a fifth or sixth of all who have embraced a life of prostitution die annually'. Captain Miller estimates that the average length of time during which prostitutes continue as such is five years, and states that 'the most common termination of their career is an early death'. Dr. Ryan has expressed opinions to the same effect.[4]

Even if pessimistic, the early part of this statement reflects more closely the life of prostitutes in York (the only town for which a detailed study of their condition has yet been made) than that put forward by the Committee itself. It is clear from the preceding Chapter that those who wished to enforce and extend the provisions of the Contagious Diseases Acts sought to present as favourable as possible a picture of the prostitute's circumstances, minimising the harmful effects on her physical health and mental well-being and emphasising her brief and temporary involvement in the activity and the ease with which she could leave it. The fact that this conflicted with traditional and other contemporary evidence and opinion on the subject was brushed aside in a complacent and sanctimonious white-washing of reality, in order that the legislation which approved and regulated a system so blatantly discriminating against one sex and class, could more palatably be passed.

Much of the evidence in this study, though limited to particular periods in prostitutes' lives – when they were breaking the law, were destitute or sick, or seeking shelter at the Refuge – shows that few of them could, in fact, have entered respectable society with the ease outlined by the Select Committee. Most, as we have seen, had had disturbed, neglected childhoods, or had been brought up in poverty and squalor with little or no education. Others, as the records of the Penitentiary show, had limited intelligence; and all, during their involvement in prostitution, must have been brutalised, humiliated and degraded, becoming accustomed to being regarded – and more important – to regarding themselves, as social outcasts. Practically all of them at some stage of their careers had been destitute or diseased, had been in trouble with the law or were addicted to drink – it is because of these characteristics that they were able to be identified for this study. How then is it possible that the vast majority of such women could have made 'good' marriages 'from the peerage to the stable' – or even been sought after as domestic servants in respectable middle-class homes? It is surely unlikely that prudent matrons would have entrusted their own daughters 'just blooming into womanhood' into the care and confidences of women such as these; or that 'decent' men, even of their own class let alone their social superiors, would seek to marry these rather than their more eligible sisters.

Since the girls most likely to have been re-absorbed into society were those who voluntarily submitted to the harsh discipline and dreary training of the many institutions operating specifically for the purpose of reforming them; and since such Homes represent society's main effort to cope with the appalling problem in the period, they are a vital, though curiously neglected aspect of any study of Victorian prostitution. The Refuge at York was one of five six such institutions in the city in the period, though it was the only 'long-term' shelter for prostitutes, and the only one for which detailed evidence has survived. Further, the other institutions were either short-lived or were set up fairly late in the period, so that throughout almost a century the Refuge remained the principal Home for fallen women in the city. Its importance in this study is based on the facts that it was representative of Shelters and Female Missions throughout the country, and also that more than forty-three per cent of recorded prostitutes in York in the period either applied to enter or were admitted to its care. In seeking to estimate what proportion of the total could have retired unscathed from the activity and successfully entered respectable society, therefore, it is necessary finally to consider this Institution in detail, and examine its history, managers and above all its inmates, at some length.

The records of the York Penitentiary in the period show – in spite of the fact that the girls admitted were carefully selected, being usually under twenty-five and, it was assumed, hopefully not too steeped in vice, neither pregnant nor diseased, of reasonable intelligence, amenable to discipline and above all, desirous of reform – that, even here, the success rate was not particularly high. In fact, by 1887, out of the total of 412 formally admitted to the Refuge since it had been opened in 1845,* the Annual Reports reveal that only 142 girls were placed in service. Some even of these, the most promising inmates, lapsed into their old habits or were led astray after leaving the Home, and, as we shall see, the Annual Reports presented a misleadingly optimistic impression of the Refuge's success rate. The Ladies' Committee Books, however, are more revealing. In May 1854, for example, the Ladies reported that 'Hoyland', who had been in the Home for two years, had been found a situation at 'Mrs. Bingley's' of Davygate, and that 'Johnson' had been placed as a laundrymaid at Crofts, in Stillington in the West Riding. By a pre-arranged plan, however, both girls had immediately left their situations and met together in York where they went into lodgings. Although they professed the intention of trying to gain a livelihood by washing, their motives were doubted by the Ladies who had

---

* This figure relates only to inmates fully admitted to the Refuge and does not include the 90 girls who did not complete their probationary period and the 40 applicants who were considered ineligible. Thus the total number of girls recorded in connection with the Refuge is 542.

discovered their deceit. Similarly, Sarah Clithero, who was described when admitted in 1854 as 'very uncouth and very ignorant' and who during her stay was guilty of unruly temper, was, in September 1856, found employment with 'a woman called Thompson who takes in washing'. Within a week, however, she had run away from her situation, the Ladies reporting: 'It is feared she has returned to her life of sin.' Another disappointment to the Ladies was 'Lawrence', who, they were informed in May 1862, was lying seriously ill in Aldershot. 'It appears that she has relapsed into sin, but it is a consolation to find that she is again brought to repentance.' Annie Ligori was another inmate who, though troublesome, had survived the rigours of the Home for two years and been placed in domestic service only to find herself in trouble almost immediately. On 3 December 1870 it was reported that the Matron, Miss Briddon, was

much distressed at the return of Ligori from her place, in the family way. She has received her into the [probation] ward until admission can be obtained to the Easingwold workhouse.

These and numerous other instances referred to below indicate that serving two years in the Refuge and being 'placed' with a good character was not, therefore, necessarily a permanent passport into respectable society; and many of the girls even who were found jobs were neither rescued nor reformed, but became pregnant, or, finding their situations unbearable, slipped back into their old ways. Further, the sort of employment they were found bore little resemblance to those refined situations as ladies' maids and children's nurses so confidently referred to by the Select Committee of the House of Lords. Such evidence as there is indicates, on the contrary, that those girls who obtained and kept situations as domestic servants were exploited even more than were other 'virtuous' women of their class. Their wages were low, even by contemporary standards, and their conditions of work poor and tedious. They were employed largely as drudges by washerwomen, commercial laundries or private families requiring cheap help in the wash-house. As one former inmate wrote to the Matron of the York Refuge regarding the situation which had been found for her at 'Mrs. Hutton's', and which she had had the good fortune to leave:*

---

* In quoting letters from inmates, the original spelling and punctuation have been used throughout.

I saw [this place] in the manchester garudiean I have everything I
want here the laundry is in the house and the wash house outside far
nicer than mrs huttons ther was nothing to your work with there a
little black hole not room to stir about in it I had a life like a crab.[5]

The attitudes of employers and other servants (if there were any) to
prostitutes attempting to reform may easily be imagined.

Before considering the statistics more closely, and examining in
detail the women themselves – the 'successful cases'; those inmates of
the Home who ran away, were dismissed or left without having
obtained a reference or a situation; and those even more unfortunate
creatures who were refused admission and considered unfit for
reform – it will be useful to give a brief outline of the history of the
Institution.

The York Penitentiary Society was one of the hundreds of
Refuges, Homes, Guardians and Asylums established throughout
the country during the period in an attempt to rescue individual
prostitutes and fallen women who, 'having followed vicious courses,
are desirous of obtaining the means of reformation'. Like all such
institutions, it was a charitable organisation, relying on voluntary
subscriptions and support, and the co-operation and willingness to
conform to the rules, of the inmates themselves.* The Penitentiary
Society had been established in 1822 though finances for permanent
premises (the 'Refuge') were not acquired until 1843.† In December
of that year Dr Stephen Beckwith of Bishophill, York, who for
several years had devoted time and energy to rescuing women from a
life of prostitution, died, leaving amongst other bequests to charities
£5,000 for the purpose of setting up a Home for fallen women. In the
following year his house in Bishophill, the gardens extending almost
down to the river at Skeldergate and two cottages in that street were
purchased by the Trustees of the Society for £2,200, and a further
£583 was spent on erecting new buildings (particularly a laundry),
making alterations to the existing property and buying furniture. At

---

* See the pledge which each inmate was required to sign (if she could) on admission, reproduced in Fig. 31, page 207.
† Prior to the opening of the Bishophill Home a small number of 'approved objects', whose
'miseries but not their deserts entitled them to pity and assistance', were sent and maintained
at the Society's expense to the Penitentiary in Hull. When that establishment was discontinued in 1826 suitable cases were sent to the Guardian Society at Leeds. A new Penitentiary
was opened in Hull in 1837, and representatives of the York Society inspected and reported in
detail on both these Homes, before opening their own establishment. See the Annual Reports
of the Committee of the York Penitentiary Society, 1822–43, and the manuscript 'Report by
Deputation to the Hull and Leeds Penitentiaries, 1845'.

the same time the Rules and General Regulations for the Society were formed, and these remained largely unaltered throughout our period. These stated that Annual Subscribers to the Society were required to pay at least one pound, donors ten pounds, Clergymen and Dissenting Ministers making Congregational Collections, ten pounds and Executors paying Bequests not less than fifty pounds. That the affairs of the Society should be conducted by a President, Treasurer, Secretary and Committee, who should elect a paid matron and assistant, a medical officer and make arrangements for the religious instruction of the inmates. That a General Meeting of the Members be held annually each February appointing officers and Committee, who should have entire control and direction of its affairs and report on their proceedings, income and expenditure each year. That the Committee should meet each month at the Refuge, and that there should also be appointed a Ladies' Committee who should present a general monthly report on and attend to and be responsible for the moral and religious improvement of the inmates. They were to assist the Matron in procuring suitable situations for those women who had satisfactorily remained within the Home for two years, and a book was to be kept in the Institution, in which the Committee Ladies entered their visits and reported on the state of the house and the girls. It is these Visitors' Books, together with the Minute Books of the Ladies' General Meetings, which provide such detailed information on the day to day running of the Home. Larger issues such as policy and finance are concentrated mainly in the printed Annual Reports. In addition to these records various other plans, reports and correspondence have been preserved, the most interesting being the letters of several former inmates, who, having left the Refuge, wrote to inform the Matron and Ladies of their new situations and circumstances.

The Matron and her assistant were required to live in the house and superintend and keep an account of all the work done by the inmates, instructing them particularly (perhaps symbolically) in laundrywork, which was the principal training they received. They were also taught how to scrub floors, make bread, do plain needlework and were given limited instruction in reading and writing by the visiting Ladies. The Matron was to conduct family worship twice daily – absence from which could be excused only by illness – and she was required to report weekly on the conduct of the inmates to the Committee of Ladies.

With regard to the inmates, as we have seen, only those considered to be hopeful cases were admitted. The first of the General Regulations stated that 'No Applicant found to be in a state of pregnancy shall be admitted or retained in the House', and examination of the monthly reports reveals that the same regulation applied too to girls found to be diseased – though these were sometimes re-admitted after a period of treatment at the Union hospital. Later in the period applicants were medically examined to ascertain their fitness to be received into the Home. During spring and summer the inmates had to rise at six and in autumn and winter at seven; they were never allowed to be up later than ten at night, after which no lighting or heating was permitted except in the Matron's room. Each girl was to be provided with a separate bed. Inmates were not allowed out of the house (except on extraordinary occasions and then in the company of a visiting Lady or other trustworthy person appointed by the Matron) and could not receive or send letters without their being scrutinised by the Matron. The father, mother, or other near relative of an inmate 'being known as such' was allowed at certain times (though later evidence reveals that such visitors were discouraged) but only at the discretion of and in the presence of the Matron. No other visitors were permitted.

Thus, though the girls entered the Home completely voluntarily, they were subjected to discipline, rules and regulations similar to that of life in a prison. Throughout their stay they were required to wear the drab uniform of 'Penitentiary dress' which obviously marked them from the rest of society; and girls with a satisfactory record were, on leaving the Home, provided with a 'plain neat dress and a bible'. Later, when additional rules for the conduct of the inmates were found to be necessary, the poster reproduced in Fig. 28 concerning lying, swearing and general insubordination was displayed in all rooms and corridors of the building.

From the beginning, the strongly religious character of the Institution was apparent, though for some years it was entirely non-denominational with Wesleyan Methodists, Congregationalists and Anglicans all being represented on the Committee. It was strongly supported by leading York Quakers such as Samuel Tuke, who was the first President of the Society and various members of the Tuke, Backhouse, Rowntree and Richardson families serving on both the Ladies' and Gentlemen's Committees. Gradually this Quaker influence was replaced by an Anglican one, so that by the end of our

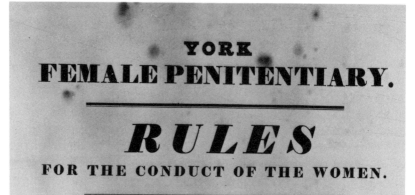

YORK FEMALE PENITENTIARY.

RULES

FOR THE CONDUCT OF THE WOMEN.

I. The directions and orders of the Matron shall at all times be promptly obeyed.

II. The women shall preserve a decent deportment, and a becoming silence, especially while at work. Reproaches for past irregularities, railing, and all angry expressions, are strictly forbidden; and if repeated after admonition from the Matron, shall be reported to the Committee, and punished at their discretion.

III. Lying, swearing, dishonesty, repeated disobedience, and gross misbehaviour, shall be punished by the Committee with expulsion, unless circumstances should induce them to mitigate the punishment.

IV. No woman shall leave her employment without the Matron's permission.

V. The father, mother, or other near relation, (being known to be such,) may be permitted to see and converse with any of the women, at the discretion and in the presence of the Matron, between the hours of eleven and twelve in the morning, and two and three in the afternoon (Sundays excepted.) —But no such person, whether male or female, shall be admitted into the wards.

VI. No Letter shall be conveyed to or from the house, without the inspection of the Matron.

Fig. 28 Poster displayed in all rooms in the Bishophill Refuge.

period the President was the Dean of York, the Secretary was Reverend Edmund S. Carter (vicar of St Michael le Belfrey) and many members of both Committees were leading Church figures. By 1902 an additional Bye-Law had been introduced: 'That there shall always be a Chaplain for the Institution who is a Clergyman of the Church of England' – for many years this being Reverend E. Bulmer, vicar of St Martin cum Gregory nearby; and when eventually the original premises were vacated in 1919 and the Society re-named the Clifton Home for Girls, it was formally merged with the Anglican Church Penitentiary Association.

Representation of the Roman Catholic Church on the Committee was noticeably absent, even though by the late eighteen-forties there was a sizeable Catholic–Irish population in the city,[6] and various Irish prostitutes have been identified – though, as has been observed, in spite of the overwhelming poverty of the vast majority of the Famine immigrants, these were disproportionately few. Nor were Catholic Priests included amongst the group of clergymen who, in rotation, preached sermons to the inmates throughout the period. The Church of Rome was, in fact, mentioned only once in the records, though this single entry is sufficient to illustrate the anti-Catholic bias of the Institution. It was reported in October 1851 that Mary Robinson, who had been living in the Home for two years was 'not in a fit state of health to be recommended to service'. It was agreed that she should return to her parents as soon as a proper situation could be found for her with a dressmaker, this having been her previous employment. The Ladies noted that her conduct had been good during her stay and that she had 'received more than an outward knowledge of the gospel'; and they added that her mother had promised that she should go to a Protestant place of worship with an aunt who lived with them. By the following month, however, they reported that:

Some circumstances [have] occurred in the home of poor Mary Robinson – the expected return of her sister and her mother's intemperance, which makes the Ladies unwilling to sanction her return to her parents.

The Ladies requested her mother to attend the Gentlemen's Committee the following week, and noted with satisfaction that:

Robinson expressed her willingness to remain, if her house is considered completely an unfit one, till she could be placed in the house of some dressmaker in the country. She will be happy to make any declaration necessary that she is advised to, as to renouncing the errors of Rome.

Her parents' house being found 'entirely unsuitable' she was eventually sent to live with an aunt at Boston, where, at the Ladies' expense, she was apprenticed for one pound to a local dressmaker.

The particular form of Anglican worship most acceptable to the Society is apparent from the church eventually chosen for its inmates to attend. There were four churches close to the Refuge, St Martin cum Gregory and Holy Trinity, both in Micklegate, and closer still St Mary Bishophill Senior and St Mary Bishophill Junior, each of which was about one minute's walk from the Home. The latter particularly, no doubt because of its high Anglican reputation, was obviously considered unsuitable, so that when in 1868 the girls were allowed to attend public services in company with the Matron, this, together with the two other neighbouring churches and various nonconformist chapels in the vicinity, was passed by in favour of St Martin cum Gregory. Elderly residents of Bishophill can still remember the 'bad' girls, sullen and peaky in their grey cloaks and bonnets, marching two by two to church each Sunday.

The highly religious character of the Institution, particularly as the less condemnatory influence of the Quakers who had been founder members of the Society diminished, undoubtedly placed an additional strain on the inmates, who were daily subjected to fierce indoctrination and constantly filled with a morbid sense of their own shame and guilt. This harsh policy, though no doubt well intentioned, often did more harm than good, resulting in many cases in the girls either running away or being dismissed or, as letters from former inmates show, in their being reduced to spiritless demoralised creatures obsessed with religion and their past sin, entirely lacking in self-confidence or self-respect and betraying a morbid and desperate dependence on the women who had lately ordered their lives. The psychological implications of such treatment are, of course, outside the scope of this study, but it is clear that many 'successful' cases were girls who were deeply disturbed and had an obsessive anxiety to gain the approval of the Matron. In some cases, she had obviously become a rather authoritarian mother figure (some girls actually addressed her as 'dear mother' in their letters) and, in view of the upbringing, background and age of the girls, this is hardly surprising. In other cases, however, the tendency for a former inmate to debase herself so entirely, to dwell on her own unworthiness and to display such abject need for the Matron's attention – whatever form that may take – seems similar to the attitude of the prostitute to her demanding but revered male protector. This is illustrated in a letter from Ellen J. Pearson written some time in the late seventies or early eighties, who, by that time, was married and expecting a baby.

Dear Miss Briddon,
I often pass and should much like to see you and Miss Waters But it seems as if your door would never open to let me see your face again. I know I have been a bad one and a wilful one also But other girls as been allowed to see you and you might give me that Permission I should like to see you I am not a Bad one now, I am sorry for what I have done But that will not mend it now. Dear Miss Briddon I am going to leave Knavesmire this week for the rates are so heavy this is six pounds a year and the one we are going to is one of the Convent houses 3/4d. a week all clear so I shall be saving something for I shall want it soon, and this house is to lodge for only to of us I have let it so it will take it off my hands Dear Miss Briddon I was very sorry Etty had to leave her place I was given to understand it was though you saying I had been in Prison, but I could scarce think you would do me harm now when I am leading a better life and striving to be a better woman what I did wrong I have had to suffer much more than Prison for it I told my husband before we where married about that and the Home as well and it has be many a (illegible) for me since and made me shed many bitter tears I hope you are well and Miss Waters for you have both been good to me I think Miss Waters will say now that some good things may come out of people.
I hope I have not offended you be writing dear Miss Briddon and believe me   Yours very humbly
Ellen J. Pearson
Mrs. H. Pearson, No. 3 St. Mary's Court, Blossom Street, York.*
P.S. Dear Miss Briddon you have gone to see other girls you might come to see me or let me come and see you.

This narrow religious indoctrination and emphasis on guilt and sin was exactly the sort of treatment so often meted out in such Homes that Gladstone – himself an authority on the problem – so deplored. He knew from his many encounters with women of the streets and his involvement in works of rescue extending over a period of more than fifty years that women desperate to turn from a life of prostitution were in need of courtesy and kindness rather than recrimination; and

---

* The cottages in St Mary's Court, now demolished, were only a few hundred yards from the Refuge. See Figure 29.

Fig. 29 St Mary's Court, Blossom Street, to which former prostitute
Ellen Pearson moved in about 1880.

that a fundamental difficulty in rescuing even a co-operative prostitute was her justifiable fear that she was past redemption and that,
even if reformed, would be shunned by the rest of society. Towards
the end of his life Mr Gladstone wrote of his rescue work:

My real failure was that not until much later in life did I fully realise that
many of these unfortunate women dreaded a return to normality. It was
not only that they dreaded the finger of scorn pointed at them, but they
actually felt a sense of shame in mixing with decent people. Only by
showing some of them that decent people could be human, lively and gay
and had emotions like themselves could they believe that they were not a
race apart.[7]

Unfortunately, the records of the York Penitentiary show that it was precisely by revealing to the inmates the depths of their sin and guilt that the managers hoped to bring about their spiritual reform. Too often, it would seem, this was at the expense of their mental and physical well-being.

In the Annual Report for 1849, for example, by which time twenty-nine girls had been admitted to the Refuge, it was stated that in the past year four of the inmates had been in the Home for two years and had been recommended to good situations. Two of these, however, had since been obliged to leave through severe illness. Another girl, who had been confined to her bed for eight months after a severe injury 'sustained in the performance of her duty in the Refuge', had been in such pain and was so weak that she had been allowed to return to her native Scotland. Three others had escaped and two of these had returned to their 'vicious courses'. One was 'soon driven by illness into the workhouse, where she died three days afterwards – it is feared in a hopeless condition'. Finally, it was reported:

One of the inmates ... has been confined several months to her bed, and is fast declining in a consumption; she came into the Refuge an orphan, very destitute, and very ignorant in June 1848. She was apparently in robust health, but in a few months time her health gave way when her mind became awakened to her sinful state.[8]

Details from the Minute Book reveal that this girl was 'Winter' who died in the following January – 'in a hopeful and peaceful state of mind, expressing a simple trust in Christ and exhibiting great patience under her suffering'. This morbid emphasis on sin and penitence continued, as we shall see, to the end of our period.

In addition to relying on subscriptions and donations, the expenses of the Institution were partly met out of the proceeds from the laundry work which was the main occupation of the inmates. The Assistant Matron was, in fact, a laundress whose main task it was to instruct the girls in the art of washing, starching and ironing. They were thus trained as laundry maids, while at the same time contributing to the cost of their keep. It is clear from the records that this work, which the girls performed for most of the day, was often exhausting – particularly for the majority of girls who, contrary to the opinions of Acton and the Select Committee of the House of Lords, had poor constitutions and entered the Home in a weak and sickly state. The work was especially hard too in the early years of the

Refuge, before even basic labour-saving equipment was acquired and improvements carried out to the wash-house and laundry. For example, it was not until September 1851, by which time laundry was being received from the 'Training School' as well as from private customers, that the Ladies requested from the Gentlemen that a 'wringing machine be procured as a valuable addition to the washing apparatus' – at a cost of five pounds. Even with a much needed mangle, however, the poor health of most of the girls meant that they could not cope with the amount of washing brought into the Home. In July 1857 a special Committee Meeting had to be held to decide what portion of the laundry was to be given up as 'the work is far too heavy for the girls and occupies their time too exclusively'. It was agreed to discontinue that from the Training School and from two of the Ladies, and that the pressure of work should be lessened to afford more time for other instruction. The Ladies agreed to devote two afternoons a week to this, in addition to other occasional visits. In spite of this the work load continued to be heavy as the Refuge was competing with other commercial laundries and with the many washerwomen in the city. At times the combination of staffing difficulties, the total inexperience of the 'succession of ignorant young women' who were fresh inmates, sickness and sudden reductions in the numbers of girls in the Home had disastrous consequences, resulting in complaints from customers about the quality of the washing, girls being overworked and unable to cope with the piles of laundry and unfavourable receipts for washing at the end of the year. Generally, however, income from the laundry went a long way towards paying housekeeping expenses.*

Although there was little relaxation in the religious indoctrination of the inmates, the rules of the Institution, though unaltered throughout the period, were gradually interpreted a little more leniently. Thus, from 1868 onwards, instead of services being held in the Refuge by various visiting clergymen, the girls were allowed to attend church services in Micklegate; and, shortly before completing their two years in the Home, trusted inmates were occasionally allowed out alone, to run errands for the Matron. Gradually too, a

* In 1863, for example, receipts for washing were £108. 1. od., while housekeeping expenses were £119. 16. 9d. with additional bills for coals £26. 16. 1½d., starch, soap, etc. £11. 5. 9d., clothing £34. 5. 2½d., gas £5. 13. od., medicine £5. 13. od., salaries and wages £71. 7. 1d. and books, advertising and printing, £6. 0. 2d. By 1878 the receipts for washing had risen to £217. 14. 4d., with outgoings being about £386. 0. od.; and in 1880 needlework and washing together brought in £263. 17. od., though the annual amount varied according to the health, training and number of inmates resident throughout the year.

more kindly attitude was adopted towards the girls, many of whom, being only fourteen or fifteen, were scarcely more than children. As girls continued to enter the Home 'entirely uneducated', illiterate or scarcely able to read, more time was spent on their education, though this still consisted largely of elementary instruction in literacy and listening to religious works being read to them while they practised plain sewing.* By the sixties, annual outings and picnics were being recorded, at Christmas each inmate was presented with a work basket, a silver thimble from the tree 'or some other equally useful article'; and towards the end of the period treats and rewards were offered as inducements to and payment for good conduct.

However, on examination of the Committee and Visitors' Books it is apparent that the printed Annual Reports, which presented an optimistic and slightly self-congratulatory account of life in the Refuge, gave little indication of the conflicts and turmoils within – both between the inmates themselves, and the inmates and staff.† Not surprisingly, with at times between twelve and twenty severely restrained one-time prostitutes closeted together – disciplined by women who at best were nervous, overworked and often taxed beyond endurance, and at worst little better than the inmates themselves – quarrels, acts of insubordination, escapes and even fights were not uncommon. The formidable strain put on these girls and the staff can be appreciated only by examining the weekly Visitors' and monthly Minute Books, which reveal the petty jealousies, squabbles, tyrannies and constant bickerings always in evidence. Occasionally events reached a climax, as in 1858, for example, when the inmates were reduced to only two – the rest either having run away or been dismissed; or in 1900, when the Annual Report urged the necessity of employing more staff, as neither the Matron nor the Laundress dared leave the other alone with the inmates, and the health of each of them was suffering as a consequence of nervous strain and lack of air and exercise. (The effect of lack of air on the inmates – who were presumably more than adequately exercised in the laundry – was not considered.) A similar request had already been made in October 1875 when the Ladies asked for a third member of staff 'so that the girls should *never* be left without

---

* In January 1847, for example, the Ladies reported that *The Churchman's Penny Magazine* and *The Friendly Visitor* were being furnished to the Society.
† Since the main function of the Annual Reports was to raise funds, they naturally presented as favourable as possible a picture of the Society's activities.

supervision, and especially at night'. This early request, however, was not complied with. On other occasions there were battles between the Ladies' and Gentlemen's Committees, as in 1861, for example, when all the Ladies threatened to resign. These flare-ups and outbursts were rarely referred to in the Annual Reports, which were too often merely financial statements and brief summaries expressing pious sentiments and soliciting funds. They emphasised the successful aspects of the Home, by publishing extracts from the devout letters of former inmates; while less favourable facets were ignored or touched on lightly. As one indignant 'lover of truth and Justice' was to complain in an anonymous letter to one of the Refuge Committee members in 1900 (and by this time the management of the Home was certainly more liberal than had formerly been the case):

I saw by the report in the *York Herald* that you are a member of the Penitentiary Committee. Your Committee reports everything very bright, they say nothing of a dark side and a dark side I feel sure there is by so many of the inmates running away. Last night Bishophill presented a disgraceful scene and one of two girls that had run away being dragged along the road by three men who saftly lodged her inside the door. The street was crowded with men, women and children some of whom passed not very complimentary remarks upon the present management of the institution.

Last week I was passing when a girl got out of one of the front windows from which she had taken a square of glass, and ran away as fast as she could. A workman that was passing said that another girl had run away last week.

Five Sundays ago I had lingered about the Minster after the service untill rather late when turning into Rougier Street I was hurridly passed by a woman whom I knew to be a Penitentiary girl by her dress. Although a bitter cold night she had nothing on to shield her from the cold and the light of the lamp showed me her white face and determined look. The river flashed into my mind at once, I turned and followed her at a distance, she rang the bell of a house in Museum Street,* she was let in. Thank God I said for I felt sure then she had not thought of drowning herself.

Pardon me for troubling you with these statements. If you are already acquainted with them I shall lose nothing and if not those poor girls may gain at least right on their side.

I am Dear Sir,
A lover of truth and Justice.[9]

* The address of Miss Crabtree who, at this time, was Secretary of the Penitentiary Society. She had also for several years been a Working Associate of the York Association for the Care of Young Girls.

A 'dark side', of course, there certainly was, as a few extracts from the Ladies' Committee Minute Books not intended for public reading, show. In May 1846, for example, they reported:

The Committee regrets that much bad temper has been evinced amongst the inmates, especially between Carter and Todd. They were reproved by the Ladies and as a punishment for their violence which has proceeded to blows, they were sentenced to keep entire silence till Monday.

By 26 June, however, since Carter and Todd continued to behave 'in a turbulent and unruly manner', the Ladies regretfully recorded that they had been dismissed. Similarly in April 1849 the Committee were grieved to find that three inmates, Shepherd, Eden and Lockwood, 'have made their escape . . . and returned into the worst neighbourhood', and in January 1851 there were further instances of 'painful discouragement'. Abbott and Wilson had to be dismissed 'from their state of health',* and Wise 'on account of her violent temper'.

In June 1852 the Ladies were disturbed by an even more 'painful subject'. They referred to accusations made against the Matron, Mrs Edwards, who had been 'plainly accused by the Assistant Matron and two of the inmates, Smith and Fothergill, of taking spirits repeatedly and often to excess'. Though the Ladies themselves had not detected anything suspicious, they were horrified to learn that 'rumours of this misconduct are afloat in the city'. Seven months later they again referred to

the painful subject of the renewed suspicion as to the Matron's conduct. Several of the Ladies have noticed a great peculiarity in her manner – an excitement beyond anything that ordinary circumstances can account for.[10]

As was occasionally to be the case in this early period, however, the Gentlemen were unmoved and the Ladies were powerless to act. By the following year the quality of the laundry work was so bad that there was not sufficient washing being sent to the Home to employ the inmates; but it was not until October 1853 that the conduct of the Matron finally led to her dismissal:

There seems no longer any doubt that she is much addicted to drinking. To many of the Ladies this was no surprise, as they have always believed her to be guilty.

* These girls, particularly Abbott, who had been in the Home for several months, were obviously diseased rather than pregnant. When Abbott originally applied in March 1850 she was already in 'so unfit a state of health' that she was recommended to go 'again' to hospital. Presumably she was thought to be cured before being admitted into the Refuge.

As we have seen, girls continued to run away from the Home until the turn of the century, partly, no doubt, because many of them were temperamentally unsuited and lacked the self-discipline necessary to remain voluntarily in such an institution; but also, it is clear, because the discipline, dreary routine and continuous religious indoctrination were equally unsuited to their needs.

In April 1856, for example, Campbell, who had never appeared to settle

made her escape over the wall. She was brought back by one of the police, but being determined in her wish to leave, was allowed to change her clothes and go.

Three months later Elizabeth Shepherd, Mary Tasker, Emma Hinley, Mary Machlochlan and Jane Steel were all reported as having escaped and gone to Leeds – the cause of their leaving was never discovered. As well as the large number who escaped there were, of course, many girls who simply insisted on leaving and had to be allowed to do so because of their unsettling influence on the rest of the inmates. Others were dismissed because of insubordination, bad temper, idleness and unwillingness to conform to the rules.

Until 1866 when Miss Briddon, who was to remain at the Refuge for thirty-one years, was appointed, the Committee was haunted by the difficulties of finding a suitable Matron. Ideally, for a demanding but comparatively poorly paid job,* they required someone experienced in rescue work, deeply religious, well educated, and, since she was constantly answerable to them, someone with whom the Ladies felt at ease. Equally important, since she was required to live on the premises and apparently rarely left the Institution, she needed to be dedicated to her absorbing work, and possess a remarkably strong constitution. Further, she was responsible for the day to day running of the Home, and had therefore, to be firm enough to cope both with the inmates and the many laundresses who came and went with alarming frequency – yet kindly and sympathetic enough to win the confidence and respect of the girls, as well as have sufficient patience and skill to look after them in their frequent illnesses. Not surprisingly, such a figure was rarely to be found, and most of the Matrons were either harsh disciplinarians or found their unenviable task completely beyond them.

* Mrs Beeton's recommended wage for a housekeeper in the eighteen-sixties was between £20 and £45 a year, though of course her duties would be much less onerous than those of the Matron of a Refuge.

Eighteen fifty-eight, for example, was an unfortunate year with regard to both staff and inmates. In February the new Matron, Mrs Macdonald, whose salary was thirty guineas a year, reported that the 'conduct of the gardener was not consistent with the rules of the institution'. In March the Laundress resigned her post, which remained vacant for some months; and by May, the rapid turnover of the girls and dwindling number of permanent inmates provoked the following comment:

> The Ladies exceedingly regret so many of the inmates having to be dismissed and would suggest whether a more conciliatory management would not be more likely to be beneficial in producing a softened mind and not bringing into constant collision with the matron, with whom the Ladies have conversed and endeavoured to state their views on the subject.

In addition to these problems the health of two of the inmates was causing extreme alarm. With the exception of poor Sarah Winter, who had died in great suffering in January 1850, no other girl throughout our period, was ever to die in the Institution. Quite simply, this was because, after that harrowing event, girls who became so seriously ill that they were in danger of dying, were removed either to the workhouse or to hospital – or in one or two instances returned to their friends. Thus in May 1858 the Ladies' report continued that Richardson, who had been ill for some months and who had already been placed outside the Institution once so that the Matron 'should not have this responsibility resting on her' was once again seriously ill. Six months previously she had returned to the Home, her health apparently being restored, but now her state had worsened to such an extent that it was decided she should no longer stay in the House. Her fare was paid to Selby, where it was stated she wished to go. Another girl, McCullock, had also become so ill that the Gentlemen dismissed her; and in addition, Whincup, Barker and Lister, being determined to leave, were allowed to do so. A few weeks later Holmes made her escape over the wall (the Ladies were of the opinion that she had been influenced by the recently departed Laundress) with the result that by June 1858 there were only two inmates in the entire Institution, and no new applicants. It was impossible to continue with the washing and the Ladies and other customers were informed that they must send their laundry elsewhere.

By July Mrs Duncan, a new Matron (at least the eleventh in as many years – and the number of sub-matrons or laundresses was even greater), was appointed and the Ladies reported the hope that she would exercise a 'kind and judicious care over the inmates'. Soon, however, there were disagreements between Mrs Duncan and the new Laundress who stated that the Matron had been unkind to yet another of the inmates who was ill, and that she was much too harsh in her treatment of the girls. The Laundress – the third appointed in less than three months – left in the following week and a replacement for her could not be found since 'the difficulties of getting a person who will exercise a judicious care over the girls and work agreeably with the Matron' were felt to be too great. At the same time, Jane Grieveson, recently admitted, was found to be in an unfit state of health for the Refuge (presumably either pregnant or diseased) and shortly afterwards, Sarah Ann Neal, who had been troublesome since entering the Home, escaped. A new Laundress was appointed in November (but was soon dismissed because of inefficiency) and in December Elizabeth Varley – whose history has already been described – was admitted by the Gentlemen's Committee but was found to be 'in such a state of disease that she had to be sent away'.

Although 1859 was a particularly bad year, similar 'painful' incidents continued throughout our period, with girls being dismissed because of their health, matrons and laundresses quarrelling, resigning or being asked to leave, and inmates continually escaping or being sent away in disgrace. Disagreements occurred too between the Ladies' and Gentlemen's Committees; the former were 'much disappointed' and obviously extremely annoyed at the Gentlemen's conduct, for example in 1857 when they dismissed Alice Crossfield who was ill and whose mother had wished to visit her. Similarly in August 1860 the Ladies were vexed to find that the Gentlemen had dismissed yet another new Laundress 'who was unequal to her task', and reported of the new Matron that 'her health will not permit her continuing in a position involving so much perplexity' – a remark obviously intended for the Gentlemen's benefit. A few months later the Gentlemen engaged a certain Mrs Milner as Laundress – the Ladies noting ominously that she had been appointed 'on the condition that she should become a total abstainer, which she has fully agreed and she signed the pledge'.[11] Needless to say, she too, soon found herself unequal to her work.

In February 1860 the Ladies were

surprised to find the Gentlemen complaining that the butcher's and bread bill was too high, and were of the opinion that if anything, rather a smaller quantity is allowed than is desirable, considering the inmates have a considerable amount of bodily labour.

By July there was more trouble between the Matron and Laundress, and a few months later the Gentlemen were complaining that the receipts from the washing were too low. In January 1861 news was received of the death of poor Margaret Richardson who had been sent to Selby. Though she died in York workhouse she was not visited there by any of the Ladies, who, however, were pleased to report that she was:

A brand plucked from the burning . . . After leaving the Penitentiary there was no return to the sin from which she had fallen. She lived in respectable service till her health, quite failing, she became paralysed, and was taken to the Union, where she died after a long season of hopeless bodily affliction . . . she had a deep sense of sin, often speaking of her former life with disgust and self-reproach.

Four months later another new Laundress, Mrs Payne, was dismissed because of drunkenness; the Ladies on this occasion, however, were so indignant that they had not been consulted, that at a special meeting they all offered their resignation. The Matron too gave in her notice – a gesture which the Gentlemen accepted. The outcome of this dispute was a new set of Bye-Laws giving the Ladies much more control over the running of the Institution. From that time the Matron and Laundress were to be examined and approved by the Ladies prior to their being appointed; the Ladies were to superintend the employment, diet and dress of the inmates and any difficulty, either with them or the staff, was to be brought in the first instance to their attention. All punishments were to be reported to the Ladies who now had the power to dismiss any inmates.

For a time things were much more settled until three girls, Steele, Partridge and Thackray, made a plan to escape for the races in August 1862. They were abusive, refused to work and demanded their clothes, and the Ladies regretted to report that, after leaving the girls were known to have returned to their former sinful life. Since another girl, Whisker, had known of their plot but had not informed on them, the Ladies asked the Matron to write to her mother asking her to remove her, 'as it was not desirable that she should stay in the Home'. Both Mary Ann Steele and Ann Partridge had been admitted to the Refuge nine months earlier in November 1861. Steele, who was nineteen, had been living in a brothel in Fetter Lane close to the Home for about five months before applying. Before that she had been in domestic service. At the insistence of the Gentlemen she had been medically examined following her application, and being found in an 'unfit state' had been required to spend some time in hospital prior to entering the Home. Partridge, who was seventeen, had already spent some time in the city jail. Harriet – or, as she sometimes called herself, 'Rose' – Thackray, had been admitted from York workhouse four months previously. The Poor Law records show that though aged only sixteen she had been received into the workhouse from the House of Correction, and was another ill prostitute.[12] According to the Ladies she had spent four months in York work-house and before that had been in the workhouse in Malton. She had lived a 'disreputable' life for three years and was thus one of the youngest girls recorded in the activity. Shortly after leaving the Refuge, Rose Thackray, an 'unfortunate girl' from Malton, was charged with the theft of a cape from a brothel-keeper in Cross Alley, and in January 1865, now living in the Water Lanes, was imprisoned for seven days for being a disorderly prostitute.[13] In the meantime, in August 1864 twenty year old Sarah Thackray 'sister to Harriet or Rose who was formerly an inmate' was admitted to the Home. The Ladies reported that, like her younger sister, Sarah Thackray had 'led a very dissolute life'. Although there is no further reference to her in the Refuge records, she too obviously left after only a short stay. In July 1865 she was sent to prison for seven days for being a disorderly prostitute,[14] and two years later she died, her death being attributed at the inquest to a 'visitation of God'.[15]

Martha Whisker, who had been in the Refuge for fifteen months, was another girl who had originally been too ill to be admitted and had had to undergo three months medical treatment before entering the Home. She was, as we have seen, returned to her mother for her rather passive part in the plot to attend York races – even though this woman was in all probability herself a prostitute or brothel-keeper, having been described by the Ladies eighteen months earlier as a disreputable woman. Within two months of this incident six more of the girls had either escaped or insisted on leaving – Flint, who was fifteen years old and had been admitted from a brothel; Ellen Lyson, who was twenty-five, had been in the Home for six months and was another former resident of a brothel in Fetter Lane and Macgee, Willis, Hodgshaw and Moore, all of whom had been in the Refuge for only a few days. The Ladies were anxious to stem this new flood of departures but only Willis provided a clue, 'stating her grievance that she "did not like to have thrown in her teeth" the idea that she was not earning her living'. They later heard 'good accounts' of Whisker, but learned that Thackray – 'the ringleader in the unsettlement' was, for the seventh time, in prison.

In January 1863 another girl, Wardale, 'under a sudden impulse made her escape over the wall'. The Ladies were pleased to report, however, that she had not gone to any of the brothels in the city, but had returned to her father, 'walking barefoot and without a bonnet'. In September Matthews, who had been an inmate for three months, ran away and eighteen year old Mary Ann Newsome who was supposed to have reported to the workhouse hospital vanished without trace. A few weeks later Elizabeth Hornsea (who appears in detail in Chapter 3), Wadmore and Biscome all left after only a short stay; and sixteen year old Ann Pybus, who had been confined to the new probationary ward, squeezed herself and a ladder through a narrow opening in the kitchen window and escaped over the garden wall. The Ladies obviously viewed her departure with some relief, as she had shown no signs of wishing to reform but had been 'troublesome and rude, singing obscene songs and using bad language'.

Unfortunately, the Ladies' Committee Book for the years 1864 to 1881 has not survived, the only available material for this period (apart from that in the printed Annual Reports) being that contained in the Visitors' Books in which reports were made by the Ladies attending the Refuge two or three times each week. Though less systematic and not reporting details such as age and background of applicants, the visitors' comments, which extend over the whole period, are often more revealing and interesting than those in the more formal monthly Committee entries. They betray, too, something of the attitudes of the individual visitors themselves. The frequent upsets and disputes in the Institution, as well as the poor state of health of many of the inmates, continue to be much in evidence in the sixties and seventies. In April and May 1864, for example, there was more calm 'than is usually the case during Race week', but Johnson was very ill with a 'return of haemorrhage' and Newsome was in a feeble state of health. By June, Johnson, having developed a 'mean and deceitful mind', was dismissed, and Newsome was sent to the workhouse hospital. In November 1866 all the girls were giving satisfaction, with the exception of Elizabeth Rooke, who was allowed to leave – 'being idle and resolved to return to bad ways'.* In 1867 a girl called Abbott was confined to bed for two months, having hurt her leg in an attempt to scale the wall. Mary Calvert was continually troublesome, Stevenson had an abscess, and Isabella Smith and Fanny Snow, who had run away, were caught by the police and imprisoned for a month with hard labour. They were subsequently sent to institutions in Hull and Leeds but escaped from these too. Visitors in 1868 recorded similar cases of insubordination, and Mary Ann Potts, who was discovered to be 'in the family way', was sent to Leeds workhouse. In November Mary Ann Murphy was insolent to the Matron, Miss Briddon, 'but begged pardon before the girls and is to return to the laundry on Monday'. In the following month, however, she showed such a 'constant exhibition of unruly temper' that she had to be dismissed – 'for the good of the Institution'.

During this period further attempts were made to brighten the inmates' dreary existence. They were treated to a missionary magic lantern show in February 1868 and in the August were taken on an excursion to Kirkham Abbey. Their 'feelings of gratitude' for such privileges were at times expressed by

presenting small articles of their own workmanship to members of the Ladies' Committee and the Matrons, and sending little parcels of tea and sugar to their mothers, tobacco to fathers, and testaments hymn-books etc., to brothers and sisters – all purchased with the price of their butter and sugar, which they preferred doing without.[16]

However, the girls' restlessness and opposition to the discipline, which continued as rigid as ever, remained much in evidence, with 1870 being a particularly trying year. Esther Williams was found to be a married woman with two children, and was dismissed; Mackenzie was troublesome, Mary Thomas was 'determined to resist any effort for her good' and left, Mary Jane Saddler was tiresome and disobedient, Emma Jackson and Sarah Binnington behaved badly and Richardson was ill with rheumatism. Comments such as these continued throughout the seventies, with Mary Ann Wilson being dismissed as 'she expressed an absolute determination to be bad', and

* This she undoubtedly did. In February 1869, living in Wesley Place, Hungate, she was charged with wandering abroad and indecency; nine months later, having moved to Peter Lane, she was sentenced to one month at York Castle for the same offence and in January 1870, having returned to Wesley Place, she faced a similar charge. In the following June, by which time she had taken up residence in a brothel in Cross Alley, Water Lanes, she was again sentenced to two months for indecency; and almost immediately following her release, and once more living in Wesley Place, she was imprisoned for seven days for the same offence.

other girls stealing, swearing, being lazy, telling lies and spending periods of confinement in the probationary ward because of obstinate temper. In October 1873 the Ladies felt especially humiliated when Sarah Agar, whom they had recommended for a situation with Archdeacon Prest, misconducted herself to such an extent that she was obliged to leave. By 1874 the Committee was pressing for separate dormitories in an attempt to end the frequent bad behaviour and insubordination amongst the inmates.

The Refuge – 43 Bishophill – had, as we have seen, originally been the private residence of a doctor. Though undoubtedly large enough for a middle-class family and its servants, in its practically unaltered state it was inadequate and unsuitable for its new purpose, which was to house up to fourteen girls, the Matron and the Laundress, and to provide the Committee Room in which monthly and weekly meetings were held and applicants interviewed. The original Georgian building, which for more than forty years fulfilled this purpose with only minor alterations is still in use, though there is little evidence of its former history. In the basement is the now disused cramped and dark kitchen in which, until 1901, all the food for the establishment was cooked and prepared, and the inmates taught to make bread. Adjoining this are various former pantries, larders and storerooms. On the ground floor is the front drawing room (which was the Matron's sitting room and the Committee Room) and a back room, used as the inmates' dining room. On the first floor, the large room at the front of the house was occupied by the Matron and that at the back by the Laundress; on the second floor are two bedrooms and above these again, two poorly lit garrets.* These four upper rooms were the original dormitories for all the inmates, many of whom, as we have seen, were often ill and confined to their beds – and there is no doubt that they must at times have been severely overcrowded. Apart from the laundry, which was built when the house was first acquired, the only addition in our period was that of the probationary ward, built in 1862 at a cost of £200. This was used to isolate those applicants whom the Committee were willing to admit to the Refuge provided they had satisfactorily served a probationary two or three week period and thus established that they were amenable to

---

* The cramped top floor of the house was not used until after September 1848 when: 'The Ladies, having examined the house, suggest that another bed might be placed in the upper garret, and also that a very small alteration would make the adjoining garret fit for two or three additional beds.'

discipline and really desirous of reform. In addition, the ward was sometimes used as a punishment block. Before 1862 applicants had been placed on probation in certain carefully selected individuals' houses, though this had proved an unsatisfactory arrangement.

Apart from minor additions to the laundry buildings in 1876, and much needed general sanitary improvements in 1882, no major alterations and extensions were made to the premises until the very end of our period; and it was not until 1888 that the Ladies' request for separate dormitories for the inmates was eventually, and then for only about half the girls, complied with. A long, two-storey wing was built facing on to Bishophill, separated at ground level from the old house by a carriage entrance, but communicating at first floor level with the original building. The architect's description of the new wing provides some indication of how inadequate the premises must have been until that date.

In the old building there were but four rooms available as dormitories for the whole of the inmates. These still remain, and in addition eight single bedrooms have been provided, all opening into one corridor which is commanded by a door from the Matron's bedroom, so that the whole is under her supervision. On the ground floor, an additional commodious sitting room with large bow-window is provided; the Probationers' Ward has also been placed on the ground floor, and is entirely cut off from the rest of the premises; it provides a sitting room and three bedrooms. A bathroom, lavatory, and other necessary accommodation are provided on both floors.[17]

The 'single bedrooms' were, in fact, no more than tiny cubicles and the probationers' ward in its entirety, only a few feet square. In addition, the wash-house and laundry were again enlarged, and alterations were made in the basement to improve the larder and kitchen accommodation. The cost of this work – slightly over one thousand pounds – was met by the sale of shares in India Stock, Great Western Railways and Consols.

Final alterations were carried out in 1902 when the Society was awarded a considerable grant by the Archbishop of York, from the Marriott Bequest. This led to the purchase of 41 Bishophill, a small house on the other side of the Refuge, which, until 1914 was used as a temporary 'Shelter' for any girl or woman in need of 'immediate protection and Christian care'. After a short stay, eligible girls could be formally admitted to the Penitentiary's probationary ward, or transferred to another long-term institution. At the same time, extensive structural repairs were made to the main building, with parts of the floors, roof and staircase being renewed, and the old basement kitchen, 'dark, cramped and inconvenient', converted into a storeroom. The former dining and workroom was now used as a spacious kitchen, in which the girls also took their meals, and part of the original probationary ward was now used for needlework classes. Other improvements were carried out:

to bring the House and Laundry into a condition that would not only satisfy H.M. inspectors, should inspection eventually be required by Law, but also to provide that healthy cheerful atmosphere which will conduce to the welfare and happiness of those who unfortunately require the restraint of such an Institution, but who – entering voluntarily – ought not to be subjected to prison rules or treatment.

It must be remembered, however, that these improvements were not carried out until fifteen years after the close of our period – by which time the Home had been in existence for almost sixty years and at least 614 girls had been formally admitted to its care. (Many others had stayed for short periods of time only.) Also, in spite of the sentiments expressed, it is significant that people old enough to recall the Home and its inmates, remember it as – and indeed are adamant that it was – a female prison whose inmates were compulsorily detained. The award from the Marriott Bequest was granted only on the condition that the Society appointed as a Chaplain for the Home an Anglican clergyman.

Thus, though the Ladies' Committee was advocating separate bedrooms for the inmates as early as 1874, these were not provided until 1889, and even these accommodated only eight girls. Since the additional rooms meant that an average of twenty rather than twelve girls could be housed in the Refuge at any one time, the four bedrooms in the old building must still have often been overcrowded. It is probable too, that one of these was used as a punishment room for those girls who, like Mary Ann Murphy, had misbehaved and were not allowed to work with the other girls in the laundry. On the outside of the door of the back garret, which has not been in use since the premises were vacated by the Society in 1919, is a heavy iron bolt – a grim reminder of its former use.

Behind the Penitentiary the large Refuge garden sloped almost down to the river at Skeldergate and was surrounded by a high wall. Though preventing the girls from seeing out, and curious eyes watching the inmates hanging out the washing, exercising, or sitting under the old pear tree, this wall, as we have seen, was not high enough to prevent girls escaping, and in May 1893 the Ladies reported indignantly that:

Some men from Skeldergate have been getting on the wall and talking to the girls in the garden and also from the laundry window. It has been going on for some time, but has only just been discovered.

Various attempts had been made to seclude the girls from the outside world, as in September 1854, for example, when:

Some alterations being desirable in the small bedroom windows, it is concluded that they should be made to open only half a pane at the top, and that they should be fresh painted on the outside as to form an effectual blind.

Similarly, the windows in the new dormitories overlooked the garden rather than the street, which was separated from the cubicles by a corridor 'commanded' by the Matron's room. In spite of these pre-cautions the Penitentiary was, to say the least, unfortunately situated. Bishophill, once a fashionable street looking out over fields and gardens, had long since been abandoned by the rich and was fast becoming hemmed in by terraces of artisans' houses stretching between it and the city wall. A few doors along from the Refuge Fetter Lane – then a 'narrow dirty street' of congested cottages and dilapidated stabling – sloped down to the river at Skeldergate; and on the same corner, but curving towards Micklegate, was the entrance to Trinity Lane. Both these streets, as has already been observed, contained several brothels in the period – some actually furnished the Penitentiary with inmates – and in addition they contained the houses and lodgings of prostitutes. Further, parallel to Bishophill and at the rear of the Penitentiary garden, Skeldergate itself contained several notorious public houses and beershops, and the congested rookeries and yards off this street, particularly Beedham's Court which ran next to the Refuge garden, housed, as we have seen, some of York's most degraded whores. North Street too, one of the principal centres of prostitution in York throughout the century, was only a few minutes walk from the Home. Perhaps most unfortunate, however, was the uninterrupted view out across the city from the back bedrooms of the Institution. Directly in line, elevated almost to the same height and separated from the Penitentiary only by its sloping garden, Skeldergate and the river were the three Water

Lanes, rising steeply to Castlegate. For many of the girls the sight of these streets, clearly visible from the Refuge, must have had an unhappy and disturbing effect.

Not until 1917 was the unsuitability of the surroundings finally referred to, when it was stated that because of this, and also the dilapidated state and general inadequacy of the Bishophill premises, the Committee had decided that an early move was absolutely imperative.[18] The property was sold in 1918 and vacated in April the following year, when the Society took possession of 'Clifton Holme', a large, early Victorian villa with seven acres of grounds, situated at Clifton on the north-west outskirts of the city. This had formerly been the home of the Munby family, one of whose sons, Frederick James Munby (1837–1914), was the prominent York solicitor who had supported Reverend Frederick Lawrence in his missionary activities, had been for many years a leading member of the Gentlemen's Committee and had handled the Penitentiary Society's legal affairs. Another son was Arthur Joseph Munby (1828–1910), the minor Victorian poet who took a life-long – if somewhat peculiar – interest in working women, and displayed too, an unusual sympathy and courtesy towards prostitutes and fallen women he encountered in London.[19]

Throughout the seventies the visiting Ladies continued to report on the difficulties of running the establishment under the conditions which then existed. Girls were repeatedly confined to the probation ward for rudeness or refusal to work, and constantly punished for bad behaviour, stealing and lies. Others continued to run away or insist on leaving, or had to be dismissed in disgrace or placed in alternative Homes. As we shall see, the health of many of the inmates too, continued to be unsatisfactory. Anxieties with regard to staff in the period, however, were probably fewer than at any other time in the Institution's history – the Society having been fortunate in 1866 in the appointment of Miss Briddon, who was to remain in the Home until her death in 1897. Both the Committees and under-matrons were able to work in close harmony with Miss Briddon and she obviously exercised a firm, but slightly more kindly influence over the girls than many of her predecessors had done. The problems and strains facing the managers, as well as the inmates of such Homes are well expressed in the Annual Report for 1897, in which the announcement of the late Matron's death and a tribute to her work

are contained. This perceptive insight also appeared in one of York's
by now daily papers.

None but those who have had experience of the inner life of these
institutions can form any adequate idea of the difficulties, dis-
couragements, and disappointments thereof. Poor human nature
which has once yielded to the influence of passion is only too liable to
become the slave, and the efforts to regain the supremacy too often
become intermittent and feeble. The impulse which has brought the
poor fallen victim into such a refuge too often soon subsides. The
ordinary monotonous routine of the daily work or occupation soon
becomes intolerable to the spirit which has lately been accustomed to
excitement. Self-control in thought, word, and action soon becomes
irritating to those who had been wont to give free vent to all the
impulses of their nature. The memories of the past life return,
divested of all which so lately rendered them intolerable, and bright
with recollections of pleasures and amusement, and the longing is
kindled for the former lot of freedom instead of the present lot of
restraint. The will and the conscience battle with each other, until the
many return to the old paths of sin, and only the few have the grace
and perseverance to succeed. For more than thirty years has Miss
Briddon patiently endured the waywardness and stubbornness of those
with whom she has had to deal. Cheered from time to time by seeing
the pure and useful and happy after-life of some of those who had
come sin-stained, defiled, and degraded, under her care, but often
pained by seeing too many resent the kindness, shake off control,
ridicule spiritual teaching, and requiting care and love with violent
conduct and bitter words go back to the streets.

In spite of the goodwill and 'inexhaustible powers of forbearance'
attributed to Miss Briddon, however, her patience must often have
been taxed during the final twenty years of the period, when she was
in immediate charge of the Institution. It was during her term of
office that a third member of staff was urgently (but unsuccessfully)
requested by the Ladies, and that because of the frequent acts of
insubordination separate dormitories (again unsuccessfully for several years) were also required. The inability of the girls, who had
previously led such irregular lives, to conform to the monotonous
routine and still strict rules of the Refuge is illustrated by the frequent number of adverse comments in both the Visitors' and Committee Books in this period. In April 1873, for example, Sarah Swann
disappeared – but since, in any case, she was to have been sent to the
workhouse to be confined, no search was made for her. In the same
month Susan Miller and H. Smith ran away, but the police were 'put
on their track' and brought them back the same day. They were

imprisoned for a few days and then discharged.* In 1874 Eveline Westerdale, Annie Wilson and Louisa Thompson refused to stay in the Institution, and Esther Vine, Elizabeth Thompson, Kate Harrison, Jane Smith and Jane Kelly were all at various times punished for bad behaviour.† During 1875 several of the girls flatly refused to work in the laundry, with Fanny Owens being the cause of so much trouble that she was confined to the ward for a month and eventually placed in another Home, Rose Palmer behaving in a similar manner, Emma Dawney being so lazy and disobedient that she was sent to the workhouse and Sarah Delaney, for some unrecorded reason, being sent to prison. Even the Christmas festivities were marred by Sarah Swann (who had apparently been found and re-admitted to the Home after the birth of her child in the workhouse). All the girls were given presents, but she 'did not behave well about hers and was unpleasant to Miss Briddon about it'. Shortly afterwards Miss Swann must have left the Refuge, as the Annual Report for 1876 stated:

S. S., who was received three years ago in a state of great destitution, and has now been above a year giving satisfaction in her situation, said, 'I can never be grateful enough for the kindness shown me, Miss Briddon was like a mother to me. It must have been the Lord in his mercy brought me to York. If you had not taken me in that day I think I should have done something to myself, and now, as long as ever I can earn anything, I hope always to have a shilling to spare for those who need it as I did, and to help to teach those who know nothing of Jesus.'

Other inmates' comments and letters less piously expressed were not published by the Society.

During the eighties the Refuge enjoyed a period of comparative calm, with fewer girls being unsettled and difficult to manage, and escapes and dismissals occurring less frequently. Notable exceptions were Jane Fallen, who in 1882 and 1883 caused the Ladies an unusual amount of trouble and who, after eight weeks in the ward, had

* In a few cases, magistrates gave young prostitutes the opportunity of entering the Refuge, rather than serve a prison sentence – providing, of course, that they were otherwise eligible for admission to the Home. If such girls left the Penitentiary without permission the police were called in to catch them, though usually if they still desired to go, they were allowed to do so. A similar arrangement existed at the Grove House Rescue Home in Monkgate, to which the police often took first offenders and young prostitutes newly emerged from prison. As Grove House was a short-term Home and provided immediate refuge, such cases were naturally received more frequently than at the Bishophill premises.
† In spite of her premature departure Eveline Westerdale obviously did not return to her former activity. A draft Ladies' Refuge Report for July 1876 reads: 'Miss Briddon requested to give Eveline Westerdale a reward for her good conduct during more than two years since she left.'

eventually to be dismissed 'for the good of the institution'; and Ethel Pollard and Mary Hindson, who in 1884 somehow got possession of the door key, let themselves out and were not heard of again. Mary Hindson, who was twenty-one, had been in service for some years and had first become a prostitute after leaving her situation which she found 'too quiet'. She was soon forced to enter Leeds workhouse where she lived for a year before obtaining another situation in service. After a short while, however, she ran away from that too, and since the Union refused to re-admit her, she drifted to Hull and prostituted herself there for three months, after which she had to go into the Leeds Infirmary. Following treatment there she was admitted to the York Refuge. Ethel Pollard was seventeen and had been brought from Canada as a servant by two ladies. She had left them on reaching England and had been a prostitute for two years. It seems unlikely that either girl had been permanently influenced by the Society's efforts to reform them, and their absence from subsequent records in York is probably due to the fact that they fled to another town rather than that they had turned from their 'lives of sin'. Another disappointment was Isabella Corkhill, who was admitted in February 1886, was determined to leave and then changed her mind, but whose violent temper and bad language were 'very injurious to the younger girls'. By the following February, however, her health was 'in such a precarious state' and causing such alarm that the doctor advised sending her 'back to the Isle of Man at once'.* This incident seems to have sparked off another of those periodic outbursts of general insubordination and staff difficulties to which the Refuge was unfortunately subject. In the following month the Ladies reported:

Three girls have run away since the last meeting. There has been an undercurrent of rebellion and disrespect in the House for many months past and it was not easy to find the cause – but things have come to light about Miss Brazil [the sub-matron] which fully account for it – her influence on the girls for evil has been very great and the deceit practised made it difficult to get to the cause of all the evil. It is hoped that things will improve now the worst girls are gone, though there are still two that must go if they do not improve. Miss Briddon's authority must be upheld with the Committee. Mrs. Burns [Miss Brazil's replacement] was so utterly incapable of managing the laundry that Sarah Kelk, another applicant has been sent for on a month's

---

* Her parents, however, were 'too poor' to receive her, and she was, in any case, too ill to be moved further than the workhouse hospital where she died a few weeks later of consumption. Miscellaneous correspondence and York Union Register of Deaths, April 1877.

trial before the other's time is up, as it was utterly impossible to carry out the work now all the trained girls are gone, unless there was someone who could iron. Miss Briddon has struggled hard to keep the work, but the strain upon her has been far too great for some time past.

During April and May there was constant trouble 'from the prevalence of bad language, quarrelling and impertinence to the Matron', and Adelaide Patterson and Mary Ellen Jones had become 'quite unbearable'. Their constant habit of swearing and their rudeness to Miss Kelk was so great that she threatened to resign if they went into the laundry. They were dismissed shortly afterwards and it was then reported that Mary Boyle and Mary Jane Fox had escaped but had been brought back by a policeman. In the following month Sarah Jane Wardle and Kate Newrey climbed the wall and ran away together and Miss Briddon had to have them brought back with the aid of the police; and a few weeks later, in August, Kate Smith, who had been found a situation as a farm servant at the nearby village of Wilberfoss, was brought back after less than a week, having been both lazy and impertinent.

Even without reference to the evidence put forward in the preceding Chapter regarding the poverty and destitution of many of York's street-walkers, it is apparent from the records of the York Penitentiary Society that many of the girls applying for admittance to the Home were utterly without friends or means. Having prostituted themselves, they had already taken what must have seemed a desperate last resort and now had literally nowhere to turn and nowhere to go but the workhouse. Some, as we have seen, could even be refused admittance there. Dismissal from the Refuge, therefore, must, to those who had no family or friends willing to receive them, have been an alarming prospect. Kate Smith was one of those whose situation was hopeless. She had been admitted to the Home in March 1885 when she was seventeen. She had been brought up in the Grey Coat School, and had lived a 'very unsatisfactory' life. Her intellect, the Ladies recorded, was below average and she was not a hopeful case, but the poor girl had promised to do her best. After a longer period than usual – two years and five months – the Ladies had eventually found her a situation in which, as we have seen, she was not a success. She was put in the ward in solitary confinement, and after a month was still there – refusing to go to the workhouse. Her only relative, an uncle, refused to receive her, and since she could be found no other employment she eventually had to be forced to go into the Union.

Applicants were often described as orphans or, as has been observed, as daughters who had suffered cruelty or neglect at the hands of a step-parent. Indifference or shame, too, could be the cause of a girl's homelessness, especially, it would seem, if she was one of the rare street-walkers who came from a more 'respectable' background. In May 1878, for example, Miss Briddon received the following letter written in a scholarly hand:

Madam,

My mother wishes me to write to you respecting my sister Maude who is an inmate of your institution. We have today received a letter from her stating that she is desirous of leaving but cannot do so without mother's consent. Before mother gives that consent she would like to hear from you personally, as to her conduct and frame of mind. Whether she is still careless and thoughtless and slovenly in her person and work, also what prospects she has of obtaining a livelihood when she quits the institution. Mother begs that you will be strict and impartial telling her.

From the tone of Maude's letter we infer that she intends coming home at once; but I may say that affairs here are at a low ebb, and mother has not a single lodger at present in the house, which you are perhaps aware is a lodging-house; so that to have to maintain another strong hearty young woman for a indefinite period would be a great strain on my mother's slender purse.

My own opinion is that Maude had better stay another year, as she must be as well off where she is as anywhere else, because even if she takes another situation she is tied almost as much as at present, and if she merely wants a change – why all I can say is she can do well without it.

Apologising for the trouble I am causing you and hoping to hear from you fully shortly.

I am Madam, Your obedient servant, J. W. Pulleyn.

P.S. Of course we understand Maude's feelings on the subject but cannot overlook the fact that she brought it upon herself.*

Other letters from the girls themselves reveal the frightening bleakness awaiting them in the world outside, even if they left the Institu-

---

* For 1876 and 1877 a few draft Ladies' Refuge Reports and hastily written Applicants' Examination Notes have survived, one of the latter providing detailed information on this untypical inmate of the Refuge, who had been brought to the Ladies by her mother. '28 May 1877. Examination of Maude Pulleyn, aged 21. Father Robert Pulleyn, was schoolmaster at Askham Bryan 14 years. Went to be station master at Leeds, died 5 years ago. Can read and write was at school at Leeds went to Mr. Crossleys at Halifax as kitchen maid – also Lady Bloomfields. Left her place a year ago. Six months with her uncle. Went with another servant to bad house in Hull. Also in Leeds. Her mother wants her to come to Refuge.'

tion 'reformed' and with a good character – explaining in some measure their dependence on the Matron, their morbid obsession with religion and sin, and the speed with which many of them reverted to drink and their former way of life. The letter from Annie Scaife, for example, who had confided to the Matron that in the situation that had been found for her at 'Mrs. Hutton's' she had had 'not room to stir about in' and a 'life like a crab', continued:

I know you will thing me very unkind and ungrateful but I thought you did not care about me . . . but it does not do for me to think it makes me look old but I would not go another day without writing give my kind love to miss waters I know she will be disgusted with me miss waters is not so forgiving as you but I know you will forgive me dear miss briddon write back to me I never get any letters from anyone else my sister next to me got married last christmas day my oldest brother is dead and my youngest brother has gone to sea and my poor dear mother died the very day I went to mrs huttons I am all alone in the world now.
      Wishing to remain your
      Humble servant,   Annie Scaif.

Another girl who corresponded in 1881 both with Miss Briddon and with the sub-matron, Miss Waters, was Elizabeth Ransome, who, after leaving the Refuge (obviously in unsatisfactory circumstances), had eventually obtained a situation as a housemaid in an Aberdeen convalescent home. She first wrote to Miss Waters:

Will you forgive the liberty I take in writing to you after I have insulted you and Miss Briddon more than any girl you have had to deal with. The reason for writing to you is to ask your forgiveness and to tell you if you remember when Miss Briddon's note being opened that was sealed in an envelope addressed to Miss Briddon and you had written some little things down on the back to remember them you asked me if I knew anything about it I did because I opened it I think I tore a piece of and lit the gas with it and I denied knowing anything about it not that you accused me of it you only asked me – I was truly sorry after and I don't think I was ever happy after it as it haunted me so and I went on from worse to worse. I don't know why I should have given way to such a temptation like that as curiosity was not one of my bad faults – will Miss Briddon and you forgive me for that and all the trouble and abuse you got from me. I dare not do the same now as I think I should put an end to myself if I thought I should ever be turned out of service. It was a kindness you did me if you only knew how the thought of it lives me as it cured me a great deal of my bad temper. I feel it just the same but it is a relief to go and tell some of the Ladies. It seems to take the passionate self will away – I have been living here a little over four months. I am housemaid here I get on very well only my back hurts me and I cannot tell anybody how bad, only them that bears the same pain themselves . . .

When Miss Waters replied to her letter she continued:

I received your kind letter and I was so glad I could not keep from crying as I did not expect an answer back I put the adress on so that if you had any doubt about me it was in your power to enquire if you liked if I was really in a situation . . . I am sorry I have not been all my life what I am now as I know too well what peace of mind and quietness I have missed. All because I wanted to do all my own way. I feel it is so pleasant and so sweet to obey and give up my own will but at times for a moment I forget and rebel in my heart but as soon as the past rises up it is enough. But I will try for a better motive than that. I am still getting on very well the Lady Superintendent as raised my wages a pound more as she says I am well worth it thanks to Miss Briddon for telling us and showing us how to scrub floors with the grain of the wood as I have a lot of scrubbing to do and I get plenty of credit and I must say I am very proud of my floors as they was grey black when I came here.

Her next letter (to Miss Briddon) provides something of the home background to which she had returned soon after leaving the Refuge, and something too, of her state of mind, both in carrying out the 'dirty trick' she describes and in relating the story to, of all people, Miss Briddon.

I feel so glad to think that either you or Miss Waters will acknowledge a letter from me. I was so surprised to know that you often wondered where I was I don't mean that you could forget me altogether but I though you and Miss Waters had ceased to take an interest in me or any girl after they have had to leave the house like I had – I won't write any more about the past I am so ashamed of it I almost hate myself sometimes when I think about it . . .

I had been [in Scarborough] eight months when my Father wrote to me asking me to come home . . . it was a sad letter too about my stepmother drinking and spending money as fast as it came in and when my father was away she used to sell anything that she could get rid of without father missing it how she carried on till her head got light or silly when she was in her proper senses she was almost mad so they got her in a cab one night and took her to the Big House and she was kept there for some time and Father had to pay 5/6 a week for her I was sorry for her when she was there but I was more sorry when she came home again when she got her head clear but she was soon as bad again . . . and her daughter was almost as bad they was so used to drinking all that they could get that one day there was some that had been standing some time on the window bottom I got I hated to see it much more to go and fetch it made my heart ache many a time the beer that had been standing about I thought I would serve them a nasty trick so I says to Charlie let us fill this jug up with something and see if they will taste the difference so you may be sure we served

them a very dirty trick anyhow when Mrs. and her daughter came in
of course they must have a drink so long as there was something they
did not notice it had increased but the dirty things enjoyed the draught . . .
I could not be happy at home when I saw my poor father's life.

Even those prostitutes who had made a sincere and successful
effort to reform then, often had little to look forward to other than a
life of loneliness and drudgery in domestic service – in all probability
being even more exploited and looked down on than their more
virtuous sisters – with few of them entering that 'respectable' society
described by Acton and his supporters. Jane Kirton, for example,
was a fallen woman who reformed to the complete satisfaction of the
Penitentiary Committee, but who nevertheless ended up both in the
workhouse and in prison, and was never allowed to shake off former
misfortune. In December 1862, aged twenty-nine years, she was
admitted to the Refuge, the Ladies reporting that she was one of a
large family of ten sons and two daughters whose father was dead and
whose mother lived in Somerset. According to her, she had lived for
twelve years with a man who had promised to marry her but had not
done so, and who had frequently 'used her very ill when he was
drunk'. She had had four children, all of whom had died. One of the
city missionaries had apparently 'awakened her mind to her sinful
state' and she had left her partner, and tried to make a living by
washing and charring. Her health giving way, however, she had
become entirely destitute and had entered the city workhouse.
Examination of other sources, however, reveals that at some stage
she had supplemented her income from washing (not apparently very
successfully) by prostitution. In September 1861 she was charged in
company with four other 'disreputable females' with wandering the
streets and annoying gentlemen;[20] and two months later she and her
companion, Henry Cowl, were, it may be recalled, fined five shillings
and costs for exposing their persons in King's Square.[21] Only a week
later, at which time her address was St Andrewgate, she was
remanded in custody for the theft of twenty-one pounds, which she
was accused of stealing from a man in a public house in Swinegate.
He claimed to have been drugged, but the charge was dismissed
through lack of evidence.[22]

In spite of her reticence regarding her past, however, she obviously conducted herself satisfactorily during her stay at the Refuge,
as in December 1863, after only a year in the Institution, the Ladies

reported that, since her health would not permit her to be placed in a situation, they wished to engage her as a servant in the new probationary ward at a wage of four pounds a year. Nothing more is recorded of Jane Kirton until June 1882, by which time she must have been about forty-nine years old. She was sentenced to six weeks imprisonment for 'decamping' from York workhouse with clothing worth one guinea. She had been given leave for a day's outing:

but had got too much to drink and remained out during the night and did not care to return and therefore went to Seamer, near Scarborough where she was found employment as a nurse . . . She had been in trouble before.[23]

As has been observed, many of the inmates of the Refuge were either totally uneducated or could barely read or write so that during the period there was, at the Ladies' request, an increasing emphasis placed on this aspect of their training. In addition, of course, as previous comments with regard to the laundry work have shown, most were very ignorant concerning ordinary domestic work such as washing, cleaning and cooking, and had to be painstakingly instructed in skills which would normally in girls and young women of their age have already been acquired. The poverty, deprivation and ignorance of these girls is clearly stated in the Annual Report for 1864:

The class of girls admitted into the Refuge needs instruction in everything – very few have even had the early training of a respectable home – the places of service they have been in, are generally of the lowest description. They come to us utterly destitute, with hardly clothes to cover them, quite ignorant of household work, often not knowing how to read, scarcely ever to write.

Indeed, the ignorance and poor backgrounds of the prostitutes applying to the Refuge was so general, that on the only occasion when a girl from a superior social class applied, she was taken only briefly into the probationary ward until 'her friends, who were in a respectable position in society . . . could make arrangements for her being received into an institution intended for the more educated class of fallen women'.[24]

Few girls, however, were admitted to the Home if they were thought to be of 'weak intellect' and Kate Smith, whose intelligence was recorded as being below average, was an exception. Nevertheless, various prostitutes such as Ann Thompson, who applied in June 1856 from the workhouse, A. Arundell, who applied in November

1859 but was returned to her parents, and Elizabeth Kilmington, who applied in March 1861 but was considered 'much more suitable for a lunatic asylum', were refused admittance because they did not even possess the very limited standard of intelligence and training required by the Refuge. This aspect of prostitution – the fact that many street-walkers were of weak intellect and simple minded, or were entirely without or possessed little fundamental education – must be regarded as an important contributory reason for a girl's initial seduction and downfall.* Girls such as Sarah Richardson, who had been twice to the Ragged School and found 'incapable of instruction', Ann Richardson, who though admitted was ill and 'in an afflicted state of body and mind . . . but very humble and requiring much care and kindness', Sarah Clithero, 'very uncouth and very ignorant', Smith, a 'young, ignorant and neglected creature', Mary Ann Richardson, 'very uncouth and has evidently been a neglected child, totally uninstructed' and poor Ellen Wilson, who at seventeen had been a prostitute in Hull, Leeds and York until 'being entirely destitute slept out of doors and wandered about until a policeman took her to the Union' and who was 'very ignorant and without education of any kind' – given the appalling experience they had acquired, and at an early age – could hardly be expected to be anything other than emotionally disturbed. Even those not actually referred to as 'hardly able to read' or 'uninstructed' must, in view of their backgrounds, invariably have been even less educated than the rest of the poor from whose ranks they were drawn. This is illustrated in the following painstakingly written and pathetic letter from a girl named Robertshaw (her Christian name is illegible) which is, after all, the outcome of two years instruction in literacy by Miss Briddon, Miss Waters and the visiting Ladies.

---

* This is demonstrated by Rescue workers' growing awareness of the need for classification of fallen women, their repeated assertions that feeble-minded girls were forming an increasing proportion of prostitutes, and their recognition that such women were amongst the most difficult to reform. In 1894, for example, the York Association for the Care of Young Girls sent a representative to the Annual Meeting of the Yorkshire Rescue Association at Dewsbury, at which a resolution was passed approving the establishment of a Yorkshire Home for feeble-minded prostitutes. The York Association's Annual Report for 1895 stated that:

'Such girls form a large percentage of those who fall to the lowest depths, they cannot be kept in ordinary Homes or Shelters, for they need permanent care and protection and it is useless to attempt to train them for service. The result is that after a few days or weeks in a Training Home or Refuge they are passed to the Workhouse, which they quickly leave, or return to their friends, who cannot guide or control them, and so they fall from bad to worse, a misery to themselves and all about them.'

October 19 1881.
Dear Madiem
    I know write these few lines to you hoping to find you Miss Swaters
hoping find you and Miss Swaters well and I thank you for what you
have done for me and you all remember me to Mrs. and Mr. Speck
and pleac to thank them for the present their gave them
    I tell you that I like my place very well and I am very comfortable
and pleac to write and tell me how Mrs. Speck is pleac to give my love
to the girls so no more at present from your
        humble servant.

It is hardly surprising, given the girls' circumstances and what
must have been generally regarded as their undesirability, that the
situations found for the inmates of the Refuge fell short of Acton's
Utopian visions – even though these were 'fallen women' genuinely
desirous of reform and amenable to discipline. The fact that they
were recommended to situations meant that they had already under-
gone two years training for their future employment, had been given
some elementary education, but, above all, that they had submitted
for a long period to an even more dreary regime than they would
hopefully experience even in domestic service. They had proved that
they were able to give up any amusement and pleasure their former
activity may temporarily have afforded them, and they were obviously not dependent on drink. At least 542 girls (43 per cent of all
recorded prostitutes in the period) applied to enter the Refuge; and
of these, only 142 were actually placed in service.* There is no reason
to suppose that those women who did not enter the Refuge, but who
are included in this study because of their prostitution combined
with drunkenness, criminality, destitution or disease, could have
entertained better prospects for their future than did the 'successful'
inmates of the Penitentiary.
    Of the 142 girls who were found employment by the Penitentiary
Society – and subsequently, various even of these returned to the
streets – all but Mary Robinson, the Catholic girl whom the Ladies
apprenticed to a dressmaker, were sent into domestic service. A few
inmates expressed a desire to set up on their own and take in washing,
but on the whole this was regarded doubtfully by the Ladies who
(sometimes with justification) feared their intentions; though an
early inmate called Marr was so 'willing' and did 'fine' washing so

---

* There is a seventeen year gap in the Ladies' Committee records from 1864 to 1881, though
this is offset to some extent by the less systematic information in the Visitors' Books. The
proportion of inmates successfully placed in service, therefore, must have been considerably
less than one quarter of the intake.

well that the Ladies considered settling her in one of the cottages owned by the Society in Skeldergate. The conditions of the girls' employment are rarely described, but, as we have seen, poor Annie Scaife worked in a dark hole of a wash-house and had a life like a crab; and another inmate Mary Burton, who in March 1848 was sent on trial to a washerwoman called Barker at a wage of three pounds a year, was in a place so 'undesirable' that the Ladies hurriedly had to find her an alternative situation.

A few girls, like Susannah Holder who left the Institution in 1883 to work for the Gunter family near Wetherby, became laundry maids in large country houses, but most went to smaller establishments either as general servants or 'maids of all work' or to do the washing of the house. Others became laundry maids or servants in institutions such as the hospital or the Blue Coat School, and a few were even temporarily employed in the Penitentiary itself. The recorded wages of those who worked as general servants in the period were between four and sixteen pounds a year, and as laundry maids between eight and twelve pounds. Neither of these rates compared favourably with those recommended by Mrs Beeton in 1867, indicating that in general girls from the Home, most of whom had already worked as domestic servants in situations of the 'lowest description', were regarded as a particularly cheap form of cheap labour.

The Society's Annual Report for 1887 stated that, of the 412 prostitutes who had been formally admitted to the Home by the end of that year, 142 had been placed in service. Of the remaining 270 inmates who sought refuge at the Penitentiary during the period, few can be considered as successful cases of reform. The reasons for their departure from the Home are listed in the Report as follows:

Restored to friends and sent to other institutions	101
Left on account of health	22
Left at their own request	63
Escaped and dismissed	71
Died in the institution	1
Dismissed insane	1
Remaining in the institution	11

However, the first three categories listed are very misleading and convey a falsely optimistic impression regarding the Home's success, which can only be corrected by analysis of the confidential Ladies' Committee and Visitors' Books. 'Restored to friends and sent to

Fig. 30 *A day out with our old girls at Hampton Court.*
Although it was comparatively rare for prostitutes who entered
Penitentiaries to be reclaimed, and the York Refuge met with
only limited success, some women, such as these former inmates
of a Home in London, obviously forsook their former profession.
A photograph from the 43rd *Annual Report of the Female Mission
to the Fallen*, Charing Cross, London, 1901.

other institutions' includes those girls who were so unmanageable or
were having such an unsettling effect on the other inmates that they
had to be sent to other Homes 'for the good of the Refuge', as well as
those who were so badly behaved that they were sent back to their
families. There is little difference, then, between this group and
those who were actually dismissed. More important, however, 'sent
to other institutions' also includes the many girls who were passed on
to the workhouse or hospital because they were diseased, ill or
pregnant and additional girls were returned to their families for the
same reasons. Thus the figure of 22 who the Report claimed, 'left on
account of health' is an entirely misleading and inadequate one, since

York Penitentiary Society,

43, BISHOPHILL.

I am wishful to abandon my sinful life and by God's grace to lead a better.

I am willing to remain two years in the Home.

I will do my best to conform to the rules and discipline of the Home.

Signed

Fig. 31 Declaration which later inmates to the York Refuge were required to sign on entering the Home.

it refers only to those poor creatures like Margaret Richardson (who was in fact dying when she 'wished' to go and work in Selby) who were too ill to be retained in the Refuge, but were neither immediately received into another institution, nor returned to their friends – presumably because they had none. 'Left at their own request' is another euphemism which refers, in fact, to those inmates who were so determined to go that they could not be prevailed upon to stay. Often, as the Ladies record, they were hysterical and abusive, and demanded their clothes. Efforts to detain them would, in all probability, merely have resulted in further escapes and dismissals and in their adversely affecting the rest of the inmates.

The above figures in the Annual Report, however, even when correctly interpreted, still present an unduly optimistic picture of the Institution's success. This is because, as has already been observed, the figure of 412 includes only those girls formally admitted into the Home after having successfully completed the necessary probationary period. It indicates nothing of those prostitutes who, having been provisionally accepted for admission, did not satisfactorily complete their initial term of trial, and, because they left after only a few weeks or days, were never regarded as or included in the Summary of Inmates. Nevertheless, the Committee and Visitors' Books show that there were at least an additional ninety girls in the period who were considered eligible for entry and allowed conditionally into the Home, but who would not or could not submit to the necessary discipline and restraint required. Added to this there were at least a further forty women who were in such a poor state of health, so mentally deficient or otherwise so unsuitable that their applications were turned down outright. The fact that there is a seventeen year gap in the surviving Ladies' Committee Books in which the names of all applicants and entrants (including probationers) were recorded means that there were undoubtedly additional girls who entered the Refuge but who remained too briefly to be included in the Summary of Inmates. This gap is only partially offset by the Ladies' Visitors' Books, which, though covering most of the period, do not provide a comprehensive record of all girls entering the Home. Even without making allowance for these omissions, hardly more than one quarter of the girls admitted to the Penitentiary were actually placed in service – though what subsequently became either of those or the remainder, is, of course, largely unknown.

In spite of these figures, however, which must, to those who appreciated their real implications, have been disheartening, the importance of the Refuge throughout the period was by no means insignificant. It is true that the Society probably rescued and permanently reformed only a small proportion of the total number of prostitutes in the city, for as the Committee itself was to report, even of those who entered – 'the many return to the old paths of sin, and only the few have the grace and perseverance to succeed'.* Neverthe-

---

* With the growing 'multiplicity' of Refuges and Shelters towards the end of the century – giving rise in some towns to open competition for inmates and an 'unseemly scramble' for cases, who were now able to 'pick and choose' which Home they entered for a few days' rest – the 'long-term' discipline of the York Penitentiary was very highly thought of by the Reformatory and Refuge Union.

less, of the 1,246 prostitutes identified between 1837 and 1887, 542 or 43 per cent sought refuge in its care and over 500 were admitted. Thus though the Home was relatively unsuccessful in its primary purpose it at least afforded many street-walkers temporary shelter and relief, and the opportunity – if they could take it – of entering a more regular course of life.

By modern standards the values expressed in the Committee Books and Annual Reports – the emphasis on the women's sin and guilt, the religious indoctrination and the strict and dreary discipline of the Institution – are harsh and inappropriate, especially when related to girls and women who, for whatever reason, must have been desperate to turn from a life of prostitution; and who, as the managers of the Refuge were aware, had invariably had poor and neglected childhoods, were almost totally uninstructed and who entered the Home utterly destitute and in a pitiful state of body and mind. Yet such treatment and values were in accordance with contemporary belief and practice, and, whatever their shortcomings, institutions such as the Refuge in York constituted society's major effort to ameliorate the evils of prostitution – as they affected the prostitute, rather than her clients – during the period. Those who ran them were sincere and well intentioned, if over zealous, and, as we have seen, often performed a thankless and unrewarding task. It is to their credit that those members of the Penitentiary Committees who interviewed applicants, visited the Institution and were called upon to reprimand insubordinate and unruly inmates, exposed themselves to uncouth, abusive and not least sickly or diseased street-walkers, from whom the rest of polite society shrank away in horror and disgust. Their courage and determination to 'pluck these brands from the burning' has to be acknowledged.* Also, it must be pointed out that in spite of its discipline, its bleakness, its religious pressures

---

* One of the most notable Ladies serving on the Committee and visiting the Penitentiary was the Quakeress Mrs Henry Richardson (1826–1911) of Cherry Hill House, York – close friend of Josephine Butler and staunch supporter of the Campaign for the Abolition of the Contagious Diseases Acts. It was with Mrs Richardson and her husband that Mrs Butler stayed when visiting York to address the National Convention in 1874, at which time, in spite of ill health, Mrs Richardson was giving practical help to prostitutes at the Penitentiary. In addition to devoting much time and energy to the Cause of Social Purity and the Abolition of the State Regulation of Vice, she advanced the cause of women's rights in other ways. For many years she was the Secretary of the York Association for the Care of Young Girls, and was also the President of the Women's Liberal Association. The Penitentiary Visitors' Books in which individual Ladies recorded their own visits reveal that she was more sympathetic in her comments regarding the inmates than were various of her colleagues – some of whom were determined to root out evil, rather than kindly or understanding. Like Reverend Frederick Lawrence who, it will be remembered, was also active in helping York prostitutes,

and its monotonous routine the Refuge, with all its faults and limitations, was for many girls the only home, the only security and the
only instruction in decency they had ever known. As the Annual
Report was to state in 1900, looking back at the 560 girls who had
been inmates of the Home, and remembering too the hundreds more
who had entered the Refuge only to leave within a few days:

> Some few of the inmates seem to admit that they have been seduced from
> their homes by the foolish solicitations of thoughtless companions,
> almost invariably girls like themselves. But the majority have known
> little, if anything, of the pure and hallowing influences which we attach
> to Home; while many have been left by the indifference of their parents
> to become the prey of temptations incident to their time of life. Many
> have had in their parents bad examples which they only too naturally
> followed; and some had been actually initiated in sin by those who
> should have been their protectors from evil influences ... There is not
> one who can be charged with having sinned in spite of opportunities for
> good, and in defiance of watchful care, and in utter disregard of sound
> teaching and loving counsel ... Who can be surprised if the natural
> impulses of youth, unchecked and uncontrolled, incite them to acts of sin
> lapsing too often in vicious courses – stimulating them to cast all restraint
> to the winds, and then, when dissatisfied therewith, to seek to escape
> from the unhappy consequences within this Home – and as soon as the
> discipline becomes irksome, to rebel against it, and, *as soon*, to regret
> with tears and protestations of amendment their waywardness and folly –
> then, in a short time, to become restless under the monotony of the life
> here, and to yearn for their former freedom, forgetful of its dangers –
> and then, when restrained or remonstrated with, associate themselves
> together, with similar and dissatisfied unchastened spirits, resent
> discipline, ignore kindness, misunderstand warnings, and determine to
> leave the shelter which they once had sought.

Obviously many girls could not cope with the discipline, restraint
and pressures of the Home, and in sudden outbursts of passion or
smouldering resentment left or were dismissed. Others, however,
actually dreaded leaving the control and shelter of the Refuge –
having (not surprisingly) little faith in their own worth or ability to
keep from sin and withstand temptation. There were those too who,
having completed their term in the Home, were frightened, lonely
and homesick for the Penitentiary in their new and often uncongenial
situations.

The sad fact that this grim and unhappy Institution really was

---

Mrs Richardson's humaneness extended from fighting injustice towards women to opposing
cruelty to animals. Neither was a popular cause.[25]

regarded as 'home' by some of the girls is demonstrated by the occasional visits of former inmates who returned to the Refuge for their 'holidays' or because they had been ill and were too weak to return to their situations. Others stayed at the Home in between jobs, as in 1872, for example, when it was reported that the probation ward had been useful in providing a temporary home for a former inmate who was briefly unemployed. In providing a substitute home or even a temporary shelter for these women, many of whom were desperate and destitute and had nowhere else to turn, the Refuge undoubtedly provided a much needed service. In the less immediate sense, however, the Penitentiary did not fulfil its purpose. It was largely unsuccessful in permanently rescuing the great majority of prostitutes who sought refuge, even though these women may be regarded as the most promising of those identified in this study. And because of the way in which they had revealed to them the extent of their sin, the depth of their defilement and the enormity of their guilt, many even of the Penitentiary 'successes' were undoubtedly casualties from anything other than the spiritual point of view – being apparently as psychologically damaged as a result of the treatment they received in the Home, as the diseased prostitutes in the workhouse were physically affected by taking part in the activity. By concentrating almost entirely on the sin and need for forgiveness of the prostitute, without reference either to the immorality and hypocrisy of her many clients, or to the injustice inherent in a society which for almost half our period upheld the infamous provisions of the Contagious Diseases Acts – and by plunging her back into that lowest paid of occupations from which so many of her kind had first turned to the streets – the managers of the York Penitentiary, like those of so many others in the period, reflected the prejudice and lack of perception of their class and time. Their undoubtedly sincere efforts were bound to fail, since they were attempting to turn individual women from a life of prostitution, without attacking the fundamental economic, social and moral issues involved.

Conclusion

As part of the general movement towards the study of history 'from below' this book has attempted to explore the reality of the Victorian prostitute's life, and, by a careful and systematic examination of all the available sources, to separate from the fiction the facts regarding her part in the activity. In doing so it has inevitably challenged recent interpretations of the subject, since these have been largely based on an uncritical acceptance of secondary material that is neither unbiased nor consistent, and which, even at the time, was regarded by many as both unjust and unsound.

Though limited to the activities of prostitutes and their associates in a particular city it is hoped that this study contributes to a greater understanding of Victorian society in general, and has a wider than local significance. Elsewhere there may well have been slight variations dependent upon the differing demand for prostitutes on the one hand, and on the type and extent of alternative forms of female employment on the other. Only if further such studies are undertaken (and, as is demonstrated here, there is an abundance of documentary evidence at local level on the details of prostitutes' lives which has been almost completely neglected by social historians) will it be possible to make comparisons. However, since all recorded and therefore low-class prostitutes have been examined here, it is unlikely that the fundamental conclusions reached regarding the circumstances of York's women of the streets would be substantially different, were another Victorian city chosen for a similar study.

This book has shown that throughout the period even in a non-industrial provincial city, low-class prostitution was so widespread and so blatantly exercised that few could have been ignorant of its existence. For though the prostitutes lived and operated in the worst slums in the city, their solicitings and 'wanderings abroad' were carried out in the more respectable thoroughfares, and their activities religiously reported in the local press. The nature of their accommodation – even by contemporary standards it was appallingly insanitary, overcrowded and in the most criminal and unsavoury neighbourhoods of York – suggests that the whores identified were catering in the main for men of their own class; a supposition borne out both by what has emerged regarding the general undesirability of the women themselves, and the limited evidence on the social status of their clients.

It seems clear that, in spite of claims to the contrary, the Victorian street-walker was not more fortunately situated than were other women of her class. Far from being more healthy, her irregular and dissipated life exposed her to general poor health, and the nature of her occupation to disease and unwanted pregnancies which, in the absence of husband or friends to support her, often resulted in destitution and commitment to the workhouse. Her street-walking, her petty criminality and her undoubted dependence on drink led to frequent and increasingly severe prison sentences from which she emerged desperate, often homeless, without means, and with no alternative but to return to the streets.

Though it is clear that prostitution was not the inevitable outcome of poverty, it is nevertheless equally obvious that poverty in some form or another was the major reason for girls initially taking to the streets, and that even after having done so, few were afforded more than a temporary relief. Though there was general agreement as to the almost invariable connection between alcohol and prostitution, few contemporary observers, with the exception of Refuge Committee members who were familiar with numerous applicants' histories, placed due emphasis on the basic poverty of that class of women from which most prostitutes were drawn. At most, those 'authorities' on the 'social evil' who were less condemnatory of the prostitute stressed the importance of the indiscriminate sleeping arrangements of the poor, bad housing, overcrowding and lack of education – all to some extent manifestations of poverty – as contributory reasons for her initial downfall. Others, as we have seen, argued that it was the prostitute's 'love of finery and dress' and disinclination to work that had made her what she was. Possibly such reasons were responsible for attracting a few individuals to the streets, though even here deprivation played a part, for had such perfectly natural desires been attainable (as they were in the more wealthy and leisured classes) then perhaps many a 'ruined' girl from the poor too, need never have ceased being respectable. The evidence in this study, however, suggests that fundamentally it was poverty which was the most powerful inducement to their becoming prostitutes. Having done so, it was overwhelmingly their reason for seeking to be rescued – an indication, as are the circumstances of those prostitutes who did not apply for admission to the Penitentiary, that low-class prostitution was not a rewarding profession, and that the majority of women who remained long enough to be recorded in the activity were rapidly reduced to their former state of need.

The fact that almost half York's recorded street-walkers in the period were sufficiently anxious to escape from prostitution that they sought shelter in the Refuge is an indication of the quality of their lives, and reveals too, their need for support and assistance in abandoning such an occupation. Their strong desire to enter such an institution for a period of two years – at the end of which they could hope for no more rewarding employment than heavy laundry work or domestic service – hardly supports the view that as prostitutes they were better off than their harder worked and more virtuous sisters. Their pitiful condition on application, their enfeebled state of health and the fact that many of them were recorded as having already spent some time in the workhouse is further proof that the harmful effects of prostitution on the women themselves were misleadingly underestimated. Obviously many were diseased and, though it is impossible to estimate the mortality rate of the group as a whole, it is clear both from the Refuge and the workhouse records that many prostitutes died at an early age as a result of their way of life.

Finally, the assertion that prostitution was engaged in by females possessing physical beauty, strong constitutions and intelligence – in short 'the finest women of their order'* – who profited from their

---

* From the Report from the Select Committee of the House of Lords on the Contagious Diseases Acts, 1866. Their Lordships were echoing Acton's opinion: 'The fact of a girl's seduction generally warrants her possession of youth, health, good looks, and a well-proportioned frame - qualifications usually incompatible with a feeble constitution.' (Nield, *Prostitution*, p. 189.) Such statements, based on the notion that only desirable and attractive young women were seduced or resorted to as prostitutes attributes to their seducers a fastidiousness and nicety of taste hardly in accordance with the facts. Matrons of Refuges, street missionaries and other contributors to the Reformatory and Refuge Union's quarterly *Notes on Work Amongst the Fallen* refer repeatedly in the eighties and nineties to the increasing number of half-witted and simple fallen women who were in need of care, many of whom were coarse featured and generally unattractive. The supplementary Cautionary Lists circulated to Homes throughout the country in an attempt to prevent unmanageable or deceitful

experience in an activity which could be abandoned with ease, has, for the majority of women in this study, been shown to be completely unrealistic. Evidence regarding the criminality and drunkenness of York's prostitutes reveals conclusively that they were brutalised and degraded by the occupation, that they suffered both physically and mentally and that they were regarded both by society and themselves as social outcasts. The confidential reports in the Penitentiary records prove beyond doubt that the young girls who had been lodged in brothels or walking the streets from the age of fourteen, fifteen or sixteen – far from having profited by their experience or attained an elevated or even lowly position in 'respectable' society – were still, for the most part, entirely illiterate or barely able to read or write, without training of any kind and even ignorant of basic domestic skills. Many were simple minded, most were uncouth and almost all during their stay at the Refuge showed signs of emotionally unbalanced or even violent behaviour. As such, they were hardly suited for the domestic service or laundry work which, in the absence of alternative forms of employment opportunities, and given their own limited abilities and the restricted facilities and finances of the Home, was the only training possible. The Penitentiary records reveal that, even with the Society's help, few in fact were permanently rescued or reformed for, since they and the remainder of York's street-walkers who wished to abandon prostitution were competing with less unstable and generally more desirable and trustworthy women, the attempts of most of them to find and keep respectable employment were unsuccessful, and many were compelled or tempted to return to their former way of life.

girls from re-entering Refuges hardly presents a more flattering picture. Cases are often described as having irregular or flat features, crossed eyes, bad or chronic complexions, unpleasing countenances, etc. Such descriptions are confirmed by the photographs of reformed prostitutes and inmates at work, in the Annual Reports of Homes throughout the country.

Notes

I INTRODUCTION

1 Quoted in Steven Marcus, *The Other Victorians* (London, 1971) pp. 31–2.
2 P. Fryer in the Introduction to his edition of William Acton, *Prostitution* (London, 1968) p. 12.
3 *Ibid.* p. 15.
4 Marcus, *op. cit.* p. 5.
5 Fryer, *op. cit.* p. 12.
6 Peter Quennell (ed.), *London's Underworld* (London, 1969) p. 25.
7 Keith Nield (ed.), *Prostitution in the Victorian Age* (Farnborough, 1973) Introduction.
8 Quoted in Fryer's Introduction to Acton, *op. cit.* p. 13.
9 Acton, *op. cit.* pp. 72–3.
10 *Ibid.* pp. 40–1 and 85.
11 William Logan, *The Great Social Evil; its Causes, Extent, Results and Remedies* (London, 1871) p. 74.
12 Acton, *op. cit.* p. 118.
13 *Ibid.* pp. 202–3.
14 See Josephine Butler, *Personal Reminiscences of a Great Crusade* (London, 1896) and Millicent G. Fawcett and E. M. Turner, *Josephine Butler, her Work and Principles, and their Meaning* (London, 1927).
15 Between January 1874 and December 1884, for example, *The National League Journal* was produced – a publication with the sub-title 'A Monthly Record of the Working Men's National League for the Repeal of the Contagious Diseases Acts'.
16 Though discontinued after the repeal of the Contagious Diseases Acts, publication of *The Shield* was resumed in 1897 and continued until 1970.
17 See, for example, Peter Cominos, 'Late Victorian Sexual Respectability and the Social System', in *International Review of Social History*, VIII, 1963: and Keith Thomas, 'The Double Standard', in *Journal of the History of Ideas*, XX, 1959.
18 *Gazette*, 3 August and 15 October 1887.

19 Logan, *op. cit.* p. 80.
20 Poor Law, September 1845.
21 *Ibid.* December 1871.
22 A description of York prostitutes in the *Gazette*, 11 February 1860.
23 *Gazette*, 2 September 1837.
24 *Gazette*, 20 December 1862.
25 *Gazette*, 1 May 1858.
26 *Gazette*, 21 April 1860.
27 *Gazette*, 15 September 1855.
28 B. Seebohm Rowntree, *Poverty: A Study of Town Life* (London, 1901).
29 Refuge Committee, December 1859.
30 Refuge Committee, April 1861.
31 Refuge Committee, May 1857.
32 *Gazette*, 21 April 1860.
33 Refuge Committee, January 1858.
34 Refuge Committee, June 1859.
35 See, for example, Francis Drake, *Eboracum* (London, 1736), p. 346 and appendix p. lxii.
36 William Hargrove, *History of York* (York, 1818) Vol. II. p. 401.
37 *Ibid.* p. 361.
38 *Gazette*, 20 May 1848.
39 *Gazette*, 7 February 1856.
40 *Gazette*, 11 February 1860.
41 *Gazette*, 19 February 1887.
42 *Gazette*, 28 May 1870.
43 *Gazette*, 4 June, 25 June, 20 August and 10 September 1870, and 16 September 1871. Poor Law, December 1871.
44 I am grateful to Major Tomlinson, Archivist and Curator of the Museum at York Barracks for this information.
45 Refuge Committee, July 1863.
46 Refuge Committee, June 1863.
47 Refuge Committee, September 1862 and June 1860.
48 *Gazette*, 26 July 1862.
49 *Gazette*, 13 July 1867.
50 *Gazette*, 25 January 1868.
51 *Gazette*, 22 May 1869.
52 *Gazette*, 7 September 1878.
53 *Gazette*, 21 May 1881.
54 See James Pope-Hennessy, *Queen Mary* (London, 1959).
55 Watch Committee, 2 January 1885.
56 Refuge Committee, January 1887.
57 Refuge Committee, March 1864.
58 Refuge Committee, September 1861. This aspect of the causes of prostitution is examined further in Chapter 6.
59 See the writer's D. Phil. Thesis, 'The Irish in York, 1840–1875'. University of York, 1977, Chapter 10.

2   HOUSES AND HAUNTS

1   See B. Harrison, *Drink and the Victorians, the temperance Question in England*, 1815–72, (London, 1971) pp. 50 and 332–3, and F. Henriques, *Modern Sexuality*, (London, 1968) Chapters 1 and 4 for discussions of the association between prostitution and drink.

2   W. Hargrove, *History of York*, Vol. II, p. 217.

3   *Annual Report*, 1870.

4   *Annual Report*, 1873. Logan, *The Great Social Evil*, p. 189 mentions the importance of the recent activities of Bible-women in the larger towns and cities in the reformation of fallen women.

5   T. Laycock, *Report on the State of the City of York. First Report of the Royal Commission for Enquiring into the State of Large Towns and Populous Districts, Parliamentary Papers*, 1844, XVII, p. 42.

6   See Chapter 10 of Beechey, 'The Irish in York'.

7   *Ibid*. pp. 350–1.

8   *Herald*, 21 August 1875.

9   City Engineer's Plans of the Castlegate Improvement Scheme, 1877.

10   *Herald*, 13 October 1914.

11   *Herald*, 21 April 1860.

12   Hargrove, *op. cit.* Vol. II, p. 149.

13   Laycock, *op. cit.* pp. 8–9.

14   *Gazette*, 16 November 1839.

15   Petition to the Ecclesiastical Commissioners for England and Wales, July 1844. Vicars' Choral Documents, York Minster Library Archives.

16   *Herald*, 4 July 1840.

17   *Gazette*, 28 November 1840.

18   *Gazette*, 3 November 1840.

19   *Gazette*, 2 February 1842.

20   *Gazette*, 24 August 1839.

21   *Herald*, 14 January 1843.

22   *Gazette*, 30 April 1870, see below page 89.

23   See below, Chapter 5, pp. 149–51.

24   See Beechey, *op. cit.* p. 154.

25   *Herald*, 14 January 1843.

26   Rowntree, *Poverty*, p. 199.

27   J. Smith, *Report to the General Board of Health on a Preliminary Enquiry into the Sanitary Condition of York*. H.M.S.O. 1850.

28   Rowntree, *op. cit.* p. 199.

29   *Ibid.* p. 202.

30   Hungate Mission Schools Minute Books, 29 March 1881.

31   *Gazette*, 18 February 1855. See also T. A. Critchley, *A History of the Police in England and Wales, 900–1926* (London, 1967).

32   Watch Committee, 14 February 1855.

33   Watch Committee, 21 February 1855.

34   *Herald*, 20 November 1858.

35 Watch Committee, 24 October 1860.
36 *Gazette*, 27 October 1849.

3 THE PROSTITUTES AND BROTHEL-KEEPERS

1 *Gazette*, 2 February 1843. (The figure of 119 was later amended to 118.)
2 *Gazette*, 10 May 1845. (This was a retrospective summary.)
3 *Ibid.*
4 *Gazette*, 17 October 1868. (Again this is a retrospective report.)
5 *Gazette*, 17 October 1868.
6 *Gazette*, 14 October 1871 and 20 October 1877.
7 *The York Society for the Prevention of Youthful Depravity*, Second Report (York, 1861).
8 Refuge Committee, December 1885.
9 W. Tait, *Magdalenism, An Inquiry into the Extent, Causes, and Consequences of Prostitution in Edinburgh* (Edinburgh, 1852) p. 32.
10 For a discussion of William Stead's exposure of child prostitution in London, see, for example, Henriques, *Modern Sexuality*. See also Figs. 16–19 for photographs of destitute children 'in moral danger', rescued by a provincial Female Mission in the 1880's.
11 Refuge Committee, February 1885.
12 Refuge Committee, June 1886.
13 For an examination of high infant mortality in a Yorkshire town see F. E. Finnegan and E. M. Sigsworth, *Poverty and Social Policy: An Historical Study of Batley*, Papers in Community Studies, University of York (York, 1978).
14 Tait, *op. cit.* pp. 251–2.
15 Tait, *op. cit.* p. 251.
16 Poor Law, December 1850.
17 Poor Law, March 1851.
18 Sessions, June 1855.
19 Sessions, August 1855.
20 *Herald*, 24 October 1855.
21 Poor Law, June 1856.
22 *Gazette*, 23 August 1856.
23 Sessions, as listed, 1857.
24 Sessions, October 1857.
25 Sessions, January 1866.
26 Poor Law, March 1875.
27 Poor Law, June 1875.
28 *Gazette*, 22 January 1870.
29 *Gazette*, 29 January 1870.
30 *Gazette*, 5 February 1870.
31 *Gazette*, 12 March and 30 April 1870.
32 *Gazette*, 30 April 1870.

33 *Gazette*, 21 May, 13 August and 8 October 1870.
34 *Gazette*, 4 March, 29 April and 8 July 1871.
35 *Gazette*, 8 July 1871.
36 *Gazette*, 18 May 1872.
37 Poor Law, June 1872.
38 *Gazette*, 24 May 1873.
39 *Gazette*, 16 January 1875.
40 *Gazette*, 30 June 1877.
41 *Gazette*, 11 August 1877.
42 *Gazette*, 29 September 1877.
43 *Gazette*, 22 July and 23 September 1882.
44 Poor Law, June 1859.
45 *Gazette*, 28 September 1850.
46 Poor Law, December 1867.
47 Rowntree, *Poverty*, pp. 156–7.
48 *Ibid.* p. 156.
49 *Gazette*, 14 December 1850.
50 *Gazette*, 15 August 1856.
51 *Gazette*, 7 August 1858.
52 *Gazette*, 7 August 1858.
53 *Herald*, 5 April 1862.
54 See, for example, *Gazette*, 28 May 1859, 8 March 1862, 24 September and 24 December 1864, and 14 January 1865.
55 Refuge Committee, October 1858.
56 Refuge Committee, September, October and November 1861.
57 See, for example, *Gazette*, 17 August 1865, 10 March and 15 December 1866 and 1 February 1868.
58 *Herald*, 11 April 1868.
59 *Gazette*, 4 May 1839.
60 *Gazette*, 6 July 1839.
61 Sessions, October 1839.
62 *Gazette*, 6 October 1838.
63 *Gazette*, 23 November 1839.
64 *Gazette*, 24 February and 30 September 1843.
65 *Gazette*, 4 May and 14 September 1844.
66 Poor Law, March 1847.
67 *Gazette*, 6 August 1870.
68 Refuge Committee, March 1848.
69 *Gazette*, 13 May 1848.
70 Refuge Committee, October to March 1848–9.
71 Refuge Committee, April 1849.
72 *Herald*, 20 April 1850.
73 See Beechey, 'The Irish in York', pp. 131–3.
74 *Gazette*, 21 August 1852, and Poor Law, June 1853.
75 *Gazette*, 7 August 1858.
76 Poor Law, April 1868.
77 Poor Law, March 1876.

78 *Herald*, 12 July 1856.
79 Poor Law, June 1860 and September 1864.
80 See, for example, *Gazette*, 10 October 1857 and 14 January 1860.
81 *Gazette*, 10 March 1866.
82 *Gazette*, 20 October 1838.
83 *Gazette*, 24 March 1855.
84 *Gazette*, 5 July 1856.
85 *Herald*, 14 April 1855.
86 *Gazette*, 1 September 1855.
87 *Gazette*, 27 October 1855.
88 *Herald*, 31 October 1863.
89 *Gazette*, 15 April 1871.
90 *Gazette*, 13 November 1869, 2 April and 4 June 1870.
91 *Gazette*, 10 January 1874.
92 *Gazette*, 4 March 1874.
93 *Gazette*, 12 February 1876.
94 *Gazette*, 24 February 1866 and 15 April 1871.
95 *Gazette*, 4 December 1874.
96 *Gazette*, 9 September 1876.
97 *Gazette*, 11 August 1877.
98 *Gazette*, 16 November 1878.
99 *Gazette*, 17 May 1879.
100 Acton, *Prostitution*. Also, see below, pages 164–5.
101 Poor Law, June 1867.
102 Poor Law, September 1867.
103 Poor Law, October 1867.
104 *Gazette*, 29 February 1868.
105 *Gazette*, 21 August 1869.
106 *Gazette*, 23 September 1837 and 15 June, 24 August and 16 November 1839.
107 See Elizabeth Hough or Huff's career as a prostitute in, for example, *Gazette*, 4 December 1858, 28 January 1865, Poor Law, June 1859 and June 1864. For her activities as a brothel-keeper see Sessions, 12 October 1868.
108 For Kendrew see, for example, *Gazette*, 21 October 1871 and 4 May 1873. For Foster, Poor Law, March 1874.
109 *Herald*, 31 October 1857.
110 *Herald*, 24 July 1858.
111 See, for example, *Gazette*, 1 September 1855, 23 February and 15 August 1856 and 21 April 1860. Poor Law, September 1866.
112 See, for example, Kate Ward, *Gazette*, 17 December 1864, 3 March 1866, 1 February 1868, 6 November 1869, etc. Sarah Douthwaite, Poor Law, June 1868 and Emma Stockhill, Sessions, 18 February 1868.
113 Poor Law, March 1851.
114 See, for example, Refuge Committee, October and November 1851, Poor Law, December 1851 and *Gazette*, 25 May 1850.

115 *Herald*, 28 October 1852.
116 *Gazette*, 21 April 1860.
117 *Gazette*, 24 February 1855.
118 Poor Law, March and June 1867.
119 See pages 25 and 132–3.
120 *Gazette*, 19 February 1887 and Watch Committee, 23 February 1887.
121 For cases involving these landlords see, for example, Sessions, 5 October 1868; Poor Law, March 1850, June 1855, June 1856, December 1859 and September 1863; and *Gazette*, 15 January 1853, 6 October 1855, 16 January 1858, 13 August 1870 and 8 January 1886.

4   THE CLIENTS

1   For an expansion of this argument see Cominos, 'Late Victorian Respectability' and Thomas, 'The Double Standard'.
2   See Acton, *Prostitution*, pp. 121–5; and for a more recent view see particularly J. A. Banks, *Prosperity and Parenthood* (London, 1954).
3   *Gazette*, 12 September 1863.
4   *Gazette*, 4 July 1863.
5   *Gazette*, 29 June 1861.
6   *Gazette*, 21 June 1862.
7   *Gazette*, 11 December 1852.
8   *Gazette*, 8 April 1854.
9   *Gazette*, 24 February 1838.
10 *Gazette*, 5 October 1839.
11 *Gazette*, 1 May 1847, 2 August 1844 and 2 August 1845.
12 *Gazette*, 20 March 1869.
13 *Gazette*, 26 November 1864.
14 *Gazette*, 27 November 1858.
15 *Gazette*, 29 November 1879.
16 *Gazette*, 20 October 1838.
17 *Herald*, 14 January 1860.
18 *Gazette*, 4 August 1876 and 26 February 1881.
19 See Beechey, 'The Irish in York'.
20 *Ibid.* pp. 174–5.
21 *Gazette*, 31 May 1862.
22 *Gazette*, 24 February 1855.
23 *Gazette*, 13 October 1877.
24 *Gazette*, 23 May 1863.
25 *Gazette*, 24 December 1853.
26 *Gazette*, 7 August 1858.
27 *Gazette*, 1 March 1856.
28 *Herald*, 31 October 1863.
29 See, for example, Logan, *The Great Social Evil*, p. 77.
30 *Gazette*, 22 January 1887.
31 *Gazette*, 11 October 1856 and 10 May 1862.
32 *Gazette*, 30 November 1839.

33 *Gazette*, 7 December 1861.
34 *Gazette*, 20 October 1855.
35 *Gazette*, 30 June 1877.
36 Tait, *Magdalenism*, p. 167. See also Logan, *op. cit.* p. 77.
37 *Herald*, 31 October 1863.
38 *Herald*, 16 April 1853.
39 *Gazette*, 30 September 1876.
40 *Gazette*, 31 October 1857.
41 *Gazette*, 23 January 1858.
42 *Gazette*, 12 September 1868.
43 *Gazette*, 19 May 1860, 24 May 1862, 7 February 1863, 28 January and 1 April 1865, and Poor Law, June 1873.
44 Acton, quoted in Marcus, *The Other Victorians*, p. 31.
45 *Gazette*, 12 and 19 December 1857.
46 *Gazette*, 16 November 1861.
47 *Gazette*, 21 October 1876.
48 *Gazette*, 14 April 1860.
49 *Gazette*, 7 December and 14 December 1861.
50 York Society for the Prevention of Youthful Depravity poster, reproduced in Fig. 25.
51 *Herald*, 4 January 1862.
52 *Gazette*, 2 September 1837.
53 *Herald*, 1 and 3 January 1878.

5 DRINK, DESTITUTION AND DISEASE

1   *Gazette*, 5 September 1863.
2   *Gazette*, 28 September 1867.
3   *Gazette*, 2 November 1867.
4   *Gazette*, 20 June 1868.
5   *Gazette*, 8 July and 15 August 1868.
6   *Gazette*, 22 February 1869.
7   *Gazette*, 17 April 1869.
8   *Gazette*, 4 September 1869.
9   *Gazette*, 6 November 1869.
10 *Gazette*, 13 May 1871.
11 *Gazette*, 27 May 1871.
12 Poor Law, December 1871.
13 *Gazette*, 9 December 1871.
14 *Gazette*, 6 April 1872.
15 *Gazette*, 25 May 1872.
16 *Gazette*, 21 June 1873.
17 *Gazette*, 8 January 1876.
18 *Gazette*, 5 May 1877.
19 *Gazette*, 10 May 1883.
20 *Gazette*, 29 March 1884.
21 *Gazette*, 10 April 1869.

22   Poor Law, September 1864.
23   See, for example, *Gazette*, 14 January 1865 and 7 April 1866. Also, Poor Law, December 1867.
24   *Gazette*, 9 May 1868.
25   Poor Law, December 1868.
26   Poor Law, March 1872.
27   *Gazette*, 9 December 1876.
28   *Gazette*, 5 February 1881.
29   Mrs Gaskell, *Mary Barton*, Everyman Edition (London, 1965) p. 154.
30   See R. Deacon, *The Private Life of Mr. Gladstone* (London, 1965).
31   Logan, *The Great Social Evil*, pp. 51–2.
32   Tait, *Magdalenism*, p. 260.
33   J. Miller, *Prostitution – Its Cause and Cure*, pamphlet, 1859; quoted in Logan, *op. cit.* p. 59.
34   Poor Law, December 1859.
35   Watch Committee, 5 August and 24 September 1846.
36   Watch Committee, 17 December 1846.
37   Watch Committee, 20 October 1849.
38   Watch Committee, 9 July 1851.
39   Watch Committee, 26 November 1856 and 7 January 1857.
40   Watch Committee, 13 March 1866.
41   Watch Committee, 7 December 1870, 4 January 1871 and 2 December 1874.
42   Watch Committee, 6 December 1871.
43   *Gazette*, 8 January 1886.
44   *Gazette*, 23 January 1864.
45   *Gazette*, 15 January 1853.
46   *Gazette*, 14 February 1857.
47   *Gazette*, 27 November 1880.
48   *Gazette*, 6 August 1870.
49   *Gazette*, 28 January 1860.
50   *Herald*, 25 October 1862.
51   *Gazette*, 2 December 1865.
52   *Gazette*, 22 October 1864.
53   *Gazette*, 20 April, 12 October and 16 November 1839, 28 November 1840, 30 September 1843 and 3 February 1844.
54   *Gazette*, 6 January 1877.
55   Margaret Riley's thirty-fifth appearance at court was reported in the *Gazette* on 23 June 1883.
56   *Gazette*, 19 June 1886.
57   *Gazette*, 29 September 1877.
58   *Gazette*, 22 and 29 November and 13 December 1879.
59   *Gazette*, 16 September 1843.
60   *Gazette*, 27 July 1878 and 5 March 1881.
61   *Gazette*, 5 January 1867 and Sessions 4 February 1867.
62   *Notes on Work Amongst the Fallen and Cautionary List*, Number 17 (London, May 1891) p. 99.

63 *Ibid.*
64 Logan, *op. cit.* p. 47.
65 Poor Law, September 1861 and *Gazette*, 10 July 1869.
66 Poor Law, September 1859 and *Gazette*, 18 April 1863.
67 Poor Law, March 1864 and *Gazette*, 23 August 1873.
68 These girls were admitted to the workhouse in March 1864, December 1853 and December 1861 respectively. They were subsequently reported in the *Gazette* as prostituting themselves in 5 December 1868, 7 November 1857 and 21 May 1871 respectively.
69 Poor Law, June 1874.
70 *Annual Report*, 1900 (York, 1901) p. 6.
71 *Ibid.*
72 See, for example, K. S. Inglis, *Churches and the Working Classes in Victorian England* (London, 1963).

6 RESCUE AND REFORM

1 Report from the Select Committee of the House of Lords on the Contagious Diseases Act, 1866; together with the Proceedings of the Committee, Minutes of Evidence and Appendix. Session 1867–8. In K. Nield, *Prostitution*, p. 200.
2 Nield, *op. cit.* p. 189.
3 Nield, *op. cit.* p. 193.
4 Nield, *op. cit.* p. 197.
5 York Penitentiary Society Miscellaneous Correspondence.
6 During the period, the post-Famine Irish community alone formed seven to eight per cent of the population in the city, and there were, of course, additional Catholics in York.
7 R. Deacon, *The Private Life of Mr. Gladstone*, p. 178.
8 *Yorkshireman*, 9 February 1850.
9 York Penitentiary Society Miscellaneous Correspondence.
10 Refuge Committee, January 1853.
11 Refuge Committee, November 1860.
12 Poor Law, March 1862.
13 *Gazette*, 18 October 1862 and 21 January 1865.
14 Sessions, 18 July 1865.
15 Sessions, 30 May 1867.
16 See, for example, *Annual Reports*, 1863 and 1883.
17 *Annual Report*, 1889.
18 *Annual Report*, 1917.
19 See D. Hudson, *Munby, Man of Two Worlds* (London, 1972).
20 *Gazette*, 28 September 1861.
21 *Gazette*, 16 November 1861. See page 129.
22 *Gazette*, 23 November 1861.
23 *Gazette*, 24 June 1882.
24 *Annual Report*, 1875.
25 *Gazette*, 4 March 1911.

Bibliography

BOOKS, ARTICLES AND PAMPHLETS

Acton, W. *Prostitution* (ed.) P. Fryer (London, 1968)

Armstrong, W. *Stability and Change in an English County Town. A Social Study of York 1801–1851* (Cambridge, 1974)

Banks, J. A. *Prosperity and Parenthood* (London, 1954)

Beechey, F. E. 'The Irish in York 1840–1875', University of York D. Phil. Thesis, 1976.

Butler, Josephine E. *Personal Reminiscences of a Great Crusade* (London, 1896)

Caine, C. *Martial Annals of the City of York* (London, 1893)

Cominos, P. 'Late Victorian Respectability and the Social System', *International Review of Social History*, VIII, 1963.

Critchley, T. A. *A History of the Police in England and Wales, 900–1926* (London, 1967)

Deacon, R. *The Private Life of Mr. Gladstone* (London, 1965)

Drake, F. *Eboracum* (London, 1736)

Fawcett, M. G. and Turner, E. M. *Josephine Butler, Her Work and Principles and their Meaning for the Twentieth Century* (London, 1927)

Finnegan, F. E. and Sigsworth, E. M. *Poverty and Social Policy: An Historical Study of Batley* (York, 1978)

Fryer, P. (ed.) W. Acton, *Prostitution* (London, 1968)

Gaskell, E. C. *Mary Barton*, Everyman Edition (London, 1965)

Hargrove, W. *History of York*, 2 Vols. (York, 1818)

Harrison, B. *Drink and the Victorians, the Temperance Question in England, 1815–72* (London, 1971)

Henriques, F. *Modern Sexuality* (London, 1968)

Hudson, D. *Munby, Man of Two Worlds, The Life and Diaries of Arthur J. Munby, 1828–1910* (London, 1972)

Inglis, K. S. *Churches and the Working Classes in Victorian England* (London, 1963)

Laycock, T. *Report on the State of the City of York. First Report of the Royal Commission for Enquiring into the State of Large and Populous Districts.* Parliamentary Papers 1844, XVII.

Logan, W. *The Great Social Evil; its Causes, Extent, Results and Remedies* (London, 1871)

Marcus, S. *The Other Victorians* (London, 1971)

Nield, K. *Prostitution in the Victorian Age* (Farnborough, 1973)

Pearl, C. *The Girl with the Swansdown Seat* (London, 1955)

Pope-Hennessy, J. *Queen Mary* (London, 1959)

Quennell, P. (ed.) *London's Underworld* (London, 1969)

Reformatory and Refuge Journal (London, 1899)

Rowntree, B. S. *Poverty: A Study of Town Life* (London, 1901)

Smith, J. *Report to the General Board of Health on a Preliminary Enquiry into . . . the Sanitary Condition of York*. H.M.S.O. 1850.

Smith, E. H. *Report on the Sanitary Condition of the Hungate District* (York, 1908)

Tait, W. *Magdalenism, An Inquiry into the Extent, Causes and Consequences of Prostitution in Edinburgh* (Edinburgh, 1841, later edition 1852)

Thomas, K. 'The Double Standard', *Journal of the History of Ideas*, XX, 1959.

Victoria County History, A History of Yorkshire, The City of York (ed.) P. M. Tillott (Oxford, 1961)

NEWSPAPERS

York Herald
Yorkshire Gazette
Yorkshireman
The Shield, 1870–6
The National League Journal, 1874–84

ARCHIVES

York Minster Library
Petition to the Ecclesiastical Commissioners for England and Wales, July 1844 (manuscript)

York City Library
Census Enumerators' Notebooks (microfilms)
1841: HO 107. 1353, 1354 and 1355.
1851: HO 107. 2353, 2354, 2355 and 2356.
1861: RG 9. 3548, 3549, 3550, 3551, 3552, 3553, 3554, 3555, 3556 and 3557.
1871: RG 10. 4743, 4744, 4745, 4746 and 4757. 4750, 4751, 4752, 4753, 4754 and 4755.
Hungate Mission Schools. Annual Reports 1864–72. Minute Books 1861–1926.
York Board of Guardians. Application and Report Books, 1840–87.
York Corporation Watch Committee. Reports, 1837–87.
Health Department Records. Hungate Area, 1907–8.

York Penitentiary Society Records. Manuscript and printed *Annual Reports*, 1822–43 and printed *Annual Reports*, 1845–1919.
Female Mission to the Fallen. *Annual Reports*, 1892 and 1901.
Ladies' Committee Books, 1845–64 and 1881–7.
Ladies' Visitors' Books.
Miscellaneous Correspondence.
Report on Female Prostitution, Edinburgh, 1857.
York Association for the Care of Young Girls. Annual Reports, 1890, 1891, 1894 and 1895.
York Society for the Prevention of Youthful Depravity, Second Report (York, 1861)
York Quarter Sessions. Minute Books.

Index

Of the prostitutes and brothel-keepers referred to in the text, only those thought to be of particular interest have been included in the index. Their names are printed in italics.

The
Nonsexist
Communicator

Bobbye D. Sorrels has published extensively on topics related to women, sexism, and the business world. She speaks often to community and academic groups on nonsexist communication and has given testimony before U.S. Senate committees on women's rights and women in business.

Prentice-Hall International, Inc., *London*
Prentice-Hall of Australia Pty. Limited, *Sydney*
Prentice-Hall Canada Inc., *Toronto*
Prentice-Hall of India Private Limited, *New Delhi*
Prentice-Hall of Japan, Inc., *Tokyo*
Prentice-Hall of Southeast Asia Pte. Ltd., *Singapore*
Whitehall Books Limited, *Wellington, New Zealand*
Editora Prentice-Hall do Brasil Ltda., *Rio de Janeiro*

Bobbye D. Sorrels

The
Nonsexist
Communicator

*Solving the Problems of Gender
and Awkwardness in Modern English*

A SPECTRUM BOOK

Prentice-Hall, Inc., Englewood Cliffs, New Jersey 07632

Library of Congress Cataloging in Publication Data

Sorrels, Bobbye.
    The nonsexist communicator.

    "A Spectrum Book."
    Bibliography: p.
    Includes index.
        1. Sexism in communication.   2. English language—
Sex differences.   I. Title.
    P86.S48S65 1983   001.54   82-24131
    ISBN 0-13-623413-5
    ISBN 0-13-623405-4 (pbk.)

10 9 8 7 6 5 4 3 2 1

ISBN 0-13-623413-5

ISBN 0-13-623405-4 {PBK.}

Editorial/production supervision by Maxine Bartow
Cover design © 1983 by Jeannette Jacobs
Manufacturing buyer: Christine Johnston

This book is available at a special discount when ordered
in bulk quantities. Contact Prentice-Hall, Inc., General
Publishing Division, Special Sales, Englewood Cliffs, N.J. 07632.

CONTENTS

PREFACE

The Nonsexist Communicator provides help for eradicating the sexist communication found in personal and organizational life. Its objectives include (1) increasing understanding of sexist communication, (2) deepening the commitment to eliminate sexist communication, and (3) providing practical suggestions for achieving a nonsexist communication style. The book will prove particularly helpful to the many people of good intention who, through years of cultural conditioning, have become unwitting transmitters of sexism.

Written, oral, and nonverbal messages of individuals and organizations teach and perpetuate sexism. Only through the direct revision and correction of sexist communication patterns can women and men begin to realize the greater potential that all people can share. As an action guide, *The Nonsexist Communicator* provides a valuable tool for effectively eliminating sexist words and nonverbal sexist behavior in all our important human encounters and relationships.

The body of the book has eight chapters. Chapters 1 and 2 define the concept of nonsexist communication, give ten reasons for using it, and introduce the world of reverse sexism. Chapters 3 through 8 provide guidelines for overcoming sexism in written, oral, and nonverbal communication. These chapters also include exercises for applying the guidelines. Appendix A contains an extensive listing of nonsexist words and phrases. Appendix B provides suggested solutions for the exercises in Chapters 3 through 8.

The Nonsexist Communicator presents many examples of messages packed artificially full of sexist expressions. It also includes a number of sweeping generalizations—to which exceptions obviously exist. However, the deliberate use of extremes should help to pull the pendulum from the opposite sexist extreme at which society has positioned it.

My thanks go to my daughter Lynne Persing for her fine suggestions; to Martha Perry and Jan Tuepker for their capable typewriting; to my family, colleagues, and students for their support of the project; and to David Gootnick for suggesting and publishing the original book from which this book was adapted.

The
Nonsexist
Communicator

NONSEXIST COMMUNICATION: THE TOOL OF SUCCESSFUL PEOPLE

False images about the relative worth of different kinds of human beings exist on many communication fronts. Race, ethnicity, nationality, culture, age, handicap, religion, occupation, appearance, and sex represent some of these fronts. However, sexist communication creates the most pervasive falsity—an image of the female as inferior to the male. Therefore, although we must attack discriminatory communication on all fronts, this book addresses the one type of negative discrimination most common to all our interactions—sexism.

SEXIST AND NONSEXIST COMMUNICATION

Broadly defined, sexist communication precasts either females or males into roles on the basis of sex alone. Conversely, then, nonsexist communication does not precast either females or males into roles on the basis of sex alone.

Existing communication patterns arose in a patriarchal culture that defines males as the norm and females as something less than the norm. Therefore, sexism in communication acts more negatively on females than on males, because it automatically both limits and subordinates them. Sexist communication assumes that anything male possesses inherent superiority over anything female; nonsexist communication does not.

Ultimately, however, sexist communication affects both sexes negatively. Therefore, although this book concentrates on the more unjust sexist communication—that heaped on females—it also accords appropriate treatment to the communication sexism that affects males specifically. In reality, all communication that debilitates females also debilitates males, for if any system diminishes a part of the species, it diminishes all of it.

WHY NONSEXIST COMMUNICATION?

Successful contemporary communicators use nonsexist patterns of expression for many reasons, including:

1. Whereas in the past society virtually restricted males to certain roles and females to others, such restrictions no longer exist. Therefore, communication symbols based on past roles simply do not portray current conditions properly. Instead, they distort reality. They constitute an anachronism in the course of human events. Cannot and do not women work as police officers, deliver mail, practice law, and serve in the army? Yet, the words *policeman*, *mailman*, *lady attorney*, and *infantryman* deny that they can and do perform these roles.

2. The use of certain words sometimes to mean males and sometimes to mean both males and females creates a great deal of confusion. For example, a national civic organization has gone to court to try to continue to exclude women from its membership, using as its major argument that the "man" words in its constitution and bylaws mean men only. Yet, to refer to all people in their public pronouncements, they use such words and phrases as *man*, *mankind*, and "brotherhood of man."

3. No set of communication symbols is permanently chiseled in stone. Humans create symbols to serve their needs for active interchange. When the symbols no longer serve those needs, humans change them. Sexist symbols do not serve human needs.

4. An old saying suggests, "Tell me a people's language, and I'll tell you the values of that people." With an English language that portrays males as the norm and females as abnormal or subnormal, those who analyze and practice the language must believe that females have less value than males.

5. A basic sense of fairness requires the equal treatment of men and women in the communication symbols that so define the lives of the people

who use them. Sexist communication limits and devalues all humans with outmoded language.

6. A basic rule for good communication involves analyzing the audience. Therefore, wise communicators understand and apply the knowledge that many people, both females and males, react negatively to sexist communication.

7. Because sexist communication tends to elevate males and debase females, it too often creates a self-fulfilling prophecy of inferiority and failure for women and aggressively insensitive machismo for men. The consequent loss of the potential contributions of both men and women represents a waste that a society can ill afford.

8. The conversion from sexist to nonsexist communication need not involve clumsy, uncomfortable, or ungrammatical expressions. Natural, graceful, and grammatically correct nonsexist patterns come relatively easily to one who has the commitment to seek them.

9. Sexist communication patterns expose their users as people who do not stay abreast of contemporary communication practices.

10. Sexist communication patterns may have legal implications. People have won lawsuits when sexist communication has contributed to discriminatory practices.

STEREOTYPING IN COMMUNICATION

Mankind	Modern man	The taxpayer should write his congressman
Brotherhood of man	Sons of man	
Forefathers	City fathers	Each manager should be sure that his secretary does her work well
Brotherly love	Lady engineer	
Businessman	Male nurse	All men are created equal
Men working	The working man	Feed your dog his favorite—Woofies
Poetess	John Q. Citizen	
King's English	Old maid	Chairman of the board
Man and wife	Dumb blonde	A commercial showing a man in a business suit and a woman in an apron
Housewife	Mrs. John Smith	

Do these words and scenes seem natural to you? If they do, take another look. You'll notice that each of these expressions reinforces a system that stereotypes the sexes, with the male in the dominant roles. The following twenty examples illustrate such stereotyping:

1. Joseph Schneider and Sally Hacker conducted research to test the hypothesis that people understand the word *man* to embrace *woman*. They asked 150 college students to find pictures to illustrate such sociology textbook

chapters as "Social Man," "Political Man," and "Industrial Man." They asked another 150 students to find pictures to illustrate corresponding chapters titled "Society," "Political Behavior," and "Industrial Life." Analysis of the collections showed that in the minds of both men and women, the use of the word *man* created, to a statistically significant degree, images of males only. The corresponding chapter titles without the word *man* created images of both females and males. Differences of 30 to 40 percent occurred.[1]

2. In spite of the admonitions of Abigail Adams and others, the founding instruments of the United States include male forms such as "all men are created equal." The Fourteenth Amendment ensured rights only to the black *man*, making the Nineteenth Amendment necessary to gain even the right to vote for women. Only the ratification of the Twenty-seventh Amendment will ensure equality of the sexes under the law.

3. Only about 4 percent of the index entries in the books *Civilisation* and *Alistair Cooke's America* refer to women.[2]

4. Documentaries about civilization such as "The Ascent of Man" communicate with both words and pictures that the male is the species and the female the subspecies.

5. Many people resist the idea of women in the clergy in the church, using the deity-as-male words in the Bible as a significant part of their argument. Yet, the root words for the deity did not have either male or female gender in Hebrew and Greek.

6. Even during the reign of Queen Elizabeth II, people still refer to the "King's English."

7. Textbooks usually contain highly sexist language, including such expressions as *businessman*, and "the doctor . . . he; the nurse . . . she." Some textbook passages even include overt sexist statements. For example, one reports that business, particularly small business, forms one of the last strongholds against women.[3]

8. A television news show item about the typical voter includes a comment about *his* wife and kids.

9. People address as *Mrs.* a woman who has a doctor's degree but

---

[1]Joseph W. Schneider and Sally L. Hacker, "Sex Role Imagery and Use of the Generic 'Man' in Introductory Texts: A Case in the Sociology of Sociology," paper presented at the section on Sociology of Sex Roles, American Sociological Association Annual Meetings, August 1973, New Orleans.

[2]Kenneth Clark, *Civilisation: A Personal View* (New York: Harper & Row, 1969), pp. 349–359; Alistair Cooke, *Alistair Cooke's America* (New York: Alfred A. Knopf, 1974), pp. 397–400.

[3]For a review of a particularly sexist treatment of the role of the woman related to the world of small business, read Clifford M. Baumback and Joseph R. Mancuso, *Entrepreneurship and Venture Management* (Englewood Cliffs, N.J.: Prentice-Hall, Inc., 1975), p. 34.

happens to be married, even after she asks her colleagues to call her *Ms.*, *Dr.*, or her first name.

10. A woman allows herself to be called "girl" in the same breath with a man's being called a "man."

11. When a woman asks not to be called "chairman," chuckles ensue. If some people agree with her, the usual compromise involves calling the man "chairman" and the woman "chairperson."

12. If both a man and woman live in the same house, society automatically considers the man the head of the household. Only if no man is present does society consider a woman the head of the household.

13. "Brotherhood," "brotherly love," and "the brotherhood of man" hold connotations as warm and encompassing words. Yet, "sisterhood," "that old sister," and "that weak sister" do not possess warm connotations.

14. Both men and women accept and defend incongruities such as "Madam Chairman."

15. The words *aggressive* and *competitive* have positive meanings when applied to a man. Yet, "an aggressive and competitive woman" has a negative meaning.

16. Such diminishing suffixes as *-ess*, *-ette*, and *-ix* appear in words that do not include *man* (*authoress, majorette, executrix*). Is the purpose to keep the key word "pure," that is, male?

17. A potential client goes into an architectural office and tells the woman there that he wants to see the architect. She says she is the architect.

18. A small girl tries to retain her identity by calling herself a "cowboy girl."

19. An old riddle asks how a baseball game could have had a score of 5 to 3 when not a man reached first base. The answer is, of course, that the players were women.

20. One of the worst things that can happen to a boy is to have a girl's name. Just think of the plight of the boy named Sue made famous by a country and western singer. Yet, many people accept a boy's name for a girl as all right.

Serious consideration of the preceding twenty situations leads to the understanding that our culture thrusts woman into the condition of the lesser, the secondary, the subspecies, the atypical, the abnormal, the adjunct. It subordinates her to the male, who is portrayed as the superior, the species, the typical, the norm, the standard. It reflects the assumption that all people are male until proven female. If we define man's humanity in terms that create less than full humanity for the woman, we damage both sexes.

For a positive solution, then, the egalitarian communicator will not use male words to include females. Nor will that communicator treat the male as the norm by using neutral words, such as *politician*, *pilot*, and *American*, as if they connote maleness.

Removing man-as-the-norm language takes concentrated effort. But belabored or unnatural-sounding words are not necessary; for example, the following expressions show nonsexist parallels to the sexist words and scenes used earlier in this section:

Humankind or humanity	Nurse	All people are created equal
Human family	The worker	Feed your dog every dog's favorite—Woofies
Forebears	Citizen	
Human love	Unmarried person or single person	
Businesspeople		Chair of the board
Working	Person	A commercial showing a man and a woman both in business suits or both in aprons or the woman in a business suit and the man in an apron
Poet	Ms. Vera Smith or Vera Smith	
Perfect English		
Husband and wife	Taxpayers should write their representatives	
Homemaker		
Modern people	Each manager should be sure that the secretary does the work well	
Children of humanity		
City leaders		
Engineer		

THE INSTITUTIONALIZATION OF SEXISM BY THE ACADEMIC COMMUNITY

Through their dictionaries, grammar rules, guidelines, handbooks, lectures, and speeches, professors, teachers, speakers, and writers have done amazingly well at institutionalizing communication sexism. If you hear academic people complain that they are not reaching students, do not believe them—they are.

History courses have their "mankind" and "man" and a dearth of coverage of the contributions of women to civilization. Business courses deal with the "businessman," "the manager . . . he," and "the secretary . . . she." Children's books paint the "typical" family picture: boys as adventurers, girls as little mothers, mothers as happy homemakers, and fathers as providers. But the greatest impact comes from the English classes. Use of the male-as-generic pronoun forms one of the most prevalent types of sexism in the language, and English learning experiences assure that communicators practice that sexism.

Studies show, however, that male pronouns usually appear more frequently than female pronouns, particularly in textbooks, simply because writers choose to write about more males than females. Thus, another form of sexism arises; society seems to view males and stereotyped male roles as more important central characters than females and stereotyped female roles.

Kate Millett extends the concept of the contributions of academia to the perpetuation of sexism. She writes,

> The continual surveillance in which she is held tends to perpetuate the infantilization of women even in situations such as those of higher education. The female is continually obliged to seek survival or advancement through the approval of males as those who hold power . . . she is customarily deprived of any but the most trivial sources of dignity or self-respect. In many patriarchies, language, as well as cultural tradition, reserve the human condition for the male. . . . general application favors the male far more often than the female as referent, or even sole referent.[4]

Not until academic leaders engage in the cause of nonsexist communication will it become the norm. Unfortunately, too many of them worship tradition to the detriment of women's psyches. Many who study communication want to expose communication patterns as a major component in the subordination of women and to shake academicians into removing the bias that pervades their work.

And changes are coming. Many publishing firms require authors to write in nonsexist fashion. Many writers, speakers, and instructors now use nonsexist language. With each new advocate, the sexism obstacle seems to become less insurmountable.

Everyone can bring her or his advocacy of nonsexism to bear on the academic community. Some of us will be asked to write articles for publications affecting the academic community, others will be asked to speak to classes, still others will enroll in classes, and all can write to authors of books, guidelines, manuals, and articles. Through all these avenues we can promote nonsexism. And, though we may sometimes feel lonely as we do so, the results reward our perseverance. A few comments to lecturers and speakers, some articles and speeches, and a few letters to authors will start ripples that will join others' ripples and eventually swell into the waves that can wash away communication sexism. With its eradication will come the tide of a self-fulfilling prophecy of a nonsexist culture.

[4]Kate Millett, *Sexual Politics* (New York: Doubleday & Co., Inc., 1969; Avon Books, 1971), p. 83. Used by permission of Doubleday & Company Inc. and Granada Publishing Limited.

2

THE COMMITMENT TO NONSEXIST COMMUNICATION

The keys to any social reform lie in the acceptance of the need for correction and the commitment to finding ways to make that correction. Thus, this book exists to help people develop or deepen their commitment to nonsexist communication and to suggest ways that it may become a reality.

Role reversal provides one vehicle for understanding how sexism reinforces the myth of male superiority and insidiously gnaws away at the female's sense of identity and self-worth. The following example, "A Tale of Two Sexes," involves a compressed satirical scene from a business office—and a reversal of sexist communication.

A TALE OF TWO SEXES

Picture the national suite of offices for a major manufacturing firm—a firm employing 50 percent women and 50 percent men in its factories scattered across the country. A top officer of the corporation enters the outer office.

9

"Good morning, ma'am," the office workers chant.

"Good morning, boys," Ms. Janesdaughter replies, as she savors the panorama of beautiful faces and bodies.[1] "Come in immediately, Freddie," she adds to a particularly attractive brunette.

As Freddie slips through the door, Janesdaughter observes the young man's well-endowed, but slender figure. Freddie sits in the chair and crosses his long and shapely legs.

Janesdaughter recites the day's tasks; Freddie writes frantically.

"First, Freddie, go out on your lunch hour today and buy my husband an anniversary gift. I've tried and I can't suit the little man; he's just a househusband, you know. And, anyway, as my right-hand woman, you're good at shopping for another boy.

"Call Dr. Anders's nurse and have him remind Anders of our church finance committee meeting. You know, Anders's nurse is so good; he supports her totally, yet knows his place.

"Make reservations for a flight to the City of Sisterly Love for the eastern district meeting." Mumbling half to herself, Janesdaughter adds: "I hope the stewards are better looking this time. You know, I learned that they're letting them marry, be fathers, and stay on till they're old—even in their forties!

"Get me a cup of coffee. I do hope it will be better than yesterday's when the women from the shop were here."

Freddie giggles apologetically, and in his haste drops a spoon on the carpet. He mutters something about being so clumsy and thinks: "Why am I such a bungler? No wonder Ms. Janesdaughter gets so irritated at me."

Janesdaughter sips the coffee and says, "That's a good boy, Freddie.

"Next, call a meeting for 2:30 for the department heads. Include the guys from personnel and that new affirmative action officer. The chairwoman of the board is coming over too, so be sure the board room is in top shape. Although the chairwoman serves only as a figurehead, he is married to the mayor, and we want to impress him because of her. Be sure that your work station is womanned while you attend the meeting. Have that new boy Joey Whitewoman at the meeting as a backup woman for you.

"Now, let's get out some letters. First, Della Knox will retire next month; thus, I'll write her husband and ask him what retirement gift would please her. Address the letter to Mrd. Della Knox, The Krauss Manufacturing Co., 203 North Seventeenth, Anywhere, Alabama, Ladies. . . .[2]

"Oh, yes, Freddie, stay for a six o'clock meeting Thursday evening. The

---

[1]In "A Tale of Two Sexes" all women have the non-marital-status courtesy title *Ms.* (pronounced "miz").

[2]In "A Tale of Two Sexes" all men have marital-status courtesy titles. *Mngl.* (pronounced "mingle"), the merging of *M* and *single*, refers to single men. *Mrd.* (pronounced "murd"), the abbreviation for "married," refers to married men.

decorators will be here, and you boys have good color sense and man's intuition about such things."

After several more letters and instructions, Janesdaughter rises and puts her hand on Freddie's shoulder, saying, "Your new suit is certainly pretty—and fits well in all the right places. I'm glad, because I want you to look good for the chairwoman."

At 3:30 that afternoon, the meeting nears an end. Seated at one end of the table is Janesdaughter and at the other end, Chairwoman Eddie Jones. The department heads (all females) sit on one side of the table, and the head of personnel (Davie Nelsdaughter), the affirmative action officer (Jimmy French), and two aides (all males) sit on the other side. Freddie and Joey hurriedly refill the coffee cups and return to their places behind Janesdaughter to continue making notes.

Janesdaughter speaks: "Now, women, let's take care of some other matters.

"I've become concerned that we've been calling Cleo the 'mail girl.' That's a put-down; she is a grown woman, after all. From now on, we'll call her the 'mail clerk.' "

At that opening, Jimmy French hesitantly says that some of the men in the firm do not like being called "boys" or "guys" or included in such terms as "women" or "chairwomen." He asks whether they might be called "men," "chairpersons," "chairmen," and similar words.

A ripple of laughter goes around the table, and for the first time that afternoon, Chairwoman Jones joins the discussion:

"That's just a lot of 'men's lib' talk. My friends and I enjoy being called 'boys.' It makes us feel young—and you know how a boy is about his age." (Mrd. Jones giggles.) " 'Chairperson' and 'chairman' sound so strange to me. A few radicals can't be allowed to destroy the Queen's English. And, if the 'men's libbers' are concerned about equal pay and such things, they should concentrate on them; words just don't make that much difference.

"We boys accept that behind every good woman, there's a good man and live our lives through our wives. We boys sometimes work through men's auxiliaries, but subordinate ourselves so that we don't destroy the female ego. Why, I've always been protected by my wife and have never been discriminated against; this idea about discrimination is just an old husbands' tale. I'm proud to be Mrd. Penelope Jones and care for her children."

Nelsdaughter says, "Oh, I agree with you. I'm sure that Jimmy does too and that he was just conveying a request from a few of the boys. He's had some three-women committees at work, and only one committee made such a recommendation."

"Yes, that's true," Jimmy replies, nervously.

Condescendingly, Janesdaughter says, "Oh, I understand. But it's just too much to expect each person to change her language habits. Would it be fair for me to have to give up being called, say, a committee 'chairwoman' when that's what I'm accustomed to being called? And, after all, parliamentary rules list 'chairwoman' as appropriate, and allow for the use of 'Sir Chairwoman' for a boy.

"Mngl. Whitewoman, what do you think?"

Squirming, Joey answers, "Well, when I was a coed in my freshwoman courses, I was taught to use the female forms; so they must be right."

Freddie adds, "I agree. My business sorority reports that most boys prefer the feminine words."

As Janesdaughter starts to move on, Lou Smith, who heads the finance department, speaks briefly about how she supports the men in their movement for liberation from stereotyped sex roles. Janesdaughter looks startled because she has known Smith only in the capacity of an outstanding finance woman, never dreaming that she embraces any part of the "men's lib" movement. The others also wonder about Smith, thinking that she must be being rooster-pecked and losing her femininity.

Janesdaughter hurries on through the rest of the meeting, with these instructions and comments.

"Allen, have your boy check with mine for completion of the report about the new womanmade fiber we're considering.

"Baker, get that memo out about the new workwomen's compensation provisions.

"Davie, I understand that some customers raise their eyebrows because the husband of a saleswoman—Gordon is the name, I believe—did not have his name changed when they married. I do feel sorry for her. Would you see if you can't have that corrected? Businesswomen are pretty conservative and just don't think it's right for a woman and her husband to have different last names, especially when they have children, as Gordon and her husband do. Even if her husband is a policewoman, I believe he should change his legal name. The woman is the head of the household, and her career is more important than her husband's. These working husbands and fathers do cause problems, don't they!

"Along that same line, Davie, do some checking on Dodd's husband. I hear he's been acting like a tramp. Excuse the expression, Mrd. Jones." (Mrd. Jones giggles and looks down shyly.) "That sort of thing does no good for the company image. I do know that he was drinking, was wearing revealing trousers, and was too loud to be masculine at the last company party.

"And that reminds me, is that new boy Alvie Seymour married? He didn't indicate marital status on his employment forms and signs his letters without the parenthetical 'Mngl.' or 'Mrd.' Freddie, get a memo out telling all boys to use the appropriate titles in all their communication. I think married men should be proud to announce to the world their marital status. After all, finding the right woman and fathering daughters form the most important accomplishments in their lives. Besides, I just like to know whether an attractive young thing like Alvie is married or single," she says as she winks at the women present. The women look slyly at one another and smile at the embarrassment shown by the men in the room.

"Speaking of children, did you hear that Selby *finally* had a daughter; she was about to give up after four sons. She's so happy; now she'll finally have someone to pass the business on to and to carry on the Selby bloodline and name.

"Compton, for the next news conference, be ready for a number of questions from the newswomen there about our new southern district acquisition. And see if you can't get the camerawomen to do some more close-ups this time. Somewhere during the news conference, stress how we support the working woman in her struggle for enough take-home pay to offset the effects of inflation and how we're working to bring labor and management together into a true sisterhood of women. Add that our sympathies are with the househusband in his efforts at stretching his household allowance.

"Baker, communicate through the company newsletter *The Workwoman* our pleasure at the way that the line forewomen and craftswomen have performed on this last crash project.

"Davie, just call Keeley Boy for some temporary womanpower for that rush job next week.

"Davie, you're simply going to have to hire some more gentleman saleswomen. But be sure that they can type. We're just not making sufficient progress toward our affirmative action plan goals. And, yes, pursue the possibility of obtaining a boy engineer trainee for the same reason. That man lawyer was over here from the local government office again the other day criticizing us for our hiring practices. I just cannot see why the government makes businesswomen do this. Don't they realize that these rules keep good women responsible for husbands and children from jobs and promotions? If boys would just stay home with their children where they belong, all our social problems would be solved. After all, every child has a right to have her father at home. I suppose we do have to hire a few boys and even pay them women's wages, but it's hard to do when they're only working for a second income, they're just working househusbands, and they're here for pin money or the fun of it.

"Compton, back to that news conference: Next week is National Sisterhood Week, so be sure to stress that the goal of our firm is the furtherance of all womankind—the improvement of the lot of the family of women and of this land that our foremothers established. And, say, so that we'll look better to the 'men's libbers' and the government, take one of our best-looking boys along and let him be the spokeswoman on some simple matter that he can handle. Be sure that his subject won't raise any difficult questions from the newswomen. Get a boy who has a bit of showwomanship in him.

"And also announce the promotion of Charlie Engels to supervisor of the typing pool, particularly stressing that he is married, has four children, is a good-looking redhead, and was a cheerleader and winner of a handsomeness pageant in high school. You might also note that in his first year with us, the women in the office chose him to be the 1967 Company Sweetheart." Janesdaughter adds as an aside: "Although the way he's let himself go, you'd never know it now." The women nod and chuckle in agreement.

"Baker, stress through a memo to all branches that the new savings plan for the workwoman is of major benefit to her because we are now matching her contribution dollar for dollar."

Turning to Nelsdaughter: "Now, Davie, for filling Louie's position in my front office, I've decided on Johnnie Green from among the applicants you sent me. I know he's a divorcé and probably less qualified than the others. I know, too, that Billy Lilsdaughter has had more experience and would, no doubt, do a better job of typing and filing. But we just can't have an old, unattractive boy like him up there. Johnnie is young and good looking and will learn, I'm sure; at least he'll not turn off the women as they enter the office. Besides, with gams like his, he doesn't need skills.

"And for the new section manager, I'm impressed with Joan Sells and her qualifications. She's a real woman's woman. But I haven't met her husband yet. Has anyone heard whether he's attractive? I surely hope that Sells doesn't let him work; our aspiring young women's husbands just must be available for entertaining customers and personnel from other districts. I suppose we could allow him to do some noncontroversial volunteer work. I'll just have to meet and know more about Sells's husband before I can decide to hire her.

"Concerning the jealousies that arise when we promote a boy to supervise other boys, I can't give you an answer. You know how boys are. I do know that boys prefer women supervisors and really can't handle power. But we'll have to keep promoting one of them occasionally. It's really too bad that their raging hormones make them so emotional and unfit for management. How fortunate we women are to have clear evidence of our hormonal cycles and climacteric so that we can better cope with them. Because boys do not understand their cycles and male menopause, they can't control their emotions and go around an office sounding like a bunch of fishhusbands. Again, Mrd. Jones, I apologize for my language." Mrd. Jones blinks his eyes demurely and makes no comment.

"Oh, yes, I've been invited to speak to the CPA Husbands next week. I'd appreciate some suggestions for a frivolous subject for that appearance. I'm afraid I don't know too much about the things that boys do.

"Each of you should consider contributing to the campaign of our state's favorite-daughter candidate for the Congress."

In closing the meeting, Janesdaughter stresses the importance of working together, saying, "For success, all it takes is a few good women and teamwork." She adds, "Thank you for joining us, Chairwoman Jones, I appreciated your comments." By way of a final instruction, she says, "Freddie and Joey, get the report of this meeting out before you leave today."

Turning to the female department heads, Janesdaughter says, "It's only four o'clock; we have time for a round of golf before dinner. However, if my husband hasn't planned a better meal than the one last evening, I'd just as soon miss it." They all laugh.

As an afterthought, Janesdaughter says, "Oh, Mrd. Jones, too bad you're not a golfer, but I do understand you're quite a fisherwoman. To each her own."

"Freddie, you and the other women's boys just say that we're in conference if we have any calls. We really are, aren't we, women?" They nod in agreement and chuckle as they leave the board room, now with only the males in it. As the men begin to clean up the coffee cups and ashtrays, they sense that something is wrong, but do not fully comprehend the power possessed by those women who have such control over their lives.

COMMENTS ON "A TALE OF TWO SEXES"

From the deliberately overdrawn "Tale of Two Sexes" comes a sense of how real the pervading influence of communication sexism is. Such sexism, whether written, oral, or nonverbal, creates self-images as second-rate in girls and women and as superior in boys and men. These images introduce all the more danger because we all subconsciously accept them as rooted in nature.

"A Tale of Two Sexes" contains over 200 sexist references that portray the way traditional forms of communication harm all people. Many believe that for a man to be a man, he must be tough, he must be the sole breadwinner, he must not be as responsible for the upbringing of children and maintenance of the home as is the woman, he must be interested in sports, and he must introduce sexual overtones to interpersonal relationships with workers— particularly in the presence of other men. They believe that for a woman to be a woman, she must be passive, she must marry and have children, she must be economically dependent on a man, she must be beautiful, and she must be serving.

The most destructive sexist communication to all people, however, lies in the message that males are superior to females. Ironically, the very myth—male superiority—that debases women also debases men. If a male's psyche rests on the belief of female inferiority—a false belief—then his psyche actually has no foundation. For men to be men, must they be superior to women? For women to be women, must they be inferior to men? No. For men to be men, they must stand on their own merits, and not on the subjugation of women. For women to be women, they must stand on their own merits, and not in a dependency relationship to men.

The myth of male superiority generally springs from the belief that females possess biological and psychological inferiority. However, analysis shows that this belief developed from invalid premises—premises that ignore or deny the impact of social conditions on human development.[3]

In consideration of psychological sex differences, Francine Gordon and Myra Strober reviewed research and reached a number of conclusions, including these four: (1) "Males and females are more alike than is commonly supposed." (2) "Even when biologically based differences are found, the variations within each sex are so large that many individuals reflect characteristics more commonly associated with the opposite sex." (3) "Some [differences] seem more than others to be attributable to social shaping." (4) "Even behavior to which an individual is biologically predisposed . . . is always subject to shaping by societal forces . . . and [does] not take the form of a generalized trait."[4]

This brief treatment of psychological sex differences does not exhaust the topic. Such exhaustion would require countless books. Instead, it establishes that environmental signals to personalities are likely to have more impact on the development of sex differences than do the genitalia and hormonal balances with which people happen to be born. Therefore, the so-called proofs of male superiority function more as self-fulfilling prophecies implicit in a male-supremacist society than as the congenital conditions associated with sex.

GENERAL GUIDELINES FOR NONSEXIST COMMUNICATION

Consciousness raising of the type introduced in "A Tale of Two Sexes" is necessary for a nonsexist communicator. However, the ultimate test lies in the ability to apply nonsexist principles to daily communication acts. To help make the transition from a raised consciousness to consistent application, the remainder of this book provides practical guidelines for overcoming sexist communication. This chapter contains general guidelines; Chapters 3 through 8 develop twenty-two specific guidelines. In addition, Appendix A includes an extensive list of sexist words and phrases along with nonsexist alternatives keyed to the specific guidelines.

[3]For a thorough dismantling of the Freudian, post-Freudian, and functionalist theories of female inferiority, see the section titled "The Reaction in Ideology" in Chapter Four of *Sexual Politics* by Kate Millett (New York: Doubleday & Co., Inc., 1969; Avon Books, 1971).

[4]Francine E. Gordon and Myra H. Strober, *Bringing Women into Management* (New York: McGraw-Hill Book Co., 1975), pp. 35–36.

The following eight general guidelines for nonsexist communication delineate rules, attitudes, and commitment:

1. Commit yourself to remove sexism from all your communication.
2. Practice and reinforce nonsexist communication patterns until they become habitual. The ultimate test is your ability to carry on a nonsexist private conversation and to think in nonsexist terms.
3. Set a nonsexist communication example and direct or persuade others to adopt your example.
4. Use familiar idiom whenever possible, but if you must choose between sexism and the unfamiliar, use the unfamiliar until it becomes familiar.
5. Take care not to arouse negativism in the receiver by using awkward, cumbersome, highly repetitious, or glaring revisions. A sufficient variety of graceful, controlled, sex-positive, dynamic revisions exist so that you can avoid entirely bland or offensive constructions.
6. Use the full range of techniques for correction of sexist communication, including reconstruction, substitution, and omission.
7. Check roots and meanings of words to be sure that the words need to be changed before changing them.
8. Check every outgoing message—whether written, oral, or nonverbal—for sexism before sending it.

3

PRONOUNS,
WORD ENDINGS,
AND NOUNS

One general guideline for conversion from sexist to nonsexist forms of communication is maintaining word patterns familiar to the receiver, at the same time removing all sexist expressions. To extend this guideline, the sincere reviser will not undermine the effort to correct communication sexism by changing already nonsexist words or by using particularly glaring expressions. If we do not wave the flags of alienating and unnecessary revisions in the faces of receivers, the transition from sexist to nonsexist forms will proceed more efficiently and painlessly.

This sexist passage illustrates unnatural expression:

The author of a suggestion for improving management should identify himself by placing his company ID number on the completed form. He should place the suggestion in the box by 5:00 P.M. on Friday for consideration during the following week. After removing the completed forms from the box, the president's secretary will hand them directly to the judging committee chairman for the committee's consideration. Only after the suggestions have been evaluated and ranked and the winners chosen will she look up the ID numbers—and then only so that awards may be distributed to the men who have won.

Now observe the negativism in this extreme revision of the paragraph:

The author/authoress of a suggestion for improving personagement should identify himself or herself by placing his or her company ID number on the completed form. He or she should place the suggestion in the box by 5:00 P.M. Friday for consideration during the following week. After removing the completed forms from the box, the president's secretary will hand them directly to the judgment committee chairman or chairwoperson for the committee's consideration. Only after the suggestions have been evaluated and ranked and the winners chosen will she look up the ID winners—and then only so that awards may be distributed to the men and/or wopeople who have won.

This is clearly an irritating and unsuccessful attempt at nonsexist writing. Let's look at its problems.

SEXIST PRONOUNS

Nonsexist communicators never use male pronouns as generic pronouns. However, they also avoid writing or speaking in a style that has "he or she," "hers or his," "her or him," and "herself or himself" line after line, paragraph after paragraph. Such repetition creates distractions and inefficiency. The preceding revision of the suggestion box passage illustrates how compressed use of paired pronouns becomes cumbersome.

When you are using paired pronouns, introduce the fairness of alphabetical or alternating order. The preceding paragraph illustrates alphabetical order. Other appropriate variations of the dual pronouns—this time in alternating order—include "she/he," "her/him," "himself/herself," and "s/he" (useful in written messages).

The combined word *s/he* illustrates the logic of the female forms as generic; for example, *she* contains *he*, *female* contains *male*, and *woman* contains *man*. However, we are interested in nonsexist communication, so we will let pass the temptation to recommend the exclusive use of such forms.

In the original suggestion box paragraph, another kind of sexist communication arises with the use of *he* and other male forms in the claimed generic sense, along with *she* with stereotyped male forms. Those who argue for male pronouns as the generic references cannot have it both ways. They cannot selectively distinguish—with the distinction always placing the male in stereotyped leadership roles and the female in stereotyped follower roles.

The words of some people who claim that they use the masculine forms in a strict, inclusive, neutral way include such references as "the president . . . he" in the same context with "the receptionist . . . she"; "the boss . . .

he" in the same context with "the clerk . . . she"; "the breadwinner . . . he" with "the homemaker . . . she"; "the principal . . . he" with "the teacher . . . she"; and "the doctor . . . he" with "the nurse . . . she." Here the traditionalist's argument that *he* is used in a purely generic sense breaks down.

In contrast to the traditionalist, the nonsexist communicator neither uses the masculine pronouns in the generic sense nor uses masculine and feminine pronouns to differentiate between dominant and submissive roles for men and women, respectively. The nonsexist communicator does use de-sexed pronoun forms—unless referring to an identified individual known as female or male.

Some people call for new pronoun forms instead of revisions. Dana Densmore recommends this set of de-sexed pronouns: *she* for *she* and *he, herm* for *her* and *him*, and *heris* for *her* and *his*.[1] Casey Miller and Kate Swift call for *tey* for *he* and *she, tem* for *him* and *her*, and *ter(s)* for *his* and her(s).[2] Other proposed pronoun sets include *ve, ver,* and *vis* (Murrell) and *co, cos,* and *coself* (Orovan).[3]

Understanding and respecting the need for neutral generic pronouns and the efforts at creating them, the realist recognizes the small probability of their widespread acceptance. Therefore, at least for the short run, the hope for nonsexist pronouns lies in adaptive measures. With these transitional methods the nonsexist communicator can satisfactorily eliminate the male-as-generic pronouns from the language. When people have removed the generic *he* from the language, then they can broach the subject of new pronouns with improved possibilities of success.

Another solution to the problem pronoun is the mixture of singular and plural forms. Some people now accept "everyone . . . their," "anyone . . . their," "none . . . their," "everybody . . . their," "anybody . . . their," and similar indefinite pronoun references in all but the most formal writing and speaking.

Some of us, even some who do not think of ourselves as extremely formal communicators, just have not been able to couple a plural pronoun with a singular antecedent. Because of other solutions, we have not had to give up a grammatical rule to become nonsexist communicators. That does not mean, however, that you cannot be comfortable without applying the traditional agreement rule. Your communication circles will determine the acceptability of the new forms for you. We who write manuals and guidelines are in communication circles that will not allow us to take liberties with subject-verb agreement—yet.

One revision for the original sexist segment illustrates two principles for correcting sexist pronouns.

[1] Dana Densmore, "Speech Is the Form of Thought." (Reprint available from Know, Inc.).
[2] Casey Miller and Kate Swift, "De-sexing the English Language," *Ms.* 1 (Spring 1972):7.
[3] Marie B. Hecht, Joan D. Berbrich, Salley A. Healey, and Clare M. Cooper, *The Women, Yes!* (New York: Holt, Rinehart and Winston. Rinehart Press, 1973), p. 59.

The authors of suggestions for improving management should identify themselves by placing their ID numbers on the completed forms. They should place the suggestions in the box by 5:00 P.M. on Friday for consideration during the following week. After removing the completed forms from the box, the president's secretary will hand them directly to the judging committee chairperson for the committee's consideration. Only after the suggestions have been ranked and the winners chosen will the secretary look up the ID numbers and then only so that awards may be distributed to the people who have won.

We can solve the problem of the male-as-generic pronoun by converting to plural pronouns. Further, when we use the singular form (as with reference to the "secretary"), we can repeat the word if the repetitions occur infrequently.

Guideline A: Sexist Pronouns

1. Use female and male pronouns only when they refer to specific females and males.

Incorrect	Correct
A sales manager should tell his staff	Janet Ellis, sales manager, told her staff
Any nurse knows about her responsibility to	As a nurse, Bill Williams knows about his responsibility to

2. Instead of male pronouns as generic (pronouns that refer to indefinite persons) and instead of female and male pronouns in stereotypes (the truck driver . . . he; and the elementary-school teacher . . . she),

  a. Use, sparingly, female and male pronoun pairs such as "he or she," "his or her," "her or him," "herself or himself," "he/she," "hers/his," "him/her," "herself/ himself," and the written combined form "s/he." The occasional deliberate insertion of such pairs often reminds the reader that both females and males constitute the population.

Incorrect	Correct
The worker must schedule his vacation at least one month in advance	The worker must schedule her or his vacation at least one month in advance

  b. Use something other than the male-first procedure for listing female and male pronoun pairs.

  i. Alphabetize the pronouns.

Incorrect	Correct
He or she will then hand the tool to him or her	He or she will then hand the tool to her or him

ii. Alternate the pronoun order but maintain nonstereotyped reference.

Incorrect

The person . . . his or her, and the manager . . . himself or herself

The flight attendant . . . she or he, and the pilot . . . he or she

Correct

The person . . . his or her, and the manager . . . herself or himself

The flight attendant . . . he or she, and the pilot . . . she or he

iii. Maintain proper pronoun order when pronouns refer to the same generic individual.

Incorrect

She or he must take his or her job seriously

Correct

She or he must take her or his job seriously

c. Change from singular to plural form.

Incorrect

An individual may check his credit records for himself

Correct

Individuals may check their credit records for themselves

d. Repeat the noun if a number of words intervene.

Incorrect

The driver must maintain a safe distance between cars. He must also

Correct

The driver must maintain a safe distance between cars. The driver must also

e. Use a different noun or pronoun, including such sex-neutral words as *person* and *one*, for repetition.

Incorrect

The machinist is responsible for his work area. He reports failures to

We have begun a new contest for the consumer. He must submit his completed entry by May 22.

Correct

The machinist is responsible for her or his work area. The person reports failures to

We have begun a new contest for the consumer. Each must submit the completed entry by May 22.

f. Use the second-person or "you" style when appropriate.

Incorrect

The taxpayer should check with his local post office to obtain the forms he needs

Correct

As a taxpayer, you should check with your local post office to obtain the forms you need

g. Reword to omit the pronouns or replace them with other words, such as *the, a, an*.

Incorrect	*Correct*
Every receptionist signs her incoming call sheet at the end of the day	Every receptionist signs the incoming call sheet at the end of the day
The average employee prefers his vacation in June	The average employee prefers a June vacation

h. Use, occasionally, the passive voice instead of the active voice.

Incorrect	*Correct*
Each employee wears his identification badge at all times. He pins his badge on his left shoulder.	Each employee wears an identification badge at all times. The badge is pinned on the left shoulder.

i. Use, occasionally, *it* and *there* as expletives.

Incorrect	*Correct*
The manager meets with all new employees. He helps them by orienting them to the organization of the office.	The manager meets with all new employees. It is helpful to orient them to the organization of the office.

j. Alternate the female and male pronouns throughout the narrative, but maintain nonstereotyped references.

Incorrect	*Correct*
A supervisor should maintain an interested, but impersonal attitude toward his workers. A manager should likewise maintain an interested, but impersonal attitude toward his supervisors.	A supervisor should maintain an interested, but impersonal attitude toward his workers. A manager should likewise maintain an interested, but impersonal attitude toward her supervisors.

k. Use, only in informal circumstances and only if acceptable to the communication receiver(s), the plural pronoun instead of the singular masculine pronoun for reference to an indefinite person.

Incorrect	*Correct*
Anybody who wants to be considered must bring his completed application blank by May 23.	Anybody who wants to be considered must bring their completed application blank by May 23.

l. Write sentence fragments initiated by verb forms, when appropriate.

Incorrect	*Correct*
He checks out supplies	Checks out supplies

The addition of *authoress* to *author* in the revision of the suggestion box paragraph is belabored and negative. *Author* is nonsexist, and introduction of *authoress* demeans the female. *Author* means "one who creates." Thus, the addition of *-ess* to denote that the "one who creates" is female implies that the true "author" is male and that the female is a subordinate imitator. Because *author* is neutral, we must not use it for the male form in conjunction with a diminished form—*authoress*—for the female. If we retain such words as *authoress* in the language, consistency demands that *author* be neutral, *authoress* female, and *author* plus some other suffix (perhaps becoming *authorepp*) male. Because that consistency will never occur, we must drop the *-ess*. Similarly, we must eliminate the suffixes *-ix, -ette,* and *-ienne/-ine,* for they too serve as diminutives.

Like *authoress,* all these words diminish females. With them the present system sets a certain word as the norm—the male—and another word ending in *-ess, -ette, -ix,* or *-ienne/-ine* as the secondary, the aberration—the female.

Poetess	Sculptress	Bachelorette
Usherette	Directress	Seductress
Priestess	Enchantress	Heroine
Tigress	Rockette	Farmerette
Hostess	Executrix	Princess
Seamstress	Majorette	Actress
Villainess	Suffragette	Temptress
Murderess	Aviatrix	Comedienne

Check your dictionary for the meaning of words with these suffixes. You will find the female form as the abnormal, diminished form of some strong, standard word. For example, if you look up *sculptor,* you will find something like "one who sculptures," followed by "sculptress, n. fem." Again, you will not find "sculptrepp, n. masc."

Because society is not likely to adopt suffixes to designate the male poet, sculptor, or whatever, the solution lies in dropping the endings that make the woman out to be something less than a full-fledged poet, sculptor, or whatever. If an actor is "one who acts," then a woman who acts is an actor. If the need arises to identify the sex of the person who acts, the appropriate identifying words can be used in conjunction with the word *actor.* Examples are (1) "The actor is a woman"; (2) "The male actor"; (3) "The actor . . . she." No great difficulty arises. In fact, such usages introduce not only equality, but efficiency.

Guideline B:
The *-ess, -ette, -ix,* and *-ienne/-ine*
Word Endings

1. Omit the *-ess* ending from words for which it denotes female (*directress, authoress, poetess*). Three *-ess* words will be difficult to eradicate in the short run: *waitress, hostess,* and *actress.* If you retain any of the three, do not also use the plural of the basic word to include the female. For example, if you use *actress,* do not use *actors* to include *actresses*; use "actors and actresses" instead.

Incorrect	*Correct*
The show featured the work of a sculptor and a sculptress	The show featured the work of two sculptors
John and Mary served as host and hostess. As hosts, they	John and Mary served as host and hostess. As host and hostess, they

2. Omit the *-ette* ending from words for which it denotes a female.

Incorrect	*Correct*
Judy has a job as an usherette at the Rig Theater	Judy has a job as an usher at the Rig Theater
The farmerette	The farmer
The bachelorettes	The singles

3. Omit the *-ix* ending from words for which it is used to denote a female.

Incorrect	*Correct*
As an aviatrix, Ellen	As an aviator, Ellen
Ms. Crowley serves as executrix	Ms. Crowley serves as executor

4. Omit the *-ienne/-ine* ending from words for which it denotes a female.

Incorrect	*Correct*
Jane Ellis, a comedienne	Jane Ellis, a comedian

SEXIST NOUNS

Use of nouns containing *man* to represent both females and males constitutes one of the major sexist communication problems. *Chairman* and *men* in the original suggestion box example illustrate this sexism.

Nonsexist alternatives to the "man" words involve several common-sense approaches. The word or suffix *person* provides one of the most important alternatives.

26

The telephone people realize that the phrase "man-to-man calls" does not describe all communication transactions. Then why cannot we transfer the "person-to-person" concept to other communication exchanges? Resistance to allowing the ending -*person* to take the place of *man* in compounds has its basis in the same resistance to change that has regularly negated attempts to bring sex equality to communication. *Person* is a perfectly legitimate word, with its roots in Latin, and it has the advantage of referring to either sex. Thus, it serves as a fine substitute for *man* in compounds referring to either a man or a woman.

Of course, other options can also preempt -*man*. If *freshperson* bothers you, use "first-year student." If *businessperson* seems a bit awkward, use "business executive" or a similar variation.

Problems may arise with -*person* or other neutral endings if they are not used universally. The most common and most serious misuse occurs when, for example, people use *chairman* for a man and use *chairperson* only for a woman. That approach perpetuates the inequity of sexism.

The intermediate solution to the misuse of -*person* as an ending is to use words such as *chairperson* for the position-holder of unknown sex, *chairpersons* or *chairpeople* for mixed sexes, *chairman* for a man, and *chairwoman* for a woman. Ultimately, we should use a neutral position title, whatever the sex of the person. But until that becomes common, we may need this intermediate solution.

In the suggestion box revision, conversions of *management* to *personagement*, *chairman* to *chairwoperson*, and "men and/or wopeople" border on the ridiculous. However, they illustrate the lengths to which some people go to sabotage the movement toward language nonsexism. They deliberately alienate receivers by leaving the impression that all nonsexist passages are necessarily clumsy and stupid. However, their exaggerations actually form the incorrect usage, for they do not reflect correct derivations.

The word *management* comes from the Latin *manus*, meaning "hand." Thus, the syllable *man* has no sex connotation.

Using *woperson* or *wopeople* to avoid *man* as a syllable in *women* is also unnecessary. *Woman* has its source in the Anglo-Saxon *wif*, meaning "female," and *mann*, meaning "human being." Thus, while *woman* came from the same word (*mann*) that evolved into *man*, the original meaning was "human being" and not "man" as used for the adult male.

Two additional illustrations show how the sincere semanticist looks at word origins. First, some who oppose nonsexist language go so far as to say that we should avoid the word *person* because it includes *son*—a male form. They ask, then, "Should it be *perdaughter*?" thinking they have made a profound point. However, a quick check shows that the word *person* comes from the Latin *persona* and means "human being." It has nothing to do with *son* as a male descendant.

Some people, much in the same vein, argue that *female* should be converted to *feperson* or *feperdaughter*. But no problem exists here either. *Female* has its basis in *femina*, a Latin word meaning "woman."

Sensitivity to language-aware people shows which words they receive well—even recommend—and which they do not. *Person* and *female* fall clearly in the category of acceptable words, at least until we develop seemingly less sexist, serious substitutes.

Observe that the following correction of the suggestion-box example converts *chairman* to *chair* and replaces *men* with *them*. *Chairperson* appears in the corrected version on page 22. *Chairone* or *chair-one* is another neutral alternative to *chairman*.

> The author of a suggestion for improving management should be identified by placing her or his ID number on the completed form. The suggestion should be placed in the box by 5:00 P.M. on Friday for consideration during the following week. After removing the completed forms from the box, the president's secretary will hand them directly to the chair of the judging committee for the committee's consideration. Only after the suggestions have been evaluated and ranked and the winners chosen will the secretary look up their ID numbers—and then only so that awards may be distributed to them.

This revision maintains the singular form at the expense of changing from the active to the passive voice in some sentences. However, if a writer or speaker needs to use the singular words, then loss of the active voice represents a small price to pay for removing female subjugation from the language. The problem lies with a language that subordinates women to men—and not with the women and men who recognize the communication sexism dilemma and firmly call for its resolution.

Sexist job titles generally include the word ending *-man*, though stereotyping also exists in other designations, such as *seamstress, newsboy*, and *maid*. Fortunately, correction of this aspect of sexist language has progressed to the point that the United States government has revised the *Dictionary of Occupational Titles* to eliminate sex- and age-referent language. Nearly 3,500 job titles listed in the third and fourth editions have been modified. Ironically, however, the *Man*power Administration (now the Employment and Training Administration) of the United States Department of Labor made the modifications. This excerpt from the publication in which the changes were introduced documents their legal basis:

> This publication brings job titles listed in the *Dictionary of Occupational Titles*, Third Edition, into conformance with equal employment legislation such as the Civil Rights Act of 1964 and the Age Discrimination in Employment Act of 1967, and with recent administration policy statements and instructions on the same subject. Included in the legislation, policy statements, and instructions is language which prohibits the use of sex- and/or age-referent language by the public employment service. As a result of these prohibitions, it is necessary to

provide the employment service and other public and private users of the *Dictionary of Occupational Titles* with revised job titles to replace existing *Dictionary* job titles now considered to be potentially sex and/or age discriminatory. This will be accomplished by the publication of this document, in which *Dictionary* job titles that have sex and/or age identification are, wherever possible, revised in favor of titles that do not connote age or sex.[4]

Guideline C: Sexist Nouns

Revise words including the syllable *man* when denoting both males and females.

1. Use *person* instead of *man*.

Incorrect	*Correct*
A committee chairman can	A committee chairperson can

2. Use syllables other than *person* to replace *man*.

Incorrect	*Correct*
The committee chairman	The committee chairone (or chair-one)
The policeman	The police officer

3. Change the word structure to avoid using *man*.

Incorrect	*Correct*
Freshman congressmen	First-year members of Congress
	or
	First-year congresspersons (or congress-people)
The participants used shrewd gamesmanship	The participants played the game shrewdly

4. Omit *man* and use root words.

Incorrect	*Correct*
The chairman should	The chair should

5. Change *man* to *woman* for the female if, during this transitional period of the language, you retain *man* for the male. Do not pair *man* for a man with *person* (or other neutral form) for a woman.

[4]United States Department of Labor, Manpower [*sic*] Administration, *Job Title Revisions to Eliminate Sex- and Age-Referent Language from the Dictionary of Occupational Titles, Third Edition* (Washington, D.C.: Government Printing Office, 1975), p. iii.

Incorrect	*Correct*
He is chairman of, and she is chairperson of	He is chairperson of, and she is chairperson of

6. Use neutral words for plurals of the original "man" words.

Incorrect	*Correct*
He is chairman of, and she is chairwoman of. As chairmen, they	He is chairman of, and she is chairwoman of. As chairpersons, they

---

APPLICATIONS

This chapter and the following chapters include exercises for you to practice nonsexist principles. They ask you to identify and correct the sexism in passages deliberately packed with sexist expressions. Suggested solutions appear in Appendix B.

The exercises focus on the applications introduced in each chapter's guidelines. However, they inevitably include other types of sexism as well.

☆ *3-1. As you read the following passage, underline the sexist words and phrases and then rewrite the sections you have marked. As you rewrite, try to find your own nonsexist words and phrases. This passage illustrates the types of sexism that might be found in brochures used by campus recruiters to introduce university students to an employer.*

Wecare Corporation has positions available for the man who wants to be in management, finance, statistics, communication, marketing, or accounting. Whether running a one-man show or working on multiple-man teams, the employee at Wecare has a great deal of freedom to engage in the kind of creativity that has brought mankind to the level of productivity it now enjoys.

Although our craftsmen, under the direction of our fine foremen, produce an outstanding manmade material, we always need bright, young men for the position of salesman so that the product can be sold. Certainly, the wife and children of the salesman must be willing to have a weekend husband and father and to move frequently as he advances from one territory to another.

The Wecare employee has his choice of several matching-fund savings plan options, including corporation stock purchases—all available after he accumulates only 2,000 man-hours. Thus, in addition to providing salaries and benefits man-sized enough to assure outstanding manpower, Wecare management also wants to assure that its workmen can establish savings accounts for the wives and children so dependent on them.

Whether a freshman or an upperclassman, a man or a coed, you will want to pursue a career with Wecare. Thousands of businessmen have done so—and express pleasure about their decision.

☆　*3-2.　Here is a segment from a hypothetical administrative manual. Underline the sexist words and phrases and write corrections.*

As a basic policy, men in the classification of foreman or higher are urged to participate in up to four of the training courses offered by the corporation each fiscal year. However, a grandfather clause states that if a man is promoted no later than May 1 of one fiscal year, one training course in addition to the basic four may be taken by him during the following fiscal year.

The training courses are offered monthly; thus, each man has twelve from which to choose. The one-week courses are announced a year in advance so that the choices and scheduling can be made then. The course topics are varied, but some that have been offered are

> "Key-Man Insurance: Worth the Investment?"
> "The Ins and Outs of Workmen's Compensation Plans"
> "Now Is the Time for Every Good Man to Come to the Aid of His Party (Or How to Be Politically Astute)"
> "How to Make the Weatherman Work for the Company"
> "Lawmen's Views of Businessmen's Political Contributions"
> "The Cattleman's Stake in the Marketplace"
> "The Pressman Has His Problems Too"
> "A Pension Plan Fit for a King"
> "The Functions of the Public Relations Advance Man"
> "Uncle Sam's 'Take' from Your Paycheck"
> "Oneupmanship in the Game Called Negotiation"
> "The Importance of Women's Auxiliaries to Business Organizations"
> "The Best-Laid Plans of Mice and Men: A Look at Forecasting"
> "Sick and Annual Leave—The Working Man's Best Friend"

Many company men are utilized as instructors for the courses. But because, all too often, a man is not without honor except in his own "company," men are frequently brought in from outside to serve as anchormen for the courses. We have had an oilman, a pressman, an aviatrix, a city councilman, a deanette from a university school of business, and a freshman congressman, among others, in the past. They add a great deal to the programs because of their fresh viewpoints.

☆　*3-3.　Following are fifteen sexist job titles. Rewrite each.*

Furnaceman	Laundress	Chambermaid
Motorman	Seamstress	Flagman
Fisherman	Hatcheck girl	Baggageman
Maintenance man	Hostess, hotel	Fireman, locomotive
Hoistman	Meter maid	Charwoman

☆   *3-4.   The two following excerpts come from hypothetical job information statements. Mark and correct their sexist passages.*

1. *Job Description*
   Lineman, Class A

   Accountability
   He reports directly to the Foreman.

   Work Performed
   Summary: He performs all duties associated with installing and maintaining telephone lines. He also helps the Foreman supervise and train Linemen, Class B, and Linemen, Class C, as those men perform those same duties.

   Details: (1) He checks out and supervises loading of equipment and supplies for the jobs or assigns to others any such activities that he himself cannot accomplish; (2) he checks right-of-way specifications before proceeding with the job; and (3) he climbs utility poles and hooks up services.

2. *Job Specification*
   Structural Metal Craftsman, II

   Education
   The job requires use of fractions, decimals, algebra, and geometry. The craftsman must possess knowledge of the structural metal field. He must be able to read blueprints, understand basic design, and apply his knowledge of foundry practice.

4

COURTESY TITLES,
SALUTATIONS,
AND SIGNATURES

Customs for courtesy titles, memoranda, and other types of messages perpetuate sexism. Therefore, this chapter focuses on these expressions.

One of the most serious examples of sexism occurs when a woman uses a courtesy title that exposes her marital status to the world; a man does not have to do so. In fact, a man has no means of doing so by courtesy title alone because of the neutrality of *Mr.*

Difficulties arise in resolving the courtesy-title issue because of the variety of preferences during transition from sex inequality to equality. Many people prefer that women, whatever their marital status, use the courtesy title *Ms.* Others want the traditional *Miss* and *Mrs.* Many want married women to use their first names (or even entire birth names) and not their husbands'.[1] Others prefer to use their husbands' names (the "Mrs. John Jones" style). Still others call for courtesy titles that do not identify either sex or marital status.

One temporary solution that begs the issue is to omit courtesy titles for both men and women. For example, we may simply omit titles by using full names (without titles) in addresses and salutations in letters and in headings in memoranda. Or we may use full names (without titles) in addresses and in headings in memoranda and first names in salutations. Or we may substitute position or status titles for courtesy titles when appropriate. Or, finally, we may omit the courtesy titles in addresses and memoranda headings or substitute status titles for them, and either omit the salutations entirely or substitute conversational phrases or subject lines for them.

Examples of these types of addresses, salutations, and headings in letters and memoranda include

To: Wanda Blair
From: Albert Wilson

Joan Smith (or John Smith)
Dear Joan Smith (or John Smith):

Joan Smith (or John Smith)
Dear Customer:

Vice-President Joan Smith (or John Smith)
Dear Vice-President Smith:

Joan Smith (or John Smith)
Dear Joan (or John):

Dr. Joan and Dr. John Smith
Dear Drs. Smith:

Professor Joan Smith (or John Smith)
Dear Professor Smith:

John Jones and Joan Smith
Dear Customers (or John Jones and Joan Smith or John and Joan):

Dr. Joan Smith (or John Smith)
Dear Dr. Smith:

Joan and John Smith
Dear Customers (or Joan and John Smith or Joan and John):

Marilyn Houston
You will be interested in the DEA Conference on June 18

George Harris
(Omit salutation)

Audrey Kline
Subject: Request for Application Blank

All the variations for courtesy-title omissions have inherent weaknesses. For example, what can be done in situations too formal for the omission of courtesy titles or for the use of first names in salutations? What about the conversational, yet not-quite-on-a-first-name-basis tone in the body of a letter achieved by using interjections of direct address such as "Now, Ms. Jones, another feature of our specialized service is . . ."? What about cases for which no

---

[1]"Birth name" instead of "maiden name" appears throughout this manual. The word *maiden* means "virgin," a sexist usage in that it applies to women and not to men.

appropriate substitute status or position title seems to exist? And what about the unacceptability in some circles of omission of or substitution for the traditional salutation?

Another stopgap treatment of the courtesy-title dilemma has us bow temporarily to cultural conditioning. This treatment calls for using *Mr.* for all men for whom other titles do not take precedence, using *Miss* or *Mrs.* and the husband's name for married women only for women who so specify, and using *Ms.* for all other women. However, this measure need not apply to notes, memoranda, and other such messages under the control of the people and organizations using them internally.

Ideally, this manual would call for removing sex-identifying courtesy titles entirely. For example, some people suggest the use of *M.* (pronounced "em") for everyone. However, receivers may think of *M.* as an initial in a name rather than as a courtesy title, although the French successfully use *M.* for *Monsieur.*

Because of the lack of satisfactory alternatives to sex-identifying courtesy titles and because of the great unlikelihood of their widespread adoption, this is the most nonsexist approach for the present.

> Use *Mr.* for all men.
> Use *Ms.* for all women.
> Use a married woman's first name, not her husband's.

For the short term, then, these forms remove some of the sexism from courtesy titles in letters and memoranda.

To: Mr. Tyrone Randall	To: Ms. Florence Page
From: Karen Elder	From: Gordon Lloyd
Ms. Joan Smith (or Mr. John Smith)	Ms. Joan and Mr. John Smith
Dear Ms. Smith (or Mr. Smith):	Dear Ms. and Mr. Smith:
Mr. John Jones and Ms. Joan Smith	Dr. Joan Allen and Mr. John Smith
Dear Mr. Jones and Ms. Smith:	Dear Dr. Allen and Mr. Smith:
Ms. Joan and Dr. John Smith	Dr. John Jones and Dr. Joan Smith
Dear Ms. and Dr. Smith:	Dear Dr. Jones and Dr. Smith:

Observe that these examples also eliminate the sexism in the traditional practice of always listing the male's name first. The basic solution lies in alphabetical order.

A particular obstacle to nonsexism arises when you are using a telephone directory, city directory, or other compilation of names as a mailing list. Such listings customarily carry entries in the names of men, with the names of women shown only when they are single. Even now that the telephone company includes married women's names for a minimal one-time charge, few women take advantage of the service.

Most who use sexist mailing lists use the exact names shown. By doing so they introduce the sexism of omission of any other adults who might live at the addresses—usually women. Such omission implies that the male to whom the communiqué is addressed forms the unit, with the woman and other members of the household as peripheral satellites.

Others who use mailing lists fall into an equally serious trap—the use of the "Mr. and Mrs." form of address derived from the man's name in the list. Not only does the "Mr. and Mrs. John Smith" style make a nonperson of the married woman but also it can lead to other types of sexism. (1) The listed man may actually be single. (2) A couple may be married, but the woman may have retained her original name. (3) A man and woman may live together, but not be married. (4) The household may include several unmarried men and/or women. (5) The listed name may not be a man's name at all, but a woman's.

The assumption that the "Mr. and Mrs." life-style represents the norm is false. When a business writer addresses a "Mr. and Mrs." letter to people who do not affiliate with that life-style, they quite rightfully will receive a negative signal. The "Mr. and Mrs." generally leaves the impression that the writer wants to force a life-style on everyone.

When using a sexist mailing list, never use the man-as-the-unit and the "Mr. and Mrs. John Jones" styles. Instead, use neutral forms, such as

John Jones and Others	John Jones and Any Others at
Dear Mr. Jones and Others:	1818 18th Street
	Dear Resident/s:
Mr. John Jones and Any Others	Mr. John Jones/Others
Dear Mr. Jones and Any Others:	Dear Mr. Jones/Others:

If you elect to use courtesy titles, try to know the sex of the recipient. Certain names and the use of initials make such knowledge difficult to gain—and the assumption that a name is male unless proven otherwise is a form of sexism in itself. Women often resent being addressed as *Mr. M.* and *Mr./Ms.* can provide useful alternatives.

These examples eliminate the sexism of listing men's names to represent entire units.

Boxholder(s)	Person(s)
Dear Boxholder(s)	Dear Person(s):
Occupant(s)	M. Insurance Buyer
Dear Occupant(s):	Dear M. Insurance Buyer:
Mr./Ms. Homeowner	
Dear Mr./Ms. Homeowner:	

Obviously, such addresses and salutations may seem cold and impersonal. Yet, if the choice is between the demeaning sexism implicit in using a man's name as defining a living unit and the less personal approaches, the egalitarian must choose the latter.

For any of the nonsexist addresses shown, we may omit the salutation or replace it with a conversational lead-in or subject line. Experiment with varying combinations to find the one that is least startling, yet totally nonsexist.

The nonsexist communicator can help overcome sexist forms of address in instruments other than letters and memoranda. For example, a writer responsible for designing forms or coupons with blanks for names should list only *Mr.* and *Ms.* as the courtesy titles to be circled by the respondents—or list no courtesy titles at all. Those who oppose *Ms.* will supply other titles, just as those of us who oppose *Miss* and *Mrs.* already supply *Ms.* when that option does not appear.

The journalistic style of reporting also perpetuates sexism in forms of address. Journalists usually use courtesy titles for women, but not for men; *Miss* and *Mrs.* instead of *Ms.*; and nonparallel structures such as a man's last name with a woman's first name (Carter speaks to graduates; Rosalyn accompanies him).

Consider this example of how to report names in a press release: "Alice Jones and Martin Phelps have been promoted. . . . Jones and Phelps. . . ." If the journalist honors the release writer's implicit nonsexist style, he or she will keep "Alice Jones and Martin Phelps" and "Jones and Phelps" as stated. However, even if the journalist uses the traditional form, the words may, at worst, become "Ms. Alice Jones and Martin Phelps" and "Ms. Jones and Phelps," for the journalist would not know the marital status of Jones. Only the most sexist of journalists would bother to determine the marital status of Jones and report it or would convert to "Ms. Jones and Martin Phelps" and "Alice and Phelps."

Guideline D: Courtesy Titles

1. Use *Mrs.*, *Miss*, and "Mrs. John Jones" format only for those who demand it, only as a last resort, only for extraorganizational addresses, and only for the short run. A sufficient number of alternatives exist to replace the sexist courtesy title in all but the most extreme circumstances.

You address a letter "Ms. Cora Hopkins" and receive a return letter from her saying that she will never do business with you again if you address her as *Ms.* instead of *Mrs.*

Incorrect	*Correct*
You address your next letter to "Ms. Cora Hopkins"	You address your next letter to "Mrs. Cora Hopkins"

2. Use *Ms.* for all women except in the extreme circumstances described in the preceding guideline.

Incorrect	*Correct*
Mrs. Neece and Miss Nye	Ms. Neece and Ms. Nye
Mrs. Grant and Miss Skelly-Frye	Ms. Grant and Ms. Skelly-Frye

3. Omit courtesy titles for both men and women.

Incorrect	*Correct*
Miss Timmons and Mr. Fry	Timmons and Fry
Price and Mrs. Tharp	Price and Tharp
Mr. John Jones and Mrs. Joan Smith	John Jones and Joan Smith
Dear Mr. Jones and Mrs. Smith:	Dear John and Joan (or omit salutation or substitute lead-in as shown in Guideline E):

4. Substitute position or status title for traditional courtesy title.

Incorrect	*Correct*
For a university teacher:	
Mrs. Helen Keith	Professor Helen Keith
Mrs. Patty Stehr, Ph.D.	Dr. Patty Stehr

5. Use *M.* or *Mr./Ms.* for names that do not clearly suggest gender or for given and middle initials only.

Incorrect	*Correct*
Mr. R. E. Thomas	Mr./Ms. R. E. Thomas
Mr. Dale Allan	M. Dale Allan

6. Control the potential sexism in courtesy titles for addresses derived from mailing lists.

a. Use the male name in conjunction with words that indicate that you know that others may reside at the same address.

Incorrect	*Correct*
Mr. Jack Phelps	Mr. Jack Phelps and Others at the Address
Dear Mr. Phelps:	Dear Residents:

b. Use inclusive terms instead of males' names.

Incorrect	*Correct*
Mr. and Mrs. Jack Phelps	Occupant(s)
Dear Mr. and Mrs. Phelps:	Dear Occupant(s):

c. Omit courtesy titles instead of assuming that those listed are males.

Incorrect	*Correct*
Mr. Gale Lewis and Others	Gale Lewis and Others
Dear Mr. Lewis and Others:	Dear Gale and Others:

SALUTATIONS

One historically sexist type of address and salutation exists when letters addressed to companies, organizations, institutions, or groups include the salutation "Gentlemen" or, improperly, "Dear Sirs" or "My dear Sirs." Such salutations obviously use *men* and *sirs* as inclusive of both men and women. Thus, we must provide nonsexist alternatives.

The immediate alternative to the salutation "Gentlemen" simply expands the form to include both females and males: "Ladies and Gentlemen" (or, alphabetically, "Gentlemen and Ladies"), "Gentlemen and Gentlewomen," "Dear Madams (Mesdames) and Sirs," "Gentlepersons," "Gentlepeople," "Gentlewo/men" and "My dear Madams (Mesdames) and Sirs." The salutation "Ladies and Gentlemen" ("Gentlemen and Ladies") represents familiar idiom and thus works satisfactorily for formal letters. Though not so familiar, "Gentlemen and Gentlewomen," "Gentlepersons," "Gentlepeople," and the written composite "Gentlewo/men" receive some acceptance. However, "Dear Madams (Mesdames) and Sirs" and "My dear Madams (Mesdames) and Sirs" are cumbersome and counterproductive. Actually, we need not deal with "Dear Sirs," because practitioners do not accept it as a proper salutation, even when sexism is not an issue.

Another acceptable alternative to "Gentlemen" calls for the use of letter forms that either omit the salutation entirely or allow conversational lead-in or subject-line substitutions for traditional salutations. A hypothetical example of a conversational lead-in is:

Shouldn't you be using the Dextrafile System?

An example of a subject-line substitution becomes

Subject: Benefits of Dextrafile

As another solution, we can change the address to direct the letter to an individual instead of an organization. To use this approach for an unknown individual, list a title instead of a name. For example, for a letter to a company about its budget, address the letter to "Executive, Finance Department" or "Finance Department Executive." With minimal effort and imagination, we can supply differing titles, such as *Head, Vice-President, Supervisor, Assistant,* and *Chairperson*. Likewise, the content of the letter dictates the area—finance, sales, service, or whatever.

Now, suppose that a letter includes as the first line of an address, "Finance Department Executive." The skeptic about nonsexist communication might say, "Aha, now we're back to 'Dear Sir' or 'My dear Sir' as the salutation, so do we use 'Dear Madam or Sir' or 'My dear Madam or Sir'?" As a moderating answer we might say, "Yes, we prefer 'Dear Madam or Sir' to 'Dear Sir,' because of its nonsexism. Moreover, we can use 'Dear Executive' and overcome the slight negativism associated with unnatural expressions such as 'Dear Madam or Sir.' In addition, we can omit the salutation or substitute a conversational lead-in for it." As established, the solutions to sexism lie in commitment and common sense.

Guideline E: Salutations

Use sex-neutral salutations.

1. Use variations of "Ladies and Gentlemen," "Gentlemen," and "Mesdames and Sirs."

Incorrect	*Correct*
Gentlemen	Ladies and Gentlemen
	Gentlemen and Ladies
	Gentlemen and Gentlewomen
	Gentlewo/men
	Gentlepersons
	Gentlepeople
Dear Sirs	Dear Madams (Mesdames) and Sirs
	Dear Sirs and Madams (Mesdames)
My dear Sirs	My dear Madams (Mesdames) and Sirs
	My dear Sirs and Madams (Mesdames)[2]

2. Omit the salutation or substitute a conversational lead-in or subject line for it.

Incorrect	*Correct*
Gentlemen (or incorrect "Sirs" variations)	(No salutation)
	Take advantage of this offer.
	Subject: A Special Offer!

3. Address the letter to an individual or position title in the organization instead of to the organization itself. When using this device, maintain nonsexism in the salutation.

[2]Some people still use the incorrect "Dear Sirs" and "My dear Sirs" variations. Therefore, nonsexist alternatives appear here.

Incorrect	*Correct*
Acme Corporation	Sales Manager Acme Corporation
Gentlemen (or incorrect "Sirs" variations):	Dear Sales Manager (or other variations shown in Guidelines E and F and elsewhere in the chapter):

4. Use the "Madam or Sir" or "Sir or Madam" format.

Incorrect	*Correct*
Personnel Department Officer	Personnel Department Officer
My dear Sir:	My dear Madam or Sir:

5. Use a nonsexist substitute for *Sir*.

Incorrect	*Correct*
Executive, Finance Function	Executive, Finance Function
Dear Sir:	Dear Executive:

6. Omit the salutation or substitute a conversational lead-in for it.

Incorrect	*Correct*
Head of Advertising	Head of Advertising
Dear Sir:	Just look at the color in the enclosed sample ads (or omit saluation)

SIGNATURES

Though echoing some of the problems of sexism discussed in preceding sections, signatures and the signature blocks of letters require special attention.

One such problem lies in the traditional requirement of a courtesy title in parentheses in front of the typewritten name of a woman although a man's name includes no courtesy title. The most serious aspect of that problem relates to the reason for the requirement: the marital-status labeling of women and the lack of it for men.

When some authorities now accept *Ms.* in parentheses, they bend somewhat under the egalitarian's cry, "Unfair." However, they do not recognize the full extent of the sexism because they retain the parenthetical courtesy title for women without requiring one for men as well. For parallelism, then, either place the courtesy title for both sexes—*Mr.* for a man and *Ms.* for a woman—in parentheses or omit the parenthetical courtesy titles for both sexes. Again, the key lies in consistency.

One argument favoring parenthetical courtesy titles for both men and women arises because initials and some first names do not clearly indicate a female or a male. Thus, as long as we use courtesy titles, the designation of *Mr.* or *Ms.* can help the recipients of letters to know which title to use.

Sexism also occurs when a married woman uses a marital courtesy title as part of her typed signature and then actually signs a name such as "Mrs. Cora Jones." Even more sexist is the use of "Mrs. John Jones" in either or both the typewritten and handwritten signatures.

Just as in the address and salutation, the problem of sexism in the ordering of names occurs in the signature block when it includes both women's and men's names. Unless some non-sex-related factor such as company rank or professional status dictates an order for names, fairness requires alphabetical order here.

As with the change to nonsexism in the address and salutation, the correction of the signature block may have to await some cultural adjustment. However, as soon as a significant number of women refuse to announce marital status through the use of *Miss* and *Mrs.*, refuse to use their husbands' names, and require nonsexist name order, the outdated forms will disappear.

When some married women use both a courtesy title and their husbands' names as part of their signatures, not only do they perpetuate sexism, but they run counter to accepted legal identification. After all, if John Jones marries and divorces several times, he leaves behind him several women named "Mrs. John Jones." Each Mrs. John Jones is a unique and distinct human being who gave up self-identification to marry John Jones. Even when a former Mrs. John Jones begins using her first name along with Jones (Elva Jones) or legally retains her birth surname after divorce, she has still left a trail of hundreds or thousands of representations of herself, in signatures, as "Mrs. John Jones."

Perhaps the most anachronistic of all these types of sexism occurs when a widow clings to "Mrs. John Jones." At marriage she gave up her identity and took his when she married John Jones. She then became the "*former* Miss Alice Voss." (Does that mean that Alice Voss died and Mrs. John Jones was born?) Now at the death of John Jones, she finds her identity in a deceased human being; she becomes a nonperson, a living memorial to a dead man.

Even obituary notices recognize the woman as an extension of her husband. "Mrs. James Colby" or, at best, "Mrs. Joanne Colby" follow her even at death. On the other hand, her husband's obituary has the head "James Colby."

Guideline F: Signatures

1. Consistently omit courtesy titles for both men and women. Those with initials or sex-neutral names should include *Mr.* or *Ms.* in parentheses in the typewritten signature line. Never use a courtesy title in the signature itself.

Incorrect	*Correct*
Cordially,	Cordially,

Myrna Gose

(Ms.) Myrna Gose

Sincerely yours,

Myrna Gose

Myrna Gose

Sincerely yours,

Mrs. Della Hess

Mrs. Della Hess

Sincerely,

Della Hess

Della Hess

Sincerely,

L. J. Waller

L. J. Waller

Yours truly,

L. J. Waller

(Ms.) L. J. Waller

Yours truly,

Chris Dobbs

Chris Dobbs

Chris Dobbs

(Mr.) Chris Dobbs

2. Married women, always use your first name and not your husband's.

Incorrect	*Correct*
Cordially,	Cordially,

Mrs. John Bayles

Mrs. John Bayles

Mary Bayles

Mary Bayles

3. For two or more names in a signature, base the order on something other than sex or sex-stereotyped criteria—alphabetical arrangement if no other criterion applies.

Incorrect	*Correct*
Cordially,	Cordially,

Max Graham
Sharon Adams

Max Graham

Sharon Adams

Sharon Adams
Max Graham

Sharon Adams

Max Graham

Sincerely,   Sincerely,

Charles and Barbara Colby   *Barbara and Charles Colby*
Charles and Barbara Colby   Barbara and Charles Colby

APPLICATIONS

Suggested solutions for these exercises appear in Appendix B.

☆ *4-1. Following are eight letter and memorandum situations. For each, write the first line of a sexist address and a sexist salutation according to traditional form. Then write a totally nonsexist address first line and salutation, being careful not to startle or offend the receiver unnecessarily.*

1. You have received a letter from a woman who signed her name "Mrs. George Rivers." In the letter she has complained about the necessity of using disposable bags in the new vacuum cleaner she purchased from your company.

2. You have drawn a random sample of names and addresses from a city directory and plan to send sales letters to those addresses. You will offer a special on home carpet installation. One name selected is Howard Harwell.

3. You address a letter to Sellwell Realty.

4. You have received a letter with a typewritten name line of "(Miss) Olivia Graham, Chairman, Finance Committee." The letter inquires about an organizational money-making product that you sell.

5. You will send a letter to a married couple listed on your mailing list as "Mr. and Mrs. David Cooper (Rita)." The purpose of the letter is to solicit a contribution from the couple toward the summer youth program your company sponsors.

6. You will send a letter to a married couple. She has retained the name with which she was born, Sara Hill, and she has an earned doctorate. His name is Jerry Selmon.

7. You will answer a letter signed "Helen Gardner."

8. You will write a memorandum to Greta Taylor. She is married to Howard Taylor.

☆ *4-2. Following are six signature-block situations. For each, identify the sexism that would occur in traditional treatment. Then write a totally nonsexist typewritten name for the signature.*

1. You are a married male named Gale Horton.
2. You are a married female named Lindsay Keller.
3. You are a single female named Ella Sells.
4. You are a single male named Jackie Howell.
5. You are a married couple named Patricia and Elwood Fraim.
6. Two of you are signing a letter. You are Vera Schell-Meyers, Manager, and your colleague is Harry Holden, Assistant Manager.

☆ *4-3. For each of the following excerpts from letters and memoranda, identify and rewrite the sexist elements.*

1. "The two supervisors are Melinda and Mr. Tryon."
2. "Mrs. George Taggert and Bill Krauss were two community leaders present."
3. A memorandum heading:
   To: Ms. Kate Brown
   From: James Courtney
4. "Mrs. Dorsey, Miss Crier, and Skelton"
5. "Miss Feeney and Mrs. Elder"
6. An address taken from a mailing list including the name Harold Arvin.
   The Harold Arvins
   Dear Arvin Family:
7. On a mail-in refund coupon included with a sales letter:
   Mr.
   Mrs.―――――――――――――――――――――――――――――――――――
   Miss

☆ *4-4. For the following sexist letter, underline the sexist words and phrases and then rewrite them.*

HAPPYDAYS HOMES PRODUCTS

Fine Products for a Man's Castle   7777 Clean Street
                                                    Nirvana, Georgia
                                                    July 8, 198X

HE WHO HESITATES . . .

. . . just may lose out on the best offer Happydays Home Products will make this year! For the next ten days only, you can buy the electric MR.

RUG SHAMPOO at 25 percent off the suggested retail price—simply by taking this letter to your local hardware man. Yes, for only $44.95, you can buy one of the finest machines on the market. And even the original price ($59.95) was considerably lower than the prices of other machines anywhere near the quality of MR. RUG SHAMPOO, because our direct-to-dealer delivery strategy cuts out the cost of using a middleman.

Just think how happy you'll make the little woman by buying her this machine to help her in her housework! After shampooing, the carpets will look as if a professional had done them—at much less than half the cost of the services of such a man. Any homemaker would be thrilled at being spoiled by her husband's thoughtfulness in buying her a MR. RUG SHAMPOO—for her birthday, Christmas, anniversary, or whatever.

The shampooer is so hefty and well constructed that your wife may even be able to sweet-talk you into operating it for her. And even if you have a cleaning girl come in, you'll be contributing to quicker and better cleaning of your home.

MR. RUG SHAMPOO has a one-year warranty on parts and service, and for a small price you can purchase a service contract at the end of the year that will assure you that a serviceman will be at your door within forty-eight hours of a telephone call. In a recent man-in-the-street survey we conducted, we found that this type of warranty is what the consumer says he wants.

When your mailman delivers this letter to your door, act immediately, because MR. RUG SHAMPOO is the finest piece of equipment of its type in this age of modern man. Not only will it allow your wife to keep your carpet clean and beautiful, but it will increase its life, thus saving you some of your hard-earned dollars.

Remember, a man is only as good as his word—and MR. RUG SHAMPOO's word can be trusted. He didn't need an adman to write this letter; he just asked us to do it because he knew his word would stand without embellishment.

Yes, don't be a man who hesitates. Show your good judgment by taking this letter to your nearest hardware store and buying MR. RUG SHAMPOO before your ten days are up. Your girl will love you for it.

Yours for a cleaner castle,

(Miss) Canday Castle
Your Happydays Home Products Girl

☆   *4-5.   For the following interdepartmental memorandum underline the sexist passages, then write nonsexist versions of those passages.*

To: Mrs. Vera Scrivner	Date: March 18, 198X
From: Gerald Chevrolet *gc*	Subject: Formation of Committees to Project Manpower Needs

As we discussed earlier, I am assigning you and Ellis to serve as cochairmen for the committee being formed to project manpower needs for your department for 198X. I have asked Miss Gibbons, Mrs. Nelms, Green, Phelps, and Reardon to serve as committeemen. Thus, the committee includes both men and ladies.

As we have done in the past in developing such projections, be sure to involve some laymen, heads of households, city fathers, and businessmen as you attempt to forecast demand for our services. You might even contact some spinsters, divorcées, and widows because of their particular need for our specialized Han-D-Man Home-Repair Service.

Pay particular attention to the impact that our new journeyman program will have on projections. I know that with a new program such as this, you are operating in a no-man's land, because you really have no empirical data base from which to work. However, do what you can, for if we find a significantly increased demand for our services, we will have to begin an extensive manhunt soon to provide the kind of men we need for the man-hours required.

Just have the girls in the typing pool take care of any report production you need. If you complete the project before vacations begin in April, all the typing stations will be manned.

Vera, would you and Ellis set a meeting for next week for the committee and me. You will also need to select a middleman for your committee and me and have him at the meeting. And, have your gal Friday present to prepare the meeting report.

5

THE ORDER OF NAMES, SEXIST MODIFIERS, AND CITING SEXIST WRITING

Sex fairness in communication includes the order of listing men's and women's names. Traditionally, the man's name comes first because of the customary male-is-the-more-important patriarchal system. The two major nonsexist approaches to ordering names are alphabetical arrangement and random alternation.

The alphabetical arrangement begins with last names when they differ and then uses first names for those with the same last name. The examples of addresses in Chapter 4 reflect this natural, unbiased approach. To alternate fairly between woman-first and man-first order, devise a formal or informal method for keeping the name rotation split about evenly.

Sometimes we cannot make the conversion from sexist to nonsexist ordering by applying these simple, straightforward rules. One example of adjustment occurs when responding to a letter with a signature block including the names of a man and a woman. In that instance, observe the order of names set by the correspondents themselves. If the woman and man take the trouble to list both names—a possible nonsexist act in itself—they may well have considered the order as well. In any case, honor the order they establish.

The ultimate solution to listing names, and all other sexism in addresses and salutations for that matter, lies with the people being addressed. And those people include all of us, for we all participate in communication chains. When we address in nonsexist fashion and insist that others address us likewise, those who correspond with us will eventually comply. Thus, we must address and sign our correspondence in sex-fair ways and take the time to correct all mailings addressed to us in sexist form. Tenacity is the key. We often have to make several contacts before those who address us will honor our insistence on sex-fair forms of address, but the results justify the effort.

Guideline G:
The Male-First Order of Presenting Names

1. Use the male-first order for those who indicate it or demand it, only as a last resort, and only for the short run. Sufficient alternatives appear in this manual so that you need use the sexist order only in the most extreme circumstances. If a woman and man sign a letter by using both names and *Ms.* or no courtesy title for the woman, honor their order.

You receive a letter signed "Kirk Jennings and Doris Adams."

Incorrect	*Correct*
You address your return letter to Doris Adams and Kirk Jennings or Mrs. Doris Adams and Mr. Kirk Jennings	You address your return letter to Kirk Jennings and Doris Adams or Mr. Kirk Jennings and Ms. Doris Adams

2. Base the order of names on something other than sex.

a. Arrange alphabetically by last names if different and by first names if the last name is the same.

Incorrect	*Correct*
Mr. Hal Keel and Ms. Lou Bly	Ms. Lou Bly and Mr. Hal Keel
George and Beverly Shay	Beverly and George Shay

b. Alternate between woman-first and man-first order by using a formal or informal method for keeping the name rotation about even.

Incorrect	*Correct*
Codirectors of a project sign all communiqués in this order:	Codirectors of a project sign communiqués in alternating order:
Ernest Tell and Alice Drew	Ernest Tell and Alice Drew
	Alice Drew and Ernest Tell

c. Observe rank if it takes precedence over sex-order fairness.

Incorrect	*Correct*
In a signature block:	In a signature block:
Jill Allison, Assistant Director	Kyle Jeter, Director
Kyle Jeter, Director	Jill Allison, Assistant Director

INCONSISTENCIES IN PAIRED REFERENCES TO FEMALES AND MALES

Inconsistency in paired references to females and males exists when we use a non-marital-status courtesy title for a man, but not for a woman. Therefore, if we use *Mr.* for a man, we must use *Ms.* (not *Miss* or *Mrs.*) for a woman.

Another particularly inconsistent form of reference is the use of courtesy titles for women and last names only for men, as in "Miss (or Mrs. or even Ms.) Kelly and Graber [a man] attended the meeting." A similar nonparallelism occurs in the use of the first name only for a woman and the last name only—or last name with *Mr.*—for a man, as in "Elaine and Anders (or Mr. Anders)."

Sexism further occurs through a mistaken impression about the courtesy title *Ms.* It is the appropriate title to supplant both *Mrs.* and *Miss*, yet people do not always understand that. Some people treat *Ms.* as the equivalent of *Miss*, but not of *Mrs.*

Age-referent terms plague both sexes. *Shoeshine boy, boyfriend, newsboy, delivery boy, houseboy, busboy, playboy, cowboy* all represent age-referent put-downs to mature males. However, the age-referent put-downs to mature females overshadow them. Special labels such as *show girl, cleaning girl, girl-friend, stunt girl, calendar girl, pinup girl, chorus girl, playgirl, cigarette girl, pom-pom girl,* even *call girl* are both age referent and sex negative. However, the most serious sexist problem here exists when phrases including *girl* are used in conjunction with phrases including *man.*

An article in a university newspaper recently appeared with a headline and several references to an upcoming appearance of the university's "Girls' Chorus," which would appear on the program with the "Men's Chorus." Even Lois Lane has the title "girl reporter," and we know she certainly doesn't run with Super*boy.* A common type of newspaper headline includes words like "Man Abducts Girl [Woman]."

When a man calls a woman "little girl" or "my baby girl," his "endear-ments" may express the subconscious desire to have a companion much like a dog—one who is "man's best friend," loyal whatever the master does to her, empty-headed, and uninclined or unable to question him. Though meanings may differ with the context, observation verifies that people are much more likely to call a woman a "baby girl" than to call a man a "baby boy." Society's enforcement of such subordination raises serious questions. However, its acceptance and support by the very women upon whom it is perpetrated puzzle many an observer.

From songs—excellent reflectors of culture—comes more proof that the culture accepts "men and girls" as a perfectly legitimate portrayal of relative sex status. Personal ballads for either sex frequently include the so-called parallel forms of *girl* and *man*. In defense of man-and-girl pairing, some would say, "But *man* and *woman* have a different number of syllables, and the rhythm of the song would be ruined by substituting *woman* for *girl*." However, several flaws exist in that argument. (1) It assumes that all songs reflect the man's point of view, so that the word *woman* is the secondary, the substitute, the one requiring adjustment. (2) It assumes that vocal musicians cannot adapt musical form to varying numbers of syllables in words. (3) It assumes that to maintain the same number of syllables the phrase would have to be "man and girl," not "boy and girl."

The last flaw exemplifies the most telling weakness of the argument. If we accept *girl* so readily, why do we not accept *boy* for a man? Could the answer be that, too often on the basis of race, calling a mature male "boy" communicates inferiority? Then, moving from racism to sexism, we must understand that calling a mature female "girl" also puts her "in her place." Minority males rightly say, "Don't you call me 'boy'!" Unfortunately, not all females demand, "Don't call me 'girl'!"

Consider these sayings: "A girl in every port," "Diamonds are a girl's best friend," "Girl watchers." Have you ever heard of a weather boy? a weather woman?

In conjunction with Sandra Day O'Connor's nomination to the Supreme Court, Tip O'Neill, Speaker of the House of Representatives, stated that he was glad a "girl" was finally going to serve as a Supreme Court judge. The furor that pronouncement sparked vindicated nonsexist communicators to some extent.

In summary, then, positive communication mandates the removal of references to female adults as *girls*, with the age of adulthood set at eighteen. That correction will eliminate the inconsistency of the girl-man dichotomy.

Guideline H:
Inconsistencies in Paired References
to Females and Males

1. Omit courtesy titles for both males and females or include them for both.

Incorrect	*Correct*
Andrew Solko and Mrs. Ina Jerome	Mr. Andrew Solko and Ms. Ina Jerome
	Andrew Solko and Ina Jerome

2. Omit parenthetical titles in the typewritten name in the signature block for both women and men. The inclusion of the parenthetical notation is logical for initials, and for names neither clearly female nor male.

Incorrect	*Correct*
(Ms.) Brenda Allen and Harry Elwood	Brenda Allen and Harry Elwood
Jan Skaggs	(Mr.) Jan Skaggs

   3. Use first names consistently.

Incorrect	*Correct*
Referring to Sheldon Andrews and Patricia Elder:	
Andrews and Patricia	Andrews and Elder
	Sheldon and Patricia

   4. Use *Ms.* for both married and single women.

Incorrect	*Correct*
Mrs. Ryerson and Ms. Clauson (Ms. Clauson is single)	Ms. Ryerson and Ms. Clauson

   5. Pair *gentleman* with *lady*.

Incorrect	*Correct*
The salesman and the saleslady	The salesman and the saleswoman
	The salesgentleman and the saleslady

   6. Use pairs of words that consistently do or do not include gender syllables.

Incorrect	*Correct*
As a businessperson, she . . ., and as a businessman, he	As a businessperson, she . . ., and as a businessperson, he
	As a businesswoman, she . . ., and as a businessman, he

   7. Maintain the parallelism of "husband and wife."

Incorrect	*Correct*
As man and wife, they	As husband and wife, they

   8. Pair *man* with *woman*.

Incorrect	*Correct*
The man and his bride	The newly married man and woman
	The groom and bride

9. Present age-referent pairs of words for females and males consistently.

Incorrect	Correct
Referring to two adults:	
The man and the girl	The man and the woman

10. Introduce nonsexist ordering of pairs involving both sexes.

Incorrect	Correct
Always:	Half the time:
Son and daughter	Daughter and son
Husband and wife	Wife and husband
Boys and girls	Girls and boys

SEXIST MODIFIERS

One major sexist use of modifiers tacks the sex-pointer adjective or noun-become-adjective on women's names and not on men's. For example, can you imagine an article in a newspaper referring to "Mr. Heller, a tall, handsome, brunette divorcé, dressed in a striking black suit"? Doubtful. Yet, "Miss Heller, a tall, beautiful brunette divorcée" or "Mrs. Heller, a rather plump, grandmotherly type of girl" are phrases common to writers, particularly journalists.

Other examples of reporting that make females the "other" or define them only in relation to males include these types of headlines.

Corporate President's Wife Takes Tour
Attractive Widow Files for Senate
Wife and Mother Named Manager
Truck Driver's Daughter Wins Scholarship
Delbert Mason's Wife Injured in Accident

Through such strings of adjectives and nouns, society makes the woman's physical being and her definition in relation to men more important than her mind and her own accomplishments.

Similarly, have you ever seen a "men's section" or even a "men's and women's section" in a news publication? However, many people consider challenging the validity of the "women's section" strange. Therefore, world news, national news, business news, financial news, the classifieds, policy statements, and sports must form "men's news," while engagements, weddings, recipes, beauty contests, social debuts, coming-out parties, style shows, volunteer work, diet and exercise programs, women's auxiliaries, sewing, decorating, child care, and how to save must form "women's news."

Another type of sexism occurs when gender words, such as *lady, woman,* and *male,* precede a neutral word. Examples of this modification of words include "male secretary," "woman manager," and "lady doctor."

The solution to sexist modifiers, of course, lies in removing them. However, a less attractive solution includes them consistently for both sexes.

Guideline I: Sexist Modifiers

1. Establish parallelism in the use of adjectives for males and females.

Incorrect	*Correct*
She is a pert young blonde programmer, and he is a supervisor	She is a programmer and he is a supervisor
	or
	She is a pert young blonde programmer, and he is a jock-type, middle-aged, brunette supervisor
He is a graduate of_____, and she is an attractive mother of four	He is a graduate of_____, and she is a graduate of_____
	or
	He is a father of five, and she is a mother of four
	or
	He is a graduate of_____ and a father of five, and she is a graduate of_____ and a mother of four
Woman superstar	Superstar
	or
	Woman superstar and man superstar
Lady lawyer	Lawyer
	or
	Lady lawyer and gentleman lawyer
Woman driver	Driver
	or
	Woman driver and man driver
Male hairdresser	Hairdresser
	or
	Female hairdresser and male hairdresser

2. Eliminate the concept of a "women's section," "women's news," a "society page," and sexist journalistic reporting style from all communication.

Incorrect	*Correct*
Mr. and Mrs. H. L. Menkin announce the engagement of their daughter Miss Helga Menkin to Jerry Post-Gardner, son of Mr. and Mrs. G. T. Post-Gardner	Helga Menkin and Jerry Post-Gardner announce that they will be married on July 22. Menkin's parents are Betty and H. L. Menkin. Post-Gardner's parents are Helen Gardner and G. T. Post.
Grandmother Wins Contest	Cooper Wins Contest
Housewife Supervises Campaign	Byers Supervises Campaign
Miss Doris Groves Named Miss Orange	Groves Named Winner
	or
	Omit all stories that diminish females

SEXISM IN CITATIONS
FROM SECONDARY SOURCES

Communicators often must cite from the sexist words of others. Serious nonsexist reporters will never use direct quotations from such words. Summaries and paraphrases usually work as well as direct quotations and allow removal of the sexism from an otherwise useful passage.

Suppose that a direct quotation of a paragraph important to a report you are writing includes these words:

> The research showed that the average citizen considers voting his most important political act. The typical respondent to the survey said he thinks that the man who does not exercise the vote is not meeting his responsibilities for the well-being of his nation. He also said the selection of the right man for president of the United States is particularly critical. And, finally, he is concerned that each man must exercise the one-man, one-vote tradition that has made America great.

Rather than quoting directly, the nonsexist writer could summarize the findings with these words.

> According to the author, the research showed that the average citizen considers the vote the most important political act a citizen can exercise. The typical survey respondent said that the citizen who does not vote, particularly for president of the United States, does not meet the responsibilities that accompany the right to vote.

If you want to retain a direct quotation yet remove the sexism from it, you may omit sexist words and insert nonsexist alternatives. This process requires ellipses for omissions and brackets around insertions. An example of such a revision for the quotation is

> The research showed that the average citizen considers voting [her or] his most important political act. The typical respondent to the survey said that . . . the

. . . [person] who does not exercise the vote is not meeting . . . responsibilities for the well-being of . . . [the] nation. . . . [The typical respondent] also said the selection of the right . . . [person] for president of the United States is particularly critical. And, finally . . . [the typical respondent] is concerned that each . . . [person] must exercise the . . . [one-person], one-vote tradition that has made America great.

Observe how cluttered the overuse of ellipses and brackets makes a passage look. Therefore, you should avoid using a direct quotation if it requires more than one omission or insertion every two or three lines. A paraphrase or summary will be a sufficient alternative.

A more difficult problem arises when the exact name of an entity required in the report is sexist. Examples include Manpower Administration, Fraternal Order of Police, Brotherhood of Railroad Workers, and honorary academic "fraternities." Also, many articles and books carry sexist words in their titles. Because we cannot change the proper names we encounter, we have no total solution. However, you can search for other equivalent sources of information to avoid the sexist names, and you can make known any offenders you must use by reporting them only in footnotes or bibliographies.

When you cannot avoid a sexist name or title, state references and lead-ins in the body of the report without using the sex-negative words themselves. For example, you can use phrases like "federal compensation laws" or "workers' compensation" instead of "workmen's compensation"; you can use lead-ins for sexist publication titles that include the author's name without the title; and you can replace names like "Manpower Administration" with such words as "a government agency" or "a division of the Department of Labor." We are not going to eradicate a phrase like "city of brotherly love," but we do not have to use it—"Philadelphia" alone communicates quite well.

When you have to use sexist words in direct quotations, footnotes, or bibliographies, insert "[*sic*]" following the offense to indicate that you use the words of another, but you recognize them as sexist. Consider this example from a bibliography:

Jetty, P. Gaul. *Any Man [sic] Can Be a Millionaire*. New York: Book Publishing, Inc., 1981.

Guideline J:
Sexism in Citations from Secondary Sources

1. Summarize or paraphrase sexist excerpts.

Incorrect	*Correct*
According to _____, "Mankind owes it to himself to"	According to _____, humans owe it to themselves to

2. Use omissions, ellipses, and bracketed insertions to eliminate sexist passages in a direct quotation. Avoid overuse of these devices.

Incorrect

Giles suggests that "our forefathers intended more for us than this law could ever provide"

Correct

Giles suggested that "our . . . [predecessors] intended more for us than this law could ever provide"

3. Use [*sic*] to indicate sexist words in direct quotations.

Incorrect

A *Newsweek* article reports: "Clergymen generally disagree"

Correct

A *Newsweek* article reports: Clergymen [*sic*] generally disagree"

4. Use only nonsexist titles and organizational names if possible; if you must use sexist ones, place them only in the footnotes and bibliography and use [*sic*] to illustrate your recognition of the sexism.

Incorrect

According to a publication of the Manpower Administration of the U.S. Department of Labor

In the book *Science and Man*, Styles wrote that

¹Jane Tiree, "Mankind's View of the Irishman's Role in War"

Correct

According to a publication of the U.S. Department of Labor

Styles wrote that

¹Jane Tiree, Mankind's [*sic*] View of the Irishman's [*sic*] Role in War"

5. Use substitutes for sexist organization names in the body of the message.

Incorrect

The Fraternal Order of Lumbermen

Correct

The lumber workers' organization

APPLICATIONS

Suggested solutions for these exercises appear in Appendix B.

☆ *5-1. For the following letter, underline the sexist words and phrases, then rewrite the letter in nonsexist form.*

WEDDING GIRL, INC.

May 14, 198X

Miss Sara Ferris
888 Fox Avenue
Wrong Number, New York 00000

Dear Miss Ferris:

So, you've caught your man and can now open that hope chest! Your wedding will be the happiest time in your entire life if you let Wedding Girl, Inc., plan it from beginning to end.

Yes, from dealing with your future mother-in-law's demands, to the "love, honor, and obey," to the final "I pronounce you man and wife," Wedding Girl, Inc., will remove all cares from your pretty little head and leave it free for dreams of the home that he will provide for you . . . for dreams of how you will make his meals and manage his home . . . for dreams of how you will mother those sons you'll give him . . . for dreams of pipe and slippers at the end of his workday . . . and for dreams of flowers and candy for you—his bride, his doll.

We'll help you make decisions about such things as who will give you away, how to place the photograph in the newspaper that will announce your upcoming MRS. "degree" (the only one you really ever wanted), arrangements for the wedding pictures, one of which will be placed in publications to show that you've changed your name to his, and how to choose the girls and men to be bride's maids or matrons, groomsmen, best man, etc. We'll even arrange for cooking lessons; after all, the way to a man's heart is through his stomach.

Call Wedding Girl, Inc., soon. Our charges are so reasonable that your father will be pleased, and our services are so complete that your mother won't spend so much time crying. Make this high point in your life all that it can be. Trust Wedding Girl, Inc., to help make the two of you into one.

Yours for a perfect wedding,

Dale Lomax, Arrangements
WEDDING GIRL, INC.

☆   *5-2.   In the following segment from a hypothetical research report, underline the sexist words, phrases, and passages that indicate sexist research procedures. Then write corrected versions of those passages.*

A stratified random sample of 400 was drawn from the population. The strata represented the classes of workmen under consideration in the research: firemen, policemen, medical emergency team crewmen, electric company linemen, and mailmen. The systematic sampling procedure was used to select the workmen from each stratum—represented by a listing of all who constituted the particular class. The number of workmen selected from each stratum represented the proportion that the particular stratum was to the whole of the population. The numbers in each class are shown as part of the findings presented in Chapter III.

After the sample was identified, clearance was obtained from the appropriate labor fraternal orders and brotherhoods. Then, each workman was contacted and asked for his permission to allow information to be taken from his personnel folder. Only 23 refused such permission, leaving 377 of the original sample.

In five instances, both a man and his wife were selected through the systematic process as members of the sample. In those instances, the man was retained, and the wife was eliminated from the sample. The wife was eliminated because data obtained from two members of the same family could have proved a biasing duplication for certain portions of the research. Thus, as head of the household, the man was retained. The final sample, then, contained 372 people (93 percent of the original sample of 400).

The personnel folder for each of the 372 workmen was inspected. If his folder was complete, the data were simply recorded on the form included as Appendix C. If, however, the folder was not complete, the workman was contacted to obtain the information needed.

As established in the report of the design of the investigation in Chapter I, the race and sex of the selected workmen were two important demographic characteristics for analysis. The numbers and proportions represented by each subclassification so determined are presented in Chapter III. Overall, however, the white man represented 81 percent of the total; the black man, 15 percent; the red man, 1 percent; and all other races, 3 percent. Ninety-two percent of the workmen were men, and 8 percent were women.

☆   *5-3.   The following excerpt from a short report is written in the informal style and uses first- and second-person pronouns. Identify the sexist passages and write corrections for them.*

After you receive approval for your new project, you will need to begin the search for the money, men, materials, market, and management necessary to complete it. Engage the support of the company wives, and you will find that the project will go more smoothly than it would without their support.

Because your project will involve the development of a new four-man trailer tent, center your marketing plan on sportsmen or outdoorsmen. You should check out the possibilities for coupling your campaign with that for the two-man canoe that was developed last year. Use appeals to the man's man, the rugged man, the man of the earth, and even the return to the common man as you develop your advertising design.

Picture primitive scenes with bewhiskered and rugged riflemen and huntsmen. However, also picture friendly scenes. Include a father and son, with man's best friend—the family dog. He should be bouncing happily beside the tent and beside the mother as she cooks the fish the fishermen have caught from the stream nearby. Show dad helping his son build a snowman in a winter scene. Stress the safety of the trailer tent against man-eating animals.

Spotlight the excitement of the wild as it is conquered by man. You might even include footprints of the Abominable Snow Man. He is, after all, a creature whose existence is not really believed, but who, like ghosts, introduces adventure into an outing. You might show the frightened mother and daughter being comforted by the strong father and son as they view the footprints. Make the father and son the men of the hour by showing how easily they can set up the tent, as the mother and daughter look on with admiration. Show the father and son pulling away from the shore in their canoe as the girls wave and wish them well.

You might feature the strength and water-tightness of the tent by picturing the family in snug comfort as the rain and wind are swirling about them. The mother is doing the dishes, the father is showing the son how to put a hook on the fishing line, and the daughter is playing with her doll. A newscaster's voice emanates from a portable radio. He says, "And the cost of living is hurting both the working man and the housewife in their battle to make ends meet."

☆ *5-4. Identify the sexist elements in the following hypothetical segments from reports. Then write nonsexist segments that could be used.*

1. The guardsmen and militiamen placed "Men Working" signs and flagmen on the highway. They called on the estate groundsmen and all local radiomen to help in the search effort.

2. Each politician promises to make every man a king. He also promises that he will not emasculate the voter by taking away his knowledge of the issues. He also assures us that Miss Liberty's principles will be upheld.

3. According to Jenks, the marketing strategy is critical: "Any good marketing plan must meet the requirements of the customer, for he has already

established his ideas in a general way. The gentlemen's agreement must be honored."

4. Englishmen and Frenchmen agree that good penmanship is an important qualification for the small law office clerk. They also establish the function of the executor or executrix as one of the most important for the lawman. They have much the same view of meeting the requirements set by Miss Justice that American men do.

☆   *5-5.   For these parts from hypothetical newspapers, magazines, or company publications, underline the sexist sections. Then write corrected versions.*

1. MISS HAMPLE NAMED MARKETING ASSISTANT

   Vice-President Jerry Klix announced the addition of Miss Sally Hample to the staff of the marketing department. Klix said that Miss Hample will be a marketing assistant.

   A gorgeous blonde, Miss Hample is a 1974 graduate of Singland University and a former Miss Singland. She was also fourth runner-up in the Miss Ogland County pageant of 1973 and was named All-College Queen in 1972 while attending Singland University.

   Klix said that Miss Hample will take over her duties January 1 and that the department is fortunate to have such an attractive girl join the staff.

2. MRS. ELLISON, SHERMAN CALLAWAY TO BE MARRIED IN LOCAL HOME

   Mr. and Mrs. William Axmore, Baconia, announce the engagement of their daughter, Mrs. Dora Ellison, to Sherman Callaway.

   Callaway's parents are Edward Callaway of Eggton and Mrs. George Attwell of Baconia. The wedding will be on December 8 in the home of the future bride's parents.

   Mrs. Ellison graduated from Baconia High School, where she was a cheerleader, basketball queen, and chairman of the usherette committee during her senior year. She is

   currently employed as a hostess at the Businessman's Lunchroom.

   Callaway, sales department, is a graduate of Baconia High School and is in the freshman year at Baconia Junior College.

3. E. A. BROWNE, MISS CLAYBORNE REPEAT VOWS IN CHAPEL

   Exchanging vows Thursday in a ceremony in the Ainsworth Chapel were E. A. Browne and Miss Dorothy Clayborne. The bride is the daughter of Mr. and Mrs. Ellis Park. Browne is the son of Mrs. Elton Bickford and the late Harry Browne.

   Honor attendants were Miss Sybil Laker and John Elton. Others were Mrs. Gene Gully, Miss Alice Drake, Donald Lancaster, and Stephen Wilt.

   The bride's mother wore. . . . The groom's mother wore. . . .

   Browne is an engineer in the Sawton District.

4. Mr. and Mrs. Richard Doakes announce the birth of a son—Richard Doakes, Jr. He weighed 7 pounds, 4 ounces. Doakes is a delivery boy in the sales department.

5. SHANNONETTES WIN BOWLING TITLE

   The Shannon Co. is proud to announce that the girls' bowling team, the Shannonettes, just won the annual bowling tournament in Mallville.

The men's bowling team—the Shannons—took second place in the same tournament. Both trophies are on display in the employee lounge.

6. CORA TO VISIT BEACON PLANT

Cora, the wife of the Shannon Co. president, Alfred Shannon, will tour the Beacon Plant on April 8. Hostesses will be the foremen's wives.

7. SHANNON TO SPEAK AT ANNUAL INDUSTRIAL CONFERENCE

President Alfred Shannon will be the featured speaker at the annual Industrial Association Conference.

Shannon's wife will accompany him to take part in the Industrial Association Wives activities.

8. MRS. DONALD ELLISON DIES

Mrs. Donald Ellison, long-time employee, died in the home on December 9 following a long illness.

Her husband is a vice-president with the Friendly Corp. He has been active in community affairs, having once served a term as a city councilman.

The funeral for Mrs. Ellison will be at the Ball Funeral Home on December 12.

Mrs. Ellison is survived by her husband; a son, Charles; two daughters, Mrs. Lowell Saul, Pretoria, and Mrs. Frank Holiday, Brookville; and six grandchildren.

☆ *5-6. The following passage includes the kind of language often used in policy statements. Underline and rewrite the sexist words and phrases found in it.*

1. Check manning standards monthly instead of bimonthly so that we can make better predictions of heavy work periods.

2. Complete workmen's compensation forms within ten days of receipt now instead of within the twenty days previously allowed.

3. The affected superior must approve any requests for a secretary's time that go beyond her normal duties. He must sign Form 9-a to confirm his approval for the girl's overtime.

4. Because of some recent airline losses of executives' suitcases with important company papers in them, put all such papers in your briefcase. Then carry the briefcase on board with you and keep it at your seat or have the stewardess stow it.

5. When arriving at the office before 7 A.M. or leaving after 7 P.M., you must now check in and out with the night watchman.

6. Couch communication with the Des Moines office in terms understandable to the layman. That office deals in support services and does not have the technical men that the other offices have.

7. The postman will no longer deliver mail by floors. Therefore, each office will need to have a mail boy.

☆   *5-7. Rewrite this sexist direct quotation. Use* [sic], *omissions and ellipses, and insertions and brackets to accomplish the revision.*

Of the twelve jurymen present, four were businessmen, one was a sculptress, two were housewives, one was a watchman, one was a deliveryman, and one was a lady computer programmer.

6

NAMES OF HUMANS AND ANIMALS; RELIGIOUS AND MONARCHIAL REFERENCES

Sexism exists implicitly in our naming customs and explicitly in the inconsistent reporting of names.[1] A person's name acts as her or his symbol of identity, virtually of existence. Yet society expects the woman to use her name to meet the rules of the culture. Unfortunately, few people—including women—recognize the psychological damage created by these customs.

Five aspects of naming will be considered here: (1) given names, (2) surnames, (3) middle names, (4) changing names at marriage, and (5) "The Joneses" concept of male names as defining units.

---

[1]For an excellent treatise on the subordination of women exemplified in our naming customs, see Una Stannard, *Mrs. Man* (San Francisco: Germainbooks, 1977).

Given Names

Culture often creates the imagery associated with being "feminine"—a socially defined "quality" of little girls—in the names given to them. The sugar-and-spice-and-everything-nice and pink-blanket connotations of girls' first names often do not stand them in good stead as they become women and desire to project the maturity, independence, and intelligence that define them as human beings.

With no intention of spotlighting, a review of such names will illustrate the point. For example, can you imagine naming a boy Fawn, Candy, Cookie, Joy, Rose, Lilly, Dolly, Precious, Sunshine, Lovie, Dovie, Ruby, Opal, Faith, Hope, Charity, Prudence, Grace, or Chastity? Yet the culture gives such names to girls in an often unwitting labeling of females as objects of beauty and dependence. Studies have shown that the names given to people can virtually create their personality types. Then the names given to females can become self-fulfilling prophecies of less-than-fully-human-potential personalities—personifications of sweets, flowers, gems, dolls, Pollyanna blandness, and gilded-cage captivity. Certainly, many women seem to overcome their names, but even for them researchers need to determine the extent of personality development attributable to their names.

Obviously, names affect boys and men too. However, strength and other positive human qualities characterize the promise in the bulk of male names: Don, Mike, Frank, Ernest, Rock, Bruce, Buck, David, Vince, Grant, Duke, John, Paul, Rod. Observe how strong names usually contain only one or two syllables.

In reality, the feminine names prove most detrimental to males. And if a female name brings psychological problems to a male, the fault lies with a system that reduces the image of the female to such a low level that penalty goes to the male for having a female name. We cannot discount the seriousness of this problem for the male. However, it represents a backlash of sexism toward the female: the myth of the inferiority of women creates the negativism associated with a feminine name for a male.

Other deprecation of females in first names appears in the use of weak suffixes as these names show: Lauretta, Juliette, Joanna, Joanie, Nellie, Sherri, Vicky, Debbie, Cindy, Suzy, Margie, Cathy, Tammie, Annie, Becky, Sandy, Julie, even Betty, Sally, Mary, Judy—all illustrate the unaccented weakness of the soft and cute endings of female names and nicknames.

Some males' names and nicknames carry the -y and, occasionally, the -ie suffixes. Examples include Johnny, Bobby, Benny, Ricky, Jimmie, Jerry, and Billy. However, most males drop the suffixes once they pass childhood. In contrast, women in their mature years still carry such little-girl names as Jonie and Angie. Think of the impact the name Jimmy may have had on Jimmy Carter's presidency. Think of how jokes and disparagement of President Reagan usually involve references to "Ronnie."

Other female-diminishing suffixes appear as variations or appendages of traditionally male names. Such names again reinforce the concept of the female as the extension of the male. Examples include Freda, Jamie, Jackie, Bobbie, Francine, Stephanie, Carla, Paulette, Jeanette, Roberta, Michelle, Josephine, Edwina, Eugenia, Charlene, Henrietta, Victoria, Wilhelmina, Geraldine, Claudette, Claudia, and Jody.

Observe how these female-weakened males' names reflect the use of devices already discussed. The unaccented terminal syllable and the *-ette*, *-etta*, and *-ine* endings form sure ways to diminish the stature of the female. Can you think of *any* examples that would weld such a suffix to a female name to convert it to a male name? Lists of names just do not yield a *Bethine* or a *Karena*, or a *Suette* for a male.

First-name sexism also exists when using a surname as a first name. The surname as first name often represents an attempt to carry on the surname from the mother's side of the family (in all likelihood a male-lineage name to begin with). Further, a surname as a first name almost always applies to a man, because society does not consider the surname "feminine" enough for a woman's first name.

The use of a surname for a first name, then, perpetuates the sexism of the naming process. It reveals the sexist attitudes of a patriarchal culture that relegates the mother's surname to an anonymous or reduced place. And weak as the surname as first name is as an approach to retaining the mother's family's surname, the culture denies even that approach to females. The culture does not accept such surnames become first names as Frank, Grant, Kirby, Langley, King, Meade, Hall, Gray, Scott, Blake, for females.

Another sexist practice in naming involves the acceptability of initials for males, but not for females. However, enough women now use initials that one cannot automatically assume that a name with initials belongs to a man.

Surnames

The use of a surname as a first name leads naturally into a consideration of how surnames exemplify historical sexism. "A Tale of Two Sexes" in Chapter 2 shows some of that sexism through its tongue-in-cheek "play" on some common surnames. Remember Nelsdaughter and Janesdaughter?

Williamson, Henderson, Nelson, Jackson, Johnson, Davidson, Thomason, Thompson, Blackman, Whiteman, Redman, Bateman: A patriarchal culture traces lineage through males, and the family "sir-names" reflect that attitude. A woman's surname—her link to the past—often derives from males' given names, as in Johnson ("John's son"), or includes *man* in it. Even when the surname itself does not include syllables of maleness, it carries with it the knowledge that females in the lineage are so unimportant that they sacrifice their names to the system.

Many people do not recognize the sexism in their birth surnames, and those who do recognize it can do little about it—in the short run at least. However, sensitivity to the system's psychological debasement of women requires knowledge of the self-perpetuating male-based derivation of those names.

Middle Names

Although the first and last names given to a female form the critical base of identity, the middle name can also contribute to or identify the sexist nature of naming customs. The middle-name problem has two facets: the feminine combination of first and second names and the quiet cry for equality that sometimes leads to use of the mother's birth surname as the middle name.

Examples of the cute, little-girl rhythm created by the paired first and second names or welded two-name first names often assigned to females include Mary Lou, Debra Lee, Sue Ellen, Betsy Ann, Sherilyn, Marianne, Marilyn, Betty Lynn, Sherry Alice, Brenda Jo, and Sally Jean. By way of contrast, try to think of double names used for men. . . . Any luck? If you think of even a few, they probably ring strong and true and include an original surname: Martin Luther, Thomas Jefferson, George Washington. Or if you thought of a name like Billy Joe or Billy Jack, you likely had difficulty thinking of any others—unless they represent the southern double-name tradition.

In the case of first and second names like George Washington, the realist must doubt that people use both names in everyday address, as they do the double names of women. For example, the family of Martin Luther King probably did not address him as Martin Luther at all times, though families do consistently call women by such names as Rita Faye.

Custom limits the use of the birth surname of the mother to the middle name for a female. A surname as a female's middle name again illustrates an attempt to retain some identity for the lineage of the mother's side of the family. But the surname is what identifies a family; it is the *family* name. Therefore, however noble the effort at maintaining the mother's surname by making it a middle name, it falls far short of offsetting the basic sexism that initiated the effort.

Consideration of surnames sets the stage for the most critical of the sexist naming problems for females. That problem involves the trauma of giving up one's name—one's very identity—to conform to the rules of society.

Changing Names at Marriage

Think about it. How would a man react if, after having one name for twenty years or so, the culture told him to give it up and take on the name of the woman he married? How would he react if he not only gave up his name, but assured her that the children would have her surname to carry on her family name? Can you imagine that a man would accept that erasure of his being? Undoubtedly not. Yet many women unquestioningly continue to accept the name-killing process for themselves.

Replacement of a woman's birth surname by that of her husband shocks her psyche enough. But the culture also expects the woman to become a "Mrs. John Jones" extension of her husband—discarding her given and middle names in all contexts except the most informal and personal. With that rule, then, does her first name become *Mrs.* and her second name *John?*

Recall how Kunta Kinte in *Roots* withstood extremes of physical and psychological pain, but finally broke under the whip to take on the name of Toby. However, he answered to Toby only outwardly, forever remaining Kunta to himself and his children. Readers or viewers of *Roots* have no trouble empathizing with Kunta Kinte's desire to hold on to his birthright—his name. Yet those same people consider women who refuse to change their names at marriage extremists of some kind. Sexism rings loud and clear: Kunta Kinte was male and his name mattered. A woman's name does not.

If names did not define people so totally, we might dismiss name changes as unimportant. However, marriage often robs a woman of the continuity of progressive growth of self. It interrupts and subverts by an act that smacks of the same type of "rights" that went with ownership of slaves. That a civilized society would engage in such a practice proves difficult to fathom.

Some women do retain their birth names after marriage. Others introduce the hyphenated surname that includes both marriage partners' surnames. However, even when a woman adopts the hyphenated form, her husband rarely does. He usually retains his original surname intact.

The names assigned to the children of such marriages vary. Some children carry the hyphenated surnames of the parents. Sometimes all children carry the birth surname of the mother. In other families, all children carry the birth surname of the father—an act that perpetuates the patriarchy. In still others, the parents randomly or alternately assign their birth surnames to the children.

No one ever said the adjustment of an ingrained system would come easily. However, the conversion to justice for both sexes requires creative adjustment.

Males' Names as Defining Units

Families have Christmas cards inscribed "The Phil Smiths." Headlines refer to "The Henry Kissingers." People put signs on mailboxes, doors, and curbs reflecting "The George Hammils" type of designation. Pollsters designate a home as 'The Albert Norman household." Directories and mailing lists are normally composed of male names to represent houses full of people—

including at least one grown woman. The government perpetuates the absorption of other people into the male by designating the head of the household as male unless a male is not present. Even sociologists classify the family's socioeconomic level as that of the male—regardless of the status of the female.

With all these procedures that make the woman a nonperson, the sexism is clear. To remove the sexism, then, could we convert the arrangement so that half the time we refer to "The Isabel Taggerts" (her birth name)? Because society rarely honors such an approach, let us instead cease to use the man's name as the unit and begin to include the woman as a cohead of household, a fully equal partner in the unit, and a human being with an individuality expressed by a unique name.

Guideline K: Names of Humans

1. Do not use the "Mrs. John Jones" style of address.

Incorrect	Correct
Mrs. Albert Grand	Phyllis Grand
	or
	Phyllis Brooks Grand
Mrs. Linda Summers	Linda Summers
	Linda Bart-Summers

2. Establish sex-fairness as parents by practicing positive naming of daughters. (The problems related to naming sons also introduce sexism toward females because of the negativism toward "effeminate" names for males.)

Incorrect	Correct
Candy, Georgette, Babette, Sugar, Lynnette, Cookie, Thomasina, Pauline, Guyleen	Any strong, one- or two-syllable name that does not diminish the female because of equation with subordination or childishness or because it springs from a male name

3. Act on and tell daughters and other women of the right to retain birth names upon marriage.

Incorrect	Correct
You speak of "changing her name to his" as if no other alternative exists	You speak of a name as a birthright and convey the information that her name does not legally have to be changed to his
Mrs. James Miller	Ms. Janet Roland (after marriage to James Miller)

4. Adopt the compound surname style that joins birth and married surnames with a hyphen.

Incorrect   *Correct*

Mrs. Robert Hensley   Betty Smith-Hensley

5. Apprise people of the sexism in *-son* and *-man* surnames and establish that little can be done about them—unless, as in more and more cases, people change them. Much as with the recognition of the fact that slavery existed, people grow by simply understanding what happened even if they can do little about it.

NAMES OF ANIMALS AND OTHER NONHUMANS

The perpetuation of the myth of the male as standard carries over into the animal world. Imagine the confusion created for the child who always hears about the "dog . . . he," only to learn later that some dogs give birth to young and that they cannot be "he's." For an animal of unknown sex or for generic reference to animalkind, use *it*, alternate between *he* and *she*, or use "he and she."

Related to the girl-man pairing and animal references is the phraseology used to call to a pet. We hear "Here, boy," and "Here, girl" up and down the block. And the age of the animal does not matter, because the dog or cat is a dumb subordinate to the human. Why, then should we retain *girl* to refer to a mature woman while we discard *boy* to refer to a mature man?

Still another female-inferiority myth occurs in the animal world. *Lion* and *tiger* form the norm words for two types of animals. But communicators use the words *lioness* and *tigress* for the females. Again, the male serves as the standard and the female as the "other."

A search of word usage indicates that we assign both female and male pronouns and nouns to nonhuman things—but usually to the detriment of the female. Generally, we assign male words to activity and dominance and female words to passivity and subordination. Even in poetry, we call the dominant meters masculine and the weak meters feminine.

Personified descriptions virtually always take the following form:

1. Mr. Internal Combustion Engine makes the car go. He . . .
2. The active verb vigorously makes his presence known, but the passive verb quietly conveys her message.
3. The captain of the ship was in complete control of her. He brought her around the bend without any problems.
4. He bought a new car last month, and she performs for him as if he'd always owned her. She purrs like a kitten at his touch.
5. The Murcan Hotel is a willing servant to her customers.

We have subconsciously established sexist images of personification—whether in speech or in the physical world. For strength and independence, as in the case of Mr. Internal Combustion Engine and the active verb, we use the male forms. On the other hand, when referring to the vehicle a human owns, controls, or manipulates, we use the female forms. Unfortunately, women are just as prey as men to the application of the male-superiority–female-inferiority myth to even the nonhuman world.

Some applications of gender to nonhuman things bring confusion. "Mother Nature" implies creation and strength at the same time that it implies the subordinated human mother—along with apple pie. Portraying justice and liberty as female introduces positiveness, yet we confuse the portrayal with the "purity" of virginity—else why *Miss* Liberty and *Miss* Justice?

Because of pressure brought by feminists, at least tropical storms and hurricanes now have male as well as female names. Historically, the weather service assigned exclusively female names to them. Now it alternates in the assignment of names.

A more serious subordination of the female occurs in the use of subhuman words to describe her. True, people often invoke the names of animals and other nonhuman forms to refer to men. But words and phrases like *buck*, *stud*, "bull of the woods," *stag*, "king of the jungle," "a real stallion," "cock of the walk," "bantam rooster," and *wolf* do not carry with them the stigma that is attached to the animal references made to women. Equating the male with any of the preceding animals casts him as the aggressive, virile, powerful epitome of sexual prowess.

By way of contrast, look at the greater number and extremely negative meanings of animal words for women: *heifer, filly, chick, mare, quail, dog, shrew, pig, sow, beaver,* "old crow," *bunny, hellcat,* "queen bee," *bat, fox,* "cold as a fish," *bitch, hen,* and words from the fowl, feline, and ape families that are not considered polite to print. To be called any of these words reduces the woman to being inferior, ugly, vexatious, nagging, chattering, ill-tempered, stupid, the game or prey or the unreasoning manipulator of the male.

Even in some of the seemingly innocent animal-world references to women, an insidious put-down exists. Words and phrases like *kittenish*, "cute as a bug," *foxy, chicken, bunny,* have an infantile, subordinated quality about them. Think about the plight of the woman who is "just a bird in a gilded cage"—an animal-like captivity that too often befalls females.

Other placements of women in the realm of animals occur when people call them "meat" and parade them like cattle in "beauty" pageants. The narration even includes the recitation of their physical measurements—just as auctioneers describe horses.

Subhuman characteristics outside the animal world also defeat females more than males. "Dumb as a doorknob," "ugly as a mud fence," and similar phrases apply to men and women alike. However, female-negating words, without parallels for the male, exist in overwhelming abundance: *wallflower, doll,* ("china doll," "paper doll," "cupie doll," "baby doll"), *dish, skirt, hag, bag, witch, hooker, wench, broad, hide, tomato, frigid, frail, built, crone, nymph, nymphomaniac, piece,* and other terms too vulgar to report. Even proclaimed endearments such as "sweetpea," "sweet petunia," "sweet potato," "a dream," "dream boat," "pretty as a picture," and "I'll place you on a pedestal" conjure up images of women as mindless pawns or toys without the ability to contribute to society in a creative way.

Nymphomaniac—a word from the nonhuman world—and *virile* make for a thought-provoking contrast. Neither has an equivalent for the other sex. The one describes the sexually aggressive female and the other describes the sexually aggressive male. The one derogates and the other congratulates.

Other animal-like sex-differentiating descriptions appear in the combination "stag or drag" and two kinds of parties, the stag party and the hen party. In the first instance, the "stag" coming to a dance alone is held in high esteem, and even when he brings a woman she is a faceless "thing" being "dragged" in by him. The stag party carries the image of an action-packed, adventurous drama; the hen party has the image of clucking prattle among members of the uncreative "weaker sex."

The subhuman references make the degradation of the female obvious. The humane communicator will exorcise such references from her or his communication through an overt act of will.

Guideline L:
Names of Animals and Other Nonhumans

1. Use something other than the generic masculine pronouns to refer to generalized animals.

a. Refer to the animal as *it*.

Incorrect

The normal dog likes his dog food to be meaty and moist

Correct

The normal dog likes its dog food to be meaty and moist

b. Alternate between female and male pronouns.

Incorrect

The average horse . . . he, but the average cat . . . he

Correct

The average horse . . . she, but the average cat . . . he

c. Use paired pronouns.

Incorrect

A typical animal . . . he

Correct

A typical animal . . . he or she

2. Use nonsexist words to refer to the female of the animal species.

Incorrect	*Correct*
The lioness cares for her young by	The lion cares for her young by
The tigress . . . she	The tiger . . . she

3. Remove the sexism that occurs because of the less serious impact of animal references on males compared with their impact on females.

Incorrect	*Correct*
He's a real stud; she's a real dog	He's sexually active; I find her unattractive
He is a wolf; she is a bitch in heat	He is sexually aggressive; she is sexually aggressive
Introduce me to that chick (fox, filly)	Introduce me to that woman
She is kittenish	She is a warm, intelligent person

4. Remove the sexism that occurs because of the less serious impact of other subhuman references on males compared with the impact on females.

Incorrect	*Correct*
Tell that frail (broad, wench, tomato, doll)	Tell that woman
He is virile; she is a nymphomaniac	He is sexually active; she is sexually active
I want to place my woman on a pedestal. [I want my woman to be beautiful, deaf, dumb, mute, and on display—a statue.]	I want the woman I care for to be sensitive, dynamic, and what she wants to be—alive.

5. Use nonstereotyped sex references to inanimate subhuman forms.

a. Use feminine forms to indicate strength and activity half the time.

Incorrect	*Correct*
Mr. Internal Combustion Engine (all the time)	Ms. Internal Combustion Engine (half the time)

b. Use masculine forms to indicate weakness and passivity half the time.

Incorrect	*Correct*
The pilot was in control of his airplane. She responded to him without a whimper.	The pilot was in control of her airplane. He responded to her without a whimper.

c. Use references other than sexist clichés.

Incorrect	*Correct*
Mother Nature, she	Nature, it

d. Replace *Miss* with *Ms.* when referring to abstract qualities as females.

Incorrect	*Correct*
Miss Liberty	Ms. Liberty
Miss Justice	Ms. Justice

RELIGIOUS COMMUNICATION

Sexism and religion—a sensitive subject, yes, but one we must broach in any attempt to identify and overcome sexist communication. For example, as one of the most influential publications in existence, the English Bible has contributed immeasurably to perpetuating the myth of male superiority and female inferiority. According to Letty Russell, "The Bible is used as a means of reinforcing . . . [women's] subordination to men through divine sanction."[2]

With the depiction of Eve, woman was cast as the evil "temptress" and still must bear that label as language ties her to that image. Such depiction from a Bible written in a patriarchal climate places women in a subservient position. This depiction clearly runs counter to the egalitarian intent of religions that consider the relationship between humans and God.

Communicators must recognize and act on the humanitarian concern for equality of the sexes in religion as well as in other facets of life. They must also act on the knowledge that sexist religious language repels many receivers. Russell summarizes the dangers of sexist language in religion.

> Our practices in traditional language run at least three risks. First, they reinforce the inferiority and superiority stereotypes. Second, they are causing the alienation of some women from the life and worship of the church because the consciousness of these women no longer allows them to accept exclusive language. Third, they run the risk of making God too small. If we think of God as a baal or idol of one group, we are forgetting the mystery of One who cares for all human beings and welcomes their love.[3]

Brief review of some movements toward sex equity in religion should satisfactorily establish the importance of nonsexist religious language for the communicator. Religious messages are so much a part of the fabric of society that some sexism derived from a false sense of their meanings has undoubtedly entered into everyone's vocabulary. Therefore, each person will need to make a deliberate effort to overcome them.

One way to overcome religious sexism is to fight the temptation to use

[2]Letty M. Russell, ed., *The Liberating Word: A Guide to Nonsexist Interpretation of the Bible* (Philadelphia: Westminster Press, 1976), p. 13. Copyright © 1976 The Westminster Press. Used by permission.

[3]Ibid., p. 18.

religious arguments to perpetuate the "woman's place." Another way is to use general, inclusive words instead of male words. Instead of "sons of man," "sons of God," "the brotherhood of man," *Lord, He, His, Him, Father, King, mankind*, use such words as "human beings," *humankind, humanity*, God, "Holy One," *One, Nurturer, Defender, Maker*, "Early One," *Creator, Spirit, Advocate, Deity*, and "Divine Force." Also eliminate the masculine pronouns in reference to the generalized human or to God.

Some feminists suggest that the word *God* itself is patriarchal and that we should return to the parallel use of *God* and *Goddess*. [4] However, others contend that in the original Greek and Hebrew, the words for the deity had no sex, thus *God* satisfies the need for a sex-neutral word.

One clear problem associated with religious sexism includes the instinctive use of words such as *lord* and *king* and monarchial references. Such references lead logically to our next section.

Guideline M: Religious Communication

Understand the male bias of the patriarchal culture out of which the Judeo-Christian religions came, and use nonsexist religious language.

Incorrect	*Correct*
Our Father, sons of God, God, Him, Lord, King, brotherhood of man	Our Creator, children of the Deity, Nurturer, Holy One, Maker, Defender, humanity

MONARCHIAL REFERENCES

What do you picture when you read the word *monarch*? Most people picture a king on his throne. Yet a check of any dictionary shows that the word is sex neutral and refers only to a hereditary sovereign. A male monarch is a king, and a female monarch is a queen. Then why do thoughts automatically go to the male when someone mentions *monarch*? They do so because of the male-as-superior concept.

As evidence of the concept, consider that Elizabeth II has been queen of Great Britain and Northern Ireland since 1952. Yet references for all those years have been and continue to be to the "King's English." One could suppose that the learned people who use those words just do not know that when a woman occupies the throne, they should refer to the "Queen's English."

As an aside, because of the sexist nature of the English language, "King's

[4]The word *feminist* means one who believes in economic, political, and social equality for females.

English" certainly does describe a male-oriented language better than "Queen's English." One play on words suggests that we really use "Manglish," not English.[5]

Encyclopedic entries illustrate sexism. For example, you will probably find that Elizabeth II is the daughter of King George VI. It is a scientific wonder that she evidently had no mother. But then, you say, King George was the parent from the sovereign lineage. But how is that consistent with another entry likely to be found: The former Princess Elizabeth married Philip, the Duke of Edinburgh, and later bore him children. In this case, though she was in the royal lineage, it was she who bore children for her nonlineage husband.

With mention of other monarchial words such as *princess* and *duchess* comes the recollection of the adjunct status for women created by *-ess* endings. Because of their historical status as titles for the nobility, the eradication of *princess* and *duchess* will be difficult indeed. But realization of their sexism and avoidance of the terms should certainly be objectives for the nonsexist communicator.

"Lord and master" uses male royalty words to describe the focal point of power. The "lady and mistress" has always been secondary to the "lord and master," but she has fallen into even less repute with current usage. Even a deck of playing cards puts the hierarchy of the royalty into sexist perspective. Does not the king "take" the queen?

Extending the understanding of sex inequality in references to monarchs, consider that the word *queen* has negative connotations because of its affiliation with the female. For example, the image of a queen is often wicked—a Jezebel. And "queen bee" is a special term assigned to a woman who climbs a little higher than her sisters in an organization, succumbs to and enjoys the attention given the only female among many males, and protects that enjoyment by keeping other females in lesser positions. (Unfortunately, we blame her for the condition, when she is, in reality, a victim herself.)

Finally, think of how we typically perceive a princess as a pampered, demanding, selfish manipulator. And of how "my little princess" refers to an adorned object. And of how the fairy tale prince saves the princess and whisks her away on his horse to live happily ever after.

The nonsexist communicator should avoid perpetuating the stereotyped monarchial hierarchy in the English language.

Guideline N: Monarchial References

Use monarchial references only if they are nonsexist.

[5]Varda One, "Manglish" (Venice, Calif.: Everywoman Publishing Co., 1971). (Reprint available from Know, Inc.)

Incorrect	*Correct*
He uses the King's English	He uses the Queen's English
She is master of the situation	She has control over the situation
God is Lord and King	God is Nurturer and Advocate
She is a little princess	She shows fine human tendencies

APPLICATIONS

☆ *6-1. The following segment represents the kind of sexist writing that often occurs in office procedural statements. Underline the sexist segments and write corrections for them. Even underline sexist proper names and offer some alternatives for them.*

1. Incoming Calls

a. Answer promptly. If the caller has to wait more than two or three rings, he may become irritated and take his business elsewhere.

b. Identify yourself and the office or department. Say something like "Mr. Johnson's office, Mrs. Blackman," "Credit Department, Claudette," or "Linoleum Sales, Davidson."

c. Avoid using "hold" for more than fifteen seconds. If the caller has to wait longer than that, he may become irritated. If the "hold" will be longer than fifteen seconds, take the caller's number and tell him that the man he is calling will return the call. (Be sure to follow up on such promises.)

d. If a call needs to be transferred, be as helpful to the caller as possible. He can become quite upset if he has to redial and still gets the wrong office.

2. Outgoing Calls

a. Have the correct number and dial it right the first time. If possible, know the man's extension as well.

b. Greet the girl who answers cordially, but in a businesslike manner, and ask her for the man you are calling by name, mentioning your superior by name, if the call is being placed for him. Use words like "Mr. Whiteman of the Delphi Corporation would like to speak to Mr. Nelson."

c. Transfer the call efficiently to your superior when the contact has been made. Do not keep either man waiting.

☆ *6-2. Identify and suggest a correction for the sexism in each of these names or nicknames.*

Doreen Jackman	The Bill Todds (Bill, Rosetta, Jeanessa, and Brad)
Adrienne Cookson	
Charletta Kay Smithson	Baby Doll Allison
Suzette Simpson Bartman	Miss Zinnia Stillman

Frank W. Dale, Jr.
Vanessa Clarkson
Miss Jonalyn Rhineman-Burk
Coramae Beetleson
Mrs. Alvin Ryanson, III
The Hobsons

Mrs. Heather Peterson
Ms. Luscious Alderman
Evan D. Friedman
Ginger Bud Klegman
Lady Bird Blakeson
Mrs. Earl Jorgenson (Birdie)
Ms. "Pet" Dyerman

☆   *6-3.   Identify and correct the sexism in these sentences.*

1. Give your favorite bird Pet-im Bird Seed. He'll sing you his favorite songs for doing so.

2. Each horse entered in the race will take his place at exactly 10:30 A.M.

3. Now, children, look at the picture and see how easily Mr. Diesel Engine pulls the rest of the train up the hill. He's so strong that he could pull a bigger train too.

4. The moment a driver takes hold of the wheel of a Newsmobile, he immediately feels her succumb to his will.

5. Every little girl should have a doll so that she can cuddle and cradle her.

6. Give your son a Mr. Owl calculator. He'll learn so much arithmetic from him.

7. Miss Elementary Teacher took her students' models of Mrs. Housewife, Mr. Executive, Captain Joe, and Sweet Darbie Doll to Mr. College Professor so he could choose the winner.

8. Ask Mr. Head of the Household to involve his wife in the discussion.

9. The lioness led the hunt.

☆   *6-4.   Identify and correct the sexism in these sentences.*

1. A benediction offered by a minister at a commencement exercise at a state-supported university. (Mark and correct religious bias also.)

> Our Father, thank you for bringing each graduate to this point in his life. Lord, let each graduate move out to take his rightful position of leadership to help man solve the problems that confront him. As Sons of God, these graduates need your Christian guidance, oh King of us all. In Christ's Name we pray. Amen.

2. As the master of ceremonies, be sure to introduce all the dignitaries and their wives. (Some dignitaries are women.) Also be sure to use the King's English.

3. Candy looked like a little duchess in her low-cut costume for the Little Miss Tigerette contest sponsored by the Edmund High School Tigers basketball team.

4. The children played King of the Hill till they tired; then they went inside to play Old Maid.

7

ROLE PLAYING, STEREOTYPING, AND NEGATIVE IMAGERY

The phrase "male as the norm" appears many times in this book, and the concept pervades it. Communication symbols created in a patriarchy reflect the values of that patriarchy. Therefore, in this culture communication establishes the male as the standard, leaving the female as something less than the standard. In this culture, virtually every verbal and nonverbal act shouts the superiority of the male and the inferiority of the female. Thus, these acts reinforce the relative status of sexes on a moment-by-moment basis.

This entire book, then, provides ways to overcome the sexism epitomized in the phrase "the male is the norm." Guidelines O, however, repeat a few suggestions to make the summary point.

Guideline O: The Male as the Norm

1. Use neutral words to refer to groups that include both females and males.

Incorrect	*Correct*
Mankind	Humankind
The brotherhood of man	The bond of humanity
The black man	Blacks

2. Maintain the sex neutrality of words.

Incorrect	*Correct*
The working man and his wife and kids	The worker and family

3. Vary references to remove the male-as-norm imagery.

Incorrect	*Correct*
John Q. Citizen	Jill Q. Citizen
The taxpayer . . . he	The taxpayer . . . she
Businessmen will be particularly affected by the new law	Businesswomen will be particularly affected by the new law
Mr. Buyer, take a look at this four-bedroom dreamhouse. She'll serve your family's needs as no other can.	Ms. Buyer, take a look at this four-bedroom dreamhouse. It'll serve your needs as no other can.

STEREOTYPING OF FEMALES

As established throughout the book—and particularly in "A Tale of Two Sexes" in Chapter 2—females exist under rather rigid stereotypes. Four broad types of stereotypes that summarize cultural views of the roles of females include (1) homemaker, (2) servant, (3) sex object, and (4) emotional, unintelligent creature.

Homemaker

Society assigns the role of homemaker to women and at the same time it devalues that role. The mass media usually portray the homemaker as the helpless, sometimes giddy woman whose major concerns in life revolve about her embarrassed husband's ring around the collar, her dull floors, cooking for the family, and buying the right toilet paper.

Nowhere does sexism assert itself more than when the woman steps out of her assigned role as stay-at-home wife and mother and into the historic domain of the man—the world of remunerated work. The stereotypes abound. Subtle and not so subtle verbal and nonverbal messages firmly entrench the stereotypes in the minds of both men and women. Such stereotyping has obvious negative effects—it limits the woman's chances of success in the work world.

A most striking example of sex-differentiating career role casting occurs in this vignette. Ask a group of little girls what they plan to be when they grow up, and you will find one or more who will say "a mother." Ask a group of little boys what they plan to be when they grow up, and you will not find even one who will say "a father." And the vignette says nothing about the stereotyped job types that the two sexes would list—even in this age of limited antidiscrimination laws.

In reality, only a small proportion of households in the United States meet the stereotype of the work-at-home wife and the work-away-from-home husband. Most women work outside the home for most or all of their lives. They work for the same reasons that men do—money and satisfaction.

To communicate as if homemaking has no value and as if the role of homemaker defines all females belies reality. Therefore, the nonsexist communicator avoids such beliefs and such imagery.

Why do we not see more of a strong woman in control of a job? Why do we not see more of women and men sharing household duties? Why do we not see little boys helping mommy—or daddy—with the cooking? Why do we not see men and women parenting instead of women mothering? Why do we not see men teaching home economics and women teaching shop? Why do we not see fewer of the forced traditional roles?

Even when women do appear in nonstereotyped roles, commercial writers usually have them play the roles in ways that demean both the roles and the women. For example, we see a woman as a cab driver giving advice to a man on which sinus medicine to take, a woman in a police uniform acting as a meter "maid" singing and dancing on the street, a woman as a truck driver being helped by a man to change a tire, a woman in a cap and gown serving soft drinks to the family gathered to celebrate *her* graduation from a university, a woman as a judge worried about what to serve her family for dinner that evening, a woman as an engineer debilitated by the limpness of her hair, and a woman as a stockbroker destroyed by a run in her stockings.

Servant

Another stereotype for the female casts her as the servant—whether as the server of food and drink, the store clerk, the housecleaner, the teacher-as-"governess," the nurse, the secretary, or the unwilling sex partner. Such concepts of a woman's place restrict horizons for all females. They do so well enough that when women work outside the home, they most often do lesser-paying "woman's work" rather than higher-paying "man's work." If an occasional young woman aspires to a nontraditional job such as plumbing or driving a bulldozer, society often succeeds in squelching such an unheard-of and "unfeminine" aspiration.

To overcome the self-fulfilling stereotype of servant, the nonsexist communicator perceives and portrays the female in dominant, leadership roles, not just the serving, following roles.

Sex Object

The sex-object status that has befallen woman also clouds her vision—and that of males—of what she can become. If society thinks of a woman as a pleasure object and not a fully capable human being, how *can* she move efficiently into and receive acceptance from a system that requires fully capable human beings?

Nothing more clearly identifies the sexism inherent in the female-as-sex-object concept than beauty-queen imagery. The parading of beautiful females is nothing more than the socially sanctioned serving up of bodies for the mental consumption of viewers. Beauty and prom queens, military ball "princesses," and class or fraternity sweethearts become the victims, but because of their conditioning they see themselves as the victors over less attractive females. Any society that places such value on woman's spirit and mind devalues all humankind.

Although pom-pom "girls"; cheerleaders; twirlers; some models; topless or bunny types; women who pose for sex-object advertisements, magazines, and movies; and exotic dancers add some varying levels of skills to their sex-object activities, they still form part of the sex-object stereotype. Some receive money for their work, but others consider as sufficient reward the "honor" of being viewed much as livestock are in a sale barn.

Second only to being mothers when they grow up, many little girls aspire to become "Miss America." To picture the centuries of wasted female mental power on such aspirations, involve yourself in this parallel. Suppose, at the urging of his parents, an Einstein focuses his energies on the highest that society holds out to him—becoming a father and a Mr. America. He plays house, watches handsomeness pageants, dresses up in his father's clothes, and struts in front of his admiring relatives, who gush about how cute he is. In school he shuns mathematics and physics as being unmasculine, enters every pageant he can, and drops out as soon as he finds a wife. Although he was disappointed at not becoming Mr. America, he did become homecoming king and a cheerleader in high school. And after all, marrying, becoming a father, and cleaning toilets are totally fulfilling activities. So who needs genius?

Sales messages epitomize the sex-object status of women. The beautiful, curvaceous, nude or near-nude, vixenish, dumb-blonde, silent, fawning, serving female appears in advertisements for products from automobiles and cigars to CB radios and beer. Rarely does she play an integral part in the story line—she just appears to be viewed. The role deliberately shrouds her humanness, mentality, and character.

Picture the kinds of advertisements that overtly use the sexuality of the woman. They feature a woman's panty hose and stockings as she dances and flourishes to expose one of the man's favorite parts of a woman's body—her legs. Of course, short shorts and skirts accomplish the same thing. Other advertisements feature some of the other favorite parts of a woman's body: tight sweaters and T-shirts, low-cut dresses and blouses, tight jeans and slacks. Jiggle and T and A contribute significantly to the image created by commercials.

Picture also the meanings associated with the bright red, petulant lips of a woman-child as her tongue flicks to lick an ice cream cone. Think of the meaning of the woman sitting or lying at a man's feet—even fondling his shoe with her face or having the shoe placed on her nude body. Not only do such poses reveal the sex-object status of the woman—and even a touch of sadomasochism—but they also show the contrast of power and powerlessness between the male and female.

One of the most destructive outcomes of the sex-object status of females lies in the use of little girls and teenage girls in suggestive poses, sexual clothes, and adult makeup for the sale of products. Such products include complete lines of cosmetics for little girls. Indeed, child pornography does not appear only in sleazy bookstores and low-grade movies.

Many of us never have direct responsibilities for beauty pageants or commercials and advertisements. However, we can refuse to acknowledge the contests conducted or won by others and oppose any attempts to have them within or sponsored by our organizations. We can write to the creators of sexist commercials, advertisements, and other such messages. Just as important, we can understand the real meaning of beauty contests and sexist advertising. And, with that understanding, we can communicate in a manner that does not treat women as sex objects.

Emotional, Unintelligent Creature

A large body of myths and associated communication surrounds the stereotype of the female as more emotional and less intelligent than the male. In truth, research shows that the female and male differ little, if at all, in the emotional and intellectual characteristics that define human beings. It also shows that when differences do appear, conditioning could explain them just as well as any innate sex-differentiating qualities.

To overcome these stereotypes, think and communicate about females as the controlled and intelligent human beings that they are or can become.

Guideline P: Stereotyping of Females

1. Portray females in positive roles as homemakers and mothers and in roles other than homemaker and mother.

Incorrect	*Correct*
Portraying a homemaker as knowing which paper towel to use, but helpless in the face of a decision about buying stocks	Portraying both female and male homemakers as decision makers for stock purchases as well as everyday consumer purchases
Portraying girls playing with dolls and tea sets, learning to sew, helping mommy in the kitchen all the time	Portraying girls playing with Erector and chemistry sets, learning to repair a car, helping mother read a blueprint half the time
Portraying women bathing babies, cooking, cleaning—all the time	Portraying women in nontraditional jobs, coming home from work—half the time

2. Portray females in other than servant roles and, when so, in positive ways.

Incorrect	*Correct*
Portraying women as homemakers, "waitresses," nurses, teachers, clerks, secretaries all the time	Portraying women as doctors, college presidents, managers, engineers half the time
Portraying women as police officers, surgeons, detectives, but "kidding" or showing them as emotionally weak and ultimately beholden to and dependent on men	Portraying women as police officers, surgeons, detectives who are in full and final control of the situation

3. Portray females in roles other than sex object.

Incorrect	*Correct*
Portraying women as beauty queens, cheerleaders, pom-pom "girls," organization sweethearts	Portraying women with brains and human tendencies, not faces and figures
Portraying beautiful women in abbreviated costumes looking adoringly and silently at macho men	Portraying women in professional, intellectual scenes as equals to men

4. Portray females as controlled, intelligent humans.

Incorrect	*Correct*
Women are emotional, jealous, soap-opera-watching, lazy, dependent creatures	Women possess the same range of emotions and intellect as men

STEREOTYPING OF MALES

The bulk of this book deals with the sexism that militates against the female because of its greater pervasiveness and negativeness. However, communication patterns also cast males in stereotypes on the basis of sex. These unfortunately form the opposites of those for the female. Thus, if the woman serves as a homemaker, the man must work outside the home. If the woman acts as a servant and sex object, then the man must be the benefactor of those two states. If the woman works in low-paying jobs, the man must work in high-paying jobs. If the woman exhibits weakness and passivity, the man must exhibit strength and aggressiveness. If the woman follows, the man must lead.

Sales writers, however, do picture the man as putty in the hands of a gorgeous woman. He smilingly purchases life insurance in anticipation of his death. He marches to his death gladly when he remembers he has purchased good insurance for his family. He pouts like a baby when sick—totally dependent on an often condescending, but serving woman. He unquestioningly accepts his role as a drudge so that he can support his wife and children.

Many people would say that the most negative portrayal of a man casts him in an effeminate role. However, that portrayal derogates women, not men. If society perceives that the worst that can happen to a man is to be like a woman, the implicit sexism disparages the woman, not the man.

Add to this partial depiction of men in sales communication, boys and men as sports nuts, automobile buffs, garbage carriers, fix-it people, furniture movers, gun collectors, financial wizards, family burden bearers, tire changers, decision makers, protectors, never-crying rocks of control, stern taskmasters, disciplinarians, virile lovers, heads of households, rugged outdoorspeople, community leaders, mechanics, yard workers, winners at all games, competitors, executive types, professionals, mental giants, all-Americans, tall and handsome woman-killers, hunters, well-heeled gift givers, military geniuses, witty entertainers. While this list provides more inspiration than the list of roles for women, it must overwhelm the ordinary boy or man. The requirements of "masculinity" must particularly overpower the boy or man who does not have physical strength; does not like guns, cars, sports, or war; does not aspire to power; likes music, art, reading, and other aspects of the humanities; is shy about his sexuality; enjoys women for their minds; does not have handsome features. The sexism of communicated roles obviously introduces difficulties for men too.

Words that conjure up negative images about males include *rounder*, *trick*, *scoundrel*, *womanizer*, *wolf*, *animal*, *rat*, *heel*, "old goat." And even the so-called generic *man* can be a disadvantage if it carries a negative meaning: *manslaughter*, "man's inhumanity to man," "man is destroying the ecological balance," "con man," "man and his wars." Because the word *man* carries with it connotations of maleness, negativism accrues to males when the claimed generic *man* relates to undesirable qualities.

Generalizations introduce unfairness for both men and women. The stereotype of the "male chauvinist pig" includes men who are not. The message that all men want only one thing from a woman introduces sexism. When we portray all men as cruel and insensitive, we do a disservice to kind and sensitive men.

Three usages deserve special treatment: "son of a bitch," *bastard*, and "mother——." The uniqueness of these terms lies in their double entendres: The surface meanings show a reduction of the male. However, the second and deep meanings actually debase the generalized female. Thus, we come full circle to the truth that we perpetrate the consummate sexism on the female.

The ultimate sexism toward the male exists in the stereotype of his superiority to the female. This stereotype destroys the male's independence by making him dependent on the psychological crutch of the inferior female stereotype. Therefore, eliminating stereotypes of male superiority and female inferiority will remove the ultimate sexism for both the female and the male.

Guideline Q: Stereotyping of Males

1. Portray males in roles as household worker and father.

Incorrect	*Correct*
Portraying boys playing with footballs and cars, learning to construct a birdhouse, helping daddy change the automobile oil all the time	Portraying boys playing with smaller children, learning to do the laundry, helping daddy in the kitchen half the time. (Note how the boy cannot be shown playing with dolls, though we want him to grow up to be the father of babies.)
Portraying men in traditional jobs, coming home from work and being greeted by a wife with the meal on the table all the time	Portraying men caring for babies, cleaning, doing the laundry, cooking half the time

2. Portray males in roles other than womanizer.

Incorrect	*Correct*
Portraying men as tall, dark, and handsome, with women in awe and available at the snap of a finger	Portraying men as ordinary-looking humans with sensitive instincts toward women as equals—not as sex objects

3. Portray males in other than dominant roles and, when so, in a positive way.

Incorrect	*Correct*
Portraying men as "bosses" and "in charge" of women all the time	Portraying men as holding positions with women "bosses" and with women "in charge" half the time
	Portraying men as comfortable and unthreatened by working for a woman

4. Portray males in roles other than working drudge, head of household, "babylike" when ill, insurance purchaser, strong hero type, and so on.

Incorrect	*Correct*
Portraying men as tough, aggressive, competitive, unemotional all the time	Portraying men as sensitive, compassionate, uncompetitive, unaggressive, emotional half the time

5. Portray males as controlled, intelligent humans.

Incorrect	*Correct*
Males are animals	Some males reveal qualities that are less than ideal
Men are male chauvinist pigs	Some men consider males superior to females
Man's inhumanity to man	The human's inhumanity to the human
Man and his pollution	Humans and their pollution

THE PROBLEMS OF BEING WOMANLY, EFFEMINATE, WOMANISH, FEMALE, FEMININE, AND LADYLIKE

"Femininity" and "masculinity" exist as qualities defined by society, and not by innate femaleness or maleness. Again, the traditional meanings of *feminine* work to the detriment of women.

Why does the culture classify intellect, strength, courage, independence, decision-making ability, leadership capability, and power as masculine qualities? Why does it classify mindlessness, passivity, self-deprecating actions, weakness, emotionalism, prettiness, perfumed sweetness, helplessness, and never-a-leader-but-a-follower-be as feminine qualities?

Some say the two sets of adjectives describing femininity and masculinity form separate, but equal categories. Then why do the words *emasculation* and *castration* and the assignment of "feminine" qualities to a man represent the worst things that could happen to him? Why do no equivalent words for *emasculation* and *castration* exist for women? And why does the assignment of male-as-the-human qualities to the female increase her stature? "Now there's a woman who thinks like a man!" How many times have you uttered or heard such a statement and considered it a compliment to the woman?

If you search your dictionary, you will not find words that describe women as full possessors of human qualities. You also will not find words that convey that the loss of female qualities has any consequence. Even the word *effeminate* has the negative denotations and connotations of weakness, delicacy, emotionalism, tenderness, and softness. And calling a man "effeminate," or a boy a "sissy," reduces him to the lowest possible state.

On a television talk show a guest brought in a laughing hyena. He noted that the hyena's sex cannot be ascertained until it is about a year old, because both the female and the male hyena have penises until then. The host made a great hoopla about the trauma involved for the hyena to go a full year thinking that "he" is "virile" and "strong," just to find out that when the penis is gone, "he" is not all those things. "He" is nothing. "He" is *only* a female.

The concepts of manliness and womanliness relate to the femininity/masculinity dichotomy and deserve extended treatment. A definition of *manly* glows with qualities such as determination, strength, courage, honor, straight-forwardness, virility, bravery. One of the clearest testimonies to the view of a woman as inferior arises from the listing of *feminine* and *womanly* as the antonyms of *manly*. In logical interpretation, then, the laundry list of the highest of human qualities describes *manly*; the opposite qualities describe *womanly*.

Consider these characteristics used in the definition of *womanly* and *womanish*: effeminate, unmanly, feminine, cowardly, weak, shrill, soft, frail, vixenish. The woman again finds herself drowning in a sea of words that dismiss her as substandard.

Because such words as *womanly, womanish, effeminate,* or *feminine* should describe human goodness, but do not, try to list specific descriptive words when referring to a woman. When describing a woman of determination, strength, courage, honor, and straightforwardness, simply say, "She is a woman of determination, strength, courage, honor, and straightforwardness." Unfortunately, you cannot say "She is a woman's woman" with the same height of meaning found in "He is a man's man."

Chapter 4 deals with the nonparallelism of the words *man* and *lady*. The meanings associated with being a lady again diminish the female. The ladylike qualities assigned to females restrict them to the ornamental, weak, retiring, dependent, genteel subordinate to the male.

When a female acts like a lady, while a male acts like a man, the female's chances of independence, accomplishment, and sense of self-worth pale beside his. Even when the male acts like a gentleman, he has more latitude than the female acting like a lady. In fact, society seems to limit the concept of gentlemanliness to the common courtesies, including opening doors and lighting cigarettes for women. It does not create for the gentleman the totally negative life-style that it creates for the lady.

When a female does not act like a lady, she runs a great risk because she steps out of her assigned role. When a woman acts from a base of independence and strength instead of dependence and weakness, the culture tells her she's too masculine. Obviously, then, the culture equates strength with masculinity. In fact, the title and thesis of a collection of fiction related to women make an unfortunately realistic summary of the two roles available to them—*Bitches and Sad Ladies*, in which *bitches* represents society's view of independent females with healthy egos and some anger at the culture's treatment of females.[1] If these two form the only roles possible for females, many now elect to become "bitches." How sad, though, that a "genteel" culture assigns such a label to a female who chooses activity over passivity, strength over weakness, and independence over dependence—who chooses not to be a "lady."

A set of contrasts seems trite on the surface, but carries deep meaning for the females who have ambitions beyond wifehood and motherhood.

A businessman is aggressive	A businesswoman is pushy
A businessman shows good taste in clothes	A businesswoman is a clothes horse
A businessman loses his temper because of the job	A businesswoman loses her temper because it's that time of the month
A businessman has a drink or two after work because of the pressure of work	A businesswoman is a lush
A businessman is a stern taskmaster	A businesswoman is impossible to work for
A businessman has lunch with his boss; he's on his way up	A businesswoman has lunch with her boss; she's having an affair
A businessman leaves for a better job because he recognizes a good opportunity	A businesswoman leaves for a better job because she's undependable.
A businessman marries, so he'll get more settled	A businesswoman marries, so she'll get pregnant and leave
A businessman talks with coworkers to discuss the latest deal	A businesswoman talks with coworkers to gossip
A businessman is confident	A businesswoman is conceited
A businessman is a man of the world	A businesswoman has really been around

Guideline R:
The Problems of Being Womanly, Effeminate, Womanish, Female, Feminine, and Ladylike

Avoid the words *womanly, effeminate, womanish, female, feminine,* and *ladylike* to describe females. Instead, use direct, specific words of description.

Incorrect	*Correct*
He is manly; she is womanly	Both are admired because of their determination and honor
She has female problems	She has not been feeling well
She's a real lady; she leaves the men to their conversation	She is a bright woman and enjoys stimulating conversation

[1]Pat Rotter, ed., *Bitches and Sad Ladies: An Anthology of Fiction by and about Women* (New York: Dell Publishing Co., Inc., 1975).

THE ABSENCE OF POSITIVE WORDS FOR FEMALES

Our language needs additional words to communicate fully about females. As discussed in the preceding section, *womanly* and *womanish* just do not make the positive impression that *manly* does. Likewise, society considers female qualities so minimal that no equivalents for *emasculate, castrate,* and *eunuch* exist for women. Can you locate a word other than *nymphomaniac* for the sexually active female? A word that is equivalent to *virile*?

Try finding a word other than *barren* for the childless woman. *Barren* has such meanings as unproductive, dull, drab, boring, tedious, and unattractive, in addition to sterile.

Try to find a positive replacement for "old maid," *spinster,* "maiden lady," or *bachelorette*. You will not be successful, for even "career woman" has a negative connotation unless combined with "and wife and mother."

Think of the meanings associated with *divorcée*. As with "old maid," no satisfactory words exist for describing a male-less woman.

We cannot, of course, wave a magic wand and cause the creation of head-held-high words for women where none now exist. But we can avoid negative ones and use reasonably constructive substitutes.

Guideline S:
The Absence of Positive Words for Females

1. Recast sentences to convey positive qualities of females.

Incorrect	*Correct*
You want to communicate that a woman is strong and courageous, so you write "She is womanly" or "She is feminine"	You want to communicate that a woman is strong and courageous, so you write "She is strong and courageous"

2. Use a series of descriptive words for communicating that a woman is stripped of her woman-defining human qualities.

Incorrect	*Correct*
She felt defeminized	She felt as if all her strength as a woman had drained from her
She felt castrated	

NEGATIVE IMAGERY ASSOCIATED WITH THE WIFE AND MOTHER

"Take my wife . . . please." The range of meanings for wifehood and motherhood shows extremes from disdain to worship—neither of which proves too healthy for the women involved. Because of the range many men have a virtual love-hate confusion about their wives, mothers, and daughters. The same confusion exists for many females about themselves, particularly in conjunction with males' attitudes toward them.

The culture expects wives to fill certain roles without questioning. The book and movie *The Stepford Wives* illustrates that expectation well. In destroying the women's independence of self, the Stepford males expect the women to meet all the standards in the automaton image they create.

Why do we call changing marital partners "wife swapping" instead of "husband swapping"? Could it have anything to do with the assumed possession of the wives by the husbands, the wives as property or chattel? Why does the man have a mistress? What does the woman have?

Why does the man ask the woman's father for her "hand" and why does the father "give her away" at the wedding? Why does she agree to "love, honor, and obey"? Why is wife abuse a serious problem?

Contrast the connotations of the unwed or divorced mother and Mother's Day. Think about this ambivalence of attitudes. Why does a marriage license change a woman who has given birth to a child from absolute disgrace to high honor? Why does it make her an "honest woman" and "give her child a name"?

The meanings of *bastard* and "son of a bitch" have roots in society's view of the unwed mother. The sexism inherent in this view transfers to the child born out of wedlock, carrying the label *illegitimate* with it.

If society considers motherhood so magnificent, why does it create the smothering, mother-hen image? Why does it not respect teenage and menopausal mothers as much as mothers in their twenties and thirties? What happens to the glow of the word *mother* when it has *-in-law* attached to it?

If conception takes place and the woman does not want the child, many in society tell her that she does not have the right to make decisions about her own body. Does woman, then, serve in only one capacity—the womb of man? Mixed emotions reveal themselves when a husband does not "allow" his wife to work, yet finds himself attracted to women who do work. The same ambivalence must exist when he cannot make enough money to support the family, accepts society's value that he would not be manly if his wife worked, but disrespects his wife because of the entrapment he attributes to her and their children.

Guideline T:
Negative Imagery Associated
with the Wife and Mother

1. Treat wife-and-mother imagery with the same respect as husband-and-father imagery.

Incorrect	*Correct*
Wifehood and motherhood form the woman's highest calling and she should want no other career. The man should have a career even to the neglect of husbandhood and fatherhood	Wifehood and motherhood and husbandhood and fatherhood can be part of the calling for a woman and a man, but they do not negate the possibility of careers for both

2. Avoid language that makes parenting the responsibility of the mother and not the father.

Incorrect	*Correct*
Mom, give your child his favorite breakfast—Crunchie Budgies	Parents, give your children their favorite breakfast—Crunchie Budgies

3. Eliminate mother-in-law jokes and other negative imagery.

Incorrect	*Correct*
My husband's parents will visit next week, and you know how mothers-in-law are!	My husband's parents will visit next week, and I look forward to their visit

4. Eliminate the negativism of such phrases as "unwed mothers" and "illegitimate children."

Incorrect	*Correct*
As a working, unwed mother, she needs a place to leave her illegitimate daughter during the day	Because she works, she needs a place to leave her daughter during the day
The common-law wife has the same legal rights as the married wife	The common-law spouse has the same legal rights as the married spouse

5. Do not define a woman in terms of her marital and childbearing status.

Incorrect	*Correct*
Did you know she is a divorcée (or widow)?	Did you know she has a degree from Matriculate University?
She is barren; she has been married ten years and has no children	They have been married ten years and have no children

---

APPLICATIONS

☆   7-1.   *For each of these statements identify and correct the sexism.*

1. The red man occupied North America long before the white man arrived.

2. Mr. Average Voter

3. Be sure that every baby has his shots by the time he reaches age two.

4. Man does not live by bread alone.

5. One small step for a man; one giant leap for mankind.

6. The military man has a right to his pension without sharing it with his divorced military wife.

7. Pioneers bravely opened new frontiers; we can't forget the contributions their wives and children made.

8. The businessman's lunch special for the day is a man-sized bowl of clam chowder.

9. Mr. Homeowner, be sure to buy this insurance so that you will leave your house free and clear to your family if you should die.

10. American wives like strong men.

11. On a birth certificate: Born to Mr. and Mrs. C. B. Belyew

12. On a form in a doctor's office:

Name of Head of Household (Mr.) _____
(The records for all members of the family are filed under the name of the head.)
Other names   Wife   _____
               Children _____
                         _____
                         _____

13. The PGA (Professional Golf Association) and the LPGA (Ladies' Professional Golf Association)

☆   *7-2.   Identify and correct the sexism in these statements and situations.*

1. Don't worry your pretty little head about it, Ellamae.

2. In a children's story: Daddy brought Jane a tiny tea set and Mike a big bulldozer from his business trip. Mommy served them milk and homemade cookies and turned Daddy's return into a party.

3. I'm so proud of my wife. She has found a low-sudsing detergent with a softener in it. It keeps my shirts clean and soft.

4. As the breadwinner, the man must move where his job takes him even if the move means that his wife must quit her job.

5. In a commercial: The male boss tells all the male sales representatives how to improve sales while the female secretaries sit silently in the background.

6. My daughter became a cheerleader, but my *son* made the football team.

7. In a commercial: A silent, beautiful, sexy woman sits at the feet of a stern, handsome 007 type as he makes all-knowing pronouncements about a product.

8. In a commercial: The wife and children stand around in awe as the husband shows them that the two-year-old batteries in the flashlight still work.

9. In a commercial: A woman who is a stockbroker misses an important customer because she's hidden behind the desk as she leans down to see what she can do about a run in her stocking.

10. As man disrupts the ecology, he once again establishes his greed.

11. Boys will be boys.

12. The man took his girl friend to the girlie show.

13. Well, my ball and chain told me I'd better be home on time tonight because she won't hold supper for me anymore.

☆ 7-3. *Describe the sexism in the following fairy tales, children's stories, and characterizations.*

1. *Cinderella*

2. *Snow White and the Seven Dwarfs*

3. *Sleeping Beauty*

4. *The Wizard of Oz*, particularly the Wizard and the Wicked Witch

5. The Muppets, particularly the number of females

6. The Smurfs

☆ 7-4. *Write positive, nonsexist alternatives to the following statements.*

1. I can't like him because he's just too effeminate.

2. I like a feminine woman, not a career woman.

3. He's too womanish for me; he clucks around like an old maid.

4. I'll never understand the mysteries of the female mind.

5. For the woman to be successful in business, she must think like a man, act like a lady, and work like a horse.

6. To a five-year-old girl in a frilly dress and hat: Now sit there and be still; act like a young lady.

7. Report to the boss lady right now.

8. My old woman can't even balance a checkbook.

9. Those women's libbers are just castrating females and lesbians.

☆   7-5.   *Check a dictionary and thesaurus for the meanings of all the "man" and "woman" words. Analyze the sexist problems in those definitions.*

☆   7-6.   *Identify the sexism in the following statements and write nonsexist versions of them.*

   1. The experience left her feeling castrated.

   2. I can't stand to be around her; my husband tells me she's a nymphomaniac.

   3. Trying to get along in a man's world is an emasculating experience for a woman.

   4. She felt like a female eunuch.

☆   7-7.   *Correct the following sexist references.*

   1. Over a gaming table: Now, where are you going to move your man? My men seem to have your men under control.

   2. In a game: Let's throw the dice to find out who's high man to see who goes first.

   3. In a card game: Hey, my king takes your queen!

   4. Mary, let's hire a maid or a cleaning lady for this place; you don't seem to be able to keep up with your housewifely duties now that you're working.

8

ORAL AND NONVERBAL COMMUNICATION

This final chapter features oral and nonverbal communication—the two categories that reflect deepset attitudes more readily than written communication. We can read and edit written communication; however, we usually must let oral and nonverbal communication remain as it is transmitted extemporaneously.

ORAL COMMUNICATION

Verbal communication—communication with words—can take the written or oral form. To the extent that both forms use the same set of words, the principles introduced in previous sections apply to oral communication. However, because the spoken word often occurs spontaneously and because we speak some words that we would never write, oral communication has some unique characteristics that call for special delineation where sexism is concerned.

Prejudices and stereotypes ordinarily expose themselves more in oral than in written communication. The serious nonsexist communicator will recognize this truth and develop a positive resolution that nothing sexist will pass her or his lips. Once the resolution exists, the communicator will mentally rehearse communication before transmitting it. Upon making a sexist error, the nonsexist communicator stores the knowledge of the error to avoid it in future exchanges. He or she also may reshape the words immediately after making the error. Granted, no one can erase something already said, but the act of immediate restatement can often reinforce correct patterns—and can communicate to the receiver the seriousness of the speaker's intent to revise sexist speech habits. With surprisingly little practice, the communicator can eliminate habitual sexist words.

Some of the words most disparaging of females exist primarily in the spoken language. Because they rarely appear in written form—and then only in tawdry novels or analytical works aimed at eradicating them—they prove all the more difficult to deal with. Rather than ignoring them, however, the committed nonsexist communicator will acknowledge their existence, and with the acknowledgement will contribute to exposing them.

Good taste does not allow many of the most sexist oral words to be put into print. However, words such as *broad, hag, dame, witch, mistress, bag, bitch, whore, prostitute, tramp, dog, slut,* and derogatory terms related to the female's genitals should call to mind the kinds of pervasive negativism toward women that regularly occur in the spoken word—even in the contexts of business, government, and industry.

Purging one's speaking vocabulary takes a committed effort. But ethics, morality, and sheer humane treatment require that we make the effort.

Speeches, meetings, small-group conferences, interviews, and conversations constitute some of the standard oral situations that perpetuate sexist communication. All involve both speaking and listening and can represent varying levels of formality and informality. And formal and informal communication often reflect different kinds of sexism. Thus, some distinction between informal and formal oral sexist expressions appears in the following sections.

Public Speaking

Speeches can range from the extemporaneous to the verbatim reading—thus from the highly informal to the extremely formal. The speaker who prepares and delivers a formal speech has complete control over it because he or she can write, rewrite, and edit. Thus, the speaker can assure the exorcism of all sexism from it. Because the speaker reads from perfected written copy, sexism remains exorcised. Therefore, the formal speech offers the best opportunity for nonsexism of all oral communication. The key to nonsexism in a formal speech lies in the writing.

One type of sexism often bursting forth in speeches is "mankind" language. Another involves the generic *he*. A third includes references to the stereotyped qualities and roles of women and men.

Other avenues for sexist expression open up when the speaker begins with an extemporaneous response to an introducer, tells a joke, deviates from the written speech, or enters into a question-and-answer interchange with the audience. All these activities allow the speaker to depart from the de-sexed printed words and interweave sexist words into the presentation. Thus, when the speaker departs in any way from the written speech, he or she must think carefully before speaking to maintain nonsexism.

Meetings

A meeting may be large or small, formal or informal. However, whatever its classification, sexist overtones or undertones are likely to shadow it unless it involves an enlightened group.

The formal meeting often rings with the patriarchal Robert's Rules of Order type of sanctioned sexism—ranging from "Madam Chairman" to the expectation that women serve as recorders to a "Now, girls" tossed in by a speaker reacting to a point being made by some women. Such sexism becomes particularly difficult to counter, much less to eradicate.

The codified rules for meetings often place active nonsexist communicators on the defensive. If the nonsexist communicators take the offensive by trying to revise the rules, the group may label them as radicals, or at least irritants. On the other hand, if nonsexist communicators implicitly accept the sexism by remaining silent, members of the group may interpret their acceptance as agreement with or support for the legitimacy of the sexism itself, or as weakness of the nonsexist communicators.

Even the informal meeting presents difficult sexist problems. Although the culture does not codify rules for sexism, they still exist. And in many ways the uncodified rules of sexism prove harder to attack than the codified ones.

One difficult situation arises because informal meetings open up the communication to sexist quips and jokes often bandied about within the dictates of culturally defined informality. In the presence of sexist "humor" another decision faces the nonsexist communicator: Laugh with the others, sit expressionless or stern faced and silent, leave the meeting in protest, or object to the so-called humor. A laugh implicitly sanctions the "humor." If one takes any of the other actions, the observers may consider him or her to be a humorless, nit-picking crank. Those who use and condone sexist, racist, and ethnic "humor" do not seem to comprehend why the objects of the "humor" don't find it side-splitting.

The informal meeting leads to even more sexist conversation and imagery than a formal meeting yields. Overcoming the flippant sexism of informal oral situations proves extremely difficult, for the corrections depend on changed attitudes. And changed attitudes and behaviors require more commitment and urgency than a few people can provide.

For the short run, nonsexist communicators will simply have to interact with sexist communicators as positively as possible. Experimentation can help us learn when to take a stand and when to let an issue pass, when to laugh at ourselves and when to challenge others who laugh for the wrong reasons, when to lead only by setting examples and when to lead by overt action, when to accept defeat and when to refuse it.

Without taking risks, the movement toward nonsexist communication will never get off the ground. Therefore, we must use as much judgment as we can bring to bear and be willing to absorb the negativism directed toward us for our actions. We must move forward—whatever the risks.

Small-Group Conferences

The small-group conference simply extends the potential for sexism described in the preceding section. Generally, the smaller the number, the more likely it is that people's veneers will be pierced. Thus, the security provided by small numbers allows conference participants to drop their guards and expose sexism that might not otherwise evidence itself.

Interviews

Whether classified by the interviewer's approach (directive or nondirective) or by the purpose (screening, hiring, orienting, appraising performance, reprimanding, counseling, settling grievances, or terminating employment), interviews introduce opportunities for sexism. The interviewer-controlled, directive interview often reeks of sexism—by act or by innuendo. The interviewee-controlled, nondirective interview may be less blatantly sexist.

The interviewer usually controls all types of interviews except the counseling interview. Add to the factor of interviewer control the knowledge that the interviewer virtually always occupies a higher position than the interviewee. And, finally, consider the high probability that the interviewer-superior is male. With such a combination of factors, the situation fairly bursts with sexist potential.

Think of some of the possible sexist attributes of a common job interview scene involving a male interviewer and a female interviewee. As the female enters the door, the male looks at her from head to toe and registers, however subtly, his impression of the shape of her body. He asks questions related to marital status or plans, childbearing plans, birth-control methods, and how much her husband earns. Even though she has applied for a supervisory position, he asks if she types. If he is substantially older than she and if she is attractive, he transmits the paternalistic attitude. If he is about the same age or somewhat older, he transmits the "are you available" attitude. Without asking her opinions or assessing her abilities objectively, he reaches stereotyped conclusions about her. Such conclusions might include that she does not want to travel, that hers is a second income, that she wants a job and not a career, that she will not be stable because she will follow her husband, that she will act more emotional than a man, that she will be absent more than a man, and so on. All these types of sexism compound the usual "man-girl" dichotomy, generic "he" language, and the male-as-the norm imagery.

The woman in the scene speaks softly, if not timidly, and unassertively. She also speaks much less often and for shorter durations than the man, and he interrupts her much more than she interrupts him.

Though this hypothetical scene is perhaps overdrawn, all these types of sexism do occur—and not as rarely as we would like to assume. Therefore, the interviewer who aspires to become nonsexist must analyze her or his techniques to recognize and remove sexist tendencies, which can become exaggerated in the superior-subordinate relationship that usually defines the interview.

Conversations

In contrast to the interview, which usually represents a formal interchange between two people at two different levels of the power hierarchy, the organizational conversation usually involves an informal exchange between or among two or more people on the same level. Thus, the sexist problems of the conversation often differ from those of the interview.

If a person ever tends to exhibit sexist communication, the framework of conversation may expose it. Thus, the organizational conversation forms the base level for the eradication of sexism. Significant amounts of information sharing and decision making take place in unstructured interpersonal interchanges during work hours, on breaks, over coffee, on the golf course, and in private time. Therefore, the conversation indeed merits serious concern by those committed to nonsexism in communication.

Because the conversation forms the critical base level of sexist communication, it provides the clearest avenue for foundational correction. Thus, the following sections and exercises concentrate on conversation. If we can cleanse the conversation of sexism, we can bring virtually all the more formal, structured classes of communication into line.

Ultimately, we can carry the correction of sexism further. Research has established that we think with verbal and nonverbal symbols. Thus, the core of correcting sexist communication lies with the thinking process itself.

Listening

Oral exchanges involve both speaking and listening. When engaging in oral transactions, the nonsexist communicator recognizes the value of listening to and observing the reactions and responses of the receiver. This feedback provides important information concerning how the receiver reacts to the communication. Thus, by coupling sensitivity to the wants of others with effective listening and observation skills, the nonsexist communicator can recognize any sexist errors made and subsequently correct them.

Guideline U: Oral Communication

1. Think before speaking so that your words do not include sexism that you cannot erase.

Incorrect	*Correct*
Did you see that one portly authoress among the other authors?	Did you notice that only one of the authors is a woman?
She is some kind of broad, though at times she acts like a Nervous Nellie	She is some kind of woman, though at times she does seem nervous

2. Use positive words in conversation instead of negative words.

Incorrect	*Correct*
She's an old hag	(Omit and speak of complaints about specific qualities)
She's a frigid old maid	She seems to be a straitlaced single woman

3. Avoid the sexism in the Robert's Rules of Order approach to formal meetings.

Incorrect	*Correct*
Madam chairman	Chairperson Phipps (Chairwoman Phipps if *chairman* is used for men occupying the position)

4. Discard sexist "humor" and do not laugh at the sexist "humor" of others.

Incorrect	*Correct*
Did you hear the one about the old bitch who . . . her (Laughter)	Did you hear the one about the old crank who . . . the (Laughter)

5. Use nonsexist methods in conducting interviews.

Incorrect	*Correct*
Asking questions of a woman related to marital status, children, birth control	Asking questions about education, experience, and training for the job
Communicating the stereotypes about women as sex objects, wives, mothers, servants	Communicating equality of assumptions for women and men

6. Cultivate sensitive listening and feedback-monitoring skills to develop awareness of sexist practices. Use this awareness to eliminate sexist practices.

Incorrect	*Correct*
You hear a woman refer to herself as a *chairperson*; you call her a *chairman* when you respond to her	You hear a woman refer to herself as a *chairperson*; you call her a *chairperson* when you respond to her

NONVERBAL COMMUNICATION

Research shows that 65 percent or more of the meaning in an oral exchange comes from the nonverbal (wordless) symbols. And, again, the weight of negative communication falls more heavily on females than males. Therefore, with such a large proportion of the impact of a transaction falling in the nonverbal realm, nonverbal components prove particularly salient in a study of sexism in communication.

Space and Territory

Humans establish bubbles around territories they claim as their own. Invasions of space by others can lead to serious problems in communication. Definitions of invasion and space differ from culture to culture, from geographic region to geographic region, from nation to nation. However, major differences tend to exist between males and females independent of these other characteristics.

Generally, those with power have more rights to invade the space of those without power. Therefore, think of the nonverbal force exhibited by males as they exercise the right to encroach on females' territories by moving closer to them for conversation than they do to males. Observe how of all the people in a home, the male is most likely to have a personal chair, room, or other defined space. Most of us grew up knowing that we could not sit in "daddy's chair," at least not when he was home.

Notice how males occupy more space when they sit and stand than women do. Contrast this with the image of females sitting primly and occupying minimal space like ladies.

Think about the male's felt need to be taller than the female or females with whom he associates. In the same vein, consider the psychological problems often encountered by females who consider themselves too tall and by males who consider themselves too short. Women slump and men wear elevator shoes. Observe how women step out of the way of oncoming men more than men step out of the way of oncoming women—just as blacks step out of the way more often than whites. The next time you sit at a conference table observe how men tend more than women to occupy the ends of the table.

In the most serious context, ponder how sexual harassment, abuse, and rape represent the ultimate invasion of territory—expression of power through violence.

Through all these illustrations the nonverbal communication rings through clearly: Males exhibit power and females exhibit powerlessness.

Touch

The skin is the most extensive tissue of the body. Therefore, touching forms a most important vehicle for nonverbal communication. Sexism occurs because the freedom to touch another indicates dominance, and males touch females more than females touch males.

One sexist nonverbal act occurs when a male makes a hands-on advance to a woman. Such touching, invading, superiority postures prove particularly difficult for women in subordinate positions in the workplace. Just what can a woman waiting tables do if a male customer lets a fondling hand stray to portions of her body he should not handle without permission? How can a female secretary deal with a male executive who considers her to be his object for standing over and touching at will? Many men parcel out pinches and pats to women as if women do not have brains or sensitivity, as if they do not mind the derogating treatment. Sexual harassment, then, often involves the assumed right of the male to touch the female whenever he wishes.

Females tend to accept the touches of others more readily than do males. This tendency again reveals female submissiveness. If women do initiate touch with men, the men often interpret the touch as having sexual overtones, rather than as connoting power.

Another kind of touch that has a sex-stereotyped meaning is the slap on the back. Men generally slap other men, not women, on the back. Similarly, the culture expects a firm handshake from males and a limp one from females. Society suspects the femininity of a back-slapping or firm-gripping woman. It expects the woman's touches to be delicate and "ladylike."

Movement

Picture the relative postures, gestures, and movements of females and males. Do they not again reinforce submissiveness and dominance, respectively?

Men put their arms over the necks of women—a dominant gesture. They lead in ballroom dancing. They clasp their hands over women's hands.

The woman walks and runs with small, high-heel-limited, delicate steps. The man strides with the confidence born of power. The woman sits in a tense position with arms close to the body, knees pressed together, perhaps with legs crossed at the ankles. The man sits in a relaxed position with his arms ajar, perhaps clasped behind his head, with the ankle of one leg planted on the knee of the other or with his feet propped on a desk. The skirted woman has to bend down to pick something up from the floor by squatting because she cannot expose herself. The man bends freely from the waist. The skirted woman sitting on a floor must go into all kinds of contortions so as not to let anything show. The man sprawls freely.

Women's hands and bodies gesture with the same smallness found in their walks and postures. Men's hands and bodies gesture with the same strength found in their walks and postures.

When men open doors, hold chairs, and light cigarettes for women, stand when women enter rooms, or hold their coats, the acts may demean the women if done in a condescending manner or if accompanied by cruel jokes about "women's lib." When done naturally by one human for another equal human, such acts contribute to nondiscriminatory interaction. However, all too often when males perform such acts, they diminish the females.

Picture the kinds of gestures that reduce a woman. One occurs when a man moves his hands in the shape of a curvaceous woman.

If women do aspire to power, then, they will take on the postures, gestures, and movements of power. If men do not want to appear forbidding or condescending, they will take on some of the more restricted postures, gestures, and movements of less power.

Time

Time adds another dimension to the nonverbal elements that have an impact on sexist communication. Stereotypes abound about the woman who keeps the man waiting or who always arrives late.

Research does not seem to establish a significant difference between the sexes in the use of time. However, if some differences do exist, they are likely to arise from the acculturated female and male roles. If society creates the picture of a woman dawdling to put on makeup and do the preening that society also requires, then the woman tends to fulfill that picture. Similarly, if society creates the picture of a businesslike man who always makes meetings on time, then the man tends to fulfill that picture.

The relative time-dimension roles of females and males also relate to work expectations. When most women stayed home with the children and most men went outside the home to work, views of time differed. Women had to keep their time schedules more flexible as they subordinated their lives to others. However, now that about half of all women work outside the home, their schedules move toward the rigidity of men's. In fact, women's workday schedules tend to be tighter than men's because the positions women occupy tend to have less flexible control. Can you imagine as many women as men able to leave work in the afternoon for a round of golf or to catch a plane to fly to another city for an evening of nightclubbing before the big football game the next day?

Some people would say that women take more time off from work than men. However, statistics show that the absentee rate for women does not differ significantly from that for men. For example, a Public Health Service study shows little difference in the absentee rate due to illness or injury: 5.6 days a year for women compared with 5.2 for men.[1]

Analysis also shows that when women do miss work, they do so because biology decrees that women have children, and society decrees that women have more responsibility toward the care of children than do men. In addition, most women do not have access to some of the kinds of time that many men have (for instance, the long business lunch or the convention in another city).

Some people suggest that women do not show as much willingness as men to work overtime—that they become clock-watchers. However, again, research does not seem to illustrate the point. And, indeed, if some women do tend to watch clocks, it may well be because they work in the dead-end, uncreative, boring jobs so often reserved for women.

Another time dimension militating against women exists in society's view of age. It expects women to remain forever young. A woman's value diminishes with age. A man just gains character. Women have face-lifts, lie about their ages, spend large amounts of money on miracle creams, and even use a certain detergent to keep young-looking hands.

Society unrealistically decrees that the husband be older than his wife, though some men and women now defy that decree. They agree that the logic of pairing older women with younger men makes more sense than the reverse, basically because women outlive men. Age and women's longer life span create other sexist ramifications. Although society discriminates against age, it does smile more favorably on older men than on older women. Therefore, because older women outnumber older men, the existing sexist patterns simply compound. Contrast the relative respect given to the "old biddy" (or *crone*) and the "old goat" (or *codger*).

Contrast the older female's preoccupation with blued or dyed hair and wigs with the male's acceptance of gray hair or baldness. Picture the older woman who either cripples around in high-heeled shoes or wears the tennis shoes or heavy shoes necessary for feet damaged by incorrect shoes over the years.

[1]U.S. Department of Labor, Women's Bureau, Employment Standards Administration, *The Myth and the Reality* (Washington, D.C.: U.S. Government Printing Office, 1974).

Think about the nonassertiveness of the societally created dependent widow who can't drive a car, balance a checkbook, or even screw in a light bulb. Picture the environment of nursing homes—dominated by older women. Think of the characteristics of "bag ladies" who live out of trash cans and sleep in the doorways of buildings.

Think of all of the nonverbal elements associated with poverty and realize that women and children form the vast majority of those in poverty. Again, older women far outnumber older men who exist in poverty.

To correct the sexist nonverbal communication associated with age and difference in female-male life span, we will have to change attitudes of both senders and receivers. Older women (the senders) must create the image and reality of strength, independence, assertiveness, and power. All people (the receivers) must encourage, recognize, and respect these same qualities in older women.

Face

The face and all its features and expressions form a fertile field for sex differentiation and nonverbal communication. Again, males tend to use their faces in power plays; females tend to use theirs in submissive acts.

As the windows of the mind, the eyes probably do as much as any other part of the body to reveal the person. Unfortunately, many males consider suggestive winking and uninhibited ogling their prerogative. At the same time, many females flirt by lowering or averting their eyes and demurely fluttering eyelashes.

Because the powerless tend to fix their eyes on the powerful, women tend to fix their eyes on men. They do so to read all the nonverbal cues that tell them how to act to gain the males' approval. At the same time, males do not have to look at females; they may look away, knowing that the females will continue to observe them. However, if males initiate eye contact, they expect females to return it. One of the reasons that males position themselves at the ends of tables arises from the eye-contact power associated with that location.

Sexism also arises in the treatment given to eyes by women through such cosmetic acts as plucking eyebrows, adding artificial eyelashes, and wearing eye shadow, eyeliner, and mascara. Again the woman spends a disproportionate amount of time on preening because society defines so much of her worth in terms of looks.

Another sexist element exists in the permission society gives to women to cry, without allowing men to do so. The ultimate solution probably lies in greater emotional openness for all people. For now, however, women who want power probably should cry less in public, and men who want improved mental health probably should cry more in private.

Similarly, the smiles of males and females differ significantly. Generally, men smile much less than women. The smiling countenances of women expresses servility. The somber countenances of men express power. A woman who does not smile becomes suspect because she does not give the assurance that she intends no aggression, that she is subservient.

Voice

As suggested in the section on oral communication, the voices of females and males conform with follower-leader categories. Women generally speak with higher pitch, tending toward shrillness, whining, or babylike helplessness. The culture believes that strength, courage, and credibility belong with low voices, probably because low voices belong to males.

Females tend to have a wider range of vocal pitch than males and to be more expressive (emotional). They tend to add more sighs, pauses, and other such timid vocal differentiators. Males tend to speak loudly and with a controlled, moderately rapid rate. Females tend to speak softly and with either an exaggeratedly slow, tentative, or sexy and sultry rate or an exaggeratedly rapid, emotional, nagging, cackling rate. Once again, the authoritative control to which the male tends exhibits a powerful stance, whereas the female's lack of that control exhibits powerlessness.

When men and women interact, the pattern generally involves men taking more turns than women, men talking for longer durations of time than women, men interrupting women more than women interrupt men. Women, when they do speak, insert tentative filler statements and questions, including tag questions and faltering patterns. For example, the socialization of women leads them to begin sentences with such phrases as "This probably isn't a good idea, but. . . ." They lift the voice at the end of a statment to turn it into a timid question, rather than an assertive declaration. They end their expression of an idea with a question such as "You don't really think so, do you?" Women laugh and giggle more at men's witticisms than the reverse. Women adapt, comply, support, resolve, and give in more than men do.

To correct nonverbal sexism in vocal patterns and interactions, then, the female who aspires to power in nonintimate interactions needs to move to a lower pitched, moderately paced and projected pattern of speech. She needs to avoid the sweet baby talk, the giggling and chattering, and the whispering sultriness that cast her in traditional powerless modes. She needs to drop tag questions, the tentative lift in the voice, and other patterns that indicate that she does not feel confident about what she says. She needs to take and hold her turns with assertive firmness.

The woman must take care to find a moderate position of strength and dynamism, because if she swings too far toward the bluff, swaggering, dominating vocal and conversational patterns of males she will put people off.

The man who aspires to more sensitivity needs to remove the gruffness from his voice. He needs to avoid the aggressive domination of conversations exercised by interrupting others, particularly women, and taking more and longer turns than women. He needs to stop the derogating whistles and gutteral sounds made toward women who pass by.

Environment

The environment contributes significantly to the sexist nonverbal interactions of humans. Both people and things form that environment. When a woman walks by a group of conversing men, her entrance often changes the conversation in a different way than a man's entrance would. The same would be true for a man entering the space of conversing women.

The concept of men's and women's conversational groups recalls the sexism inherent in the automatic sexual separation of a group of men and women into conversational groups. This separation arises primarily because the culture assigns more importance to "men's talk" than to "women's talk." Indeed, if women want to remove themselves from the "women's room," they must not limit themselves to talk about recipes, children, and home furnishings. Instead, they must learn and converse about an extensive body of knowledge, for instance, world events. Men, too, need to broaden their horizons. Recipes, children, home furnishings, and other topics often relegated to the world of "girl talk" have as much importance as football games, dirty jokes, sexual feats, and power trips. The key, then, lies in moderation for both females and males. Both must work to remove the imagery that a woman's place is in the kitchen or bedroom and begin to enjoy each other's minds.

Even colors in the environment carry sexist connotations. Society expects the woman to have a pastel, weak personality, for it tells her to become pink from birth. In contrast, it tells the boy to begin with blue—already a stronger color than pink—but to move quickly to dominant colors in clothing and furnishings. Can you imagine a teenage boy with a pale yellow bedspread and flounce under a frilly pale yellow canopied bed? His parents would fear that he would grow up to be a *sissy* or a *wimp*—again casting a sexist aspersion on the female, whom society expects to grow up to be a *sissy* or a *wimp* because her bedroom has such furnishings.

Other aspects of sexist furnishings include their textures, design, and arrangement. The culture reinforces the female's roles of sex object and servant by decreeing for her furnishings that reflect softness, fluffiness, cuteness, sweetness, airiness, floweriness, lightness, and sexiness. In contrast, the culture reinforces the male's roles of leadership and dominance by giving him furnishings of strength, angularity, firmness, and power. When a member of either sex flies in the face of society's decrees, he or she risks negative reactions. Why should not a woman want to express the power that comes from sharp corners, firm cushions, and hard, solid fabrics? Why should not a man want to express the sensitivity that comes from curved corners, soft cushions, and sheer fabrics? Both men and women have buried within them the full range of feelings. Why does society not allow them to express that full range without labeling them aberrations?

The office scene suggests a great deal about sexism in the environment. It usually involves a male status figure in the most powerful location relative to the female subservient figures. The most powerful male occupies the largest, highest corner office with the most windows. He sits behind a massive executive desk so that those who approach him understand his authority. His furnishings all exude power. He probably has his own marked parking place near the entrance of the building and may have a private elevator.

In contrast, most women find themselves in pools behind secretarial desks but subject to the male power figures in the scene. Their furnishings may be businesslike, but they often include a little feminine touch, such a the bouquet of flowers sent by the boss on National Secretaries Day. (Think of the range of meanings in that act. It parallels the Bosses' Night sponsored by many women's groups; the bosses are virtually always male.)

An interesting twist arises in the display of family pictures on an office desk. For the man such pictures portray him as a caring family man. For the woman with or without status such pictures portray her as preoccupied with domestic matters.

Even in the matter of odors, sex differences exist. The culture requires different types of fragrances to express its views of femininity and masculinity. Thus, men's shaving lotions have a "manly" scent; women's perfumes, colognes, soaps, and deodorants have a sweet or sexy scent.

Society wants both females and males to mask unpleasant human odors with deodorants. However, even in this realm, the culture condones males' sweat and natural odors as part of the macho image at the same time that it runs commercials on "feminine" deodorant products on television. It permits men to be men, but it does not permit women to be women.

The power of the sexist environment compounds the pressures on females. The barrage overwhelms so thoroughly that many females unconditionally surrender just to survive.

Dress and Appearance

This section title—dress and appearance—conveys the sexism inherent in attitudes toward the dress and appearance of women. It also spotlights the sexism of the man-girl inequality, the sex-object status of women, and the implied conflict between attractiveness and intellect.

The most handicapping kind of sexism exists in the criteria of beauty and form for determining the worth of a woman. Such sexism appalls because woman has no control over the genes that shape her countenance and body. If she happens to be born ugly, whatever "ugly" means, she spends a lifetime doing what she can cosmetically and feeling less worthy than her more comely sisters. Or she throws off the shroud society has imposed on her and decides that she, like all human beings, is worthwhile. Unshackled by sex-object status, she becomes strong for having overcome the unreasonable cultural criteria.

Think of the story of Cinderella. Can you agree that the tale would have held out more hope for society if Cinderella had been large footed and ugly, had never had beautiful clothes, had never gone to a ball, and had found a genuine love—not a love based on appearance and dress? Instead, children learn that ugliness (embodied in the stepsisters and mother) is bad and always "loses," and that prettiness is good and always "wins."

Think of how the bride wears white—for purity and virginity. The "bridesmaids" and even "matron" of honor wear pastels. The groom and "best man" often wear black.

Briefly picture the sexism associated with each of these elements of appearance and dress: frilly, flimsy, sheer, low-cut dresses; tight-fitting clothing; dresses instead of pants; jeans with clear vinyl seats; high heels; miniskirts; silicone injections; face-lifts; bras that lift and separate; the cult of unreasoning dieting accompanied by the disease anorexia nervosa; pocketless garments; permanents; long, straight hair; sprayed hairdos; tanned skin; preening; shaving legs and underarms; girdles; cosmetics; deodorants; Easter hats; hair coloring; wigs; perfumes; expensive furs; jewelry; pierced ears. True, we are past binding feet to make cripples of women, but we still move in and out of periods of binding bosoms, cinching waists, wearing high heels, and requiring skirts, not pants suits, in offices.

The types of dress for females and males again reflect powerlessness and power. Therefore, if women want power, they will dress in a powerful way. Obviously, women would find it difficult to deny cultural conditioning in one fell swoop by throwing off all sexist, nonfunctional garb and cosmetics. Instead, they will have to make some adjustment as they phase out their powerless appearance. Indeed, as men give more attention to hair, cosmetics, and clothing, and women give less attention to them, the sexist gap will decrease. Perhaps we will reach some middle ground of reason and the shell of the person will become less important than the core.

Silence

The mythical talkative woman actually talks less on the average than the typical man. With subordination for women in conversations, then, comes a sexism in silence—an important nonverbal contributor to communication. Indeed, men remain silent at times, but their silences come less often and often involve strength or even intimidation; they are not the reticent silences of submissive women. When a man uses silence to intimidate, the woman often fills the silence with disorganized chatter.

From another viewpoint, women often have less opportunity than men for the kind of private silence that leads to good thinking and rehabilitating meditation. Humans require privacy, yet the heightened serving responsibilities of women—particularly married women—place them constantly in contact with husbands, children, bosses, working peers, and the consuming public. They do not have that special room or special time that society permits the man to take—if only behind the newspaper over breakfast.

Guideline V: Nonverbal Communication

1. Express sex-positive treatment of territory and space.

Incorrect	*Correct*
A man moves close to a woman he has just met or whose bearing suggests that she does not want encroachment into her territory	A man avoids invading the space of a woman he has just met or whose bearing suggests that she does not want encroachment into her territory
A man sits back in his executive chair with his feet planted on his desk and his hands and arms behind his head. He talks with a woman who sits primly in her straight-backed chair with her arms close to her body, her hands folded in her lap, her knees pressed together, and her feet flat on the floor and touching. The man's executive desk separates them.	A man and woman talk as they face each other without an intervening desk. Both sit in the same kind of chair in relaxed positions. Both have their arms away from their bodies. The woman crosses her legs at the ankles or knees, but in an assertive arrangement. The man plants his feet flat on the floor or crosses his legs.
Several members of a committee gather around a table for a meeting. The members have not yet selected their chairperson. The women sit on the sides, and two of the men occupy the end positions.	At least one woman occupies an end position at a meeting table

2. Use touch in a nonsexist way.

Incorrect	*Correct*
A man puts an arm around a woman just above her waist when her feedback for such a move has been negative in the past	A man does not touch a woman who gives negative feedback about such acts
A woman either does not offer her hand for a handshake at all or shakes limply when she does	A woman offers her hand for a handshake and makes it a firm one

3. Cultivate nonsexist postures, gestures, and movements.

Incorrect

A man holds a door for a woman and comments (with half a chuckle) that he should not do that anymore, because "women's lib" is ruining everything

A woman wears spike-heeled, open-toed, and open-heeled shoes and walks with a small-stepped, forward-tilted, weak gait

A woman wears a tight, short skirt and low-cut, tight sweater to her work as a file clerk; the work requires a great deal of bending and climbing ladders to get to the files

A man sits and strides with gross movements so that he intimidates the people whose favors he wants to curry

Correct

A man does not hold a door for a woman or holds it without verbal or nonverbal comment. A woman holds a door for a man when circumstances call for it.

A woman wears low- to medium-heeled, closed-toed, and closed-heeled shoes and walks with a firm, graceful, moderate stride of strength

A woman wears tastefully fitting slacks and tailored blouse to her work as a file clerk when it requires bending and climbing

A man sits and walks with moderate but assertive movements so that he does not intimidate the people whose favors he wants to curry

4. Treat time in a nonsexist fashion.

Incorrect

A personnel officer says, "I think we should hire a man instead of a woman because men have fewer absences than women"

A woman thinks she's cute and meeting society's expectations when she arrives late for meetings or keeps men waiting

Businesses require all employees to come to and leave work at the same time each day, thus making schedules difficult for working parents

A younger man and older woman decide not to marry because of the age difference

An older woman lives her life under the intensified sexism that comes with age

Correct

A personnel officer says, "I disagree with the myth that women have more absences than men; we should make our decision about hiring on bases other than such myths"

A woman knows that people observe and react negatively to the misuse of time. Therefore, she arrives on time for meetings and does not keep people waiting unnecessarily.

Businesses institute flexible working hours, thus freeing up work schedules—a particularly helpful scheme for working parents

A younger man and older woman make the decision about whether to marry on the basis of factors other than the age difference

An older woman lives her life by overcoming the intensified sexism that comes with age

5. Cultivate nonsexist facial expressions.

Incorrect	*Correct*
A woman plays society's "feminine" role by averting and fluttering her eyes, tilting her head, and fixing a sweet, coy smile on her face	A woman wants success; thus, she looks people in the eye, holds her head at a strong angle, and smiles sincerely at only appropriate times
A woman who aspires to power wears artificial eyelashes, heavy makeup, and thinly plucked eyebrows. She puts on makeup in public.	A woman who aspires to power wears no artificial eyelashes, minimal makeup, and moderately shaped eyebrows. She does not put on makeup in public.
A man uses his eyes to wield power over a woman; he initiates eye contact, expecting her to respond, but haughtily gazes away when she initiates eye contact	A man works for mutual and equal eye gaze with a woman, just as he does with a man

6. Develop nonsexist use of the voice as a nonverbal transmitter.

Incorrect	*Correct*
A woman speaks with high pitch, tense rapidity, and baby-talk softness	A woman speaks with moderate to low pitch; moderate, dynamic rate; and unaffected, moderate, but projected volume
A man talking with a woman interrupts frequently and dominates the conversation	A man talking with a woman does not interrupt and takes turns so that she speaks about half the time
A woman always includes a lift in the voice at the end of a statement, asks tag questions, or initiates a statement with a disclaimer about its quality	A woman speaks with firm declaration, without tag questions, and without disclaimers about the quality of her statement
A woman giggles or laughs no matter what the male says or does	A woman laughs with naturalness and sincerity—and only when the situation warrants it
A man speaks so loudly and stridently that he puts people off	A man moderates speaking patterns so that he becoms approachable

7. Recognize and correct the sexism in the environment.

Incorrect	*Correct*
After a dinner party the men move to one room and the women to another for conversation	After a dinner party the conversational groups form on a basis other than sex
Women talk only about children, husbands, and recipes	Women include such items as world and community news and financial market considerations in the conversation

Men talk only about yesterday's football game, the last big deal, and sexual exploitations	Men include such items as children, wives, and recipes in the conversation
A woman furnishes her office with frills, pastels, and silken fabrics. She displays pictures of her husband and children.	A woman furnishes her office with straight corners; warm, strong colors; and hard-finished fabrics. She does not display pictures of her husband and children.
A commercial shows a working father, a homemaking mother, a daughter in a restrictive dress holding a doll, and a son in comfortable jeans holding a military tank	A commercial of a family shows a working mother and one child (either female or male) holding an object, toy, or game of a sex-neutral or sex-"opposite" nature
A newspaper will not report a wedding unless it pictures the bride in her white wedding gown and uses the "Mr. and Mrs." style of reporting	A newspaper respects and suggests the use of nonsexist photographs and language

8. Develop and support nonsexist attitudes and actions about dress and appearance.

Incorrect	*Correct*
A manager says, "Hire a sexy girl for the front desk"	A manager says, "Hire a capable person for the front desk"
A business executive wears a chiffon dress and dangling earrings to the office	A business executive wears a dark-skirted business suit and gold stud earrings (if any) to the office

9. Cultivate sex-neutral patterns of silence and privacy.

Incorrect	*Correct*
A man uses the ten-second silence to intimidate a woman	A man uses logic to try to win his argument. A woman does not fall prey to the intimidating silence.
A husband and children expect the woman to be available to them during all working hours	A husband and children understand the human's need for regular privacy and fulfillment of personal thoughts and needs. Thus, they respect the woman's periodic removal from the family scene.

APPLICATIONS

The exercises for this section provide the opportunity to recognize and correct sexist oral and nonverbal communication. For each, identify the sexism and then suggest ways to remove it.

☆   *8-1.   Following is a sexist conversational scene. Identify the sexism and suggest a nonsexist revision.*

Cast:

Fred Guthrie, Manager, Media Development. He is developing a media package for Forgan and another for Clancey. He does not like working for Clancey because she is a woman, and he feels that women belong in the home. He plans to spend more time on Forgan's project than Clancey's; in fact, he would like to see Clancey's project fail.

Danny Forgan, Manager, Sales Department. Forgan, too, resents having to work with a woman as an equal in the organization—especially in management of a nontraditional field for a woman. He likes Guthrie's assurance that his media package comes before Clancey's. He particularly resents his company's affirmative action plan, which forces him to hire women in sales.

Rita Clancey, Manager, Export Department. Clancey senses the negativism toward her as the only woman manager in the firm. A great deal of her credibility as an export manager depends on the success of the media campaign. Its success depends a great deal on Guthrie's work. She would like to spend more time with Guthrie discussing the project.

Ellie Gibson, Waitress, Coffee Shop. Gibson is working as a waitress while attending night school and majoring in business administration. She would like to move into management in a major firm in another city. As a divorced woman financially responsible for two children, she cannot go to school full time. She resents sexual advances by males, but must keep her job.

Scene: The coffee shop in the building housing the offices of the large corporation employing Guthrie, Forgan, and Clancey. Guthrie and Forgan converse as they enter the coffee shop.

FORGAN: Hey, let's sit here where we can watch the hides come in the door. (Snaps fingers.) Waitress, two cups, please.

GUTHRIE: (Nods in agreement as they sit down.) Well, as I was saying, I just don't see what the girls are complaining about. After all, we men are the ones who have to carry the load for our families. They just work for pin money. Besides, they don't have the emotional stability to cope with the demands of management positions. (Gibson brings two cups of coffee. Guthrie puts an arm around her below the waist.) You're looking foxy today, Ellie.

GIBSON: (Emits an appropriate, if insincere, giggle, extricates herself from the arm, and walks away.)

FORGAN: I'll bet Ellie was a cheerleader and a prom queen in high school. I'm glad that Al hires only good-looking girls and won't let them wear pants suits. Oh, for the good old days when girls were girls and men were men.

GUTHRIE: Right; but when girls don't get married, have babies, and stay home, they're all bitchy that time of the month—unless they're going through the change, and then they're bitchy all the time. Take that broad Rita who they had to promote to supervisor. Oh, I guess she knows her work, but she can't really expect men to be willing to have a girl for a boss or work with her. As I was telling you, I'm supposed to develop a media package for her, but I don't see why I should spend my time on a project for her when you have one going too. Besides, she's just a plain Jane, and I like to see good-looking dames in short skirts in the office where I have to spend eight hours a day. Speaking of broads, did you just see that set walk by? (Looking at the woman from head to toe.)

FORGAN: Now, why couldn't we have a doll like her in the office instead of that castrating female Ida. Why doesn't Ida give up that women's lib stuff? She's built well enough that she could get a man, so I don't see why she's so uptight about women's rights.

GUTHRIE: Man, I don't either. Take Rose. She's advanced to be Mr. Allen's secretary by knowing her place, by using feminine gamesmanship, and by having all her friends among the men instead of among the girls. She doesn't complain about making and serving the coffee and doesn't expect to move into management. She told me that she can't understand why a woman would want to take a man's job. She agrees with us that the jobs ought to go first to men with wives and children, but these libbers seem to think that they should get them. And when Rose does pout about something, candy and flowers have her purring like a kitten in no time. I'm sure when Rose finds a husband, she will leave us to have babies.

CLANCEY: (Clancey enters the coffee shop, notes Forgan and Guthrie sitting at a table that could hold two more, makes a move toward them and speaks.) Good morning, Fred and Danny. I'm ready for a cup of coffee—and see you evidently have had such a morning too. I'm having some trouble with that media package you're helping me with, Fred. (She pauses at the table, clearly wanting an invitation to join them.)

FORGAN: (Glances up, but makes no receptive motion toward Clancey. Speaks in voice that closes out Clancey.) Yes, Mrs. Clancey, it has been a long one; but at least we can get away from it all and be alone for a few minutes now and then.

CLANCEY: (Moves awkwardly away from the men's table.) I'll talk to you later. (Sits at a table alone—some distance from Forgan and Guthrie.)

GUTHRIE: Damn, do these libbers who take jobs away from men really expect us to fall all over ourselves to do their work for them? And I certainly am not going to give up my break time for any of them.

FORGAN: Well, as we were saying, from what I've seen of the feminists, they're either such dogs that they can't have a man or so (holds hand out flat and moves it up and down from side to side) that they don't want a man. If I were a normal gal, I sure wouldn't want to be affiliated with them. I told my wife this morning that she's going to have to stop going to those so-called women's rights meetings or she's going to become a libber and ruin our marriage. By the way, she's having some sort of hen party at my house this very afternoon. (Pauses.) My dinner had better be on time. I just don't know what it's coming to. When the day comes that I don't wear the pants in my family, we'll have to cease being a family.

GUTHRIE: True. An aggressive, pushy broad is impossible to live or work with. In an office she's usually one who has been around, a frustrated divorcée, or an old maid who just can't accept that she has no place in a man's world.

GIBSON: (Overhears comment about a "frustrated divorcée"; fills cups.)

GUTHRIE: (Perplexed and nervous look on face.) You know, though, there are getting to be more and more girls who bother me. Take Rita. (Glances toward her and notes that she is reading something as she drinks her coffee.) She thinks like a man and acts like a lady, and some of the men are actually saying that she is doing a good job.

FORGAN: Man, we sure don't need our brothers deserting us and supporting a girl—the turncoats.

GUTHRIE: Isn't that the truth! She just comes on too confident for me, and I do feel sorry for her husband.

FORGAN: Right. He must be some kind of henpecked frail to stay married to her.

GUTHRIE: But, much as I hate to admit it, she doesn't seem to be absent, doesn't seem to complain, travels willingly, and, worst of all, is working in career planning with other women so that they, too, can be promoted. She has children, but she and her husband jointly take care of the house and see that the children are cared for. Is a couple like that ever hurting our cause!

FORGAN: Right, and I'm frightened that business may be one of the last strongholds against females. And, like Rita, they're pounding away at our defenses—just because of the fem lib bunch and their hold on the government. It frightens me.

GUTHRIE: (Looking at watch.) Me too. But on that sad note, I guess we'd better get back to the office and pay homage to that bitch-goddess success. (Leaves tip and pays check.)

GIBSON: Thank you, Mr. Forgan and Mr. Guthrie.

CLANCEY: (Glances up to note the men leaving.)

☆ *8-2. Picture these skeleton scenes. Identify the sexism in them and suggest nonsexist alternatives.*

1. A meeting of five line managers: four men and one woman. The woman is taking the minutes. The men ask her about the "woman's" view of an issue.

2. A TV commercial. A mother acts horribly embarrassed when her pie crust is not flaky because she used the wrong shortening in it. Her daughter also expresses embarrassment because her home economics teacher and class-mates (all young women) are giving her and the crust disdainful "looks."

3. A group of women calling themselves the Acme Wives discuss money-making projects. One woman suggests a toddler's beauty contest. Another suggests compiling a recipe book and selling it. Still another suggests a homemade bake sale. And, finally, another suggests that they volunteer to cook and serve the monthly meal for a men's club.

4. At the annual company picnic the women and older girls set up the tables and watch after the younger children. The men and older boys pitch horseshoes, play baseball, and play volleyball.

5. A man offers the invocation at a business luncheon. He asks all to bow their heads. He uses these words in the prayer: "Father," "Lord," "He," "His," "Him," "In Christ's Name," and "Amen." (Be sure to identify the religious bias in this one.)

6. A female secretary and her male boss. She sits in a short skirt with her legs crossed. He is admiring her legs. He stands up and puts his hand on her shoulder as he passes her chair. He returns to his chair and she gets his coffee for him.

7. Magazine advertisement: A strikingly handsome bikini-clad man stares aloofly as he enjoys his cigarette. Three beautiful women hover about him, touch him, and admire him.

8. A military recruiting poster includes one white male, one black male, and one white female, in that order. The full name tag of the white male shows; the first name on the tag of the black male shows; none of the name tag on the female shows.

9. The living room of a home: The husband talks to a salesperson about life insurance. The wife dries dishes, but listens. The daughter cuts out paper dolls. The son plays with a truck.

☆   *8-3.   Describe the sexism in each scene. Then suggest a parallel nonsexist version for it.*

1. Office: Four men. One is small in stature, plain in appearance, does not care for football or golf and does not pretend to, does not treat women as objects, does accept and respect women as coworkers, speaks of his liberated, working wife in positive terms. The other three, through postures, avoidance, and comments do not accept the maverick.

2. Office: Six men and one woman. Woman enjoys her role as the only woman in the group. She makes comments about how she has never been discriminated against and how she prefers to be around men. She puts down women in lesser positions than she holds saying that they cannot keep secrets, have too many absences, and just work to find husbands. She urges that if a woman prepares herself, she can advance. She flirts with the men and uses baby talk. They reply in kind.

3. Commercial: Chattering wife makes a fuss over her sick "baby boy" husband and administers a product that will help cure his cold. He sniffles and feels sorry for himself.

4. Four little girls talking: One wonders why Santa Claus is a man. Another wonders what "Mrs." Santa Claus's first name is. All speculate on whether "Mrs." Claus ever gets to ride in the sleigh or just has to stay home during all the fun.

5. Commercial: The speaker says that you only pass through this life once, so you ought to live with bravado. Men sail ships, climb mountains, and womanize. Women are womanized.

6. Commercial: Woman talks as her husband mops the kitchen floor. Impression is left that only a weakling man, under the sway of a domineering woman, would do such a thing.

7. Commercial: Man looks on in condescension as his mother-in-law makes a fool of herself over toilet paper. Little girl uses some of the toilet tissue on her doll and extols its superior qualities.

☆   *8-4.   Identify and correct the sexism in actual advertisements and commercials.*

APPENDIX A: ALTERNATIVES TO SEXIST USAGE

Sexist Symbols	Suggested Alternatives	Guidelines
Act like a lady and think like a man	Act and think sensitively and clearly	H, O, P
Actress(es) (deeply ingrained)	Actor(s) (if *actress* is eliminated) Actress(es) and actor(s) (if *actress* is retained)	B, O, Q
Adman(men)	Ad agent(s) Ad writer(s) Ad creator(s) Adwo/man; adwo/men[1] Ad woman (women) and man (men)	C, O

[1]For many "man" words in this list the alternatives include the printed inclusive "wo/man" form, the alternated "-woman and -man" endings, and the alternated "man and woman" words. When the "-woman and -man" endings are used, the form "adman and woman" is incorrect. The word beginning must be repeated so that parallelism is maintained: "adwoman and adman." Only when the root word is separated from the ending is the "man and woman" combination correct: "ad woman and man." Note the alternation of "man and woman" and "woman and man," so that nonsexist ordering is observed. The "man and woman" concept runs counter to some writers' ideas of de-sexing the language, but is necessary for at least a transitional period. It should be used sparingly and as a last resort, however. When an exact job title is incorporated into the list, the "woman and man" words are not listed. See "advance agent."

Sexist Symbols	Suggested Alternatives	Guidelines
Adulteress	Adulterer	B, O
Advance man (men)	Advance agent(s)[2]	C, O
Adventuress	Adventurer	B, O
Age and age differences (powerlessness for females; power for males)	Females use age and age differences for power	O, P, Q, V
Airman	Flier, pilot, aviator	C, O
Airplane steward	Airplane flight attendant*	B, O
Airplane stewardess	Airplane flight attendant*	B, O
Alderman	Alderperson Council member	C, O
All-girl orchestra	Orchestra All-woman orchestra (if *all-man* orchestra is used)	H, O
All men are created equal	All men and women are created equal All people are created equal	O
All the king's men	All the monarch's personnel (men and women; people)—or eliminate	C, N, O
All work and no play make Jack a dull boy	All work and no play make people dull	O
Alumnus (alumni) (for women)	Alumna (alumnae) Alumnae and alumni	O
Ambassadress	Ambassador	B, O
Anchorman(men)	Anchor(s) Anchorperson(s)(people) Anchorwo/man; anchorwo/men Anchorwoman(women) and anchorman(men) Anchor man (men) and woman (women)	C, O
Appearance (powerlessness for females; power for males)	Females take on appearance of power	O, P, Q, V
Assemblyman (crafts)	Assembler*	C, O
Assemblyman(men) (government)	Assemblyperson(s)(people) Assembly member(s) Assemblywo/man; assemblywo/men Assemblyman(men) and assemblywoman(women) Assembly woman (women) and man (men)	C, O

[2]U.S. Department of Labor, Employment and Training Administration, *Dictionary of Occupational Titles*, 4th ed. (Washington, D.C.: Government Printing Office, 1977). Hereafter an asterisk indicates alternative job titles from this source.

Sexist Symbols	Suggested Alternatives	Guidelines
Authoress	Author	B, O
Aviatress	Aviator	B, O
Aviatrix	Aviator	L
Baby (for woman)	Eliminate	H, R
Baby . . . his (for baby of unknown gender)	Baby . . . her or his Baby . . . its Babies . . . their	A, O
Baby doll (for woman)	Eliminate	H, L, P, R
Bachelor of Business Administration degree and other bachelor's degrees (deeply ingrained)	BBA (acronym only, never words) Eventually change to mean Baccalaureate Business Administration degree	O
Bachelor's degree (deeply ingrained)	Undergraduate degree	O
Bachelorette	Single	O
Bag (for woman)	Eliminate	L, P
Baggageman	Baggage checker*	C, O
Ball and chain (for woman)	Eliminate	L, P
Barren (for woman)	That couple has no children	P, R, T
Bastard	Eliminate	P, Q
Bat (for woman)	Eliminate	L, P
Bathing beauty	Sunbather	P
Battle-ax (for woman)	Eliminate	L, P
Be your own man	Be your own person Be your own individual To thine ownself be true To yourself be true	C, O
Bearcat (for woman)	Eliminate	L, P
Beauty contests; beauty pageants	Eliminate	P
Beauty queen	Contest winner—or eliminate	N, P
Beaver (for woman)	Eliminate	L, P
Behind every good man there is a good woman	Behind every good woman or man is another good man or woman—or eliminate	O
Bellboy	Passenger attendant*	H, O
Bellman	Bellhop*	C, O
The best-laid plans of mice and men	The best-laid plans of mice and people (persons)	C, O
Best man and matron of honor (or maid of honor)	Best man and best woman	H, O, P
The best man for the job	The best person for the job	C, O
Better half (for woman)	Eliminate	L, P
Bitch, bitchy (for woman)	Eliminate	L, P
Bitch-goddess Success	The god Success	B, L, P

Sexist Symbols	Suggested Alternatives	Guidelines
Black man (men)	Black(s)	O
	Black person (persons, people)	
Blonde (for woman)	Woman with blonde hair	P, R
Bookman(men)	Booksalesperson(s)(people, personnel)	C, O
	Publisher's representative(s)	
	Book dealer(s)	
	Bookwo/man; book wo/men	
	Bookwoman(women) and bookman(men)	
	Book man (men) and woman (women)	
Boss man	Boss	C, O
Boy (as sex-opposite) adjective	Eliminate	I
Boy (for a man)	Man	H, Q
-boy (a syllable in words used for men and women)	Use nonsexist, non-age-referent syllables, including -person	H, O
Boy and girl (always in this order)	Girl and boy (half the time)	G, H
Boyfriend (for man)	Friend	H, Q
	Man friend (if "woman friend" is used)	
	Gentleman friend (if "lady friend" is used)	
Boys will be boys	Children will be children	C, O
Breadwinner . . . he	Breadwinner . . . he or she	A, O
	Breadwinners . . . they	
Brethren	Brothers and sisters	O
Brewmaster	Brewing director*	O
	Head brewer	
Bridesmaid	Bridal attendant	P
Brinkmanship	Courting catastrophe	C
Broad (for woman)	Eliminate	L, P
Brood mare (for woman)	Eliminate	L, P
Brotherhood	Humanity	O
	The bond of humanity	
Brotherhood of man	Humanity	O
	Humankind	
	Bond of humanity	
Brotherly love	Human love	O
	People love	
	Love of people	
	Love of others	
	Other love	
Buck (for man)	Eliminate	L, Q
The buck deer fights off any challenge to his property (a doe deer)	The buck deer fights off any challenge	L, O

Sexist Symbols	Suggested Alternatives	Guidelines
Buddy (for woman)	Eliminate unless *sissy* is used positively for man (*buddy* is derived from *brother* and *sissy* from *sister*)	O, R
Built (for woman)	Eliminate	L, P
Bull (for man)	Eliminate	L, Q
Bullish on America	Strong on America	L, O
Bull market	Rising market Improving market	L, Q
Bull session	Rap session Brainstorming session	L, O
Bunny (for woman)	Eliminate	L, P
Busboy	Dish carrier* Room service assistant* Dining room attendant*	H, O
Bushman(men)	Bushperson(people, persons)	C, O
Businessman(-men)	Businessperson(s)(people, personnel) Business executive(s) Businesswo/man); businesswo/men Businessman(men) and business-woman(women) Business woman (women) and man (men)	C, O
Busman's holiday	Bus driver's holiday	C, O
Calendar girl	Eliminate	H, P
Call girl	Eliminate	H, P
Camera girl	Photographer*	H, P
Cameraman	Camera operator*	C, O
Candy stripers (hospital volunteers)	Volunteers Teen volunteers	K, P
Can you type? (for woman, but not man)	Ask questions about skills necessary for position, not on basis of sex	H, P
Career woman/girl	Woman whose career is (or add "career man/boy")	H, I
Castrate (for woman)	Destroy strength and sexuality	S
Castrating female/woman	Eliminate unless equivalent form is introduced to describe a male who saps and destroys the woman's strength and sexuality	I, P
Cat (for woman)	Eliminate	L, P
Cattleman(men)	Cattle grower(s) Cattle producer(s)	C, O
Cattlemen's Association	Cattle Owners' Association	C, O
Catty (for woman)	Eliminate	L, P

Sexist Symbols	Suggested Alternatives	Guidelines
Caveman(men)	Caveperson(s)(people)	C, O
	Cave dweller(s)	
	Cavewo/man; cavewo/men	
	Cavewoman(women) and caveman(men)	
Centerfold girl	Eliminate	H, P
Chairman(men)	Chairperson(s)(people)	C, O
	Chair(s)	
	Chairone(s)	
	Chair-one(s)	
	Chairer(s)	
	Head(s)	
	Chairwo/man; chairwo/men	
	Chairman(men) and chairwoman-(women)	
	Chair woman (women) and man (men)	
Chairperson(s) (for women, but not men)	Chairperson(s); chairone(s); chair-one(s); head(s) (for women and men)	H
	Chairwoman (for woman) and chairman (for man)	
Chambermaid	Room cleaner*	P
Charwoman	Charworker*	P
Chaste; chastity (for woman, but not man)	Apply equally to women and men	H, P
Chauvinist pig (for man, but not woman)	Chauvinist (apply equally to man and woman)	H, Q
Checkroom girl/woman	Checkroom attendant*	H, P
Chef (for man, but not woman)	Chef (for man and woman)	O
Chick (for woman)	Eliminate	L, P
Chicken (for woman)	Eliminate	L, P
Chickie-baby (for woman)	Eliminate	L, P
The child is father to the man	The child is parent to the adult	C, O
Child . . . he	Child . . . he or she	A, O
	Children . . . they	
China doll (for woman)	Eliminate	L, P
Chinaman(men)	Chinese	C, O
	Citizen(s) of China	
	Chinese citizen(s)	
	Chinese person(s)(people)	
	Chinese wo/man; Chinese wo/men	
	Chinese woman (women) and man (men)	
Chippie	Eliminate	L, P
Chorus boy	Chorus member	H
	Member of the chorus	

Sexist Symbols	*Suggested Alternatives*	*Guidelines*
Chorus girl	See "Chorus boy"	H, P
Chubbette (for woman)	Eliminate	B, H
Churchman(men)	Church member(s)	C, O
	Churchperson(s)(people)	
	Churchgoer(s)	
	Church worker(s)	
	Churchwo/man; churchwo/men	
	Churchman(men) and church-woman(women)	
	Church woman (women) and man (men)	
Cigarette girl	Cigarette vendor*	H, P
City of brotherly love	City of human love	O
	Philadelphia	
City father(s)	City officeholder(s)	O
	City founder(s)	
Cleaning girl	Cleaner	H, P
	Housecleaner	
Cleaning lady	See "Cleaning girl"	H, P
Cleaning woman	See "Cleaning girl"	H, P
Clergyman	Clergy*	C, O
Clerk . . . she	Clerk . . . he or she	A, P
	Clerks . . . they	
Coal miner's daughter/son	Refer to both parents (the son of a coal miner and a bus driver)	O
Coast Guardsman(men)	Coast Guarder(s)	C
	Coast Guardswo/man; Coast Guardswo/men	
	Coast Guardsman(men) and Coast Guardswoman(women)	
	Coast Guard woman (women) or man (men)	
Cock of the walk (for man)	Eliminate	L, Q
Coed (for woman but not man)	Student	H
	Coed (for man and woman)	
Cold as a fish (for woman)	Eliminate	L, P
Comedian(s)	Comedian/comedienne*	B, O
	Comedian(s) and comedienne(s) (if *comedienne* is retained)	
Comedienne(s) (deeply ingrained)	See "Comedian(s)"	O
Commercials that stereotype by sex	Eliminate	P, Q
Committeeman(men)	Committeeperson(s)(people, personnel)	C, O
	Committee member(s)	
	Committeewo/man; committeewo/men	

Sexist Symbols	Suggested Alternatives	Guidelines
	Committeewoman(women) and committeeman(men)	
	Committee man (men) and woman (women)	
Common Joe	Common citizen	O
	Common person	
	Common human	
Common man	Common Joe	O
Confidence man (con man)	Confidence operator	O, Q
	Operator	
Congressman(men)	Congressperson(s)(people)	C, O
	Member(s) of Congress	
	Congresswo/man; congresswo/men	
	Congressman(men) and congresswoman(women)	
	Congress woman (women) and man (men)	
Copy boy/girl	Copy carrier	O, Q
Cosmetics used in excess	Cosmetics used in moderation	P, R
Cotton maid	Eliminate	H, P
Councilman(men)	Council member(s)	C
	Councilperson(s)(people)	
	Councilwo/man; councilwo/men	
	Councilwoman(women) and councilman(men)	
	Council man (men) and woman (women)	
Counter girl	Counter attendant*	H, P
Country gentleman and country girl	Country people	H
Countryman	Citizen	C, O
Cow (for woman)	Eliminate	L, P
Cow (to intimidate)	Eliminate	L, P
Cowboy (may be too ingrained to eliminate)	Cowpuncher	H, O
	Cowboy and cowgirl (if *cowboy* is retained)	
Cowboy girl	Cowpuncher	H, O
	Cowgirl (if *cowboy* is retained)	
	Cowboy(s) and cowgirl(s) (if age-referent form is retained)	
CPA wives	CPA spouses	O
	CPA friends	
Craftsman(men)	Skilled worker(s)	C, O
	Crafts worker(s)	
	Craftswo/man; craftswo/men	
	Craftsman(men) and craftswoman(women)	

Sexist Symbols	*Suggested Alternatives*	*Guidelines*
	Crafts woman (women) and man (men)	
Craneman	Crane operator	C, O
Crewman	Crew member	C, O
Cro-Magnon man	Cro-Magnons Cro-Magnon people	C, O
Crone	Eliminate	P
Cupie doll (for woman)	Eliminate	L, P
Curse (for woman's menstrual cycle)	Eliminate	L, P
Cute as a bug (for woman)	Eliminate	L, P
Dame (for woman)	Eliminate	P
Damsel (in distress)	Eliminate	P
Dancing girl	Dancer	H
Daughter of a prominent banker, and so on	Just name her	H, O
Deaconess	Deacon	B, O
Deanette	Dean	B
Dear Sir (salutation)	Dear Madam or Sir Dear Executive Substitute conversational lead-in Omit	E
Dear Sirs (salutation)	Eliminate	E
Debutante	Eliminate	P
Defeminize	Destroy qualities of strength and courage	S
Delivery boy/man	Deliverer* Delivery person	H, O
Diamonds are girl's best friend	Diamonds are a good investment	P
Directress	Director	O
Distaff	Eliminate	L, O, P
Divorcée	Eliminate (unless *divorcé* is used for man)	H, P
Doctor . . . he	Doctor . . . she or he Doctors . . . they	O, Q
Doctor, lawyer, Indian, chief, rich man, poor man, beggarman, thief	Doctor, lawyer, chief, rich, poor, beggar, thief	C, O
Dog (for woman)	Eliminate	L, P
A dog is man's best friend	A dog is the human's best friend	O
Doll (for woman)	Eliminate	L, P
Dowager	Eliminate	P
A dream (for woman)	Eliminate	L, P
Dreamboat (for woman)	Eliminate	L, P

Sexist Symbols	Suggested Alternatives	Guidelines
Dress (powerlessness for females, power for males)	Females take on dress of power	O, P, Q, V
Duchess (deeply ingrained)	Use only for nobility	B, N
Dumpling (for woman)	Eliminate	L, P
Dutchman(men)	Dutch citizen(s) Dutch person(s)(people) Dutchwo/man; Dutchwo/men Dutchwoman(women) and Dutchman(men) Dutch man (men) and woman (women)	C, O
Effeminate	Eliminate because ultimate sexism is to female	S
Emasculate (for woman)	Destroy strength and sexuality	S
Empress (deeply ingrained)	Use only for nobility	B, N
Enchantress	Enchanter	B, O
Englishman(men)	English citizen(s) English person(s)(people) Englishwo/man; Englishwo/men Englishman(men) and English-woman(women) English woman (women) and man (men)	C
Enlisted man (men)	Enlistee(s) Enlisted person(s)(people, personnel) Enlisted wo/man; enlisted wo/men Enlisted woman (women) and man (men)	O
Environment (powerlessness for females; power for males)	Females establish environment of power	O, P, Q, V
Eve (as "temptress")	Eliminate	M, P
Everybody pulls his weight	Everybody pulls her or his (their) weight	A, O
Ewe (for woman)	Eliminate	L, P
Executrix	Executor	B, O
Eyes (powerlessness for females; power for males)	Females use eyes for power	O, P, Q, V
Facial expressions (powerlessness for females; power for males)	Females use facial expressions for power	O, P, Q, V
Fair sex (for women)	Eliminate	L, P
Fairy godmothers	Eliminate (or create fairy godfathers)	P
Fallen woman (for sexually active woman)	Eliminate	P, S
Family of man	Humanity Humankind	O

Sexist Symbols	Suggested Alternatives	Guidelines
Farmer . . . he	Farmer . . . she or he Farmers . . . they	A, O, Q
Farmerette	Farmer	B, O
Father (for God)	Being God Creator Nurturer Holy One Maker Defender	L, O
Fatherland	Homeland Native land	O
Favorite-son candidate	Favorite-citizen candidate Favorite-daughter or -son candidate	O, Q

Fellow (for woman)	Fellow (originally "partner")
	  (reasonably satisfactory for
	  woman, but avoid)
		O

Fellowship	Association Companionship	O
Fem lib	Feminism Female liberation movement Women's liberation Women's movement	P, S
Female (as sex-marking adjective)	Eliminate	I
Female lawyer	Lawyer	I, O

Feminine (as defined as patriarchal
  culture)
	Use words descriptive of strong
	  character until *feminine* means
	  that
		P, S

Feminine institution	Institution	P
Feminize	Make strong and confident	P, R, S
Fickle (for woman)	Fickle (for man and woman)	P
Filly (for woman)	Eliminate	L, P
Firecracker (for woman)	Eliminate	L, P
Fireman	Fire fighter	C, O
Fireman, locomotive	Firer*	C, O
The first lady	The first lady or gentleman	O, P
Fisherman	Fisher*	C, O
Fishwife	Eliminate	P
Fix-it man	Fix-it person Fix-it expert Fixer Fix-it wo/man Fix-it woman and man	C, O
Fixture (for woman)	Eliminate	L, P
Flag girl	Flag bearer	H, L, O

Sexist Symbols	Suggested Alternatives	Guidelines
Flagman	Flagger*	C, O
Flower girl	Flower seller	H, P
A fool and his money are soon parted	A fool and her or his money are soon parted	
For a woman, she performs well	She performs well	O, P
Forefather(s)	Forebear(s) Ancestor(s) Forefather(s) and foremother(s)	O
Foreman	Supervisor*	C, O
Founding father(s)	Founder(s) Founding mother(s) and father(s)	O
Fox, foxy (for woman)	Eliminate	L, P
Fraternal order of (for organization)	Order of	O, S
Fraternal twins	Nonidentical twins	O
Fraternity (for organization of women and men)	Organization Society Fraternity and sorority	O
Fraternize	Associate	O
Frenchman(men)	French citizen(s) French person(s)(people) Frenchwo/man; Frenchwo/men Frenchwoman(women) and Frenchman(men) French man (men) and woman (women)	C, O
Freshman(men)	Beginner(s) First-year student(s) Freshperson(s)(people) Freshwo/man; freshwo/men Freshman(men) and freshwoman(women) Fresh woman (women) and man (men)	C, O
Frigid, frigidity (for woman)	Impaired sexual feeling[3]	L, P, S
Frontiersman	Frontier person	C, O
Furnace installer-and-repairman	Furnace installer-and-repairer*	C, O
Furnaceman	Furnace installer*	C, O
Gal(s)	Woman(women)	H, P
Gal Friday	Person Friday Man/woman Friday Right hand	H, P
Gamesmanship	Gaming Playing games	C, O
Gam(s)	Eliminate	

[3]David Reuben, *Everything You Always Wanted to Know about Sex—But Were Afraid to Ask* (New York: David McKay Company, Inc., 1969), p. 99.

Sexist Symbols	Suggested Alternatives	Guidelines
Gas-producer man	Gas operator producer*	O
Gentleman (as sex-opposite adjective)	Eliminate	I
Gentlemen (salutation)	Ladies and Gentlemen Gentlewo/men Gentleperson(s)(people) Substitute conversational lead-in Address to individual	E
Gentlemen's agreement	Honorable agreement Gentlemen's and ladies' agreement Gentlewo/men's agreement	C
Gestures (powerlessness for females; power for males)	Females adopt the gestures of power	O, P, Q, V
Girl (as sex-opposite adjective)	Eliminate	I, O, P, Q
Girl (for female 18 years of age or older)	Woman Lady (only if paired with gentleman)	H, P
Girl cowboy	See "Cowboy girl"	H, O
Girl Friday	See "Gal Friday"	H, P
Girl friend (for woman)	Friend Woman friend (if "man friend" is used) Lady friend (if "gentleman friend" is used)	H, P
Girlie	Eliminate	H, P
A girl in every port	A woman in every port (or eliminate)	H, P, Q
Girls and men	Girls and boys (for those under eighteen) Men and women (for those eighteen and older)	H, P, Q
Girl watching	Eliminate	P, Q
Give away the bride	Eliminate	P
Glamor girl	Glamorous woman (or eliminate)	H, P
Goddess(es)	God(s) God(s) and goddess(es)	B, O
Gossip (as noun for woman)	Eliminate	P
Governess	Instructor	B, O
Grandfather clause	Escape clause	O
Grantmanship	Getting grants	C, O
The groundhog saw his shadow, so it's six more weeks of winter	Its shadow Her or his shadow	L, O
Groundsman(men)	Grounds worker(s) Groundsperson(s)(people) Groundswo/man; groundswo/men Groundswoman(women) and groundsman(men)	C, O

Sexist Symbols	Suggested Alternatives	Guidelines
	Grounds man (men) and woman (women)	
Gunman(men)	Gunner(s)	C, O
	Gunperson(s)(people)	
	Gunwo/man; gunwo/men	
	Gunman(men) and gunwoman(women)	
	Gun woman (women) and man (men)	
Guy(s) (for men)	Man (men)	H
Guy(s) (for women)	Eliminate	O
Hag (for woman)	Eliminate	L, P
Handyman(men)	Repairer(s)	C, O
	Handyperson(s)(people)	
	Handywo/man; handywo/men	
	Handywoman(women) and handyman(men)	
	Handy man (men) and woman (women)	
Harlot	Eliminate	H, P
Harpy (for woman)	Eliminate	L, P
Hatcheck girl	Hatcheck attendant*	H, P
Hatchet man (men)	Hatchet(s)	C
	Hatchet person(s) (people)	
	Hatchet wo/man; hatchet wo/men	
	Hatchet man (men) and woman (women)	
He (as generic pronoun)	Eliminate	A
He (for generic animal)	It	A, L
	Sh/e	
	He/she	
	He or she	
He (for generic child)	Eliminate	A
He (for God)	Eliminate *He*, *His*, and *Him* for God. See "Father (for God)"	A, M, O
Headmaster	Principal*	O
Head of household (for man unless none are present in household)	Joint or cohead(s) of household (for women and men in same household)	O
	Head of household (for single man or woman in household)	
Heifer (for woman)	Eliminate	L, P
Heiress	Heir	B
Hellcat (for woman)	Eliminate	L, P
Hen (for woman)	Eliminate	L, P
Hen party	Party	L, P

Sexist Symbols	Suggested Alternatives	Guidelines
Henpecked (for man)	Eliminate	L, P
Heroine	Hero (or raise heroine to same level)	B, O
He who hesitates	She or he who hesitates He or she who hesitates	A, O
Hide (for woman)	Eliminate	L, P
Him (as generic pronoun)	Eliminate	A
Himself (as generic pronoun)	Eliminate	A
His (as generic pronoun)	Eliminate	A
History of man	History of humanity History of humankind	C, O
Hoistman	Hoist operator*	C, O
Homemaker . . . she	Homemaker . . . he or she Homemakers . . . they	A, O, P
Homeowner . . . he	Homeowner . . . she or he Homeowners . . . they	A, O, Q
Homeroom mother	Homeroom parent Homeroom father or mother	P
Homo sapiens	Humans Humanity Humankind	O
An honest woman (for pregnant woman who marries)	Eliminate	P
Honey bunny (for woman)	Eliminate	L, P
Hooker	Eliminate	H, L, P
Hostess(es)	Host(s) (if *hostess* is eliminated)* Host/ess; host/esses Hostess(es) and host(s) (if *hostess* is retained)	B
Hostess, hotel	Social director*	B
Hostess, train	Passenger attendant*	C
Hot potato (for woman)	Eliminate	L, P
Housewife	Homemaker	O, P, Q, S
Hunk (for woman or man)	Eliminate	L, P
Huntress	Eliminate	B, O
Hurricane names (formerly all female)	Now female alternated with male names	L
Iceman	Ice deliverer	C, O
Illegitimate child	Eliminate	P, R, T
Infantryman(men)	Infantryperson(s)(people) Infantrywo/man; infantrywo/men Infantryman(men) and infantry-woman(women) Infantry woman (women) and man (men)	C, O
Insurance man(men)	Insurance person(s)(people)	C, O

Sexist Symbols	Suggested Alternatives	Guidelines
	Insurance sales representative(s)	
	Insurance wo/man; insurance wo/men	
	Insurance woman (women) and man (men)	
Jack of all trades, master of none	Good at all trades, expert at none	O
Jewess	A woman who is a Jew (only if such specific identification is appropriate)	B, O
Jezebel	Eliminate	P
John Q. Citizen	Jill and John Q. Citizen	O
Journeyman	Beginner	C, O
	Trainee	
	Use nonsexist name of actual postapprenticeship position, such as "potter," "machine setter," "inside jointer")	
Junior (for academic level)	Third-year student	O
Junior (for first-level position)	Trainee	O
Junior (for son of father with same name)	II	K, O
Junior Miss	Eliminate	D, O, P
Juryman(men)	Juror(s)	C, O
Key man(men)	Key executive(s)	O
	Key person(s) (people, personnel)	
King (as tops in checkers, chess, playing cards, bowling, kingpin, and so on)	Commander	N, O
	President (with pictures and images split equally between the sexes)	
King (for God)	See "Father (for God)"	M, N, O
King (for top position)	Monarch	N, O
Kingdom	Monarchy	N, O
	Realm	
	Domain	
King of the jungle	Monarch of the jungle	L, N, O
	Queen of the jungle	
	Queen and king of the jungle	
Kingmaker	Executive maker	N, O
	Power creator	
Kingpin (as main person)	Main one	N, O
	Top person	
	Monarch	
	Leader	
King's English	Queen's English (when queen is on throne)	N, O
	King's and Queen's English	
Kinsman	Kin	C, O

Sexist Symbols	Suggested Alternatives	Guidelines
Kittenish (for woman)	Eliminate	L, P
Knockers (for woman)	Eliminate	L, P
Ladies and men	Ladies and gentlemen	H
	Women and men	
Lady (as noun)	Eliminate	H, P
Lady (as sex-opposite adjective)	Eliminate	I, O
Lady luck	Luck	P
Ladylike (in traditional terms of sitting primly, and so on)	Describe strong human traits	R
Lady of the evening	Eliminate	H, P
Landlord	Owner	N, O
	Manager	
Laundress	Launderer*	B, O
	Laundry worker, hand*	
Laundryman	Launderer*	C, O
	Laundry-machine tender*	
	Laundry worker, hand*	
Lawman(men)	Attorney(s)	C, O
	Judge(s)	
	Sheriffs (or whatever law group is referred to)	
Layman(men)	Layperson(s)(people)	C, O
	Laywo/man; laywo/men	
	Laywoman(women) and layman(men)	
	Lay man (men) and woman (women)	
Leading lady	Lead	H
Letterman(men)	Letterholder(s)	C, O
	Letterearner	
	Letterwo/man; letterwo/men	
	Letterman(men) and letterwoman(women)	
	Letter woman (women) and man (men)	
Libber	Liberationist	P, S
	Feminist	
Librarian . . . she	Librarian . . . he or she	A, P
	Librarians . . . they	
Lineman (telephone)	Line installer-repairer*	C
Linesman	Lines tender*	C
Lioness	Lion	L, O
Little men don't cry	Eliminate	Q
Little Miss ——ette	Eliminate	B, D, P
Little woman (wife)	Woman	I, P
	Wife	

Sexist Symbols	Suggested Alternatives	Guidelines
A living doll	Eliminate	L, P
Loose woman	Eliminate (or add "loose man")	P, S
Lord it over someone	Dominate someone	N, O
Lord (for God, Christ, or other deity)	See "Father (for God)"	M, N, O
Lord and master	Eliminate because "lady and mistress" does not have equality of status	N, O
Love, honor, and obey (in wedding ceremony)	Develop mutual love and respect	O, P
Lumberman(men)	Tree cutter(s) Woodchopper(s) Lumber cutter(s) Lumberperson(s)(people) Lumberwo(man); lumberwo(men) Lumberwoman(women) and lumberman(men) Lumber man (men) and woman (women)	C
Ma'am	Use only with *sir*	H, P
Ma Bell (in derogation of Bell Telephone)	Ma and Pa Bell Pa and Ma Bell	P
Machine . . . he (as in control; as in "The internal combustion engine is a strong machine . . . he")	Machine . . . it Machine . . . she or he Machines . . . they	L, Q
Machine . . . she (as possessed and controlled by a human)	Machine . . . he	L, P
Madam	Eliminate because of negative connotation (except in tandem with *sir*)	H, P
Madam Chairman	Eliminate Call person by name If *chairman* is changed to nonsexist term, use *madam*, but only if *sir* is used: "Madam Chairperson and Sir Chairperson"	C, H, P
Maestro	Expert	C
Maid	Houseworker*	C
Maiden lady	Single	H, P
Maiden name	Birth name	K, P
Maiden voyage	First voyage Premiere voyage	P
Maidenly	Eliminate	P
Maid of honor	Attendant of honor Honor attendant Best woman	H, P

Sexist Symbols	Suggested Alternatives	Guidelines
Mail boy	Messenger, mail*	O, P
Mailman	Letter carrier Mail carrier Mail deliverer Postal worker	C, O
Maintenance man	Maintenance repairer* Maintenance specialist* Maintainer*	C, O
Majorette	Major Twirler	B, O
Male chauvinist pig	Chauvinist (apply equally to woman and man)	H, Q
Male ego	Ego Female ego and male ego	O
Male and female (always in this order)	Female and male (half the time)	G, H
Male menopause	Climacteric	I
Male nurse	Nurse	I
Man/manned stations	Occupy stations; stations occupied Take stations; stations taken Supply with personnel; personnel supplied Staff, staffed	O
Man (men) (for human(s))	Human(s) Humanity Humankind Human race Person(s) (people)	O
Man (as sex-opposite adjective)	Eliminate	I
Man (as token or pawn in games)	Pawn	O
-man (as in surnames) (deeply ingrained)	Recognize sexism in names Change if possible Do not perpetuate	K

-man (as syllable in words used for
    men and women)
	Use nonsexist syllable or
	    substitutions, including -person
		C, O

Manageress	Manager	B, O
Man and bride	Groom and bride Man and woman	H
Man and female	Female and male Man and woman	G, I
Man and wife	Man and woman Wife and husband	G, H
Man and woman (always in this order)	Woman and man (half the time)	G, H
Man does not live by bread alone	Humans do not live by bread alone	C, O

Sexist Symbols	Suggested Alternatives	Guidelines
Man-eater (plant, shark, or other animal)	Human-eater	O
Man-eating (plant or animal)	Human-eating	O
Every man for himself	All for themselves	C, O
Manhandle	Subdue	C, O
Manhole	Sewer hole	C, O
Manhood (in generic sense)	Adulthood	C, O
Man-hours	Labor-hours	C, O
Manhunt	Person hunt	O
	Wo/man hunt	
	Man or woman hunt	
	Woman or man hunt	
Man in the moon	Face in the moon	C, L, O
Man in the street	Citizen	C, O
	Person in the street	
	Wo/man in the street	
	Woman and man in the street	
A man is only as good as his word	A person is only as good as her or his word	A, O
Mankind	Humankind	C, O
	Humanity	
Manly/womanly	Retain, but bring *womanly* to full positive meaning	O, P, Q, S
Manmade	Synthetic	C, O
	Manufactured	
	Simulated	
	Human constructed	
Manning	Staffing	C, O
Man of the hour	Human of the hour	C, O
	Person of the hour	
	Wo/man of the hour	
	Woman or man of the hour	
Man of the year	Citizen of the year	O
	Member of the year	
	Wo/man of the year	
	Man or woman of the year	
Man overboard	Person overboard	C, O
Manpower	Labor	C, O
	Staff	
	People	
	Personnel	
Manpower Administration	Do not quote exactly. Use "United States Department of Labor," or similar general term	C, J, O
This man's army	This army	C, O
Man's best friend	Human's best friend	C, O
	Person's best friend	

Sexist Symbols	*Suggested Alternatives*	*Guidelines*
A man's home is his castle	A person's home is her or his castle	A, C, O
Man's inhumanity to man	Humans' inhumanity to humans—or eliminate	C, O
Man-sized	Big	C, O
Manslaughter	Humanslaughter Personslaughter Wo/manslaughter Manslaughter or womanslaughter	C, O
Man's law	Humans' law Humanity's law	O
A man's man	Retain, but develop positive meaning for "a woman's woman"	O, P
Man's wages	Good wages	C, O
A man's world	A human's world	C, O
Man-to-man defense (sports)	Player-to-player defense	C, O
Man-to-man talk	Person-to-person talk	C, O
Mare (for woman)	Eliminate	L, P
Marketing man (woman)	Marketer(s) Marketing wo/man; marketing wo/men Marketing woman (women) and man (men)	C, O
Marksman(men)	Sharpshooter(s) Marksperson(s)(people) Markswo/man; markswo/men Marks(men) and marks-woman(women) Marks woman (women) and man (men)	C, O
Marksmanship	Sharpshooting ability	C, O
Master (as noun)	Head Expert	O
Master (as verb)	Conquer	O
Master builder	Contractor	O
Master of Business Administration degree and other master's degrees (deeply ingrained)	MBA (acronym only, never words) Eventually change to something like SBA (Second Business Administration)	O
Master of ceremonies	Leader of ceremonies Coordinator of ceremonies Emcee (if retained for short run)	O
Master's degree (deeply ingrained)	First graduate degree	O
Mastermind	Intelligent person One who can develop and carry out project skillfully	O
Masterpiece	Great work Best work	O

Sexist Symbols	Suggested Alternatives	Guidelines
Matron of honor	Best woman Honor attendant	P, R
May the best man win	May the best person (contestant, competitor, individual) win	C, O
Her measurements are	Eliminate	L, P
Meat (for woman)	Eliminate	L, P
A meat-and-potatoes man	A meat-and-potatoes person (individual, eater)	O
Medicine man	Medicine person Medicine wo/man; medicine wo/men Medicine man and woman	O
Men of goodwill	People of good will	O
Men, machines, money, and materials	Wo/men . . . Women and men . . . Men and women . . . Personnel . . . Labor . . .	O
Men are men and girls are glad of it	Men are human and women are glad of it	H, P, Q
Men Working (sign)	Operators Working Workers Working Persons Working People Working Working	C, O
Merchantman	Merchant Merchant ship	C, O
Meter maid	Meter attendant*	O, P
Mickey Mouse Club	What about Minnie?	L, O
Middleman(men)	Middleperson(s)(people) Middlewo/man; middlewo/men Middleman(men and middlewoman(women) Middle woman (women) and man (men)	C, O
Military wife	Her husband is in the military	O
Militiaman(men)	Militia Militiaperson(s)(people) Militiawo/man; militiawo/men Militiaman(men) and militia-woman(women) Militia woman (women) and man (men)	C, O
Milkman	Driver, milk route*	C, O
Miss (courtesy title for single woman)	Ms. Use *Miss* only for those who demand it and only during transitional period	D, H, P

Sexist Symbols	*Suggested Alternatives*	*Guidelines*
Miss America	Eliminate Ms. America (if retained)	D, H, P
Miss Jones and Smith	Jones and Smith	H, K
Miss Justice	Justice Ms. Justice (if courtesy title retained)	D, H, P
Miss Liberty	Liberty Ms. Liberty (if courtesy title retained)	D, H, P
Mistress	Eliminate (original meaning perverted)	D, P
Mistress of ceremonies	See "Master of ceremonies"	D, P
Modern man	Modern humanity Modern civilization Modern people	C, O
Monarch . . . he	Monarch . . . she or he Monarchs . . . they	N, O
Mothering	Parenting	P, Q
Mother-in-law jokes and aspersions	Eliminate	P
Motherly (for government)	Protective	P, R
Mother Nature	Nature	L, P
Motorman	Motor-power connector* Dinkey operator* Streetcar operator* Motor operator*	C, O
Movements (powerlessness for females; power for males)	Females develop movements of power	O, P, Q, V
Mr. and Miss CHS (for high school "favorites" or whatever)	Eliminate	O, H
Mr. and Mrs. (always in that order)	Mr. and Ms. *or* Ms. and Mr. Mrs. and Mr. *or* Mr. and Mrs. (if "Mrs." retained)	D, H, O
Mr. Employer	Employer	O, Q
Mr. Fix-it	The Fix-it Ms. and Mr. Fix-it	O, Q
Mr. Grocer	The Grocer Mr. and Ms. Grocer	O, Q
Mr. Homebuyer	Homebuyer	O, Q
Mrs.	Ms. Use *Mrs.* only for those who demand it and only during transitional period	D, H, P
Mrs. John Doe	Meg Doe Meg Rory (her birthname)	O, Q
Mrs. O'Connor and Justice Rehnquist	Justice O'Connor and Justice Rehnquist	D, H, O
Mrs. Santa Claus	Give her a name	O, Q

Sexist Symbols	Suggested Alternatives	Guidelines
Ms. for single woman; Mrs. for married woman	Ms. for both	H, P
Murderess	Murderer	B, O
My brother's keeper	My sister's and brother's keeper	O
My dear Sir (salutation)	My dear Madam or Sir My dear Executive Substitute conversational lead-in Omit	E
My dear Sirs (salutation)	Eliminate My dear Madams (Mesdames) and Sirs (if retained)	O
My old lady	Wife	P
Nag (for woman)	Eliminate	L, P
Nanny	Nurse	L, P
Necessity is the mother of invention	Necessity is the parent of invention	P
Negress	Black Black woman	B, O
Nervous Nellie	Nervous person	P
Newsboy	Newspaper vendor*	O
Newsman(men)	Newsperson(s)(people) Newswo/man; newswo/men Newswoman(women) and newsman(men)	C, O
Night watchman	Night guard*	C, O
Nobleman	Nobility	C, O
No man is an island	No one is an island	C, O
No man's land	Unclaimed land Noncombatant land (zone) Buffer zone No one's land No person's land	C, O
Not fearing any man	Not fearing any person	C, O
Nurse . . . she	Nurse . . . he or she Nurses . . . they	A, P
Nurseryman	Nursery operator	C, O
Nymph (for woman)	Eliminate	L, P
Nymphomania	Sexual aggression	L, P
Nymphomaniac	Sexually aggressive woman	L, P
Office girl	Office helper*	H, P
Oilerette	Oiler	B, O
Oilman(men)	Oil executive(s) (or appropriate noun) Oilperson(s)(people) Oilwo/man; oilwo/men	O

Sexist Symbols	Suggested Alternatives	Guidelines
	Oilman(men) and oilwoman(women)	
	Oil man (men) and woman (women)	
Old goat (for man)	Eliminate	L, O
Old maid	Eliminate	P, S
Old wives' tale	Tale	P
	Misconception	
Ombudsman(men)	Investigator(s)	C, O
One man, one vote	One voter, one vote	C, O
	One citizen, one vote	
	One person, one vote	
One-man show	One-person show	C, O
	One-wo/man show	
	One-man or -woman show	
Outdoorsman(men)	Outdoorsperson(s)(people)	C, O
	Outdoorswo/man; outdoorswo/men	
	Outdoorswoman(women) and outdoorsman(men)	
	Outdoors man (men) and woman (women)	
Paper boy	Paper carrier	O
	Paper deliverer	
	Paper boy and girl (if under eighteen)	
Paper doll (for woman)	Eliminate	L, P
Parade women like cattle (in beauty pageants)	Eliminate	L, P
Patrolman(men)	Police officer(s)	C, O
Patroness	Patron	B, O
Penmanship	Handwriting	C, O
Pert blonde	Eliminate	P
Pet of the month (for woman)	Eliminate	L, P
Piece (for woman)	Eliminate	L, P
Pig (for woman)	Eliminate	L, P
Pink ladies (hospital volunteers)	Volunteers	P
Pinup girl	Eliminate or add "pinup boy"	H, P
Pioneer . . . he	Pioneer . . . she or he	O, Q
	Pioneers . . . they	
Pioneer women (as if the real pioneers are men)	Eliminate	O
Plain Jane	Eliminate	P
Poetess	Poet	B, O
Policeman(men)	Police officer(s)	C, O

Sexist Symbols	Suggested Alternatives	Guidelines
Pom-pom girl	Eliminate	H, P
	Pom-pom artist (if retained)	
Postman	See "Mailman"	C, O
Postman's holiday	Mail carrier's holiday	C, O
Postures (powerlessness for females; power for males)	Woman adopts postures of power	O, P, Q, V
Powder Puff Derby	Eliminate this sort of "cute" name for women's activities	P
President . . . he	President . . . he or she	O
	Presidents . . . they	
Pressman	Press tender*	C, O
	Press feeder*	
	Press operator*	
Pretty little head (for woman)	Eliminate	P
Priestess	Priest	B, O
Princess (deeply ingrained)	Use only for royalty	B, O
Professional man (men)	Professional	C, O
Prom queen	Eliminate	P
Proprietress	Proprietor	B, O
Pussy (for woman)	Eliminate	L, P
Quail (for woman)	Eliminate	L, P
Queen	Make equal to *king*	N, O
Queen (as secondary in chess, playing cards, and other games)	Vice-Commander	N, O, P
	Vice-President	
	(with pictures and images divided equally between the sexes)	
Queen bee (for woman)	Eliminate	L, N, P
Radioman	Radio operator	C, O
Red man(men)	Native American(s)	C, O
	First American(s)	
	American Indian(s)	
	Indian(s)	
	Red wo/man; red wo/men	
	Red woman (women) and red man (men)	
Repairman	Repairer*	C, O
Rich man's sport	Rich person's sport	C, O
Right-hand man	Right hand	C, O
Ring around the collar (as woman's responsibility)	Eliminate	P
Rockette	Rocket	B, O
The Ronald Reagans	Ronald and Nancy Reagan	K, O
Saleslady	Salesperson	P
	Sales associate*	
	Sales representative*	
	Sales agent*	

Sexist Symbols	Suggested Alternatives	Guidelines
Saleslady and salesman	Salespersons Saleslady and salesgentleman Saleswoman and salesman	H, O
Salesman	Salesperson Sales associate* Sales representative* Sales agent* Sales clerk	C, O
The Sandman	The Sander	C, O
Scarlet woman	Eliminate	P
Scatterbrained woman	Eliminate	P
Schoolmarm	Teacher	H, P
Sculptress	Sculptor	B, O
Seaman	Sailor Mariner	C, O
Seamstress	Sewer* Mender*	B, O
Secret Service	Secret Service person(s) (people, personnel) Secret Service agent(s) Secret Service wo/man; Secret Service wo/men Secret Service man (men) and woman (women)	C, O
Secretary . . . she	Secretary . . . he or she Secretaries . . . they	P
Selectman	Representative Board officer	C, O
Seminal work	Original work Creative work	C, O
Senior (for academic level)	Fourth-year student	O
Senior (for father of son with same name)	I Pass down *full* female names as well as male names	C, K, O
Senior (for top-level position)	I Use nonsexist name of position ("executive" instead of "senior executive")	O
Separate the men from the boys	Separate the best from the good (good from the bad, mature from the immature, strong from the weak)	C, O
Serviceman	Servicer*	C, O
Serviceman(men) (military)	Member(s) of the service Servicewo/man; servicewo/men Servicewoman(women) and serviceman(men)	C, O

Sexist Symbols	Suggested Alternatives	Guidelines
	Service man (men) and woman (women)	
Set (referring to woman's bosom)	Eliminate	L, P
Settler . . . he	Settler . . . she or he	A, O
	Settlers . . . they	
Sex kitten	Eliminate	L, N
Sexism in direct quotations	Change to paraphrase or summary	J
	Use omission and insertion	
	Use [sic]	
She bore him three children	She gave birth to three children	O, T
She goat (for woman)	Eliminate	L, P
She knows her place	Eliminate	P
Shoeshine boy	Shoeshiner	Q
Shop girl	Shop owner	H, P
	Shop clerk	
Showgirl	Dancer	H, P
Showman(men)	Showperson(s)(people)	C, O
	Showwo/man; showwo/men	
	Showman(men) and showwoman (women)	
	Show woman (women) and man (men)	
	Show manager	
Showmanship	Showpersonship	C, O
	Showwomanship and showmanship	
	Showiness	
Shrew (for woman)	Eliminate	L,P
Sign your John Hancock here	Sign your name here	O
Silence (powerlessness for females; power for males)	Females use silence for power	O, P, Q, V
Single lady	Single	H, R
	Single woman (if "single man" is used)	
Siren (for woman)	Eliminate	L, P
Sissy	Eliminate (sexist toward female)	K, S
Sister (for woman—as in "that old sister," "weak sister")	Eliminate	P, R
Skirt (for woman)	Eliminate	L, P
Slattern	Eliminate	L, P
Slut	Eliminate	L, P
Smiling (powerlessness for females; power for males)	Females adopt smiles of power	O, P, Q, V
Son(s) (as representative of generations to come)	Child/children	O
	Daughter(s) and son(s)	

Sexist Symbols	Suggested Alternatives	Guidelines
-son (as in Johnson) (deeply ingrained)	Recognize sexism in names	K
Songstress	Singer	B, O
Son of a bitch	Eliminate (sexist toward female because *bitch* refers to female)	L, P
Sons of God	Children of God	M, O
Sons of man	Children of humanity	M, O
Sophomore	Second-year student	H
Sorceress	Sorcerer	B, O
Sow (for woman)	Eliminate	L, P
Snowman	Snow figure Snow person Snow wo/man Snow man or woman	C, O
Space (powerlessness for females; power for males)	Females use space for power	O, P, Q, V
Spaceman(men)	Spaceperson(s)(people, personnel) Spacewo/man; spacewo/men Spacewoman(women) and spaceman(men) Space man (men) and woman (women) Astronaut	C, O
Spinster	Eliminate	P
Spokesman(men)	Speaker(s) Spokesperson(s)(people, personnel) Spokeswo/man; spokeswo/men Spokesman(men) and spokeswoman(women)	C, O
Sport of kings	Sport of monarchs	N, O
Sportsman(men)	Sports lover(s) Sportspersons(s)(people) Sportswo/man; sportswo/men Sports man (men) and woman (women)	C, O
Squaw (as derogatory toward woman)	Eliminate	P
Stacked (for woman)	Eliminate	L, P
Staff man (men)	Staff person(s)	O
Stag (for man)	Eliminate	O, Q
Stag or drag (for dance or party)	Eliminate	P, Q
Starlet	Star	B, R
Statesman(men)	Statesperson(s)(people) Stateswo/man; stateswo/men Stateswoman(women) and statesman(men)	C, O

Sexist Symbols	Suggested Alternatives	Guidelines
Stewardess	Airplane flight attendant*	B, O
Stock in a stable (for humans, as a stable of models)	Eliminate	L
Straight man	Straight person	C, O
Strawman	Straw person	C, O
Stud (for man)	Eliminate	L, Q
Stuff (for woman)	Eliminate	L, P
Stunt girl	Stunt woman	H
Suffragette	Suffragist	B, O
Sugar and spice and everything nice	Eliminate	L, P
Sugar daddy	Eliminate	L, P, Q
Sugar pie (for woman)	Eliminate	L, P
Sugar plum (for woman)	Eliminate	L, P
Superman	Eliminate concept	P, R
Sweetpea (for woman)	Eliminate	L, P
Sweet petunia (for woman)	Eliminate	L, P
Sweet talk (for woman)	Eliminate	P
Switchman	Switcher	C
Tarzan—Lord or King of the Jungle	Tarzan (Observe how Tarzan—the strongest in the jungle—is both white and male)	N, O
Taskmaster and taskmistress	Overseer	H, O
Territory (powerlessness for females; power for males)	Females use territory for power	O, P, Q, V
Testatrix	Testator	B, O
Thing (for woman)	Eliminate	L, P
Tigress	Tiger / Female tiger (if "male tiger" is used)	B, O
Time (powerlessness for females; power for males)	Females use time for power	O, P, Q, V
To a man	To a man and woman	O
To each his own	To each her or his own—or eliminate	A
Tomato (for woman)	Eliminate	L, P
Tomboy (for girl)	Active child	O
Touch (powerlessness for females; power for males)	Females use touch for power	O, P, Q, V
Tradesman	Trader / Tradesperson	C, O
Tramp (for woman)	Eliminate	L, P
Tribesman(men)	Tribesperson(s)(people) / Tribe member(s)	C, O
Trick (for man)	Eliminate	L, Q

Sexist Symbols	*Suggested Alternatives*	*Guidelines*
Trollop	Eliminate	L, P
Turn taking in conversation	Make equal for men and women	U, V
Two-man plane (tent, canoe, and so on)	Two-place Two-person Two-seated Two-seater	C, O
Uncle Sam (deeply ingrained)	Aunt Lee and Uncle Sam	O
Union man	Union member Union person	C, O
Unwed mother	Mother	P, R
Upperclassman	Upperclassperson	C, O
Usherette	Usher	B, O
Vestal (for woman)	Eliminate	L, P
Villainess	Villain	B, O
Virgin	Use equally for men and women	P, R
Vixen (for woman)	Eliminate	L, P
Voice (powerlessness for females; power for males)	Females use the voice for power	O, P, Q, V
Waitress(es)	Waiter(s)* Waitress(es) and waiter(s) if *waitress* retained)* Waitperson(s)	B, O
Wife of Dr. Joe Bloke	Betty Bloke-Sayres	H, K, O
Wallflower (for woman)	Eliminate	L, P
War-horse (for woman)	Eliminate	L, P
Watchman	Crossing tender* Patroller* Guard*	C, O
The way to a man's heart is through his stomach	The way to a man's heart is through his heart	P, Q
Weaker sex	Eliminate	O, P
Weathergirl	Weather reporter(s) Weatherperson(s)(people) Weatherwo/man; weatherwo/men Weatherwoman(women) and weatherman(men) Weather man (men) and woman (women)	H, O
Weatherman	See "Weathergirl"	H, O
Wench (for woman)	Eliminate	L, P
What evil lurks in the hearts of men?	What evil lurks in the hearts of humans?	C, O
What is the measure of a man?	What is the measure of a human (or person)?	C, O

Sexist Symbols	*Suggested Alternatives*	*Guidelines*
White man (men)	Caucasian(s) White(s) White person(s)(people) White wo/man; white wo/men White man (men) and woman (women)	C, O
Truman's widow has stroke	Bess Truman has stroke	O
Wife-swapping	Spouse-swapping	H, O
Wise men	Wise people	C, O
Witch (for woman)	Eliminate	L, P
Wolf (for man)	Eliminate	L, Q
Woman (as sex-opposite adjective)	Eliminate	I, O
Woman did as well as a man	Woman did as well as anyone	O, R
Woman did well for a woman	Woman did well	O, R
Woman doing dishes; father reading paper	Man and woman doing dishes Woman and man reading paper	P, Q
Woman driver	Driver	I, P
Woman farmer	Farmer	H, J
Womanlike	Name specific characteristic(s)	R
Woman policeman	Police officer	C, I
A woman's place is in the home	A human's place is to develop to fullest potential	O, P
Woman's work	Eliminate	O, P
Women and children first	Children, elderly, and infirm first	O
Women cry; men do not cry	Humans cry	P, Q
Women's auxiliary	Eliminate	O, P
Women's lib	See "Fem lib"	P
Women's section (in newspaper)	Eliminate	O, P
Working man	Worker	O
Working mother/wife	Worker	O, R
Workman	Worker	C, O
Workmen's compensation	Workers' compensation	C, O
Yardman	Yard laborer* Yard worker* Yard supervisor*	C, O
A "yes" man	A "yes" person	C, O
Youthfulness (as special preoccupation of females)	Eliminate	P, R

APPENDIX B:
SUGGESTED SOLUTIONS
TO EXERCISES

These solutions to the application exercises in Chapters 3 through 8 are examples of nonsexist alternatives to the sexist passages. Other nonsexist versions exist, of course.

When appropriate, the solutions include two parts: (a) the original sexist passage with the sexist words and phrases italicized and numbered, and (b) the corrected versions with the italics and numbers identifying the corresponding corrected words and phrases.

Exercise 3-1 illustrates a wide range of sex-referent expressions, with particular emphasis on "man" words, pronouns, and sex-role stereotyping.

Sexist Words and Phrases

Wecare Corporation has positions available for the *man* (1) who wants to be in management, finance, statistics, communication, marketing, or accounting. Whether running

155

a *one-man* (2) show or working on *multiple-man* (3) teams, the employee at Wecare has a great deal of freedom to engage in the kind of creativity that has brought *mankind* (4) to the level of productivity it now enjoys.

Although our *craftsmen* (5), under the direction of our fine *foremen* (6), produce an outstanding *manmade* (7) material, we always need bright, young *men* (8) for the position of *salesman* (9) so that the product can be sold. Certainly, the *wife* (10) and children of the *salesman* (11) must be willing to have a weekend *husband* (12) and *father* (13), and to move frequently as *he* (14) advances from one territory to another.

The Wecare employee has *his* (15) choice of several matching-fund savings plan options, including corporation stock purchases—all available after *he* (16) accumulates only 2,000 *man-hours* (17). Thus, in addition to providing salaries and benefits *man-sized* (18) enough to assure outstanding *manpower* (19), Wecare management also wants to assure that its *workmen* (20) can establish savings accounts for the *wives* (21) and children so *dependent* (22) on them.

Whether a *freshman* (23) or an *upperclassman* (24), a man or a *coed* (25), you will want to pursue a career with Wecare. Thousands of *businessmen* (26) have done so—and express pleasure about their decision.

Corrected Words and Phrases

Wecare Corporation has positions available for the *graduate* (1) who wants to be in management, finance, statistics, communication, marketing, or accounting. Whether *working alone* (2) or *with others* (3), the employee at Wecare has a great deal of freedom to engage in the kind of creativity that has brough *humanity* (4) to the level of productivity it now enjoys.

Although our *workers* (5), under the direction of our fine *supervisors* (6), produce an outstanding *synthetic* (7) material, we always need bright, young *people* (8) for the position of *sales representative* (9) so that the product can be sold. Certainly, the *sales representative leads an exciting life that involves travel and a variety of homes as advancements from one territory to another come along* (10) (11) (12) (13) (14).

The Wecare employee has *a* (15) choice of several matching-fund savings plan options, including corporation stock purchases—all available after accumulating (16) only 2,000 *hours on the job* (17). Thus, in addition to providing salaries and benefits *excellent* (18) enough to assure outstanding *employees* (19), Wecare management also wants to assure that its *employees* (20) can establish savings accounts for *their futures* (21) (22).

Whether a *first-year student* (23) or a *graduating student* (24), a man or a *woman* (25), you will want to pursue a career with Wecare. Thousands of *businesspeople* (26) have done so—and express pleasure about their decision.

EXERCISE 3-2

The hypothetical administrative manual section in Exercise 3-2 provides an excellent opportunity for recognizing and removing male-as-norm sexism. The word *deanette* appears almost tongue in cheek; yet it has actually been used—with an accompanying chuckle—to refer to an academic dean who happens to be female.

Sexist Words and Phrases

As a basic policy, *men* (1) in the classification of *foreman* (2) or higher are urged to participate in up to four of the training courses offered by the corporation each fiscal year. However, a *grandfather clause* (3) states that if a *man* (4) is promoted no later than May 1 of one fiscal year, one training course in addition to the basic four may be taken by *him* (5) during the following fiscal year.

The training courses are offered monthly; thus, each *man* (6) has twelve from which to choose. The one-week courses are announced a year in advance so that the choices and scheduling can be made then. The course topics are varied, but some that have been offered are

"*Key-Man* (7) Insurance: Worth the Investment?"

"The Ins and Outs of *Workmen's* (8) Compensation Plans"

"Now is the Time for Every Good *Man* (9) to Come to the Aid of *His* (10) Party (Or How to Be Politically Astute)"

"How to Make the *Weatherman* (11) Work for the Company"

"*Lawmen's* (12) Views of *Businessmen's* (13) Political Contributions"

"The *Cattleman's* (14) Stake in the Marketplace"

"The *Pressman* (15) Has *His* (16) Problems Too"

"A Pension Plan Fit for a *King* (17)"

"The Functions of the Public Relations Advance *Man* (18)"

"*Uncle Sam's* (19) 'Take' from Your Paycheck"

"*Oneupmanship* (20) is the Game Called Negotiation"

"The Importance of *Women's Auxiliaries* (21) to Business Organizations"

"The Best-Laid Plans *of Mice and Men* (22): A Look at Forecasting"

"Sick and Annual Leave—The *Working Man's* (23) Best Friend"

Many company *men* (24) are utilized as instructors for the courses. But because, all too often, a *man* (25) is not without honor except in *his* (26) own "company," *men* (27) are frequently brought in from outside to serve as *anchormen* (28) for the courses. We have had an *oilman* (29), a *pressman* (30), an *aviatrix* (31), a city *councilman* (32), a *deanette* (33) from a university school of business, and a *freshman* (34) *congressman* (35), among others, in the past. They add a great deal to the programs because of their fresh viewpoints.

Corrected Words and Phrases

As a basic policy, *employees* (1) in the classification of *line supervisor* (2) or higher are urged to participate in up to four of the training courses offered by the corporation each fiscal year. However, an *exception clause* (3) states that if an *employee* (4) is promoted no later than May 1 of one fiscal year, one training course in addition to the basic four may be taken by *her or him* (5) during the following fiscal year.

The training courses are offered monthly; thus, each *employee* (6) has twelve from which to choose. The one-week courses are announced a year in advance so that the choices and scheduling can be made then. The course topics are varied, but some that have been offered are

"*Key-Executive* (7) Insurance: Worth the Investment?"

"The Ins and Outs of *Workers'* (8) Compensation Plans"

"Now Is the Time for Every Good *Citizen* (9) to Come to the Aid of *the* (10) Party (Or How to Be Politically Astute)"

"How to Make the *Weather Forecaster* (11) Work for the Company"

"*Attorneys'* (12) Views of *Businesspeople's* (13) Political Contributions"

"The *Cattle Owner's* (14) Stake in the Marketplace"

"The *Print Shop* (15) Has *Problems* (16) Too"

"A Pension Plan Fit for the *Best—You* (17)"

"The Functions of Public Relations Advance *Work* (18)"

"*The Government's* (19) 'Take' from Your Paycheck"

"*How to Be a Step Ahead* (20) in the Game Called Negotiation"

"The Importance of *Community Organizations* (21) in Business"

"The Best-Laid Plans *Can Go Astray* (22): A Look at Forecasting"

"Sick and Annual Leave—The *Employee's* (23) Best Friend"

Many company *people* (24) are utilized as instructors for the courses. But because, all too often, a *person* (25) is not without honor except in *her or his* (26) own "company," *people* (27) are frequently brought in from outside to *anchor* (28) the courses. We have had an *oil executive* (29), a *press operator* (30), an *aviator* (31), a city *council member* (32), a *dean* (33) from a university school of business, and a *first-year* (34) *member of Congress* (35), among others, in the past. They add a great deal to the programs because of their fresh viewpoints.

EXERCISE 3-3

Job titles are emphasized in this exercise. All the titles appear in a government publication, cited in the chapter, designed to remove their sex- and age-referent components.[1] The government's revisions for these and other job titles appear in Appendix A. Its revisions for these fifteen titles also appear here.

Sexist Version	*Corrected Version*
Furnaceman	Furnace installer
Motorman	Motor operator
Fisherman	Fisher
Maintenance man	Maintainer
Hoistman	Hoist operator
Chambermaid	Room cleaner
Flagman	Flagger
Baggageman	Baggage checker
Laundress	Launderer
Seamstress	Sewer
Hatcheck girl	Hatcheck attendant
Hostess, hotel	Social director
Meter maid	Meter attendant
Fireman, locomotive	Firer
Charwoman	Charworker

[1] United States Department of Labor, Employment and Training Administration, *Dictionary of Occupational Titles*, 4th ed. (Washington, D.C.: Government Printing Office, 1977).

Exercise 3-4 provides practice in rewriting sexist job information statements. The fragment initiated by an active verb provides a revision for many of the sexist statements.

1. *Job Description*
   Lineman (1), Class A

   Accountability
   He (2) reports directly to the *Foreman* (3).

   Work Performed
   Summary: *He* (4) performs all duties associated with installing and maintaining telephone lines. *He* (5) also helps the *Foreman* (6) supervise and train *Linemen* (7), Class B, and *Linemen* (8), Class C, as those *men* (9) perform those same duties.
   Details: (1) *He* (10) checks out and supervises loading of equipment and supplies for the jobs or assigns to others any such activities that *he himself* (11) cannot accomplish; (2) *he* (12) checks right-of-way specifications before proceeding with the job; and (3) *he* (13) climbs utility poles and hooks up services.

2. *Job Specification*
   Structural Metal *Craftsman* (1), II

   Education
   The job requires use of fractions, decimals, algebra, and geometry. The *craftsman* (2) must possess knowledge of the structural metal field. *He* (3) must be able to read blueprints, understand basic design, and apply *his* (4) knowledge of foundry practice.

Corrected Words and Phrases

1. *Job Description*
   Line-Installer-Repairer (1), Class A

   Accountability
   Reports (2) directly to the *Supervisor* (3).

   Work Performed
   Summary: *Performs (4)* all duties associated with installing and maintaining telephone lines. *Also helps* (5) the *Supervisor* (6) supervise and train *Line-Installer-Repairers* (7), Class B, and *Line-Installer-Repairers* (8), Class C, as those *workers* (9) perform those same duties.
   Details: (1) *Checks* (10) out and supervises loading of equipment and supplies for the jobs or assigns to others any such activities that *are necessary to complete the job* (11); (2) *checks* (12) right-of-way specifications before proceeding with the job; and (3) *climbs* (13) utility poles and hooks up services.

2. *Job Specification*
   Structural Metal Crafts Worker (1), II

   Education
   The job requires use of fractions, decimals, algebra, and geometry. The *crafts worker* (2) must possess knowledge of the structural metal field. The *worker* (3) must be able to read blueprints, understand basic design, and apply *knowledge* (4) of foundry practice.

The eight address/salutation situations contrast traditional and correct forms. Because some new ground is being plowed here, differences of opinion on the proper way to remove sexism exist.

Traditional Form	*Correct Form*
1. Mrs. George Rivers	Ms. Rivers
Dear Mrs. Rivers:	Dear Ms. Rivers:
2. Mr. and Mrs. Howard Harwell	Mr. Howard Harwell and the Other Residents of
Dear Mr. Harwell:	Dear Mr. Harwell and Other Residents:
	or
	Dear Residents:
3. Sellwell Realty	Sellwell Realty
Gentlemen:	Gentlemen and Ladies:
	or
	Gentlewo/men (Gentlepersons):
	or
	Substitute conversational lead-in for salutation
4. Miss Olivia Graham, Chairman	Ms. Olivia Graham, Chairwoman (Chairperson)
Finance Committee	Finance Committee
Dear Miss Graham:	Dear Ms. Graham:
	or
	Olivia Graham
	Finance Committee:
	or
	Substitute conversational lead-in for salutation
5. Mr. and Mrs. David Cooper	Mr. David and Ms. Rita Cooper
Dear Mr. and Mrs. Cooper:	Dear Mr. and Ms. Cooper:
6. Mr. and Mrs. Jerry Selmon	Dr. Sara Hill and Mr. Jerry Selmon
Dear Mr. and Mrs. Selmon:	Dear Dr. Hill and Mr. Selmon:
7. Miss Helen Gardner	Ms. Helen Gardner
Dear Miss Gardner:	Dear Ms. Gardner:
8. To: Ms. Greta Taylor (or Greta Taylor)	
From: (Your name without courtesy title)	

The signature blocks provide opportunities for correcting six different sexist forms. Because we have control over our own signature blocks, we can remove the sexism from them immediately.

Traditional Form	*Correct Form*
1. Gale Horton	(Mr.) Gale Horton
2. (Mrs.) Lindsay Keller	(Ms.) Lindsay Keller
3. (Miss) Ella Sells	(Ms.) Ella Sells
	or
	Ella Sells
4. Jackie Howell	(Mr.) Jackie Howell
5. Elwood Fraim	Elwood Fraim
Mrs. Elwood Fraim	Patricia Fraim
or	or
(Mrs.) Patricia Fraim	(Mr.) Elwood Fraim
	(Ms.) Patricia Fraim
6. (Mrs./Miss/Ms.) Vera Schell-Meyers	Vera Schell-Meyers
Manager	Manager
Harry Holden	Harry Holden
Assistant Manager	Assistant Manager

EXERCISE 4-3

Exercise 4-3 provides practice in reporting names in a consistent, nonsexist way.

1. "The two supervisors are Ms. _____ [her last name] and Mr. Tryon."

   or

   "The two supervisors are Melinda and _____ [his first name]."

2. "Ms. _____ [her first name] Taggert and Mr. Bill Krauss were two community leaders present."

   or

   "Ms. Taggert and Mr. Krauss were two community leaders present."

   or

   "_____ [her first name] Taggert and Bill Krauss were two community leaders present."
   Reverse the names in any of the preceding to alphabetical order.

3. Acceptable, but for interoffice memorandum, would also be acceptable as:
   To: Kate Brown
   From: James Courtney

4. "Ms. Dorsey, Ms. Crier, and Mr. Skelton"

   or

   "Dorsey, Crier, and Skelton"

5. "Ms. Feeney and Ms. Elder

   or

   "Feeney and Elder"

6. Harold Arvin/Others
   Dear Mr. Arvin/Others (or omit or replace with conversational lead-in or subject line)

7. Ms.
   Mr. _____

   or

   _____

   (Name)

This sales letter is a concentrated, nearly satirical attempt to expose many sexist clichés. Such clichés appear in communication on a regular basis—to the extent that many people consider them right and proper.

Sexist Words and Phrases

HAPPYDAYS HOME PRODUCTS

Fine Products for a *Man's Castle* (1)

7777 Clean Street
Nirvana, Georgia
July 8, 198X

HE WHO HESITATES (2) . . .

. . . just may lose out on the best offer Happydays Home Products will make this year! For the next ten days only, you can buy the electric *MR. RUG SHAMPOO* (3) at 25 percent off the suggested retail price—simply by taking this letter to your local *hardware man* (4). Yes, for only $44.95, you can buy one of the finest machines on the market. And even the original price ($59.95) was considerably lower than the prices of other machines anywhere near the quality of *MR. RUG SHAMPOO* (5), because our direct-to-dealer delivery strategy cuts out the cost of using a *middleman* (6).

Just think *how happy you'll make the little woman* (7) *by buying her* (8) *this machine to help her in her housework* (9)! After shampooing, the carpets will look as if a *professional* (10) had done them—at much less than half the cost of the services of such a *man* (11). Any *homemaker* (12) would be *thrilled* (13) at being *spoiled by her husband's thoughtfulness in buying her* (15) a *MR. RUG SHAMPOO* (16)—for her *birthday, Christmas, anniversary, or whatever* (17).

The shampooer is *so hefty and well constructed* (18) that *your wife may even be able to sweet-talk* (19) you into *operating it for her* (20). And even if you have a *cleaning girl* (21) come in, you'll be contributing to quicker and better cleaning of *your home* (22).

MR. RUG SHAMPOO (23) has a one-year warranty on parts and service, and, for a small price you can purchase a service contract at the end of the year that will assure you that a *serviceman* (24) will be at your door within forty-eight hours of a telephone call. In a recent *man-in-the-street survey* (25) we conducted, we found that this type of warranty is what the consumer says *he* (26) wants.

When your *mailman* (27) delivers this letter to your door, act immediately, because *MR. RUG SHAMPOO* (28) is the finest piece of equipment of its type in this age of *modern man* (29). Not only will it allow *your wife* (30) *to keep your carpet* (31) clean and beautiful, but it will increase its life, thus saving you some *of your hard-earned dollars* (32).

Remember, *a man is only as good as his word* (33)—and *MR. RUG SHAMPOO's* (34) word can be trusted. *He* (35) didn't need an *adman* (36) to write this letter; *he* (37) just asked us to do it because *he* (38) knew *his word* (39) would stand without embellishment.

Yes, *don't be a man who hesitates* (40). Show your good judgment by taking this letter to your nearest hardware store and buying *MR. RUG SHAMPOO* (41) before your ten days are up. *Your girl* (42) will *love* (43) you for it.

Yours for a cleaner castle,

(Miss) (44) *Canday Castle* (45)
Your Happydays Home Products *Girl* (46)

Corrected Words and Phrases

HAPPYDAYS HOME PRODUCTS

Fine Products for a *Castle* (1)

7777 Clean Street
Nirvana, Georgia
July 8, 198X

DON'T HESITATE . . . (2)

. . . you just may lose out on the best offer Happydays Home Products will make this year! For the next ten days only, you can buy the electric *SHAMPOO YOUR RUG* (3) at 25 percent off the suggested retail price—simply by taking this letter to your local *hardware store* (4). Yes, for only $44.95, you can buy one of the finest machines on the market. And even the original price ($59.95) was considerably lower than the prices of other machines anywhere near the quality of *SHAMPOO YOUR RUG* (5), because our direct-to-dealer delivery strategy cuts *costs* (6).

Just think *how the housework will be made easier by using this machine* (7) (8) (9). After shampooing, the carpets will look as if a *professional* (10) rug cleaner had done them—at much less than half *the cost of such services* (11). *Anyone* (12) *would be pleased* (13) *to own* (14) (15) (17) a *SHAMPOO YOUR RUG* (16).

The shampooer is *hefty and well constructed for long life and sure performance* (18). *Anyone* (19) *would gain satisfaction from operating it* (20). And even if you have a *professional house cleaner* (21) come in, you'll be contributing to quicker and better cleaning of the *home you're so proud of* (22).

SHAMPOO YOUR RUG (23) has a one-year warranty on parts and service, and for a small price you can purchase a service contract at the end of the year that will assure you that a *service representative* (24) will be at your door within forty-eight hours of a telephone call. In a recent *survey* (25) we conducted, we found that this type of warranty is what the *consumer* (26) wants.

When your *letter carrier* (27) delivers this letter to your door, act immediately, because *SHAMPOO YOUR RUG* (28) is the finest piece of equipment of its type in this *modern age* (29). Not only will it allow *you* (30) *to keep your carpet* (31) clean and beautiful, but it will increase its life, thus saving you some *hard-earned dollars* (32).

Happydays Home Products gives you its word (33) that *SHAMPOO YOUR RUG* (34) is all that it is advertised to be. *We* (35) didn't need an *advertising agency* (36) to write this letter; *we* (37) did it ourselves because *we* (38) know *our products* (39) are good enough to stand without embellishment.

Yes, *don't hesitate* (40). Show your good judgment by taking this letter to your nearest hardware store and buying *SHAMPOO YOUR RUG* (41) before your ten days are up. *You* (42) will *gain a great deal of satisfaction* (43) from owning and using one.

Yours for a cleaner castle,

(44) *Joan Bryan* (45)
For Happydays Home Products (46)

EXERCISE 4-5

Exercise 4-5 calls to task some of the so-called generic "man" words. This memorandum also shows lack of parallelism in the treatment of men's and women's names and in the use of *girl* and *gal* with *man*. It illustrates other sexism as well.

Sexist Words and Phrases

To: *Mrs.* (1) Vera Scrivner   Date: March 18, 198X
From: Gerald Chevrolet *gc*   Subject: Formation of Committee to Project
                                                  Manpower (2) Needs

As we discussed earlier, I am assigning *you and Ellis* (3) to serve as *cochairmen* (4) for the committee being formed to project *manpower* (5) needs for your department for 198X. I have asked *Miss Gibbons, Mrs. Helms, Green, Phelps, and Reardon* (6) to serve as *committeemen* (7). Thus, the committee includes both *men and ladies* (8).

As we have done in the past in developing such projections, be sure to involve some *laymen* (9), *heads of households* (10), *city fathers* (11), and *businessmen* (12) as you attempt to forecast demand for our services. You might even contact some *spinsters* (13), *divorcées* (14), and *widows* (15) because of their particular need for our specialized *Han-D-Man* (16) Home-Repair Service.

Pay particular attention to the impact that our new *journeyman* (17) program will have on projections. I know that with a new program such as this, you are operating in a *no-man's land* (18), because you really have no empirical data base from which to work. However, do what you can, for if we find a significantly increased demand for our services, we will have to begin an extensive *manhunt* (19) soon to provide the kind of *men* (20) we need for the *man-hours* (21) required.

Just have the *girls* (22) in the typing pool take care of any report production you need. If you complete the project before vacations begin in April, all the typing stations will be *manned* (23).

Vera, would you and Ellis (24) set a meeting for next week for the committee and me. You will also need to select a *middleman* (25) for your committee and me and have *him* (26) at the meeting. And, have your *gal Friday* (27) present to prepare the meeting report.

Corrected Words and Phrases

To: *Ms.* (1) Vera Scrivner

From: Gerald Chevrolet *ap*

Date: March 18, 198X

Subject: Formation of Committee to Project *Labor* (2) Needs

As we discussed earlier, I am assigning *you and Mr. Ellis* (3) to serve as *cochairpersons* (4) for the committee being formed to project *labor* (5) needs for your department for 198X. I have asked *Ms. Gibbons, Ms. Helms, Mr. Green, Mr. Phelps, and Mr. Reardon* (6) to serve as *members of the committee* (7). Thus, the committee includes both *women and men* (8).

As we have done in the past in developing such projections, be sure to involve some *laypersons* (9), *household representatives* (10), *city leaders* (11), and *businesspeople* (12) as you attempt to forecast demand for our services. You might even contact some *homeowners* (13)(14)(15) because of their particular need for our specialized *Han-D* (16) Repair Service.

Pay particular attention to the impact that our new *trainee* (17) program will have on projections. I know that with a new program such as this, you are operating *somewhat blindly* (18), because you really have no empirical data base from which to work. However, do what you can, for if we find a significantly increased demand for our services, we will have to begin an extensive *search* (19) soon to provide the kind of *workers* (20) we need for the *work-hours* (21) required.

Just have the *employees* (22) in the typing pool take care of any report production you need. If you complete the project before vacations begin in April, all the *typists will be available* (23).

Vera, would you and Tom (24) set a meeting for next week for the committee and me. You will also need to select a *liaison person* (25) for your committee and me and have *her or him* (26) at the meeting. And, have a *secretary* (27) present to prepare the meeting report.

EXERCISE 5-1

This letter illustrates the kinds of sexism that dull our senses. Such expressions bombard us daily.

WEDDING GIRL (1), INC.

Miss Sara Ferris (2)
888 Fox Avenue
Wrong Number, New York 00000

May 14, 198X

Dear Miss Ferris (3):

So, you've *caught your man (4)* and can now open that *hope chest (5)*! Your wedding will be the *happiest time in your entire life (6)* if you let *Wedding Girl (7)*, Inc., plan it from beginning to end.

Yes, from *dealing with your future mother-in-law's demands (8)*, to the "*love, honor, and obey (9),*" to the final "*I pronounce you man and wife (10),*" *Wedding Girl (11)*, Inc., will *remove all cares from your pretty little head (12)* and leave it free for dreams of the home that *he will provide for you (13)* . . . for dreams of how *you will make his meals (14)* and *manage his home (15)* . . . for dreams of how you will *mother (16) those sons (17) you'll give him (18)* . . . for dreams of *pipe and slippers (19)* at the end of *his work day (20)* . . . and for dreams of *flowers and candy (21)* for you—*his bride (22)*, *his doll (23)*.

We'll help you make decisions about such things as who will *give you away (24)*, how to *place the photograph in the newspaper that will announce your upcoming MRS. "degree" (the only one you really ever wanted) (25) (26)*, arrangements for the wedding pictures, one of which will be placed in publications to show that *you've changed your name to his (27)*, and how to choose the *girls and men (28)* to be the *bride's maids or matrons, groomsmen, best man, etc. (29)* We'll even arrange for *cooking lessons (30)*; after all, *the way to a man's heart is through his stomach (31)*.

Call *Wedding Girl (32)*, Inc., soon. Our charges are so reasonable *that your father will be pleased (33)*, and our services are so complete that your *mother won't spend so much time crying (34)*. Make this *high point in your life (35)* all that it can be. Trust *Wedding Girl (36)*, Inc., to help *make the two of you into one (37)*.

Yours for a perfect wedding,

(38) Dale Lomax, Arrangements
WEDDING GIRL (39), INC.

Corrected Words and Phrases

MARRIAGE (1), INC.

Ms. Sara Ferris and Mr. Brad Hilton (2)
888 Fox Avenue
Wrong Number, New York 00000

May 14, 198X

Dear Ms. Ferris and Mr. Hilton (3):

So, *the two of you (4) have made the decision (5)*! Your wedding will *reflect the commitment and joy of that decision (6)* if you let *Marriage (7)*, Inc., plan it from beginning to end.

Yes, *from relating to the concerns for your loved ones* (8) to the final *mutually supportive* (9) *vows* (10), *Marriage* (11), Inc., will *help in the decision making* (12) and leave you more time for plans for the home the two of you will establish (13) . . . for plans of how *you will share the daily responsibilities of that home* (14) (15) . . . for plans for *proper parenting* (16), *if you should decide to have children* (17) (18) . . . for plans *for growth* (19) as you *hot hend your day's work* (20) . . . and for plans of the *mutual giving of oneself to the other in the interchange that is marriage* (21) (22) (23).

We'll help you make decisions about such things as the *type of ceremony you want* (24), *any announcements you want to make* (25) (26), *arrangements for the wedding pictures* (27), and how to choose your *wedding attendants* (28) (29). We can even arrange for *premarital counseling* (30) to *help you make the human adjustments that are necessary for two people who marry* (31).

Call *Marriage* (32), Inc., soon. *Our charges are reasonable* (33); *our services are complete* (34). Make this *important ceremony* (35) all that it can be. Trust *Marriage* (36), Inc., to help *two unique individuals embark upon the cooperative, sharing experience called marriage* (37).

Yours for a perfect wedding,

(Mr.) (38) Dale Lomax, Arrangements
MARRIAGE (39), INC.

EXERCISE 5-2

Exercise 5-2 concentrates on male-as-norm sexism in the formal research report. Note that substituting passive for active voice is one possible method for correcting male-as-norm sexism. The loss of the active voice is a small sacrifice for the greater good of nonsexism. Nevertheless, passive voice in formal reports should not be cause for complaint by sexist report writers—they frequently use the impersonal passive voice in their own formal writing.

Sexist Words and Phrases

A stratified random sample of 400 was drawn from the population. The strata represented the classes of *workmen* (1) under consideration in the research: *firemen* (2), *policemen* (3), *medical emergency team crewmen* (4), electric company *linemen* (5), and *mailmen* (6). The systematic sampling procedure was used to select the *workmen* (7) from each stratum—represented by a listing of all who constituted the particular class. The number of *workmen* (8) selected from each stratum represented the proportion that the particular stratum was to the whole of the population. The numbers in each class are shown as part of the findings presented in Chapter III.

After the sample was identified, clearance was obtained from the appropriate labor *fraternal* (9) orders and *brotherhoods* (10). Then, each *workman* (11) was contacted and asked for *his* (12) permission to allow information to be taken from *his* (13) personnel folder. Only 23 refused such permission, leaving 377 of the original sample.

In five instances, both a *man and his wife* (14) were selected through the systematic process as members of the sample. In those instances, *the man was retained* (15), and the *wife was eliminated from* (16) the sample. The wife was eliminated because data obtained from two members of the same family could have proved a biasing duplication for certain portions of the research. Thus, *as head of the household, the man was retained* (17). The final sample, then, contained 372 people (93 percent of the original sample of 400).

The personnel folder for each of the 372 *workmen* (18) was inspected. If *his* (19) folder was complete, the data were simply recorded on the form included as Appendix C. If, however, the folder was not complete, the *workman* (20) was contacted to obtain the information needed.

As established in the report of the design of the investigation in Chapter I, the race and sex of the selected *workmen* (21) were two important demographic characteristics for analysis. The numbers and proportions represented by each subclassification so determined are presented in Chapter III. Overall, however, *the white man* (22) represented 81 percent of the total; *the black man* (23), 15 percent; *the red man* (24), 1 percent; and all other races, 3 percent. Ninety-two percent of the *workmen* (25) were men, and 8 percent were women.

Corrected Words and Phrases

A stratified random sample of 400 was drawn from the population. The strata represented the classes of *workers* (1) under consideration in the research: *fire fighters* (2), *police officers* (3), *medical emergency team members* (4), electric company *field workers* (5), and *letter carriers* (6). The systematic sampling procedure was used to select the *workers* (7) from each stratum—represented by a listing of all who constituted the particular class. The number of *workers* (8) selected from each stratum represented the proportion that the particular stratum was to the whole of the population. The numbers in each class are shown as part of the findings presented in Chapter III.

After the sample was identified, clearance was obtained from the appropriate *labor organizations* (9) (10). Then, each *worker* (11) was contacted and asked for (12) permission to allow information to be taken from *her or his* (13) personnel folder. Only 23 refused such permission, leaving 377 of the original sample.

In five instances, both *the husband and wife in a single family* (14) were selected through the systematic process as members of the sample. In those instances, *a coin was tossed to determine which would be retained in* (15) (16) the sample. Only one was retained because data obtained from two members of the same family could have proved biasing duplication for certain portions of the research (17). The final sample, then, contained 372 people (93 percent of the original sample of 400).

The personnel folder for each of the 372 *workers* (18) was inspected. If *the* (19) folder was complete, the data were simply recorded on the form included as Appendix C. If, however, the folder was not complete, the *worker* (20) was contacted to obtain the information needed.

As established in the report of the design of the investigation in Chapter I, the race and sex of the selected *workers* (21) were two important demographic characteristics for analysis. The numbers and proportions represented by each subclassification so determined are presented in Chapter III. Overall, however, *whites* (22) represented 81 percent of the total; *blacks* (23), 15 percent; *native Americans* (24), 1 percent; and all other races, 3 percent. Ninety-two percent of the *workers* (25) were men, and 8 percent were women.

EXERCISE 5-3

As an excerpt from a short informal report, Exercise 5-3 provides opportunity for eliminating the pervasive sexism that occurs in informal writing. Because the report discusses an upcoming advertising project, the removal of stereotyped sexism is particularly important. Observe that the corrected version uses the active voice—this is possible because the personal style prevails.

Sexist Words and Phrases

After you receive approval for your new project, you will need to begin the search for the money, *men* (1), materials, market, and management necessary to complete it. Engage the support of the company *wives* (2), and you will find that the project will go more smoothly than it would without their support.

Because your project will involve the development of a new four-*man* (3) trailer tent, center your marketing plan on *sportsmen* (4) or *outdoorsmen* (5). You should check out the possibilities for coupling your campaign with that for the two-*man* (6) canoe that was developed last year. Use appeals to the *man's man* (7), the rugged *man* (8), the *man* (9) of the earth, and even the return to the *common man* (10) as you develop your advertising design.

Picture primitive scenes with *bewhiskered and rugged riflemen* (11) and *huntsmen* (12). However, also picture friendly scenes. Include a *father and son* (13), with *man's* (14) best friend—the family dog. *He* (15) should be bouncing happily beside the tent and beside *the mother as she cooks the fish* (16) the *fishermen* (17) have caught from the stream nearby. Show *dad helping his son* (18) build a *snowman* (19) in a winter scene. Stress the safety of the trailer tent against *man-eating* (20) animals.

Spotlight the excitement of the wild as it is conquered by *man* (21). You might even include footprints of the Abominable Snow *Man* (22). *He* (23) is, after all, a creature whose existence is not really believed, but who, like ghosts, introduces adventure into an outing. You might show the *frightened mother and daughter* (24) being comforted by the *strong father and son* (25) as they view the footprints. Make the *father and son the men of the hour* (26) by showing *how easily they can set up the tent* (27), as the *mother and daughter look on with admiration* (28). Show the *father and son* (29) pull away from the shore in their canoe as the *girls* (30) wave and wish them well.

You might feature the strength and water-tightness of the tent by picturing the family in snug comfort as the rain and wind are swirling about them. The *mother is doing the dishes* (31), the *father is showing the son how to put a book on the fishing line* (32), and the *daughter is playing with her doll* (33). A newscaster's voice emanates from a portable radio. *He* (34) says, "And the cost of living is hurting both the working *man* (35) and the *housewife* (36) in their battle to make ends meet."

Corrected Words and Phrases

After you receive approval for your new project, you will need to begin the search for .the money, *personnel* (1), market, and management necessary to complete it. Engage the support of the company *spouses* (2), and you will find that the project will go more smoothly than it would without their support.

Because your project will involve the development of a new four-*person* (3) trailer tent, center your marketing plan on *sports people* (4) or *outdoors people* (5). You should check out the possibilities for coupling your campaign with that for the two-*person* (6) canoe that was developed last year. Use appeals to the *strong individual* (7), the rugged *person* (8), the *human* (9) of the earth, and even the return to the *basic person* (10) as you develop your advertising design.

Picture primitive scenes with *earthy rifle carriers* (11) and *hunters* (12). However, also picture friendly scenes. Include a *family* (13), with *its* (14) best friend—the family dog. *It* (15) should be bouncing happily beside the tent and beside the *father and daughter as they cook the fish* (16) the *family* (17) has caught from the stream nearby. Show *all members of the family* (18) building a *snow figure* (19) in a winter scene. Stress the safety of the trailer tent against *human-eating* (20) animals.

Spotlight the excitement of the wild as it is conquered by *people* (21). You might even include footprints of *Big Foot* (22). *It* (23) is, after all, a creature whose existence is not really believed, but which, like ghosts, introduces adventure into an outing. You might show the *frightened children* (24) being comforted by the *parents* (25) as they view the footprints. *Show how easily all members of the family can set up the tent* (26) (27) (28). Show the *mother and son* (29) pull away from the shore in their canoe as the *father and daughter* (30) wave and wish them well.

You might feature the strength and water-tightness of the tent by picturing the family in snug comfort as the rain and wind are swirling about them. The *father and mother are doing the dishes* (31), and *the children are putting hooks on their fishing lines* (32) (33). A newscaster's voice emanates from a portable radio. *She* (34) says, "And the cost of living is hurting both the *worker* (35) and the *consumer* (36) in their battle to make ends meet."

EXERCISE 5-4

These segments illustrate correction of the kinds of sexism found in reports and other formal writing.

Sexist Words and Phrases

1. The *guardsmen* (1) and *militiamen* (2) placed "*Men Working*" (3) signs and *flagmen* (4) on the highway. They called on the estate *groundsmen* (5) and all local *radiomen* (6) to help in the search effort.

2. Each politician promises to make every *man* (1) a *king* (2). *He* (3) also promises that *he* (4) will not *emasculate* (5) the voter by taking away *his* (6) knowledge of the issues. *He* (7) also assures us that *Miss Liberty's* (8) principles will be upheld.

3. According to Jenks, the marketing strategy is critical: "Any good marketing plan must meet the requirements of the customer, for *he* (1) has already established *his* (2) ideas in a general way. The *gentlemen's agreement* (3) must be honored."

4. *Englishmen* (1) and *Frenchmen* (2) agree that good *penmanship* (3) is an important qualification for the small law office clerk. They also establish the function of the executor or *executrix* (4) as one of the most important for the *lawman* (5). They have much the same view of meeting the requirements set by *Miss Justice* (6) that American *men* (7) do.

Corrected Words and Phrases

1. *Members of the Guard* (1) and the *Militia* (2) placed "*Workers Working*" (3) signs and *flaggers* (4) on the highway. They called on the estate *grounds workers* (5) and all local *radio operators* (6) to help in the search effort.

2. Each politician promises to make every *citizen* (1) a *queen or king* (2). *He or she* (3) also promises that *the voter* (4) will not *be weakened* (5) by taking away *the* (6) knowledge of the issues. The *politician* (7) also assures us that *liberty's* (8) principles will be upheld.

3. According to Jenks, the marketing strategy is critical: "Any good marketing plan must meet the requirements of the customer, for the *customer* (1) has already

established (2) ideas in a general way. *The gentlewo/men's agreement* (3) must be honored."

    4. *English* (1) and *French people* (2) agree that good *writing* (3) is an important qualification for the small law office clerk. They also establish the function of the *executor* (4) as one of the most important for the *attorney* (5). They have much the same view of meeting the requirements set by *justice* (6) that *Americans* (7) do.

EXERCISE 5-5

The devices for correcting the sexism in the journalistic reporting style form the focus for this exercise.

Sexist Version	*Corrected Version*
1. *MISS* (1) HAMPLE NAMED MARKETING ASSISTANT	*HAMPLE* (1) NAMED MARKETING ASSISTANT
Vice-President Jerry Klix announced the addition of *Miss Sally Hample* (2) to the staff of the marketing department. Klix said that *Miss Hample* (3) will be a marketing assistant.	Vice-President Jerry Klix announced the addition of *Sally Hample* (2) to the staff of the marketing department. Klix said that *Hample* (3) will be a marketing assistant.
A gorgeous blonde (4), *Miss Hample* (5) is a 1974 graduate of Singland University and a *former Miss Singland* (6). She was also *fourth runner-up in the Miss Ogland County pageant* (7) of 1973 and was named *All-College Queen* (8) in 1972 while attending Singland University.	*Hample* (4) (5) is a 1974 graduate of Singland University where she *majored in marketing* (6). She was *president of the Marketing Club in 1973* (7) and *a member of the Society for the Advancement of Management* (8) chapter in Singland.
Klix said that *Miss Hample* (9) will take over her duties January 1 and that the department is fortunate to have such an *attractive* (10) *girl* (11) join the staff.	Klix said that *Hample* (9) will take over her duties January 1 and that the department is fortunate to have such a *qualified* (10) *woman* (11) join the staff.

Sexist Version	*Corrected Version*
2. *MRS. ELLISON, SHERMAN CALLAWAY* (1) TO BE MARRIED IN LOCAL HOME	*CALLAWAY AND ELLISON* (1) TO BE MARRIED IN LOCAL HOME
Mr. and Mrs. William Axmore (2), Baconia, *announce the engagement* (3) of their daughter, *Mrs. Dora Ellison* (4), to Sherman Callaway.	Sherman Callaway, sales department, *announces his engagement* (3) to *Dora Ellison* (4), who is *employed at a local lunchroom* (13) (14).
Callaway's parents are *Edward Callaway of Eggton and Mrs. George Attwell of Baconia* (5). The wedding will be on December 8 in the home of the *future bride's* (6) parents.	Callaway's parents are *Sharon Attwell of Baconia* (5) *and Edward Callaway of Eggton. Ellison's parents are Marie and William Axmore* (2) of Baconia. The wedding will be on December 8 in the home of *Ellison's parents* (6).
Mrs. Ellison (7) was graduated from Baconia High School, where she was a *cheerleader* (8), basketball *queen* (9), and *chairman* (10) of the *usherette* (11) committee during her *senior* (12) year. She is currently employed as a *hostess* (13) at the *Businessman's* (14) Lunchroom.	*Callaway and Ellison* (7) were both graduated from Baconia High School. Callaway is in his *first year* (15) at Baconia Junior College. [(8) (9) (10) (11) (12) omitted because of inappropriateness; could have supplied some appropriate experiences for Ellison.]

Callaway, sales department, is a graduate of Baconia High School and is in his *freshman* (15) year at Baconia Junior College.

Sexist Version

3. *E. A. BROWNE, MISS CLAYBORN* (1) REPEAT VOWS IN CHAPEL

Exchanging vows Thursday in a ceremony in the Ainsworth Chapel were *E. A. Browne and Miss Dorothy Clayborn* (2). *The bride* (3) is the daughter of *Mr. and Mrs. Ellis Park* (4). *Browne* (5) is the son of *Mrs. Elton Bickford and the late Harry Browne* (6).

Honor attendants were *Miss Sybil Laker and John Elton* (7). Others were *Mrs. Gene Gully, Miss Alice Drake, Donald Lancaster, and Stephen Wilt* (8).

The bride's mother wore (9). . . . *The groom's mother wore* (10). . . .

Browne is an engineer in the Sawton District.

Corrected Version

E. A. BROWNE, DOROTHY CLAYBORN (1) REPEAT VOWS IN CHAPEL

Exchanging vows Thursday in a ceremony in the Ainsworth Chapel were *E. A. Browne and Dorothy Clayborn* (2). *Ms. Clayborn* (3) is the daughter of *Ellis and Fran Park* (4). *Mr. Browne* (5) is the son of *Althea Bickford and the late Harry Browne*.

Honor attendants were *Sybil Laker and John Elton* (7). Others were *Ida Gully, Alice Drake, Donald Lancaster, and Stephen Wilt* (8).

[Omit (9) and (10) entirely—unless you report what the fathers wore. Also, never include what the bride and the female attendants wore.]

Browne is an engineer in the Sawton District. [What is Clayborn?]

Sexist Version

4. *Mr. and Mrs. Richard Doakes* (1) announce the birth of a son—Richard Doakes, *Jr.* (2) He weighed 7 pounds, 4 ounces. Doakes is a *delivery boy* (3) in the sales department.

Corrected Version

Lois and Richard Doakes (1) announce the birth of a son—Richard Doakes, *II*. (2) He weighed 7 pounds, 4 ounces. Doakes is a *deliverer* (3) in the sales department. [*Jr.* was changed to *II* because of the strong association of *Jr.* with the patriarchy.]

Sexist Version

5. *SHANNONETTES* (1) WIN BOWLING TITLE

The Shannon Co. is proud to announce that the *girls'* (2) bowling team, the *Shannonettes* (3), just won the annual bowling tournament in Mallville.

The men's bowling team—the Shannons— (4) took second place in the same tournament. Both trophies are on display in the employee lounge.

Corrected Version

SHANNONS (1) WIN BOWLING TITLES

The Shannon Co. is proud to announce that the *women's* (2) bowling team, the *Shannons* (3), just won the annual bowling tournament in Mallville.

The *men's Shannons bowling team* (4) took second place in the same tournament. Both trophies are on display in the employee lounge.

Sexist Version

6. *CORA* (1) TO VISIT BEACON PLANT

Cora (2), the wife of the Shannon Co. president, Alfred Shannon, will tour the Beacon Plant on April 8. *Hostesses* (3) will be the *foremen's* (4) *wives* (5).

Corrected Version

CORA SHANNON (1) TO VISIT BEACON PLANT

Cora Shannon (2), the wife of the Shannon Co. president, Alfred Shannon, will tour the Beacon Plant on April 8. *Those responsible for the visit* (3) will be the *supervisors'* (4) *spouses* (5).

Sexist Version

7. SHANNON TO SPEAK AT ANNUAL INDUSTRIAL CONFERENCE

President Alfred Shannon will be the featured speaker at the annual Industrial Association Conference. *Shannon's wife* (1) will accompany him to take part in the *Industrial Association Wives* (2) activities.

Corrected Version

SHANNON TO SPEAK AT ANNUAL INDUSTRIAL CONFERENCE

President Alfred Shannon will be the featured speaker at the annual Industrial Association Conference. *Cora Shannon* (1) will accompany him to take part in the *Industrial Association* (2) activities.

Sexist Version

8. *MRS. DONALD ELLISON* (1) DIES

Mrs. Donald Ellison (2), long-time employee, died in the home on December 9 following a long illness.

Her husband is a vice-president with the Friendly Corp. (3). *He has been active in community affairs, having once served a term* (4) as a city councilman (5).

The funeral for *Mrs. Ellison* (6) will be at the Ball Funeral Home on December 12.

Mrs. Ellison (7) is survived by her husband; a son, Charles; two daughters, *Mrs. Lowell Saul* (8), Pretoria, and *Mrs. Frank Holiday* (9), Brookville; and six grandchildren.

Corrected Version

MARTHA ELLISON (1) DIES

Martha Ellison (2), long-time employee, died in the home on December 9 following a long illness.

[Omit (3) (4) (5)]

The funeral for *Ms. Ellison* (6) will be at the Ball Funeral Home on December 12.

Ms. Ellison (7) is survived by her husband, Donald; two daughters, *Elva Saul* (8), Pretoria, and *Jane Holiday* (9), Brookville; a son, Charles; and six grandchildren.

EXERCISE 5-6

Exercise 5-6 affords practice in revising several types of sexist expressions.

Sexist Words and Phrases

1. Check *manning* (1) standards monthly instead of bimonthly so that we can make better predictions of heavy work periods.

2. Complete *workmen's compensation* (2) forms within ten days of receipt now instead of within the twenty days previously allowed.

3. The affected superior must approve any requests for a secretary's time that go beyond *her* (3) normal duties. *He* (4) must sign Form 9-a to confirm *his* (5) approval for the *girl's* (6) overtime.

4. Because of some recent airline losses of executives' suitcases with important company papers in them, put all such papers in your briefcase. Then carry the briefcase on board with you and keep it at your seat or have the *stewardess* (7) stow it.

5. When arriving at the office before 7 A.M. or leaving after 7 P.M., you must now check in and out with the *night watchman* (8).

6. Couch communication with the Des Moines office in terms understandable to the *layman* (9). That office deals in support services and does not have the technical *men* (10) that the other offices have.

7. The *postman* (11) will no longer deliver mail by floors. Therefore, each office will need to have a mail *boy* (12).

Corrected Words and Phrases

1. Check *labor* (1) standards monthly instead of bimonthly so that we can make better predictions of heavy work periods.

2. Complete *worker's compensation* (2) forms within ten days of receipt now instead of within the twenty days previously allowed.

3. The affected superior must approve any requests for a secretary's time that may go beyond (3) normal duties. The *superior* (4) must sign Form 9-a to confirm *such* (5) approval for the (6) overtime.

4. Because of some recent airline losses of executives' suitcases with important company papers in them, put all such papers in your briefcase. Then carry the briefcase on board with you and keep it at your seat or have the *flight attendant* (7) stow it.

5. When arriving at the office before 7 A.M. or leaving after 7 P.M., you must now check in and out with the *security officer* (8).

6. Couch communication with the Des Moines office in terms understandable to the *layperson* (9). That office deals in support services and does not have the technical *personnel* (10) that the other offices have.

7. The *letter carrier* (11) will no longer deliver mail by floors. Therefore, each office will need to have a mail *clerk* (12).

EXERCISE 5-7

Though one would choose to paraphrase such a sexism-packed passage, this exercise provides practice with devices to remove the sexism within a direct quotation.

Of the twelve jurymen [*sic*] present, four were . . . [businesspeople], one was a . . . [sculptor], two were housewives [*sic*], one was a . . . [guard], one was a deliveryman [*sic*], and one was a . . . computer programmer.

EXERCISE 6-1

Exercise 6-1 focuses on stereotyped relative ranks of women and men in organizations and nonparallelism in using names.

1. Incoming Calls

a. Answer promptly. If the caller has to wait more than two or three rings, *he* (1) may become irritated and take *his* (2) business elsewhere.

b. Identify yourself and the office or department. Say something like "*Mr.* (3) Johnson's office, *Mrs.* (4) Blackman," "Credit Department, *Claudette* (5)," or "Linoleum Sales, *Davidson* (6)."

c. Avoid using "hold" for more than fifteen seconds. If the caller has to wait longer than that, *he* (7) may become irritated. If the "hold" will be longer than fifteen seconds, take the caller's number and tell *him* (8) that the *man* (9) *he* (10) is calling will return the call. (Be sure to follow up on such promises.)

d. If a call needs to be transferred, be as helpful to the caller as possible. *He* (11) can become quite upset if *he* (12) has to redial and still gets the wrong office.

2. Outgoing Calls

a. Have the correct number and dial it right the first time. If possible, know the *man's* (13) extension as well.

b. Greet the *gril* (14) who answers cordially, but in a businesslike manner, and ask *her* (15) for the *man* (16) you are calling by name, mentioning your superior by name, if the call is being placed for *him* (17). Use words like "*Mr. Whiteman* (18) of the Delphi Corporation would like to speak to *Mr. Nelson* (19)."

c. Transfer the call efficiently to your superior when the contact has been made. Do not keep either *man* (20) waiting.

Corrected Words and Phrases

1. Incoming Calls

a. Answer promptly. If the caller has to wait more than two or three rings, *he or she* (1) may become irritated and take *the* (2) business elsewhere.

b. Identify yourself and the office or department. Say something like "*Ms.* (3) Johnson's office, *Mr.* (4) Black," "Credit Department, *Ms. Younger* (5)," or "Linoleum Sales, *Ms. David* (6)."

c. Avoid using "hold" for more than fifteen seconds. If the caller has to wait longer than that, *he or she* (7) may become irritated. If the "hold" will be longer than fifteen seconds, take the caller's number and tell *her or him* (8) that the *person* (9) *being called* (10) will return the call. (Be sure to follow up on such promises.)

d. If a call needs to be transferred, be as helpful to the caller as possible. *The caller* (11) can become quite upset if *he or she* (12) has to redial and still gets the wrong office.

2. Outgoing calls

a. Have the correct number and dial it right the first time. If possible, know the *person's* (13) extension as well.

b. Greet the *person* (14) who answers cordially, but in a businesslike manner, and ask (15) for the *person* (16) you are calling by name, mentioning your superior by name, if the call is being placed for *her or him* (17). Use words like "*Mr. White* (18) of the Delphi Corporation would like to speak to *Ms. Neill* (19)."

c. Transfer the call efficiently to your superior when the contact has been made. Do not keep either *party* (20) waiting.

EXERCISE 6-2

Though significant changes in surnames will take generations to accomplish, we can at least eliminate sexist first and middle names and revise methods of reporting names to remove the sexism.

Sexist	*Nonsexist*
Doreen Jackman	Dorn Jank
Adrienne Cookson	Adren Cook
Charletta Kay Smithson	Kay Smith
Suzette Simpson Bartman	Sue Simpel Bart

Frank W. Dale, Jr.	Frank W. Dale, II
Vanessa Clarkson	Ann Clark
Miss Jonalyn Rhineman-Burk	Lyn Rhine-Burk
Coramae Beetleson	Cora Beetle
Mrs. Alvin Ryanson, III	Lucille Ryan
The Hobsons	Clarence Hobbs and Linda Curell
The Bill Todds (Bill, Rosetta, Jeanessa, and Brad)	Mildred, Bill, Jean, and Brad Todd
Baby Doll Allison	Jan Allis
Miss Zinnia Stillman	Ms. Rachel Still
Mrs. Heather Peterson	Ms. Karen Peters
Ms. Luscious Alderman	Ms. Janice Alder
Evan D. Friedman	Evan D. Fried
Ginger Bud Klegman	Elizabeth Kleg
Lady Bird Blakeson	Carol Blake
Mrs. Earl Jorgenson (Birdie)	Mary Jorgens
Ms. "Pet" Dyerman	Doris Dyer

EXERCISE 6-3

These sentences illustrate corrections of the sexism in references to nonhumans.

1. Give your favorite birds Pet-em Bird Seed. They'll sing you beautiful songs.

2. All horses entered in the race will take their places at exactly 10:30 A.M.

3. Now, children, look at the picture and see how easily Ms. Diesel Engine pulls the rest of the train up the hill. She's so strong that she could pull a bigger train too.

4. The moment drivers take hold of the wheel of a Newsmobile, they immediately feel in control of its wonderful power.

5. Every child should have a toy to hold close.

6. Give your children a Ms. Owl Calculator. They'll learn so much arithmetic from her.

7. The elementary teacher took his students' models of Ms. Executive, Captain Betty, and Bruce Doll to a college professor so she could choose the winner.

8. Ask all adult members of the family to participate in the discussion.

9. The female led the lions' hunt.

EXERCISE 6-4

These nonsexist versions illustrate how to avoid the sexism in monarchial and religious references.

1. Let us be thankful that these graduates have reached this point in their lives. May these graduates move out to take positions of leadership to help solve the problems of humanity.

2. As the coordinator, be sure to introduce all the dignitaries and their spouses. Also be sure to use good English in your presentation.

3. Elaine looked so pleased at her selection as a member of the Edmund High School Tigers basketball team.

4. The children played tag till they tired; then they went inside to play Go Fish.

EXERCISE 7-1

These corrections illustrate the removal of sexism from statements portraying the male as the norm.

1. The American Indians occupied North America long before the Europeans arrived.

2. The average voter

3. Be sure that all babies have their shots by the time they reach age two.

4. The human does not live by bread alone.

5. One small step for a human; one giant leap for humankind.

6. The military person has a right to a pension over which he or she has complete control.

7. Pioneers bravely opened new frontiers; we can't forget the contributions these women, men, and children made.

8. The business lunch special for the day is a giant bowl of clam chowder.

9. Homeowner, be sure to buy this insurance so that you will leave your house free and clear to your family if you should die.

10. Of 100 American women who responded to a survey, 52 said they like strong men.

11. Born to Sybil and Carl Belyew

12. Your name _____

     Address _____

                    _____

                    _____

13. The GPGA (Gentlemen's Professional Golf Association) and the LPGA (Ladies' Professional Golf Association)

EXERCISE 7-2

These nonsexist versions show how to correct sexist stereotypes.

1. I don't think we have to worry, do you, Ella?

2. Mommy and Daddy brought Jane a doctor kit and Mike a paint set from their business trip. They ate milk and fruit and turned the reunion into a party.

3. I'm so pleased that I have found a low-sudsing detergent with a softener in it. It keeps my shirts clean and soft.

4. Breadwinners sometimes have to move where their jobs take them, even if the moves hurt the others in the family.

5. The female boss tells a mixture of female and male sales representatives how to improve sales while female and male workers sit silently in the background.

6. My daughter just became a member of the debate team, and my son was elected president of the Art Society.

7. A man and a woman jointly and equally make strong statements about a product.

8. A woman, man, and children jointly discover that the two-year-old batteries in the flashlight still work.

9. A woman who is a stockbroker grooms well before coming to work, but then does not think about the grooming process any more during the day. If she does discover a run in her stocking, she simply waits until she has time to change in a private place.

10. As humans upset the ecology, they once again establish their greed.

11. Children will be children.

12. The man and woman went to a nude nightclub show.

13. Well, I want to get home on time tonight because my periodic lateness justifiably disappoints Helen.

EXERCISE 7-3

These lists suggest some of the key sexist elements in the stories and characterizations.

1. *Cinderella:* Beautiful, poor, mindless woman saved by handsome, rich, confident prince. Ugly, mean stepmother and stepsisters who lose because of their ugliness. Fair godmother.

2. *Snow White and the Seven Dwarfs:* "Mirror, mirror on the wall, who's the fairest of them all?" A crone who tries to kill Snow White when she learns Snow White is more beautiful than she. Male dwarfs who go to work in the mines while Snow White stays home and sweeps, cleans, and cooks. Handsome prince saves mindless, sweet Snow White. The ugly, mean woman loses again.

3. *Sleeping Beauty:* A sleeping, beautiful, characterless woman saved by the kiss of an active, handsome prince.

4. *The Wizard of Oz:* The male wizard controlling Oz. The female Wicked Witch. The dingy female witch. The three kindly male friends to Dorothy.

5. The Muppets: Though Miss [*sic*] Piggy is a strong characterization, virtually all the rest of the Muppets are male.

6. The Smurfs: Only one of the characters is female, and she is called a "Smurfette." She plays a stereotyped female role.

EXERCISE 7-4

Exercise 7-4 illustrates the negative imagery associated with being labeled with the "feminine" adjectives.

1. I like him; he seems to be a thoughtful, sensitive person.

2. I like a woman who has a good self-image, can carry on an important conversation, and is sensitive and thoughtful.

3. I don't like him; he is too meticulous for me.

4. I find it difficult to understand Jill's innermost thoughts—or anyone's innermost thoughts for that matter.

5. For people to be successful in business, they must use their minds, develop their human relations skills, and work very hard.

6. To a five-year-old girl dressed in a free and comfortable fashion: Be active so that you will develop your mind and body.

7. Report to Ms. Abel right now.

8. Joan has had no experience in financial matters, but, of course, now that she has the opportunity, she'll learn in no time.

9. I've noticed that those in the women's movement come from all walks of life, with the bulk made up of men and women representing the same basic types of moderate people found anywhere.

EXERCISE 7-5

This exercise provides a most telling summary of society's view of the relative worth of females and males. These words actually appear in dictionaries and thesauruses in conjunction with the identification of each sex.

Female

Feminine

Womanhood

Emasculated

Lady—falsely genteel, old-fashioned

Unmanly

Lacking in many qualities

Effeminate

Unsuitable to a man or to a strong character of either sex

Womanish

Traits inappropriate to a man

Vixen, tigress, lioness, cow

Characterized by weakness, overrefinement, cowardice, shrillness, softness, gentleness, delicacy, modesty, lack of dynamism, decadence, docility, dutifulness

Wife, goodwife, squaw, frail, fair sex, weaker sex

Femme, donna, belle

Matron, matronly

Dowager

Maiden, maidenly

Sister

Tomato

Antonym: See Male

Male

Masculine

Manhood

Gentleman—considerate, courteous, and socially correct

Manly

The state of being human

Qualities such as straightforwardness, strength, courage, determination, honor, valor, resoluteness, spirit, daring, gallantry, heroism, confidence, self-reliance, prowess, chivalry, nerve, pluck, firmness, stability, fortitude, achievement

Android

Blade, swain

Virility

Anthropoid

Cock, drake, stag, bull, rooster

Antonym: See Female

This exercise illustrates the lack of words to describe women in a positive light.

1. The experience left her feeling stripped of power.

2. I'm uncomfortable around her because she seems to have more interest in sex than I like.

3. Trying to get along in "a man's world" can be a defeating experience for a woman.

4. She felt as if she had been stripped of her strength.

EXERCISE 7-7

This exercise provides additional opportunity to exorcise the sexism from common communication.

1. Now, where are you going to move your pawn? My pawns seem to have your pawns under control.

2. Let's throw the dice to find out who's high to see who goes first.

3. My card takes your card. (The king-takes-the-queen syndrome is quite ingrained. However, some decks of cards now have the queen take the king. We at least can refuse to use the words that create the imagery.)

4. John, let's hire someone to clean this place; we just don't seem to be able to keep up with our housework now that we both work outside the home.

EXERCISE 8-1

Exercise 8-1 compresses the kinds of sexism found in all-too-common scenes. Because of the wide variety of nonsexist alternatives available, this section does not include a nonsexist version.

FORGAN: Hey, let's sit here where we can watch the *hides* come in the door. (*Snaps fingers*.)[1] "*Waitress*,"[2] two cups, please.

GUTHRIE: (Nods in agreement as they sit down.) Well, as I was saying, I just don't see what the *girls* are complaining about. After all, we *men are the ones who have to carry the load for our families. They just work for pin money.* Besides, *they don't have the emotional stability to cope with the demands of management positions.* (Gibson brings two cups of coffee. *Guthrie puts an arm around her below the waist.*) You're *looking foxy* today, *Ellie.*[3]

GIBSON: (Emits an *appropriate, if insincere, giggle,* extricates herself from the arm, and walks away.)

[1] If used equally for males who wait table, not sexist, but superiorist.
[2] "Waiter/waitress" was retained in the *Dictionary of Occupational Titles* even after revision.
[3] All right if she calls them by first names.

FORGAN: I'll bet Ellie was a *cheerleader* and a *prom queen* in high school. I'm glad that Al hires only *good-looking girls* and *won't let them wear pants suits*. Oh, for the good old days when *girls were girls and men were men*.

GUTHRIE: Right; but when *girls don't get married, have babies*, and *stay home*, they're *all bitchy that time of the month*—unless they're going through the *change*, and then they're *bitchy all the time*. Take that *broad* Rita who *they had to promote* to manager. Oh, *I guess she knows her work*, but she can't really *expect men to be willing to have a girl for a boss or work with her*. As I was telling you, I'm supposed to develop a media package for her, but *I don't see why I should spend my time on a project for her when you have one going too*. Besides, she's just *a plain Jane*, and I like to see *good-looking dames* in *short skirts* in the office where I have to spend eight hours a day. Speaking of *broads*, did you just see that *set* walk by? (*Looking at the woman from head to toe.*)

FORGAN: Now, why couldn't we have a *doll* like her in the office instead of that *castrating female* Ida? Why doesn't Ida *give up* that *women's lib* stuff? She's *built* well enough that she could *get a man*, so I don't see why she's so *uptight about women's rights*.

GUTHRIE: *Man*, I don't either. Take Rose. She's advanced to be *Mr. Allen's secretary* by *knowing her place*, by *using feminine gamesmanship*, and by *having all her friends among the men instead of among the girls*. She *doesn't complain about making and serving the coffee* and *doesn't expect to move into management*. She told me that *she can't understand why a woman would want to take a man's job*. She *agrees with us* that *the jobs ought to go first to a man who has a wife and children*, but these *libbers seem to think that they should get them*. And when *Rose does pout* about something, *candy and flowers* have her *purring like a kitten* in no time. I'm sure when *Rose finds a husband*, she will *leave us to have babies*.

CLANCEY: (Clancey enters the coffee shop, notes Forgan and Guthrie sitting at a table that could hold two more, makes a move toward them, and speaks.) Good morning, Fred and Danny. I'm ready for a cup of coffee—and see you evidently have had such a morning too. I'm having some trouble with that media package you're helping me with, Fred. (She pauses at the table, clearly wanting an invitation to join them.)

FORGAN: (Glances up, but *makes no receptive motion toward Clancey*. Speaks in *voice that closes out Clancey*.) Yes, *Mrs. Clancey*, it has been a long one; but at least we can get away from it all *and be alone* for a few minutes now and then.

CLANCEY: (Moves awkwardly away from the men's table.) I'll talk to you later. (Sits at a table alone—some distance from Forgan and Guthrie.)

GUTHRIE: Damn, do these *libbers* who *take jobs away from men* really expect us to *fall all over ourselves* to *do their work for them*? And *I certainly am not going to give up my break time for any of them*.

FORGAN: Well, as we were saying, from what I've seen of the feminists,[4] they're either such *dogs* that they *can't have a man* or so (*holds hand out flat and moves it up and down from side to side*) that *they don't want a man*. If I were a *normal gal*, I sure *wouldn't want to be affiliated with them*. *I told my wife* this morning that *she's going to have to stop going to those so-called women's rights meetings* or she's *going to become a libber* and *ruin our marriage*. By the way, she's having some sort of *hen party* at my house this very afternoon. (Pauses.) *My dinner had*

---

[4]The word *feminist* is not italicized because it is not sexist. A feminist is simply one who works actively for equal political, economic, and social rights for females.

better be on time. I just don't know what it's coming to. *When the day comes that I don't wear the pants in my family, we'll have to cease being a family.*

GUTHRIE: True. An *aggressive, pushy broad* is *impossible to live* or *work with.* In an office she's usually *one who has been around,* a *frustrated divorcée* or an *old maid* who just *can't accept* that *she has no place in a man's world.*

GIBSON: (Overhears comment about a "frustrated divorcée"; fills cups.)

GUTHRIE: (Perplexed and nervous look on face.) You know, though, there are getting to be more and more *girls* who *bother me.* Take Rita. (Glances toward her and notes that she is reading something as she drinks her coffee.) *She thinks like a man and acts like a lady,* and *some of the men are actually saying that she is doing a good job.*

FORGAN: *Man,* we sure don't need our *brothers deserting us and supporting* a *girl*—the *turncoats.*

GUTHRIE: Isn't that the truth! She just comes on *too confident* for me, and I do *feel sorry for her husband.*

FORGAN: Right. He must be some kind of *henpecked frail* to *stay married to her.*

GUTHRIE: But, *much as I hate to admit it, she doesn't seem to be absent, doesn't seem to complain, travels willingly, and worst of all, is working in career planning with other women so that they, too, can be promoted.* She has children, but she and her husband jointly take care of the house and see that the children are cared for. *Is a couple like that ever hurting our cause!*

FORGAN: Right, and I'm frightened that *business may be one of the last strongholds against females.* And, like Rita, they're *pounding away at our defenses*—just because of the *fem lib* bunch and *their hold on the government. It frightens me.*

GUTHRIE: (Looking at watch.) Me too. But on that sad note, I guess we'd better get back to the office and pay homage to that *bitch-goddess success.* (Leaves tip and pays check.)

GIBSON: Thank you, *Mr. Forgan and Mr. Guthrie.*

CLANCEY: (Glances up to note the men leaving.)

EXERCISE 8-2

These scenes represent unfortunately typical oral and nonverbal sexism. A wide variety of nonsexist alternatives exist. Therefore, this section does not include nonsexist versions.

   1. A meeting of five line managers: four men and one woman. *The woman is taking minutes. The men ask her about the "woman's" view of an issue.*

   2. A TV commercial. *A mother acts horribly embarrassed when her pie crust is not flaky because she used the wrong shortening in it.* Her *daughter also expresses embarrassment* because *her home economics teacher and classmates (all young women)* are *giving her and the crust disdainful "looks."*

   3. A group of women calling themselves the *Acme Wives* discuss money-making projects. One woman suggests a *toddler's beauty contest.* Another suggests *compiling a recipe book and selling it.* Still another suggests a *homemade bake sale.* And, finally, another suggests that they *volunteer to cook and serve the monthly meal* for a *men's club.*

   4. At the annual company picnic *the women and older girls set up the tables and watch*

after the younger children. The men and older boys pitch horseshoes, play baseball, and play volleyball.

5. A man offers the invocation at a business luncheon. He asks all to bow their heads. He uses these words in the prayer: *"Father," "Lord," "He," "His," "Him," "In Christ's Name,"* and *"Amen."* (The religious bias exists because references to deities exist in a secular situation. In addition, "In Christ's Name" assumes that all believers present are Christians.)

6. *A female secretary* and her *male boss*. She sits in a *short skirt* with her legs crossed. *He is admiring her legs. He stands up* and *puts his hand on her shoulder* as he passes her chair. He returns to his chair and *she gets his coffee for him.*

7. Magazine advertisement: A strikingly handsome bikini-clad man *stares aloofly as he enjoys his cigarette.* Three beautiful women *hover about him, touch him,* and *admire him.*

8. A military recruiting poster includes one white male, one black male, and one white female, *in that order.* The full name tag of the white male shows; the first name of the tag of the black male shows; *none of the name tag on the female shows.*

9. The living room of a home: *The husband talks to a salesperson about life insurance. The wife dries dishes,* but listens. *The daughter cuts out paper dolls. The son plays with a truck.*

EXERCISE 8-3

Exercise 8-3 identifies some of the sexism exemplified in everyday situations. Because of the wide variety of nonsexist alternatives available, this section does not include nonsexist versions.

1. Office: Four men. One is small in stature, plain in appearance, does not care for football or golf and does not pretend to, does not treat women as objects, does accept and respect women as coworkers, speaks of his liberated, working wife in positive terms. *The other three, through postures, avoidance, and comments do not accept the maverick.*

2. Office: Six men and one woman. *Woman enjoys her role as the only woman* in the group. She makes comments about how *she has never been discriminated against* and how *she prefers to be around men.* *She puts down women in lesser positions* than she holds, saying that *they cannot keep secrets, have too many absences,* and just *work to find a husband.* She urges that *if a woman prepares herself, she can advance.* She *flirts with the men* and uses *baby talk. They reply in kind.*

3. Commercial: *Chattering wife* makes a fuss over her *sick "baby boy" husband* and administers a product that will help cure his cold. *He sniffles and feels sorry for himself.*

4. Four little girls talking: One wonders why *Santa Claus is a man.* Another wonders what *"Mrs." Santa Claus's* first name is. All speculate on whether *"Mrs." Claus ever gets to ride in the sleigh* or *just has to stay home during all the fun.*

5. Commercial: The speaker says that you only pass through this life once, so you ought to live with bravado. *Men sail ships, climb mountains, and womanize. Women are womanized.*

6. Commercial: Woman talks as her husband mops the kitchen floor. Impression is left that only a *weakling man, under the sway of a domineering woman, would do such a thing.*

7. Commercial: *Man looks on in condescension* as his *mother-in-law makes a fool of herself over toilet paper. Little girl uses some of the toilet tissue on her doll* and *extols its superior qualities.*

SELECTED BIBLIOGRAPHY

Addendum to Style Guide for Authors, Academy of Management Review. Madison, Wis.: Academy of Management Review, July 1976, pp. 150–152.

American Psychological Association Task Force on Issues of Sexual Bias in Graduate Education. "Guidelines for Nonsexist Use of Language." *American Psychologist*, June 1975, pp. 682–684.

BURR, ELIZABETH, SUSAN DUNN, and NORMA FARQUHAR. *Guidelines for Equal Treatment of the Sexes in Social Studies Textbooks*. Los Angeles: Westside Women's Committee, 1973.

CLARK, KENNETH. *Civilisation: A Personal View*. New York: Harper & Row, 1969.

COOKE, ALISTAIR. *Alistair Cooke's America*. New York: Alfred A. Knopf, 1974.

"Desexing the Language." *Managementips* Special Edition, (n.d.)

Editorial and Graphics Criteria for Art and Design. Lexington, Mass.: Ginn & Co., 1975.

Fair and Balanced Treatment of Minorities. Cincinnati, Ohio: South-Western Publishing Co., 1976.

GORDON, FRANCINE E., and MYRA H. STROBER. *Bringing Women into Management.* New York: McGraw-Hill Book Co., 1975.

GRAHAM, ALMA. *Non-Sexist Language Guidelines.* New York: Alma Graham.

Guidelines for Creating Positive Sexual and Racial Images in Educational Materials. New York: Macmillan Publishing Co., Inc., 1975.

Guidelines for Equal Treatment of the Sexes. New York: McGraw-Hill Book Co., 1972.

Guidelines for Improving the Image of Women in Textbooks. Glenview, Ill.: Scott, Foresman & Co., 1972.

Guidelines for Multiethnic/Nonsexist Survey. New York: Random House, Inc., 1976.

Guidelines for Richard D. Irwin Authors and Copy Editors for Equal Treatment of Men and Women. Homewood, Ill.: Richard D. Irwin, Inc.

" 'He' Is Not 'She.' " Los Angeles: Westside Women's Committee, 1972.

Headquarters Staff of National Council of Teachers of English. "Guidelines for Nonsexist Use of Language in NCTE Publications." *NCTE,* March 1976, pp. 23–26.

HECHT, MARIE B., JOAN D. BERBRICH, SALLEY A. HEALEY, and CLARE M. COOPER. *The Women, Yes!* New York: Holt, Rinehart and Winston, Rinehart Press, 1973.

HENLEY, NANCY M. *Body Politics: Power, Sex, and Nonverbal Communication.* Englewood Cliffs, N.J.: Prentice-Hall, Inc., 1977.

HENLEY, NANCY, and BARRIE THORNE, *She Said/He Said: An Annotated Bibliography of Sex Differences in Language, Speech, and Nonverbal Communication.* Pittsburgh, Penna.: Know, Inc., 1975.

MEHRABIAN, ALBERT. *Silent Messages.* Belmont, Calif.: Wadsworth Publishing Company, Inc., 1971.

MILLER, CASEY, and KATE SWIFT. *Words and Women.* Garden City, N.Y.: Doubleday & Co., Inc., Anchor Press, 1976.

MILLETT, KATE. *Sexual Politics.* New York: Doubleday & Co., Inc., 1969; Avon Books, 1971.

MONTAGU, ASHLEY, and FLOYD MATSON. *The Human Connection.* New York: McGraw-Hill Book Co., 1979.

National Education Association. *Sex Role Stereotyping in the Schools.* Washington, D.C.: National Educational Association, 1973.

ONE, VARDA. "Manglish." Venice, Calif.: Everywoman Publishing Co., 1971. Reprint available from Know, Inc.

OROVAN, MARY. *Humanizing English.* New York: Mary Orovan, 1972.

PERSING, BOBBYE SORRELS. *Business Communication Dynamics.* Columbus, Ohio: Charles E. Merrill Publishing Co., 1981.

———. *The Nonsexist Communicator: An Action Guide to Eradicating Sexism in Communication.* East Elmhurst, N.Y.: Communication Dynamics Press, 1978.

———. "Sticks and Stones and Words: Women in the Language." *Journal of Business Communication* 14 (Winter 1977):11–19.

PICKENS, JUDY E., PATRICIA WALSH RAO, and LINDA COOK ROBERTS, eds. *Without Bias: A Guidebook for Nondiscriminatory Communication.* San Francisco: International Association of Business Communication, 1977.

ROTTER, PAT, ed. *Bitches and Sad Ladies: An Anthology of Fiction by and about Women.* New York: Dell Publishing Co., Inc., 1975.

RUSSELL, LETTY M., ed. *The Liberating Word: A Guide to Nonsexist Interpretation of the Bible.* Philadelphia: Westminster Press, 1976.

SCHNEIDER, JOSEPH W. and SALLY L. HACKER. "Sex Role Imagery and Use of the Generic 'Man' in Introductory Texts: A Case in the Sociology of Sociology." *American Sociologist* 8 (February 1973): 12–18.

STANNARD, UNA. *Mrs. Man.* San Francisco: Germainbooks, 1977.

STEAD, BETTE ANN. "The Semantics of Sex Discrimination." *Oklahoma New Woman,* 25 April 1976, pp. 4–5. Reprinted from *Business Horizons.*

———, ed. *Women in Management.* Englewood Cliffs, N.J.: Prentice-Hall, Inc., 1978.

STONE, JANET, and JANE BACHNER. *Speaking Up.* New York: McGraw-Hill Book Co., 1977.

THORNE, BARRIE, and NANCY HENLEY, eds. *Language and Sex: Difference and Dominance.* Rowley, Mass.: Newbury House Publishers, Inc., 1975.

Treatment of Women and Minority Groups. Lexington, Mass.: Ginn & Co., 1975.

U.S. Department of Labor, Employment and Training Administration. *Dictionary of Occupational Titles,* 4th ed. Washington, D.C.: Government Printing Office, 1977.

U.S. Department of Labor, Manpower [sic] Administration. *Job Title Revisions to Eliminate Sex- and Age-Referent Language from the Dictionary of Occupational Titles, Third Edition.* Washington, D.C.: Government Printing Office, 1975.

U.S. Department of Labor, Women's Bureau, Employment Standards Administration. "The Myth and the Reality." Washington, D.C.: Government Printing Office, 1974.

WENDLINGER, ROBERT M., and LUCILLE MATTHEWS. "How to Eliminate Sexist

Language from Your Organization's Writing: Some Guidelines for the Manager and Supervisor." In *Affirmative Action for Women: A Practical Guide*, by Dorothy Jongeward, Dru Scott, et al. Reading, Mass.: Addison-Wesley Publishing Co., Inc., 1973, pp. 309–320.

INDEX